# IN BLACK AND WHITE: AUSTRALIANS ALL AT THE CROSSROADS

# By the Editors

*Teaching the Teachers Indigenous Australian Studies:*
*Framework Statement* (1996)

*Survival: A History of Aboriginal Life in New South Wales* (2005)

*The Croc Festival* (2007)

*The Education Movement: A People's History of the AECG* (2010)

*Teaching Aboriginal Studies* (2011)

*Deadly Australians* (2011)

*Indigenous Peoples: Education and Equity* (2013)

# In black & white

*Australians All
at the Crossroads*

Edited by
Rhonda Craven, Anthony Dillon,
and Nigel Parbury

Published in 2013 by Connor Court Publishing Pty Ltd

Copyright © Rhonda Craven, Anthony Dillon, Nigel Parbury 2013

ALL RIGHTS RESERVED. This book contains material protected under International and Federal Copyright Laws and Treaties. Any unauthorised reprint or use of this material is prohibited. No part of this book may be reproduced or transmitted in any form or by any means, electronic or mechanical, including photocopying, recording, or by any information storage and retrieval system without express written permission from the publisher.

Connor Court Publishing Pty Ltd.
PO Box 1
Ballan VIC 3342
sales@connorcourt.com
www.connorcourt.com

ISBN: 9781922168511 (pbk.)

Cover design by Ian James

Printed in Australia

# CONTENTS

### Real Statistics and History

1. The Undercover Guide to Indigenous Statistics......................... 1
   *Helen Hughes and Mark Hughes*

2. Why History Matters..................................................... 21
   *Paddy Cavanagh*

### Some Elephants in the Room

3. Promised Brides and the Insolence of Freedom: Aboriginal Australia and Violence During Cultural Transition.................. 37
   *Stephanie Jarrett*

4. Who are You to Speak? Silencing Aboriginal Dissent............... 57
   *Kerryn Pholi*

5. No More Victims........................................................ 75
   *Anthony Dillon*

6. Indigenous Scholarship and Values-formation........................... 91
   *Brian Roberts*

### Illuminating Iniquities

7. Dispossession: Neo-Liberalism and the Struggle for Aboriginal Land and Rights in the 21st Century....................... 105
   *Jeff McMullen*

8. The Problem of Over-Representation of Indigenous Australians within the Western Australian Criminal Justice System: Possible Solutions....................................................127
   *Brian Steels and Dot Goulding*

9. On Nudging and Fudging: Paternalism and its Variants in Remote Aboriginal Australia............................................. 145
   *Ernest Hunter*

## Communities and Well-being

10. A Life Remote: My Own Cultural Journey........................157
    *Patricia Shadforth*

11. Politics of Difference............................................................173
    *Sara Hudson*

12. Good Culture – Bad Culture, Where Do We Go From Here?....191
    *Dave Price and Bess Price*

## Education

13. 'You *are* Boss for Me!' A Case Study of the Erosion of Indigenous Self-Determination in Education................................. 209
    *Jerry Schwab*

14. A Short Critique of Indigenous Education Research....................229
    *Geoffrey Partington*

15. Indigenous Education – Policy, Pedagogy, and Place....................247
    *Bill Fogarty*

16. Whatever the Problem, Education is the Key: The Scots College Experience............................................................. 267
    *Jonny Samengo*

## Employment

17. Gambling Spaces and the Paradox of Aboriginal Social Inclusion..................275
    *Martin Young, Francis Markham, and Bruce Doran*

18. A Key Role for Indigenous Peoples in Australia's Sustainable Future..................287
    *Seán Kerins*

19. The Social Benefits and Costs of Indigenous Employment......303
    *Nicholas Biddle and Kirrily Jordan*

20. The Rose that Grew from Concrete..................321
    *Thomas Draper*

## Forging Australia's Future

21. Our People Need Careers..................333
    *Warren Mundine*

22. Real Education, Real Jobs..................339
    *Alison Anderson*

23. Towards a Reconciled Australia..................353
    *Mick Gooda*

24. Together We Can't Lose: Seeding Success to Ensure Australia Flourishes.................. 367
    *Rhonda Craven and Nigel Parbury*

Bibliography.................. 376

Contributors.................. 407

# Foreword[1]

Aboriginal Affairs is hard work, in the fullest sense. It's not just hard yakka (an Aboriginal word) but also at times exhausting and frustrating because so much effort often seems to bring about so little progress. Trying to 'fix' entrenched Indigenous disadvantage is the real 'hard yards'.

Aboriginal Affairs is a place of passion. This is because it matters: it is about extraordinary opportunity and debilitating despair, pride and prejudice, life and death. People in Aboriginal Affairs are not 'mercenaries, missionaries and misfits'. They are generally people with real passion for what they aspire to achieve. That's just the whitefellas. For the Indigenous brothers and sisters, it's about the survival of their people. And for Australia, it's about our collective sense of nationhood and the single greatest test of our participatory democracy.

In my 20 years as an Australian Public Servant, no area of public policy was more significant to me than seeking to influence and administer government support to Aboriginal people and Torres Strait Islanders. As CEO of ATSIC, and successively as Departmental Secretary of Employment, then Education, and finally Prime Minister & Cabinet, I had significant responsibility for the design and oversight of Indigenous programs. It was rewarding. It was also demanding and wickedly complex.

I learned a great deal, made abiding friendships and took comfort in modest but real achievements. Overall, however, I look back on those years as a period of failure, judged against the criteria of equal opportunity, economic and social mobility, human rights and civic responsibilities, control and empowerment.

---

[1] References relating to this Foreword are provided in the Bibliography. See Shergold (2009) and (2012).

I believe that all the governments I served – led by Bob Hawke, Paul Keating, John Howard and Kevin Rudd – wanted, in different ways, to improve the lot of Australia's first peoples. Certainly I feel that the great majority of relevant Ministers, of widely varying political persuasions, all sought to make a positive difference. Most of the public servants I worked alongside did their best. Yet, after two decades, the scale of relative disadvantage suffered by Indigenous Australians remained as intractable as ever. I can think of no failure in public policy that has had such profound consequences.

Since I left the Australian Public Service, I have reflected at length on that failure, personal and systemic. Three key things I have learned.

First, far too many government initiatives, generally well meant and often well implemented, simply end up compounding the problem of passive welfare and learned helplessness. Programs meant to alleviate social exclusion are all-too-frequently delivered in such a way as to reinforce a sense of dependence and marginalization. Too often the best of intentions create the worst of outcomes. Stripped bare of the rhetoric of self-determination or mutual responsibility, what is too often provided is 'sit-down money', training to nowhere, and an array of financial disincentives and administrative barriers to people taking control of their own lives.

Second, the structure of bureaucratic programs tends to ossify over time. Programs are often designed and regulated to the most exacting of ethical standards, meet every guideline, tick every box – but still end up disconnected from the 'outcomes' they were meant to deliver. Time after time, publicly-funded training leads to little sustainable employment, inevitably fuelling cynicism amongst Indigenous participants. 'Go-round-in-circles' training is no solution – it is part of the problem.

Third, government programs tend to be designed for administrative convenience rather than centred on the needs of the individual. They offer little diversity of choice. The particular problems of Indigenous communities – whether in remote parts of Australia, regional centres or inner cities – are treated as uniform. There is far too little willingness to tailor services to local need or to devolve responsibility and decision making to the community level. There are also too few opportunities for individuals and families to direct and manage their own publicly-funded support.

As I become older I seem to become more old-fashioned. I do believe that work is the path to dignity and a sense of purpose. Education and training are the key. Giving Aboriginal people a real chance to take control of their lives means enabling them to find a job, earn a wage and support their family. The delivery of training has to be inextricably bound to the experience of work and, most importantly, tied to the actual job requirements of employers or industries. The workplace is not an easy place. Certified training alone is not enough. Work-readiness, combined with employer support, is equally important.

Over the years I increasingly recognized the unintended consequences of public policy. Too often in the period since I've sounded like a broken record (to use a vinyl-age metaphor). My recurring theme has been the need to support people who, even at a time of low unemployment, remain welfare dependent, mired in the morass of sit-down money which Noel Pearson and others aptly call "welfare poison". We need to financially support Indigenous Australians to address their multiple needs but also – and even more essentially – encourage and incentivise them to become self-reliant.

At present the vast sums spent on benefits too often entrench the poverty the payments are intended to eradicate. Surely it's far better to spend the money on providing assistance to help people get off benefits? People – our fellow-citizens – need to be given the chance to take full control of their lives. Finally, it's absolutely vital that political risk aversion or administrative caution does not stand in the way of public and social innovation. There are occasions when we should 'just do it'. We need to explore our appetite for risk, trial new approaches, learn by doing and carefully evaluate the results.

That is why it is important to bring fresh eyes, sharp minds, a range of experience and a no-holds-barred honesty to debates on Aboriginal Affairs. Orthodoxies and rigidities in public policy develop with remarkable rapidity and nowhere faster than in Aboriginal Affairs. Policy prescriptions quickly become entrenched, in part, because the issues appear so intractable. Yet we know that if we continue to do what we always did, we'll always get what we always got.

That's why I am so delighted by this provocative and stimulating collection of essays. This volume sets out to illuminate diverse and at times diametrically opposed viewpoints – and to find the common ground that is prerequisite for effective solutions. Some of the essays raised my spirits. Others raised my ire. All engaged me and, together, made me reflect anew on the public policy of Indigenous Affairs.

I commend the editors of *In Black and White: Australians All at the Crossroads*. They have taken on a task that is difficult and potentially thankless, but their efforts are critically important. They have done a great job.

Finally, I am proud that this important volume has been conceived and brought to fruition at the University of Western Sydney, of which I am honoured to be Chancellor.

**Professor Peter Shergold**
**Chancellor**
**University of Western Sydney**

# Editors' Preface:
# Which Way at the Crossroads?

Though more and more Indigenous Australians are realising their potential, in general Aboriginal Australians remain significantly, in fact radically, disadvantaged on all socio-economic indicators. What is worse, aggregating statistics across the country buries Aboriginal achievement in the mainstream of Australian life, and even worse, masks appalling outcomes in some areas, especially, but by no means only, in remote Australia – most particularly on Aboriginal lands. The real potential and talents of Indigenous Australians continue to be wasted rather than contributing as they could and should to individuals', families', communities' – and Australia's well-being. Despite widespread agreement that this disadvantage needs to be eradicated and Aboriginal success achieved, effective solutions remain elusive and the road to such solutions unclear – to the extent that any resolution, and indeed much debate, remains stuck at the crossroads.

This volume is to more widely disseminate established and new Indigenous and non-Indigenous thinkers' diverse, even diametric, perspectives on what needs to be addressed (including some 'elephants in the room') and suggest potent ways forward for building Indigenous success to fix disadvantage. Not all perspectives are easily accessible to all interested in understanding. Some opinions are given disproportionate space in popular media, including social media (especially if there is a hint of conflict). In many cases balancing opinions are only found in specialised journals and forums, not readily accessible to all Australians. A further problem is that much of what passes for informed debate on Indigenous issues is conducted from entrenched positions, too often proceeding from or degenerating into heresies and hostilities.

We seek to present informed opinion, written in an engaging and accessible style, that will advance understandings of the issues and point the way to fresh strategies to achieve commensurate socio-economic and well-being outcomes for Indigenous people such as most other Australians can take for granted. A primary goal is to make widely available (e.g., to university students in diverse disciplines; policy makers; education, health, employment stakeholders; social commentators; community members; and the general public) a dynamic compilation resource of some current thinking, of the voices of informed and respected Indigenous and non-Indigenous leaders, thinkers, and social commentators from a variety of relevant fields and walks of life.

It is our devout hope that this volume will contribute to establishing common ground which is prerequisite for finding effective solutions. Our subtitle, *Australians All at the Crossroads*, makes the vital point that these issues concern all Australians. For all of us, it is imperative to seed success, to put an end to the wastage of Aboriginal talents and Aboriginal lives that has blighted the potential of Australia for far too long.

We thank our authors for offering fresh, astute, and candid insights in an accessible style, and commend their expertise and perspectives to you the reader for your consideration. We also thank Connor Court for publishing the work, with particular thanks to Dr Anthony Cappello.

We also would like to acknowledge the excellent job done by our reviewers.

| | |
|---|---|
| Jon Altman | Hannah McGlade |
| Andrew Baker | Janet Mooney |
| Gawaian Bodkin-Andrews | Lynette Riley |
| Benjamin Herscovitch | Marjorie Seaton |
| Helen Hughes | Peter Sutton |
| Benjamin Jones | Sarah Taylor |
| Joe Lane | Kirhi Euloo Wiree |
| Kurt Marder | |

We trust the volume will help readers consider which way at the crossroads will seed success.

**Professor Rhonda Craven**
**Dr Anthony Dillon**
**Nigel Parbury**
**Centre for Positive Psychology and Education**
**University of Western Sydney**

# 1
# The Undercover Guide to Indigenous[1] Statistics

*Helen Hughes and Mark Hughes*

*The past 40 years of Aboriginal policy has been a sort of experiment; an experiment with human lives costing billions of dollars.*[2]

## Introduction

Most Australians are poorly informed about the Aboriginal and Torres Strait Islander population. They are not aware that New South Wales has the highest Indigenous population, or that most Aborigines and Torres Strait Islanders live and work in capital cities and regional towns. They do not understand that the most dysfunctional communities are primarily on the 20% of Australia that is Indigenously owned or controlled land. Separate 'apartheid' government policies have made these lands another country within Australia.

Official Indigenous statistics present averages of mainstream Australia and Indigenous lands. They minimise the achievements of working Aborigines and Torres Strait Islanders while grossly understating the deprivation on Indigenous lands.

## Population Size

Every five years, the ABS (Australian Bureau of Statistics) census records data about Australian individuals and households.

---

[1] For simplicity, the word Indigenous, despite its ambiguity, has been used for persons identifying as Aborigines and/or Torres Strait Islanders.

[2] Anderson, A. 'Address in Reply to the Northern Territory Assembly', delivered in Darwin, 23 October 2012. See also Anderson, this volume.

## 'Apartheid' Census Forms

Across mainstream Australia, two census forms are used:

1. In households, one or more residents, and any overnight visitors, complete/s the *Household Form*.
2. In accommodation such as hotels and motels, persons staying there on census night complete the *Personal Form*.

But in a few remote Indigenous communities on Indigenous lands, there is a special Indigenous form called the *Interviewer Household Form*. The differences for the 2006 census were:

- *Household Form* – up to 6 people, any more people on extra *Personal Forms*; *Interviewer Household Form* – up to 12 people, any more on extra *Interviewer Household Forms;*
- *Household Form* – 61 questions; *Interviewer Household Form* – 55 questions with different question wording, different question order, and different possible responses;
- *Household Form* – separate forms can ensure privacy of residents' data; *Interviewer Household Form* – no privacy of residents' data is possible.

A 'justification' for the separate *Interviewer Household Form* is poor literacy in remote Indigenous communities. In mainstream Australia, however, illiterate householders, such as recent migrants, do not get the *Interviewer Household Form*.

The differently worded questions, in a different order and with different response options, between the *Household Form* and the *Interviewer Household Form* mean that data are not statistically comparable.

The ABS does not make public the *Interviewer Household Form* or the communities where it is used.

## Recording Ethnicity

The Australian Census has two questions on ethnicity. Question 7 of the Household Form asks about a person's Indigenous status, that is, if they are of Aboriginal or Torres Strait Islander origin, Question 18 of the Household Form asks about a person's ancestry. It is therefore possible for census respondents to be recorded as Indigenous, and at the same time, for example, German, Chinese, or Czech, or up to two of these. This data is not published.

## Population Growth

Table 1.1 Population, 2001, 2006 and 2011 census, pre PES.

|  | 2001 | 2006 | + or - % | 2011 | + or - % |
|---|---|---|---|---|---|
| Identified as Aboriginal | 366,429 | 407,700 | 11.3% | 495,756 | 21.6% |
| Identified as Torres Strait Islander | 26,046 | 29,516 | 13.3% | 31,406 | 6.4% |
| Identified as Aboriginal and Torres Strait Islander | 17,528 | 17,811 | 1.6% | 21,206 | 19.1% |
| Total Aboriginal and Torres Strait Islander | 410,003 | 455,027 | 11.0% | 548,368 | 20.5% |
| Did not answer this question | 767,757 | 1,133,445 | 47.6% | 1,058,583 | -6.6% |
| **Total Australia** | 18,769,249 | 19,855,288 | 5.8% | 21,507,719 | 8.3% |

After the date of the census (8th August for 2011) the ABS carries out a Post Enumeration Survey (PES). In the PES:

- "around 10% of the respondents who identified themselves as Indigenous in the 2006 Census, via a self-completion form, stated they were non-Indigenous"[3] during the PES.
- A much larger number who identified themselves as non-Indigenous on the Census form identified as Indigenous on the PES.

---

[3] ABS. *National Aboriginal and Torres Strait Islander Social Survey* (no. 4720.0) (2010a).

High-level data such as state and territory totals are adjusted for the PES, but other data are not adjusted. The effect is that different data is available for the same measure. For example, the initial Indigenous count in the 2006 census was 455,027. The net effect after the PES was an adjusted total 517,043 Indigenous Australians, an increase of 13.6%. The 455,027 number, however, still appears in many ABS reports such as those including geographic levels below state or territory. The PES for 2011 was not yet available in February 2013.

To sum up, census Indigenous counts are in effect rough estimates. Trend data must be interpreted very carefully. For example, comparing the 2006 and 2011 census data could imply a large Indigenous population move to cities and towns. In fact, data changes appear to have been driven by changes in self-identification in urban areas. Only DNA testing could objectively and definitively identify Australia's Indigenous population.[4]

## *Indigenous Population by State and Territory*

Table 1.2 Indigenous population by state and territory, ABS census data

|  | 2006 | 2011 | % growth 2006-2011 | % of Australian Indigenous population 2011 | % of state/territory population 2011 |
|---|---|---|---|---|---|
| NSW | 138,507 | 172,621 | 24.6% | 31.5% | 2.5% |
| VIC | 30,143 | 37,990 | 26.0% | 6.9% | 0.7% |
| QLD | 127,582 | 155,825 | 22.1% | 28.4% | 3.6% |
| SA | 25,556 | 30,431 | 19.1% | 5.5% | 1.9% |
| WA | 58,711 | 69,664 | 18.7% | 12.7% | 3.1% |
| TAS | 16,767 | 19,626 | 17.1% | 3.6% | 4.0% |
| NT | 53,663 | 56,776 | 5.8% | 10.4% | 26.8% |
| ACT | 3,875 | 5,185 | 33.8% | 0.9% | 1.5% |
| **Australia** | **455,026** | **548,369** | **20.5%** | **100.0%** | **2.5%** |

---

[4] Hughes, H. 'Who are Indigenous Australians?' (2008).

Contrary to popular perception, ABS data shows there is no Indigenous population explosion. Indigenous fertility is slightly above the rate for non-Indigenous Australians. The high proportion of youngsters in Indigenous demographics is the result of lower Indigenous life expectancy rather than a 'population explosion'.

In the 1980s and 1990s increased self-identification was a significant contributor to increasing Indigenous population counts at each census. The 20.5% increase between 2006 and 2011 was also primarily the result of increased self-identification.

The less remote the location, the higher was the recorded Indigenous population growth. Only in the Northern Territory was non-Indigenous population growth (10.4%) higher than Indigenous population growth (5.8%).

## *Intermarriage*

Australia has a high rate of intermarriage between Indigenous and non-Indigenous. The ABS and other government organisations commonly treat all children of intermarriage as Indigenous. Australians with any Indigenous ancestors commonly self-identify as Indigenous. The result is a rapid Indigenous population growth. As Joseph and Maria Lane saw:

- With each generation, a higher proportion of Australians are Indigenous.
- With each generation, most individual Indigenous Australians have a lower proportion of Indigeneity.
- This trend can be expected to continue until 100% of Australians (except immigrants) have some Indigenous ancestry.[5]

This effect is already evident in school enrolment data. Whereas in

---

[5] Lane, J. & Lane, M. 'Hard Grind – The Making of an Urban Indigenous Population' (2008).

the 2011 Census, Indigenous Australians were 2.4% of the population, 4.8% of school students in 2010 were identified as Indigenous. There is no fertility increase to account for this difference. Shorter longevity contributes, but does not account for the difference, which is smallest in the Northern Territory where longevity is the shortest.[6]

### *Population Distribution by Location*

ABS classifies remoteness using five Accessibility/Remoteness Index of Australia (ARIA) groupings: Major Cities, Inner Regional, Outer Regional, Remote, and Very Remote.

The ARIA Remote and Very Remote geographical classifications are misleading. 'Remote' includes substantial towns such Mt Isa, Alice Springs, and Port Hedland which have mainstream economies with commercial facilities including shopping malls and cinemas as well as social facilities such as major hospitals and public libraries. In common parlance, however, when 'remote Aboriginal' or 'remote Indigenous' terms are used, they mean communities on Indigenous lands.

The 2006 Census classified 76% of the Indigenous population as urban residents of major cities and regional towns. Only 24% of the Indigenous population was Remote or Very Remote. More than 85% of Indigenous Australians are urban when the population of mainstream Remote towns is added to 'cities and regional towns'. Less than 15% of Aboriginal and Torres Strait Islanders – about 75,000 – live on remote Indigenous lands.[7]

## Socio-Economic Status

The Indigenous population ranges from those living in remote communities on Indigenous lands to those living in 'leafy' suburbs in capital cities. Averaging this population (as the Productivity Commission's

---

[6] Hughes, H. & Hughes, M. *Indigenous Education 2012* (2012), has a more detailed discussion of these issues.

[7] Taylor, J. & Biddle, N. 'Locations of Indigenous Population Change' (2008).

*Overcoming Indigenous Disadvantage* does for all data) may be mathematically correct but is highly misleading. It is like averaging the per capita income of Australia and Afghanistan. Indigenous averaging masks both the successes of the cities and the failures of remote communities.

Three Indigenous socio-economic groups can be identified: urban working, urban welfare dependent, and those living on Indigenous lands.

## Urban Working Aborigines and Torres Strait Islanders

About 65% – some 350,000 – of Indigenous families are working in cities and towns. These urban working Aborigines and Torres Strait Islanders are still skewed toward less skilled occupations (and hence lower earnings) but include professionals, managers, and entrepreneurs.

Working Indigenous Australians are over-represented in public-sector employment because affirmative action programs stream well educated Aborigines and Torres Strait Islanders away from going into business. Rather than becoming entrepreneurs, Indigenous graduates are appointed to public service jobs where they write 'development plans' for Indigenous businesses in need of entrepreneurs.

Socio-economic characteristics – income, education, health (alcoholism), longevity – for the working urban Indigenous population are probably similar to those of non-Indigenous Australians in similar occupations. For example, home ownership does not appear to differ greatly between Indigenous and non-Indigenous urban working households. With award pay rates, working Aborigines and Torres Strait Islanders earn much the same incomes as their non-Indigenous co-workers. However, there is little research comparing similar Indigenous and non-Indigenous socio-economic groups.

Joseph and Maria Lane described how people struggled to get into the labour force, moving up from generation to generation. They pointed out that Indigenous families became members of mainstream society without 'losing a sense of difference and pride in one's Indigenous background:

their ancestors will forever be Indigenous, and their ancestral places will always be Indigenous'.[8]

Many families with both Indigenous and non-Indigenous backgrounds take pride in both their heritages – Indigenous and Anglo-Celtic, Chinese, Jewish, or whatever the origin of their parents and grandparents.

A 2004-2005 survey of Aboriginal and Torres Strait Islander people reported that 84% had not experienced racial discrimination in the previous 12 months.[9]

## Urban Welfare Dependent Aborigines and Torres Strait Islanders

Urban welfare dependent Aborigines and Torres Strait Islanders are probably about 20% – some 130,000 – of the Indigenous population; a significant reduction from 25% in 2006. Some live in discrete Indigenous ghettoes like Toomelah but most are scattered in suburbs like Mt Druitt where they live side-by-side with other welfare dependent Australians, often in public housing.

Urban welfare dependent Indigenous Australians are a small proportion of Australia's total 1.2 million welfare dependents. There are both Indigenous and non-Indigenous welfare dependent single parents, long-term unemployed, and disability pensioners. There has been a transfer from unemployed to disabled, but assessments of disability are so subjective that there is no reliable data on the number of able-bodied welfare dependent Australians who could be working and the number who are in genuine need of a safety net. While some NGOs have a serious concern for poverty and disadvantage, there are many whose existence in the 'welfare industry' is dependent on continuing large numbers of welfare recipients.

Although it is possible that low expectations and perceptions

---

[8] Lane, J. & Lane, M. op. cit.
[9] AIHW 2009, 'Measuring the Social and Emotional Well-being of Aboriginal and Torres Strait Islander Peoples', Cat No IHW 24, quoted in Pholi, K. 'The Final Insult' (2013).

of victimhood contribute to worse indicators for some welfare dependent Indigenous Australians, there is no evidence that long-term unemployment, literacy and numeracy, ill health, alcoholism, and violence are different for these families than for non-Indigenous welfare dependent families. Research comparing Indigenous and non-Indigenous welfare dependent urban populations is virtually non-existent.

## *Remote Communities on Indigenous Land*

Over the last 50 years, about 20% of Australia has been returned to Indigenous ownership and control. On these lands, 75,000 Indigenous Australians are subject to 'apartheid' government policies that treat them differently from their fellow citizens in the rest of Australia.

These communities concentrate the most dismal social indicators – lack of literacy and numeracy (some 45,000 men and women), poor health (diabetes, trachoma, otitis media, etc.) and low life expectancy. Alcoholism and violence are the result of welfare dependence, as Noel Pearson has so ably demonstrated.[10]

## *Townships and Outstations/Homelands*

The population of Indigenous lands is distributed between townships and outstations/homelands. Townships have populations between about 350 and 2,500. Governments have identified the larger ones as priorities for improved 'remote service delivery'. The Commonwealth government has prioritised 29 remote towns of which 15 are in the Northern Territory. Meanwhile, the Northern Territory government has prioritised 20 'growth towns'.

The objective of government policies is to develop these priority townships into 'mainstream country towns'. Large amounts of taxpayer funds are being expended. Bob Beadman, as Northern Territory Coordinator General for Remote Services, produced biannual reports that exposed the difficulty of trying to change townships to 'mainstream country towns' without addressing 'apartheid' policies. Most significantly,

---

[10] Pearson, N. *Up from the Mission* (2009b).

individual secure titles for private housing or business premises are not available. Without a private sector there are no jobs and no rateable properties to pay for infrastructure.

Outstations/homelands have less than 350 people. There are perhaps 750 small outstations/homelands – 500 plus in the Northern Territory. Many are not occupied all year round. Some are within an hour's drive of an Indigenous township or mainstream country town. Many families prefer to live in outstations away from the gambling, violence, and dysfunction in townships.

As in townships, on outstations/homelands individual secure titles for private housing or business premises are not available. Governments have decided that no new public housing will be built in outstations/homelands, and are avoiding decisions on whether new infrastructure will be built or how it will be funded. Outstations/homelands have been left in limbo.

## 'Apartheid' Policies

Despite large expenditures and programs such as the Northern Territory 'Intervention', the data show very little improvement on Indigenous lands. In January 2013, former Northern Territory Administrator, Ted Egan, said he had "never been more despondent about the prospects for Aboriginal people in the Northern Territory".[11]

The discriminatory policies responsible for individual, family, and community dysfunction are still in place:

- Education: Indigenous schools with separate curriculum, 'pretend' bilingualism, and Homeland Learning Centres (without qualified teachers) have resulted in generations who can't read and write. A handful of schools where good Principals are making the effort are the exception.
- Property rights: All prosperous societies have private property rights (houses, businesses) side-by-side with

---

[11] Egan, T. 'Indigenous Policies 'Demeaning, Wasteful'", *The Australian*, 3 January 2013.

communal property rights (roads, parks, schools). But on Indigenous lands traditional owners cannot own their home and are not eligible for benefits such as the *First Home Owner Grant*. Without private property side-by-side with communal, there is no private economy and therefore no employment. There are no coffee shops, newsagents, petrol stations, clubs or the other facilities found in mainstream towns. Public housing is expensive to build and cannot meet demand, resulting in substandard overcrowded houses. This is directly responsible for poor Indigenous health. First world health cannot be delivered in a third world slum.

The right 'to own property alone as well as in association with others' is guaranteed by the *United Nations Declaration of Human Rights* and *International Convention on the Elimination of All Forms of Racial Discrimination*. By not taking action to enable private housing on Indigenous land, Australian governments are contravening these United Nations commitments and the *Racial Discrimination Act*.

- Democratic processes: Communal ownership of housing and business is compounded by an absence of democratic processes and regulations that apply in mainstream Australia. Because land was returned to Indigenous groups without identifying group members, there can be no democratically elected governance. In contrast, in mainstream Australia body corporates and companies must meet probity standards.
- Regulatory supervision: The Commonwealth government operates ORIC (Office of the Registrar of Indigenous Corporations) specifically to enable Aboriginal corporations to avoid having to comply with ASIC requirements. The two largest Northern Territory Outstation Resource Agencies, despite receiving considerable taxpayer funds to provide services to remote homelands/outstations, have gone

bankrupt in the last two years.

- Royalties: Because individual Indigenous land owners have not been identified, royalties cannot be fairly distributed to individuals. Instead, they fund Indigenous bureaucracies and mostly failed communal projects. The Northern Territory Aboriginals Benefit Account has over $400,000,000 in the bank.[12] If land owners were identified, it could fund superannuation or housing trust accounts. In this way, royalties could fund home ownership rather than drugs or gambling.

- Additional Indigenous-only welfare programs: Compounding the lack of jobs is the additional income received by those on Indigenous land. CDEP (Community Development and Employment Projects) 'wages' and 'pretend' jobs such as assistant teachers, Indigenous health workers, and Indigenous rangers are all welfare by another name. With welfare income mostly higher than entry-level wages, there is little incentive to work in the private sector. When Colin Baker, a hard working Principal of a remote school, told kids wagging school that they had to learn to read to get a job, they replied: "No we don't. You can get a CDEP job without being able to read and write and you do not have to do anything for it."[13]

- Services to communities on private land: In mainstream Australia, private landowners such as cattle stations and 'gated estates' have to pay the capital cost of roads, water, power and sewerage. In contrast, communities on Indigenous land expect governments to pay for infrastructure development. Without private property, Indigenous communities have no ratepayers, so that government is forced to cover the operational costs as well as capital costs of services.

---

[12] DFHCSIA. *Annual Report, 2010-2011* (2011).
[13] Colin Baker. Personal Communication (2011).

# Education

## History

In 1996 Australian governments set a target to 'close the gap' between Indigenous and non-Indigenous educational achievement within 4 years. Little progress was made. So in 2008, following Prime Minister Kevin Rudd's Apology, COAG halved the target to 'close half the gap', and extended the time frame to achieve this to 10 years.

In 2008, national NAPLAN literacy and numeracy tests replaced state and territory testing. The results showed a significant majority of Indigenous students achieve national standards. The exception was the Northern Territory where the majority of Indigenous students fail.

Table 1.3 Percentage of Year 3 Indigenous students passing NAPLAN in 2011.[14]

| Indigenous Students | Reading | | Numeracy | |
|---|---|---|---|---|
| NAPLAN Year 3 (2011) | Pass rate | Pass rate adjusted for absent | Pass rate | Pass rate adjusted for absent |
| New South Wales | 85% | 81% | 89% | 85% |
| Victoria | 88% | 80% | 90% | 80% |
| Queensland | 80% | 76% | 87% | 81% |
| South Australia | 72% | 62% | 79% | 67% |
| Western Australia | 70% | 60% | 80% | 68% |
| Tasmania | 86% | 82% | 90% | 86% |
| Northern Territory | 40% | 32% | 59% | 47% |
| Australian Capital Territory | 87% | 84% | 89% | 85% |
| **Australia** | **76%** | **70%** | **84%** | **76%** |

## Enrolment

Comparisons of census cohorts and enrolment data show no evidence of significant numbers of school age Aborigines and Torres Strait Islanders

---

[14] Hughes, H. & Hughes, M. op. cit.

not being enrolled in school. School funding is tied to enrolment numbers, ensuring that even in very remote areas, schools work hard to ensure all kids are enrolled.

Of the 168,803 enrolled Indigenous students in 2010:

- about 110,000 were children of working Indigenous families in cities and regional towns attending mainstream government and non-government schools;
- about 40,000 were children of urban welfare dependent families mostly attending 'residualised' schools side-by-side with children of non-Indigenous families from similar socio-economic backgrounds. These schools have high absenteeism and high failure rates. There has been no research to determine whether there are significant differences in NAPLAN results between Indigenous and non-Indigenous students in these schools;
- about 20,000 were children on Indigenous lands attending Indigenous schools. These students had by far the worst results, with failure rates often exceeding 90%.

## *COAG Education Targets*

In 2008, Council of Australian Governments (COAG) set three education targets.

The first target was for all four-year-olds to be in pre-school taught by qualified teachers by 2013. This target will not be achieved. Higher socio-economic pre-schoolers will be in such pre-schools this year, but attendance by pre-schoolers on Indigenous lands will be a long way from 100%.

The second target is to halve the literacy and numeracy gap by 2018. This target will also not be achieved. Although the COAG Reform Council has 'cherry picked' results to show that 4 of 20 NAPLAN indicators were on target in 2011,[15] there was little progress on the other 16 indicators. Queensland and WA have made the most progress.

The third target is to halve the gap in Year 12 completion. This loosely defined target implies 'passing the year 12 curriculum'. But COAG data are based on enrolment and attendance more than educational achievement. In some Indigenous schools the majority of students 'completing Year 12' cannot meet year 5 NAPLAN literacy and numeracy standards.

## Causes of Failure

We know the cause of Indigenous Education failure. It is not:

- Indigeneity – the majority of Indigenous students pass NAPLAN;
- remoteness – there are many instances of remote locations that have both a high-performing mainstream school and an underperforming Indigenous school;
- school funding – some schools with the highest per-student funding have the worst NAPLAN results and vice versa;
- size of school – many non-Indigenous small schools have excellent results.

As Pearson, Denigan, and Göttesson pointed out in their seminal book on Indigenous Education, it is school ethos and teaching that makes the difference between good and bad education.[16] Attendance is a chronic problem in Indigenous schools and in 'residualised' schools. Overcrowded housing, travel to funerals etc., and the lack of work commitments contribute to high mobility and high rates of absenteeism on Indigenous lands. But so do schools that do not teach. Experience in the Northern Territory and Queensland shows that schools that have good teaching have good attendance.

---

[15] COAG Reform Council. *Indigenous Reform 2010-2011* (2012).
[16] Pearson, N. Denigan, B. & Göttesson, J. *The Most Important Reform* (2009).

## Post-Schooling Education

### Vocational Education

National Centre for Vocational Education Research data show that 15% of the Indigenous population participates in vocational education, compared to only 7% of the non-Indigenous population.[17] Although Indigenous data includes some 'pretend' courses delivered in remote communities, the enrolment of some 80,000 Indigenous students in vocational courses in 2010 shows remarkable success.

### University Education

In 2012, the government released the *Behrendt Report*.[18] Its 300 pages bemoan the lack of Indigenous university participation. But the data tell a different story:

- There are now more than 30,000 Indigenous graduates.
- About 10,000 Indigenous students were enrolled in universities in 2011. This does not include those enrolled in 'higher education non-University' courses. Most university students were children of working Aborigines and Torres Strait Islanders. More than 75% were not from low socio-economic backgrounds and 44% were not the first in their families to attend university.[19] The university participation rate of working-family Indigenous children appears to be about the same as that of non-Indigenous working-family children.
- Joseph Lane has shown that Indigenous students have left

---

[17] National Centre for Vocational Education Research. *Australian Vocational Education and Training, Indigenous Students* (2010).

[18] Behrendt, L. *Review of Higher Education Access and Outcomes for Aboriginal and Torres Strait Islander People* (2012).

[19] Asmar, C. *et al.* 'Dispelling Myths' (2011).

sub-professional degrees and moved up from primary to secondary teaching, from nurses to doctors and so on.[20]
- There were more than 1,000 Indigenous postgraduate students. Although some may not be doing rigorous graduate degrees, neither are many non-Indigenous graduate students.
- Youngsters on Indigenous lands are missing out on the growing Indigenous university participation.

## Employment and Income

### *Indigenous Unemploymernt*

Most Aborigines and Torres Strait Islanders are in the labour force, working and living in capital cities and country towns. Like most other Australians, they move between jobs but are not welfare dependent or long-term unemployed.

Indigenous unemployment and low labour force participation are not caused by a shortage of jobs. The lowest Indigenous labour force participation is in the areas with the strongest overall labour markets. Aborigines and Torres Strait Islanders, even in remote areas, live within reach of jobs.

Indigenous non-labour force participation is a much greater problem than unemployment. The difference between Indigenous and non-Indigenous participation rates is twice as large as the difference in unemployment rates.

Indigenous unemployment is three times that of other Australians. Almost 40% of Indigenous unemployment is in New South Wales, which has the largest Indigenous population.

Unemployment and not in the labour force rates are surprisingly consistent across states and between cities, regions, and remote locations

---

[20] Lane, J. *Indigenous Participation in University Education* (2009).

such as Alice Springs and Mount Isa. The exception is Indigenous lands, where unemployment is virtually 100%.[21]

The policies required to bring these welfare-dependent Aborigines and Torres Strait Islanders into the labour force and jobs are essentially the same as those for non-Indigenous welfare dependent Australians. On Indigenous lands, however, the pervasive unemployment is the result of separatist government policies that deny these lands a normal economy. Where jobs exist, for example in mines or communities neighbouring Indigenous lands, welfare incomes that are above entry level wages discourage movement from welfare to jobs.

CDEP is a government program that primarily operates on Indigenous lands. It is commonly regarded and referred to – even by Indigenous leaders – as the 'Indigenous work for the dole'. But unlike work-for-the-dole programs in mainstream Australia, the ABS records CDEP as employment. This significantly overstates employment in communities on Indigenous lands.

Like other Indigenous measures, employment and workforce participation statistics are based on self-identification, and data should be used with caution. Increases in employment from the 2006 to 2011 census reflect changes in self-identification as well as changes in employment status.

## *Income*

Welfare incomes, including Indigenous-specific welfare, are so high that there is no relationship between employment and household income. The median Indigenous Australian household income at the 2011 census was $51,000 per year. Median household incomes of $80,000 per year and higher are found in remote communities on Indigenous lands where unemployment is virtually 100%. Like the working Aborigines and Torres

---

[21] Hughes, H. & Hughes, M. *Indigenous Employment* (2010).

Strait Islanders who own their homes, many families on Indigenous lands with incomes above the median could own their home if they were allowed access to secure land title.

## Conclusion

Indigenous lands are 'another country' – a world apart from mainstream Australia. The endless repetition of 'the intractability of Indigenous problems' avoids acknowledging that dire conditions on these lands are caused by discriminatory policies. Poor health, poor housing, and violence are the result of the 'Indigenous experiment'.

Aborigines and Torres Strait Islanders deserve the same rights and responsibilities as other Australians. On Indigenous lands, they are denied basic rights such as education and home ownership – and robbed of the most basic responsibility of caring for themselves.

Effective policy requires honest data. Data that covers up the actual situation has been combined with spin to distract attention. Billions of dollars have been spent each year, but there has been virtually no change in government policy. This is why there has been no progress on Indigenous lands.

# 2
# Why History Matters

*Paddy Cavanagh*

*History is more or less bunk ... We want to live in the present, and the only history that is worth a   tinker's damn is the history that we make today.*
(Henry Ford, reported in *Chicago Tribune*, 1916)

*History is so last Century*
(B.Ed. student, tutorial, University of Sydney, 2012)

The history that Aboriginal and non Aboriginal people have shared in Australia since 1770 matters because it influences our understanding of who we are and how we relate to each other. If we have no knowledge of it we can have little understanding of either our personal identity or of the national identity.

Yet many Australians, including many of those I lecture in pre-service teacher training courses, profess little interest in history and have always 'found it dull'. Moreover, they have little conscious awareness of the historical baggage that they, like all of us, carry: that *sense of history* that Simon Schama suggests flows through us as *part of our cultural bloodstream, the secret of who we are* which we all begin imbibing it at a very early age – from our parents and families, from the small enclaves in which we live, and from the schools that we attend.[1]

To understand our relationship with Aboriginal people, we must first recognise the source of the *sense of history* that flows through us and then unpack the *historical baggage* that we all carry. Let me illustrate with reference to my own experience.

---

[1] Schama, S. *A History of Britain* (2000).

Like many Irish Australians of my generation, I grew up with a sense of being apart from the mainstream of Australian society, carrying a subconscious sense of exile and of historic injustice inflicted on Irish Celts by the dominant Anglo Saxons. This manifested itself in various ways that now seem harmless and quaintly humorous but which, in the 1950s, were really manifestations of the sectarian divisions in Australian society then.

We attended parties where the adults sang *Danny Boy* and maudlin versions of *I'll Take You Home Again, Kathleen* – which left no doubt that the *home* being sung about was Ireland itself. We proudly celebrated the Saint Patrick's Day holiday by wearing green sashes and brooches depicting harps and shamrocks – and we were sure to get out early to taunt the kids trudging off to the local state school with childish chants of *Proddy dogs eating frogs* or some such nonsense. On Saturday afternoons we refused to stand for the playing of *God Save the Queen* before the start of the show at the local flicks. At Easter we attended a service at the 1798 Irish Monument in Waverley Cemetery where the Rosary was recited in Irish and reminiscences of Michael Collins and other heroes of 1916 were shared. We still felt under siege.

Fortunately, the Catholic schools we attended, though not totally out of the bog of sectarian division, set expectations for us that were based on a slightly more sophisticated view of society. In many ways they were *Irish* schools rather than *Catholic* schools and asserted the validity of our new Irish-Australian identity. In other words they celebrated our *Irishness* but also insisted that we had a place to fill in Australian society. So successful were they that hordes of us, though often losing *the Faith* in the process, achieved respectability of a sort through careers in the public service, education, nursing, the police, the trade unions, and the ALP. We knew we belonged.

Like all school students of that era, we learned little at all of Aboriginal people or their history – certainly no suggestion that our new sense of belonging had come at a cost to them. The very little we were taught focused on those *good* Aboriginal people who had assisted explorers and settlers – the unnamed man who ran along the river bank to warn Sturt of armed Aboriginal men waiting further down the Murrumbidgee and later acted as an intermediary; the assistance given by Wylie to Eyre on his long trek across the Bight; and the loyalty of *Jacky Jacky* in staying with the fatally wounded Kennedy in North Queensland.

There was certainly no mention at all of terms like *invasion* or *dispossession*. On the contrary, I well remember a good nun using the iconic Emanuel Phillips Fox painting, *The Landing of Captain Cook at Botany Bay, 1770*, to demonstrate the benign impact of colonisation: Cook was bringing civilisation to this new land, extending his arm to tell his men not to fire their muskets at the two Cadigal men confronting them – though I am sure she did not say *Cadigal,* a term then barely known.

Many, many years later I realised that Aboriginal people might have a very different interpretation of this event, even later that Phillips Fox's painting did not even tally with Cook's own record.

Figure 2.1 E. Phillips Fox: The Landing of Captain Cook at Botany Bay, 1770 (1902), Courtesy National Gallery of Victoria.

In fact, of course, Cook did not restrain his men but actually ordered them to fire at the two Aboriginal warriors. Impatient to get ashore, he first ordered that they fire above the heads of the two men. Momentarily alarmed by this first volley of gunshots in eastern Australia, they dropped their spears and withdrew; but when they returned almost immediately, Cook ordered that shot be fired into their legs.[2] Only then did the men withdraw so that Cook and his party were able to land.

This is absent from Phillips Fox's painting which was commissioned to celebrate Federation in 1901. The omission is perhaps understandable – by challenging the right of the British to land, these Cadigal men had, at least symbolically, undermined the notion of *terra nullius* which was the basis of Cook's claim of the eastern half of Australia and the subsequent colonisation of the entire continent. Those celebrating Federation would hardly have wanted to be reminded of this.

It took even longer for me to become aware of how different were the family histories of those Aboriginal children attending school in the 1950s – many at La Perouse just a few miles from where I was with the nuns at Clovelly – from mine.

They were not newly arrived migrants but could trace their family histories back thousands of years. They too had a sense of being apart from the mainstream of Australian society. Indeed they were much further from the mainstream than any Irish Australians – for their dispossession, from which the rest of us had benefited, had made them exiles in their own land.

Moreover, the Aboriginal students of that era did not benefit from attending schools that reinforced the strength of their identity by celebrating their history, and insisting that they had a role in contemporary Australian society. Instead they were given the same *settler's perspective* on Australian history as we were – Captain Cook bringing civilisation to a wild land from which Aboriginal people faded into the background – as indistinct as the two Aboriginal figures in the Phillips-Fox painting.

---

[2] See Nugent, M. *Captain Cook Was Here* (2009).

The *settler's* view of the past left little room for Aboriginal people in the Australia of that time. At best they were quaint tourist attractions from a disappearing past who might entertain us with exhibitions of boomerang throwing or diving off the Bare Island jetty for the pennies thrown by day-tourists at La Perouse. There was no place for them in mainstream society and most Aboriginal students of my generation dropped out of school even before completing the old Intermediate Certificate, to eke out a living as best they could on the margins of society.

It took me quite a few years to realise that Aboriginal people did not *buy* the Australian history that I was teaching, and understand why my Aboriginal students in the Riverina, Darwin, and elsewhere would not engage with it. Then, beginning with the 1970 Bicentenary celebrations of Cook's arrival at Botany Bay, a series of events made me aware that the vast majority of Aboriginal people had retained a very healthy cynicism and mistrust of the received wisdom about Cook, *terra nullius*, subsequent British *settlement* and the way Australian history was taught in schools.

First, the protests at the 1970 Cook bicentenary when Aboriginal and non-Aboriginal people – including Kath Walker (later Oodgeroo), Faith Bandler, and the ABC journalist Alan Ashbolt – spoiled the celebrations by taking a boat into the bay and throwing a mourning wreath into the water as the re-enactment was taking place. Most people at the time had no appreciation of this protest.

Little had changed 18 years later when Aboriginal people responded to the Bicentennial Celebrations by insisting that *White Australia Has a Black History*. My own experience in the NSW Department of Education then suggests that Aboriginal people had every reason to be insistent. Resources in use at that time were still patronising, stereotypical, and partial in representing Australian history, but complaints by Aboriginal parents were typically brushed aside and ignored. On one occasion in 1982 this paternalistic approach resulted in a group of concerned parents storming into Cleveland Street High school and simply removing an entire class set of an offensive and outmoded History text.

A 22-page resource booklet I prepared for the Department's Aboriginal Education Unit caused some controversy when a complaint about its use of the term *invasion* was made by a dispatch clerk who had time to read one of the 20,000 copies about to be sent to schools. The booklet was recalled, pulped, then reissued with several passages deemed potentially offensive deleted.[3] These included Pemulwuy *daring to resist the invasion of his land* in the section describing Governor Phillip's orders to a punitive expedition after Pemulwuy's killing of the Governor's gamekeeper. A phrase suggesting the establishment of the Aboriginal Legal Service in the 1980s was *'in response to the treatment of Aborigines in the Redfern area by the police'* was also deleted. The concluding paragraph was also deleted, suggesting the determination of Aboriginal people, referring to the Land Rights struggle by citing verbatim the words the Aboriginal activist, Chicka Dixon, used to end the documentary, *Lousy Little Sixpence*:

> *"The struggle goes on, and will continue to go on, until justice prevails. Because we are the first Australians and this is our land."*

Another indication of departmental ignorance and hyper-sensitivity to controversy was its initial failure to purchase *Lousy Little Sixpence* when it was originally offered to them on very favourable terms by the producers, Alec Morgan and Gerry Bostock. Two senior officers in the Department's Special Programs Unit, then still responsible for Aboriginal Education, flatly rejected the possibility that Aboriginal children had been removed from their homes and families in the 1920s, 1930s, and 1940s. Dumbfounded, the producers took the documentary to Charles Perkins at DAA (Department of Aboriginal Affairs) in Canberra. Within months the film was so widely acclaimed that the Department then had to purchase the rights for a much more expensive fee.

---

[3] *The Aborigines in Australian History – Some Background Notes for NSW Teachers* (Directorate of Special Programs, NSW Department of Education, c. 1983).

Departmental ignorance and obstructiveness changed in the 1990s. Following the adoption of Reconciliation under the Hawke and Keating governments, the momentous Mabo decision by the High Court in 1992, and even the History Wars during the Howard years that followed, we saw new levels of awareness of the place of Aboriginal people in Australian History and some appreciation of the benefits of incorporating multiple perspectives into a *shared history*. But that progress already seems to be disappearing as, for a variety of reasons, interest in this history has declined – no longer as relevant as it was in the 1980s and 1990s.

The post-Mabo generation has become blasé in the belief that the ideological and social struggles of the movement for Aboriginal rights are no longer relevant. Instead there seems a complacent belief that all resolved by legislation for Native Title, the emotion of the 2008 Apology, or a sentimental tear or two during a screening of *Rabbit Proof Fence*. Teacher trainees are certainly no longer as interested in the historical struggle between *coloniser* and *colonised* as were students in the 1980s and 1990s when the Bicentennial, the Royal Commission into Aboriginal Deaths in Custody, *Bringing Them Home*, and *triumphalist* vs. *black armband* interpretations of history stoked the fires of intense debate.

The emergence of an Aboriginal middle class, stimulated in part by increasingly broad interpretations of Aboriginal identity, may also be blurring distinctions and dampening interest in the historical struggle between Aboriginal and *settler*. Much less restrictive, less discriminatory immigration policies over the past 30 years have produced a much more open and diverse society and a remarkable flowering of multiculturalism. However, it has also contributed to a rapid decline in general knowledge of the previous 220 years of Australian history – both the traditional Anglo-centric *settlers' histories* that earlier generations were force-fed and the *shared history* since the Bicentennial. To understand the newer *shared history*, one must understand the influence of earlier approaches to telling the nation's story.

So great has been the decline in what was previously thought to be common knowledge that the significance of Cook and Phillip can no longer be assumed knowledge in second year teacher trainees. Much less can it be assumed that they will know anything at all of Bennelong and Barangaroo – or why an understanding of the subsequent relationship between Aboriginal and non-Aboriginal peoples is necessary in contemporary Australia.

All of these factors make it even more imperative to develop more detailed knowledge and understanding of the historical baggage that we carry and which influences our attitudes. This historical baggage very quickly morphs into *received wisdom* about the past through pervading commemorative art, public ceremony, political discourse, the media, and the arts. Examples of this can be seen in the commemorative art that adorns Sydney's Macquarie Street precinct around the State Library and the Mitchell Library. In a prominent position outside the library immediately opposite the entrance to the Botanic Gardens is an 1846 monument, built by public subscription to honour Sir Richard Bourke, Governor of NSW 1831-1837.

The inscription clearly demonstrates the blithe disregard of colonisers of the 19th century for any Aboriginal claims to the land: the unstated assumption that all of Australia was in a state of terra nullius. It begins by lauding Bourke as a man of judgement, urbanity, and fairness who comprehending at once the vast resources peculiar to this colony … applied them for the first time systematically to its benefit. He also founded the flourishing settlement of Port Phillip (Melbourne) and threw open the unlimited wilds of Australia to pastoral enterprise.

Bourke is justifiably regarded as one of NSW's more effective and enlightened Governors and his achievements certainly earned him popularity and praise from the colony's citizens. But his monument represents a major element of received wisdom about Australian history – the wild lands of Australia were unoccupied and awaiting the enterprise of the colonisers; Aboriginal people were irrelevant – not even worthy of mention, nor of consultation about the seizure of their lands for development by pastoral enterprise.

A nearby 1925 monument to Matthew Flinders, the British navigator who first circumnavigated and mapped the entire Australian coast, is also revealing. Flinders' achievement was extremely significant and is widely recognised in public memorials around Australia. But neither the Sydney monument nor any of the others acknowledge that Flinders was accompanied on his circumnavigation by an Aboriginal man, Bungaree. Such an omission was perhaps understandable in 1925 when it might be attributed to ignorance of Bungaree – even though Flinders referred to him as a worthy and brave fellow who had assisted in bringing about a friendly intercourse with the inhabitants of other parts of the coast.[4]

However, a recent addition, fixed on the wall of the Library immediately behind the original memorial, is more difficult to explain. Sponsored by the women of the North Shore Historical Society and completed in 1996, it is a John Cornwell sculpture of *Trim*, Flinders' cat of which he was fond and which also accompanied him. Apparently this quaint memorial is so popular with visitors to the library that *Trim* merchandise sells well in the library bookshop and the cafe has been named after the little moggy. There is still no mention of Bungaree – despite the supposed impact of all the positive changes to Australian historiography since the 1980s, Aboriginal people are still largely irrelevant to the main story of Australia's past.

This message of the superiority of the colonisers is reinforced by the art work on the commemorative doors at the main entrance to the Mitchell Library. This was completed between 1934 and 1942, funded by a £4000 donation from Sir William Dixson, the library's principal benefactor to honour the library's founder, David Scott Mitchell. Dixson made the donation on condition that the art work at the entrance depict Australian themes; Nita Bernice, the library's then director of Research

---

[4] Flinders, M. *A Voyage to Terra Australis* (1814), 235.

Services, scoured the collections for appropriate images of explorers and Aboriginal people.

The images of Aboriginal people and their way of life came from a variety of sources that today could well be regarded as insensitive, narrow, and ethnocentric. They included material from Ion Idriess, the novelist; anthropologists Herbert Basedow and A.P. Elkin; Herbert Finlayson, a writer whose book *The Red Centre* had just been published; and *Walkabout* magazine. Bernice then commissioned a young Queensland sculptress, Daphne Mayo, who produced the door covered in images of Aboriginal people as 'primitives'. The door was acclaimed and enthusiastically described as *preserving the primeval majesty of Stone Age man*.[5]

The suggestion that these 'primitives' were supplanted by a *superior* race was emphasised by a second door depicting Australian explorers. This featured busts of: Torres, Cook, La Perouse, Bass, Tasman, Baudin, Dampier, Flinders, Hovell, Sturt, Major Mitchell, and Stuart as well as Tasman's ships, the *Heemskerck* and the *Zeehan*, and two of Cook's ships, the *Adventure* and the *Resolution*. It was produced by the Czech Jewish refugee Arthur Fleischmann whose gaining of the commission caused some controversy when he was accused of being an enemy alien. More controversy when Fleischmann proposed to depict the near fatal 1790 Aboriginal attack on Governor Phillip at Manly – but such a scene was beyond the pale in the Australia of 1940.

The two doors emphasise the supplanting of a *primitive* race by the arrival of *civilised* Europeans. The message of the land being opened up and *civilised* by the coming of the Europeans is further reinforced by the replica of Tasman's 1642 maps on the marble floor, showing the incomplete European outline of the Australian coast at that time.

Changes in university education and technology over the years mean not all today's students are necessarily familiar with the environs of the Mitchell Library and hence not necessarily susceptible to their received

---

[5] *ABC Weekly*, cited in Jones, D.J. *A Source of Inspiration and Delight* (1988).

wisdom. However, the decimal currency banknotes that we carry around every day are another source of *received wisdom* about Australian history. A quick examination of these notes reveals that, though at least two represent Aboriginal themes, their depiction of Australian history and culture is also very much from a *coloniser's* or *settler's* perspective.

The very first issue of notes in February 1966 represented a view of the nation's past that was very similar to the History textbooks used in schools. The original $1 note proudly displayed the nation's coat of arms and our Head of State, a youngish Queen Elizabeth II in impressive robes and regalia. However, the reverse side showed images of an Arnhem Land bark painting and rock art.

The Governor of the Reserve Bank at that time was H.C. (*Nugget*) Coombs, a prominent advocate of Aboriginal rights. Like the opening chapter of school history books, the note acknowledged the long history of Aboriginal occupation prior to the arrival of Europeans. Usually titled 'Pre-History' these chapters reflected the stirring of new understandings,

Figure 2.2 The original 1966 $1 Note.

acknowledging the long Aboriginal occupation of the continent, at that time estimated to be around 20,000-30,000 years before the present (BP).

But the Reserve Bank's attempt at inclusiveness backfired. Despite Coombs's standing as an advocate of Aboriginal rights, no one at the Bank had considered any obligation to pay a copyright fee for the use of an Aboriginal artist's work, or get permission. The story broke only a few days before the introduction of the new currency and caused considerable controversy. Fortunately for all involved, the artist, David Malangi, accepted an apology and the issue of the new currency went ahead as scheduled. Later that year Malangi received a modest compensation payment – *$1,000, a fishing kit and a silver medallion in recognition of the nation's appropriation of his work.*[6]

The rest of the decimal banknotes depict the story of Australia in a very similar way to the bland, boring, and often smug way the nation's story since 1788 is recounted in school textbooks. The now defunct $2 note, like the $1 a victim of inflation, celebrated colonial pastoralism and farming with portraits of John Macarthur and his merino sheep and William Farrer and his rust-free wheat.

The $5 note demonstrated again the nation's links to Britain with another portrait of Queen Elizabeth II backed by illustrations of the old and new parliament houses in Canberra – symbols of the development of a thriving democracy.

The $10 note provided further reminders of the pioneering, colonial past with images of two poets renowned for celebrating the struggles of the pioneers – poets Mary Gilmore, known for support of Aboriginal people, and Banjo Paterson, with an extract from and illustration of *The Man From Snowy River* – learned by generations of students from the 1930s. A Bicentennial special $10 (the first revolutionary polymer) featured an Aboriginal youth in bodypaint backgrounded by a Morning Star Pole by the Arnhem Land artist, Yumbulul; at his right shoulder a

---

[6] Sackville, R. *Traditional Knowledge* (2002).

rock painting of a woman in Deaf Adder Gorge (Arnhem Land), with handprint stencils as in rock drawings across the country as background pattern on the left.

The $20 and $50 notes also refer to the colonial or pioneering past, both promoting the idea of a history in which progress and the *fair go* went hand in hand. The $20 features Mary Reiby, the convict woman who *made good* by engaging in colonial commerce. She is pictured against a background of a trading ship at anchor at Circular Quay. On the reverse side is a picture of John Flynn – *Flynn of the Inland* – with the small aircraft and camels that he used to establish the Flying Doctor Service and ensure medical assistance for the pioneers developing Central Australia in the middle years of the 20th Century.

The $50 note reinforces the theme of social justice, the *fair go*, and equality in Australian History. It features Dame Edith Cowan on one side and an Aboriginal man, David Unaipon, on the other. Cowan became the first woman elected to an Australian Parliament – indeed one of the first women elected to a parliament anywhere in the world – when elected to the West Australian parliament in the 1920s. Unaipon was a clergyman, first published Aboriginal writer, and an inventor of some repute and from the 1930s to the 1950s a gentle and conservative advocate of social justice for Aboriginal people through assimilation.

The $100 note concludes the currency's history by referring to some of Australia's international achievements and our military tradition. The people featured on this note are Sir John Monash, the Jewish-German-Australian who commanded the Australian forces in World War One, regarded by some as one of the more effective commanders of that wasteful and tragic war, and world renowned opera singer from the 1890s to the 1920s, Dame Nellie Melba.

In such ways is a collective view of Australian history inserted into the consciousness of Australians. Like much history taught in schools, it is bland, simplistic, and not a little smug: a history of progress and achievement with no meaningful reference to any losers and only superficial references to the most accommodating of Aboriginal people.

The pervasiveness of this *received wisdom* about the past is a major influence in shaping the popular view of the *national identity*; the extent to which one's own personal identity connects with this collective view of the past can determine how comfortable an individual feels as a member of Australian society. Needless to say, most Aboriginal people still do not feel particularly comfortable.

Despite the apparent ongoing resilience of the Eurocentric *colonisers'* view of Australian history, it is foolish and churlish to deny that there have been enormous changes in Australian historiography since the Cook Bicentenary of 1970 and the Bicentennial celebrations in 1988.

Aboriginal activism and a new approach to history by academic historians[7] has led to the development of *shared history*: an approach to history that allows multiple perspectives – from the Aboriginal side of the frontier as well as from the settlers' side. The visual and performing arts are significant sources of Aboriginal perspectives on history, an example being *We Call them Pirates Out Here*, Daniel Boyd's 2007 parody of *The Landing of Captain Cook at Botany Bay*. A comparison of this artistic representation of history with the 1901 painting by Phillips Fox highlights the different perspectives that are incorporated into the new *shared history*.

This *shared history* is now a feature of school curriculum, particularly in NSW where the Board of Studies has incorporated extensive Aboriginal perspectives not only in History but in almost all Key Learning Areas. But the effectiveness of these perspectives depends very much on the historical knowledge and understanding of teachers and their ability to teach historical skills rather than emotive responses. As with Australian History generally, there is a danger of counter-productive *overkill* with the repetition of perspectives throughout the curriculum resulting in content being broadly spread, but not very deep – an approach that inevitably results in superficial knowledge but little understanding.

---

[7] Among others these include Rowley, Henry Reynolds, Heather Goodall, Lyndall Ryan, Bain Attwood, Richard Broome, Andrew Markus, and James Miller.

Figure 2.3 Daniel Boyd: We Call Them Pirates Out Here (2006), Museum of Contemporary Art. Courtesy of the artist and Roslyn Oxley9 Gallery, Sydney.

There are other issues as well. One of the strengths of Aboriginal culture is the widespread attachment to family and communal histories. This reflects and reinforces the strength of kinship ties and the oral tradition. It may also be a response to the loss and disorientation suffered by many of the Stolen Generations and the realisation, as a Lakota proverb puts it, that *a people without history is like wind on the buffalo grass*.[8] But while Aboriginal parents and lobby groups like the Aboriginal Education Consultative Group (AECG) encourage teachers and schools to help educate their students about these family and communal histories, typically transient teachers know little of them. Moreover, their pre-service training encourages them to empower their students through a broader

---

[8] Trimble, Sommer & Quinlan (2008; fn.21) attribute this to Amos Bad Heart Bull, Oglala.

analysis of issues and policies by focusing on state, national, or global levels rather than on local issues.

Somehow teachers need to develop the skills that will allow them to combine both approaches – to reinforce the local identity of their students by fostering pride in local history and culture while at the same time empowering their students so that they will have the ability to engage in issues at national and global levels. To not do both will ultimately promote either paternalistic or assimilationist outcomes and further undermine the identity and self-confidence of both students and communities.

Clearly, History matters. It is crucial to understanding and developing the relationship between ALL Aboriginal and ALL non-Aboriginal Australians. Whether we are Aboriginal Australians, Anglo-Australian, Celtic or Euro-Australian, or part of the rapidly growing Asian-, Arabic-, African- or Islamic-Australian population – knowing where we come from and where others come from is essential both to our understanding of who we are and to the establishment of relationships with all of multicultural Australia.

# 3

# Promised Brides and the Insolence of Freedom: Aboriginal Australia and Violence During Cultural Transition

*Stephanie Jarrett*

*Where women are promised to men they have to go with them. If they do not there is shame. Sometimes there are bashings to wash out the breach when these women marry others than those to whom they were promised.*[1]

### Introduction: The Dangerous Time of Cultural Transition

As with various cultures across the world, interpersonal violence within traditional Indigenous Australia occurs not just in the context of an angry domestic setting, but since traditional times, is viewed as an instrument to maintain or restore the correct order of social and sacred life. This renders it difficult for many remote Indigenous communities to reach a threshold of effective opposition to violence, and the threshold of support needed to protect and empower Aboriginal victims of violence. Moreover, traditional law is considered not human-made, but from Creation time, unchanging, eternal: "Aboriginal law always stays the same";[2] "Tribal punishment, blackfella way, never change".[3]

Despite the fixed nature of Indigenous traditional law, and despite geographical remoteness, self-determination policies, and the permit

---

[1] Law Reform Commission of Western Australia (LRCWA). (2004), 29. Comment from Kimberley region.
[2] Ibid., 49, Comment from Kimberley region.
[3] Ibid., 8, Comment from Pilbara region.

system, all of which are intended to further enhance traditional continuity, there is a cultural transition occurring across remote Aboriginal Australia. Young Indigenous people are becoming more familiar with the choices available to men and women in mainstream Australia, particularly in those most precious spheres: freedom to choose a partner; and freedom to leave a violent relationship without the threat of violent community or family enforcement to stay. This awareness is likely to increase, as remote young people in greater numbers experience mainstream norms during school semesters in the city away from the community. In addition, even on the most isolated communities with strictly enforced permit systems, young Indigenous people are rapidly adopting mobile phones, internet and social networking technology, thereby bringing them into daily contact, in their very homes, with once distant mainstream lifestyles and choices. Concerns from remote community people in Western Australia portray a society in transition:

- (Kimberley) Women and others were subjected to controlled punishments by men. This was often seen as a way of showing the men's concern for their women. Now we see an increase in women in prison for bashing up their men.[4]

- (Kimberley) Aboriginal women have moved on, but the men have been left behind. The men often don't know how to do things traditionally, and they have lost much self-esteem.[5]

- (Pilbara) The problems start when young people refuse to be bound by the law ... More youths are complaining about law, which may lead to the situation where a young person goes through law and then lays charges. In traditional society, people did not give consent to be put through law.[6]

---

[4] Ibid., 29.
[5] Ibid., 29.
[6] Ibid., 4.

During these transitional times, Elder community members witnessing women's and young people's more assertive behaviour are responding in several ways. Some call for greater application of white law to protect women and young people from the violent enforcement of male authority. Some have a sad resignation to young people's loss of respect and compliance with traditional law, and because of this, transition times can be heart-breaking for them, particularly when they see their young people go to towns and break white law as well, accessing the physically, mentally, and emotionally damaging aspects of mainstream life such as alcohol and drugs. Other Elder community members use violence and blackmail in a bid to enforce 'unchanging' traditional law onto increasingly non-compliant women and young people. This latter response can mean intense gender and intergenerational conflict, rendering cultural transition prolonged, violent, and dangerous. The plight of remote Aboriginal women and young people during cultural transition has placed our nation at ideological and practical crossroads. Self-determination and cultural 'rights' ideology supports traditional practice and law, with its punishment-enforced male and Elder authority and exacting marriage laws. Some young people will comply out of respect for their culture, others to avoid violent punishment. However such compliance appears to be increasingly unbearable. For Indigenous women and young people, non-compliance to tradition, and the choice of freedom, are worth pursuing, even at the risk of family and community ostracism and punishment. Indeed, the escape road to the mainstream and its freedom of choice can be perilous.

What does our nation need to do to uphold young Indigenous people's universal rights to freedom of choice and freedom from violence, in the face of ancient, respected, but unbending Indigenous laws, invoked against an increasingly defiant younger generation? Can we empower Aboriginal women and youth in communities to stand up for freedom of choice and freedom from violence, without those attempts being perceived as an expression of 'cultural genocide', or 'assimilation', or 'paternalism'? These are tough issues which need discussing.

## Oppressions of a Traditional Patriarchy

In Lisa Tuttle's *Encyclopedia of Feminism*, a definition of patriarchy is:

> The universal political structure which privileges men at the expense of women ... Literally it means 'rule by the father', and was originally used by anthropologists to describe the social structure in which one old man (the patriarch) has absolute power over everyone else in the family ... Under some systems women have more privileges, even token power, than in others, but everywhere men are dominant, and the basic principles ... remain the same: 'men shall dominate female; elder male shall dominate younger'.[7]

In the past, human societies demonstrated a tendency to have separate social and economic roles for men and women, and greater power and status for men. Some of these role differences were largely unavoidable due to women's child-bearing and breastfeeding years. How societies elaborated on male and female roles beyond these innate physical differences was through 'artefact' or culture, and not determined by nature. This enabled a huge diversity in male and female roles and power relations between cultures. As presented by David Levinson in his global survey of domestic violence, even across traditional cultures there was great variation.[8]

In Australia's traditional Indigenous cultures, gender roles, both ceremonial and everyday, were separate, clearly defined, and patriarchal. Their traditional sacred roles and practices, while both important, were separate and unequal, with older, initiated male sacred roles typically

---

[7] Tuttle, L. *Encyclopedia of Feminism* (1987), 242.
[8] Levinson, D. *Family Violence in Cross-Cultural Perspective* (1989).

of higher status, and women and uninitiated males subordinate.[9] The traditional domestic or economic domains for men and women were also distinct and separate, and fathers, brothers, and husbands had considerable control over daughters, sisters, and wives.[10,11]

Another feature of traditional Aboriginal Australia that reflects a patriarchal system, particularly its gerontocratic (rule by Elders) aspects, is the pre-contact practice of polygamy across much of the continent, which while no longer typical, still occurs in parts of remote Australia. This caused additional subjugations of women, and also of young men due to the resultant dearth of women available for marriage. To partially correct for the gender imbalance arising from polygamy, while men were commonly mature, even elderly, when they married, girls frequently married just after or even before puberty. In addition, because polygamy rendered women a scarce and valuable commodity, a girl could be a promised bride from even before birth. Men with more status, fighting ability or in more recent years greater wealth, were better able to acquire a wife. Typically, older men were the winners in this traditional competition for scarce brides, with inevitable distress among young men.[12]

There were also strictly enforced 'correct skin' marriage rules, defining and limiting whom one could marry, and giving additional scope to Elders as law-keepers to punish young people for attempting to form a love marriage.

Along with polygamy, promised brides and the forced marriages of young girls to mature men, anthropologists and other early observers

---

[9] Jarrett, S. *Liberating Aboriginal People from Violence* (2013), Chapter 4.
[10] Warner, W. L. *A Black Civilization* (1958), 110.
[11] While Diane Bell in *Daughters of the Dreaming* (1983), argues that women's traditional status and role were more equivalent than subordinate, men nevertheless wielded violent-enforced control over women. See Kimm, J. *A Fatal Conjunction* (2004), 44-54; and Jarrett, S. op. cit., Chapter 5.
[12] Mary Bennett, evidence to Moseley Royal Commission March 1934, quoted in Windschuttle, K. *The Fabrication of Australian History* (2009), 462.

reported gender relations typical of a harsh, patriarchal system. There were legitimised reasons that husbands could beat their wives, fathers and brothers could physically punish daughters and sisters, and more sacred transgressions for which women could be punished, even executed.[13] In sum, classical cultures across pre-contact Australia were structured for men's control of women, and for older men's benefit at the cost of younger men. It was a harsh, patriarchal society.

## "People change it but law never changes":[14] Traditional Patriarchy in a Time of Transition

Traditional Aboriginal culture and the fundamental belief in its unchanging nature remains a patriarchy with perils for women, as shown by the high assault and homicide victim rates of women on remote communities.[15] This is the kind of patriarchy one expects would enrage women's rights activists.[16] In recent decades, there has been a growing national awareness and alarm at the high rate of serious Aboriginal family or domestic violence. Reports on the severity of violence against women on Aboriginal communities have raised national concern, but not enough. For instance, at the 1993 *Violence Against Aboriginal Women* seminar in Darwin the (then) Northern Territory Police Commissioner Mick Palmer said, "We cannot afford to sweep this problem under the proverbial rug and pretend we are in control because, in my view, we are not". Palmer also criticised the wider community, including the feminist lobby, for regarding Aboriginal violence as either "too hot to handle" or "just the Aboriginal way". He further stated, "There is nowhere near the same sense of outrage in the community as there is when there is violence against a European woman."[17]

---

[13] Jarrett, S. op. cit.
[14] LRCWA. op. cit., 6. Note: Comment from Pilbara region.
[15] Productivity Commission, *Overcoming Indigenous Disadvantage: Headline Indicators* (2007).
[16] Tuttle, L. op. cit., 242.
[17] Nason, D. 'Black Laws 'Force Abuse Victims Home" *The Weekend Australian*, 18-19 September 1993.

Paucity of academic and activist interest in exploring the cultural underpinnings of this heightened violence across much of remote Indigenous Australia delays effective remedies. The primary focus is on western impacts such as alcohol and the decades of Aboriginal suffering, disruption, and loss under colonial regimes. Even when acknowledged, there is scant concern about tradition's oppressive aspects underpinning much of this violence. Indeed, there have been recent equivocal, even apologist, arguments for traditional Indigenous customs being oppressive to very young women, including some from surprising voices. Here are some examples:

Sharon Payne, when she was director of the North Australian Aboriginal Legal Aid Service stated:

> there was usually nothing wrong with promised marriages as such. Promised brides are really about keeping kinship systems here, making sure the story continues as it should.

She conceded,

> the issue of forcing somebody to have sex against their will is a different matter altogether.[18]

Hetty Johnston, founder of the child protection group Bravehearts, commented in an article about a remote Aboriginal man in his 20s convicted of carnal knowledge against his 13-year-old customary marriage wife. The case appears challenging, in that the girl is now in her late teens, the couple live in the home of the girl's supportive parents, and the couple are raising their child together since its birth. Nevertheless, clarification from Johnston is warranted for her ambiguous and unhelpful statement on young Indigenous women's rights:

> there was room to allow indigenous people to have their own enforceable laws. But she said all current laws should be respected

---

[18] Hughes, H. *Lands of Shame* (2007), 31.

until that happened. "We can't have decisions being made and exceptions being made without that process having taken place".[19]

In his speech to the National Indigenous Legal Conference, Tom Calma, then Aboriginal and Torres Strait Islander Social Justice Commissioner, emphasised his opposition to violence against women and young people. In reference to the infamous *The Queen v GJ* "'promised bride' case", Calma sought to clarify that culture cannot be used as a mitigating circumstance in cases of violent physical and sexual enforcement of a promised bride:

> Now I want to make clear, taking promised wives by force is not customary. In 2003, the Northern Territory Law Reform Commission undertook an inquiry into Aboriginal law in the NT. It found the following about promised marriage:
>
>> Generally speaking, the child is expected to understand the nature of the contract when she reaches puberty (say 12 or 13) ... The girl can choose not to comply with the marriage agreement at any time prior to living with the husband. However it should be noted that the social expectations of all the families involved are that the marriage would normally proceed. Love marriages are recognised as a fact of life for the girl, her family and the community and thus the process for the girl and her family repaying benefits received in anticipation of marriage is also dealt with under traditional law.[20]

Along with ignorance or denial that the traditional promised marriage agreement could involve force against resistant girls, these three examples also share an ideology that child abuse is relative, depending on cultural context. Hence, parents promising their young daughter to a much older man for marriage when she is barely out of puberty, and sex in marriage with underage girls, being ancient aspects of Indigenous customary

---

[19] Schliers, M. 'Appeal Likely in Case of Wife, 13' *The Australian*, 14 April 2011.
[20] Calma, T. 'Integration of Customary Law into the Australian Legal System' (2006a).

practice and law, are to be defined as not abusive. This conflicts with the liberal democratic and United Nations principle of the universal rights of women and girls.

Rendering such perspectives more disturbing, violence as punishment surrounding promised marriage and women's subjugated status continue, as evident in community perspectives from the Kimberley and the Pilbara, Western Australia:

> (Kimberley) Where women are promised to men, they have to go with them. If they do not there is shame. Sometimes there are bashings that wash out the breach when these women marry others than those to whom they were promised.[21]
>
> (Pilbara) Marriage is strong – separation is not allowed without parents' consent, if wife does separate she will be punished.[22]

The equivocal statements of Payne, Johnston, and Calma also contrast with some traditional women's pleas to override customary law where necessary, to protect underage young women. In 2003, these pleas were read to the Northern Territory Parliament for a Bill for legal protection of underage Indigenous girls, triggered by the notorious assault on a 15 year promised bride, *Hales vs Pascoe*:

> a 19-year-old girl sought refuge from the then member for Nightcliff, Dawn Lawrie, after the girl had been beaten regularly by her promised husband. The 19-year-old alleged, back then, 20 years ago, that many young women were running away from unhappy promised marriages. She said they were often beaten, and pack raped in an effort to make them accept their marriages. In relation to the 15-year-old girl, Dawn Lawrie put out a press release saying:
>
> *I am sick and tired of what I see as a conspiracy of silence on this issue, and call on Territory politicians to make their views known to us all. For*

---

[21] LRCWA. op. cit., 29.
[22] Ibid., 3.

> *too long, too many have pretended that the slavery of child brides just does not happen.*

Although I expect some objections to this amendment, ... support will come from the people ... most affected in this debate: Aboriginal women and girls. I will quote from a letter I received from the Aboriginal Women's Group in Central Australia ...

> *...The women felt very strongly the court should not have any regard to Aboriginal Customary Law where the victim is under 16 years of age.*

They are all too aware of the abuse that is inflicted on children and young girls in their communities. The letter goes on to say:

> *One of the main objectives has been to ensure that the Australian legal system protects Aboriginal women and children from violence.*[23]

In apologist statements about children being promised into marriage, there is possibly an assumption that because these Indigenous marriage laws are customary and thousands of years old, they are not experienced as abusive by young girls living in a traditional society. Evidence indicates otherwise, and when they did not comply, force entered the situation. There are reports of young traditional girls fleeing to missions for protection from forced, promised marriage to older men. One young Bathurst Island girl, Martina, was rescued by Bishop F.X. Gsell in 1921 from a promised marriage to a much older man. Years later Martina sought help from Bishop Gsell again, this time to rescue her six year old daughter, who was kidnapped into a promised marriage and taken 50 miles away from her distraught parents:

> "it is the tribal custom," Martina explained amidst her tears, "that all baby girls are given a son-in-law who will be the husband of all her daughters ... this son-in-law, now a young man, came to us in the forest ... and although I protested, ... We could not stop them from taking Elizabeth away".[24]

---

[23] Northern Territory Second Reading Speeches, Sentencing Amendment Bill 2003.
[24] Gsell, F.X. *"The Bishop with 150 Wives": Fifty Years as a Missionary* (1956), 88. See also, Franklin, J. 'The Missionary with 150 Wives' (2012); and Jarrett, S. op. cit.

Elizabeth was rescued. There was joy among 150 Indigenous Bathurst Island girls rescued by Bishop Gsell over the years from promised marriages, freeing them to court and marry young men of their own age and choosing. In the words of Bishop Gsell:

> In the bush there are no engagements, there is no courtship. When the time comes there is merely an automatic transfer from the mothers of girls to their "sons-in-law" ... The change we instituted was revolutionary to our young charges and, at first, they hardly knew what to do about it nor how to behave themselves.[25]

The thwarting of young people's freedom by Elders upholding ancient laws continues to cause suffering in remote Indigenous Australia. The notorious, often discussed Northern Territory *Hales vs Pascoe*[26] and *The Queen vs GJ*[27] cases are about traditional, older male sense of right to kidnap and assault a resistant young promised bride, echoing aspects of the kidnapping of Martina's daughter about 80 years earlier.[28] In *The Queen vs GJ*, the 55-year-old offender's kidnap and sexual assault of his 14-year-old promised bride was triggered by his suspicion that she was having sex with a young male school friend.[29] While these cases are well-known, others remain anonymous, or never get reported at all, because of fear of consequences to victims if they are reported.

Fear of reporting domestic violence is also common among non-Aboriginal victims. Women in all cultures, including Australia's suburban (disadvantaged through to upper-class) white households, are subjected to controlling behaviour by violent husbands. These may include blackmail threats by the perpetrator against his wife's family, pets, or property unless she complies with his will. These too are isolating, silencing, physically and mentally dangerous situations. Women

---

[25] Ibid., 98-99.
[26] *Hales v Jamilmira* [2003] NTCA 9.
[27] *The Queen v GJ* [2005] NTCCA.
[28] Gsell, F.X. op. cit., 88-9.
[29] *The Queen v GJ* [2005].

across cultures have much in common through such shared, patriarchal oppression as women. Indeed, to presume one woman's experience as a domestic violence victim is invariably worse than another woman's on the basis of their different race and cultural settings is to presume too much.

However, along with greater rates of severe domestic violence among Aboriginal Australians, there are cultural and other differences that make it more difficult particularly for remote area Aboriginal women to escape. At the 1993 *Violence Against Aboriginal Women* seminar in Darwin, it was reported that:

> Aboriginal women who have suffered from often extreme violence are returning to their homes to protect family members from retribution or "payback" that can occur under traditional law.[30]

One wonders how women victims are ever meant to become 'empowered' and forge their own liberation in such a violent, silencing, and isolating cultural setting. The words of Eileen Cummings of the Northern Territory Office of Women's Affairs, reinforce this pessimism:

> In traditional (Aboriginal) law women cannot leave the family without the approval of the tribal elders ... If they do, they risk retribution against family members. The result is that Aboriginal people have a higher level of acceptance of family violence than the rest of the community.[31]

A woman cannot leave "without the approval of the tribal Elders"? In Australia? Are these women not Australian citizens? The victimised woman's love and fear for her family moreover, engenders greater resignation or adaptation to violence against herself. What a choice, what a cruel form of control and blackmail: stay for further serious violence; or flee, and beloved family members get abused. This forced

---

[30] Nason, D. op. cit.
[31] Ibid.

'choice', even though traditional, deserves no respect, dignity, or right to continuity. Women's right to these most fundamental of freedoms is far more important than that. As an abuse of a person's freedom of movement, it too is domestic violence, and should trigger outrage among women's rights groups and effective action by police. Such restriction of an adult's freedom of movement would also contravene the Northern Territory's *Domestic and Family Violence Act* as a action of intimidation, defined by the Act as a form of domestic violence which includes "any conduct which has the effect of unreasonably controlling the person or causes the person mental harm".[32]

## The 'Wrong Way' is a Broken Heart

The cost for young people for breaking the rules of customary law can be debilitating, indeed unbearable. Increasing numbers of young Aboriginal people on remote communities are engaging in 'wrong way' relationships, in conflict with customary marriage rules, as documented in the 2008 Mullighan Inquiry:

> An anthropologist informed the Inquiry that a wrong way relationship occurred if the basic rule that governed the kinship system was broken ... the whole reason for the moiety system is to avoid incest, to make sure you're marrying the right way and surviving ... But what was always very heavily punished, even by death, was marrying the wrong person.[33]

The Mullighan Inquiry includes cases of at-risk under-age girls in sexual relationships, some consensual, others forced, and some violent. Additional problems arose for these troubled young people when it was a 'wrong way' relationship.

One depressed, suicidal 14-year-old girl faced additional stress

---

[32] Department of the Attorney General and Justice, Northern Territory. (2012). *Northern Territory Domestic Violence Act*, Table of Provisions, 5 (c) and 6 (1) (c).

[33] Mullighan, Hon. E.P. QC. *Children on Anangu Pitjantjatjara Yankunytjatjara (APY) Lands: Commission of Inquiry: A Report into Sexual Abuse* (2008), 28.

because her relationship with a 21 year old man was 'wrong way'. It was recorded that by age 15:

> she has become ostracised by what family supports she did have (in the community) due to her wrong way marriage ... the couple were evicted ... after a protracted marital dispute that escalated and involved threats of self harm.[34]

In another case a 14 year old pregnant girl was deemed at risk "because of her young age, limited supports, and substance abuse":

> Medical records indicate there were pressures by relatives to have a termination because of the "wrong skin" relationship but the pregnancy was detected too late. The pressure on the girl by relatives to terminate the pregnancy allegedly continued after it ceased to be medically possible.[35]

The following instance is particularly tragic, also involving a 14-year-old pregnant girl and her teenage husband:

> Aged 14, the girl had a 'wrong way' marriage to an older teenager. The girl became pregnant and the youth committed suicide. Welfare records suggest that fear of punishment under traditional law for the 'wrong way' relationship and pregnancy may have contributed to the youth's suicide. The girl was allegedly told that she would be punished when the child was born, or to a lesser extent if the pregnancy was terminated. The girl was considered responsible for the youth's death and an assault on her carer had occurred as part of payback.[36]

The Inquiry recorded that payback rarely occurred for 'wrong skin' relationships anymore, with such relationships among young people on the APY Lands so common that "the old people were 'tired of young

---

[34] Mullighan, Hon. E.P. QC. op. cit., 43.
[35] Ibid., 66.
[36] Ibid., 69.

people doing it and don't try to stop it'".³⁷ Nevertheless, the Inquiry documentations indicate widespread conflict between older and younger people on the APY Lands over this issue. Older people feel shamed by 'wrong way' relationships, young people are forced away from their community, and pressured by families to abort or adopt out the 'wrong way' baby. Indeed, "In one such instance a health professional noted that the family were more concerned with the baby being 'wrong skin' than the sexual exploitation of the girl".³⁸

'Wrong skin' marriage causes transitional tension between old and young across remote Australia. In the Kimberley and Pilbara regions, community people want the right to punish. For example, one woman indicated that:

> in cases of "wrong way" marriage (marriage outside of skin group) then people should be able to punish and it should not be classified as physical abuse. "It is just punishment and the people punishing under Aboriginal law should not be punished by white law."³⁹

And the frightened, ostracised young people leave, to 'mess up' in the towns:

> The community gets the blame when young people leave the community and mess up in Nyaparu Town ... Many went to live there because they were involved in "wrong" relationships and these relationships would not be tolerated in the community.⁴⁰

In his speech to NILC when he was Aboriginal and Torres Strait Islander Social Justice Commissioner, Tom Calma emphasised that:

---

³⁷ Ibid., 68.
³⁸ Ibid., 173.
³⁹ LRCWA. op. cit., 49. A 2012 report on the high rate of suicide in the Kimberley community of Mowanjum depicts the high level of service concern and response, but despite this, the suicides continue. See Herbert, B. 'Spate of suicides grips Aboriginal community', ABC News, 6 September 2012 (located on the Australian Database of Indigenous Violence: www.indigenousviolence.org/dnn)
⁴⁰ LRCWA. op. cit., 4.

> ... marriage into the right skin group is still extremely important in many Indigenous communities. A wrong marriage disrupts the social order and makes it difficult for people to maintain good relationships. It can have implications in terms of customary law. By the same token, traditional marriage also requires consent – it requires a process of education whereby those who are betrothed go through careful preparation before marriage.[41]

What would Calma recommend to these young people? Older people's adherence to correct skin law runs counter to the reality of young people's lives and loves. Banishment, punishment, and the pressure to abort or adopt out their baby, place these already at-risk young men and women at additional peril of substance abuse, neglect, homelessness, criminal activity, and suicidal despair.

## A Search for Remedies in a Time of Transition

In the early decades of the 20th Century, Bishop Gsell rescued many young women from forced, promised marriage to older men, and brought happiness to as many young men by enabling them to marry their chosen young partner. Moreover, he did this with a cultural sensitivity that avoided shaming the Elders, and he gained their co-operation to release the girls from their traditional marriage promise.[42] As a nation we seem to have lost that kind of art, or perhaps it would no longer be workable. Many hard working and caring Aboriginal and non-Aboriginal service providers for remote communities look on in alarm at the suffering of young people caught in the clash of traditional requirements with modern world freedoms.

We also seem stuck at resignation to traditional subordination of women as we search for means of protecting them from domestic violence. This is reflected in the provision of local respite centres in

---

[41] Calma, T. op. cit.
[42] Gsell, F.X. op. cit., Chapter V.

response to remote Indigenous women's calls for temporary shelter from partner violence, rather than provide shelters as part of an effective pathway for permanent escape.[43] Problems with remote area safe houses are outlined in the *Women, Homelessness and Domestic Violence: A Synthesis Report*:

> Solutions to family violence and the provision of housing are best provided within the communities as Aboriginal women have strong kinship ties and in the main will not leave their community…'Safe houses' in the Australian context refers to the Indigenous concept of a 'place where women can go before or after crisis, and stay for a time, without actually "leaving" their partner'.[44]

Certainly, the love and sense of belonging these women have for their family, community, home, and country, would make leaving very hard.[45] However, how much is 'strong kinship ties and in the main will not their leave community' code for the patriarchal intimidation, parental punishment, and blackmail threats from tribal Elders that force domestic violence victims on remote lands to stay? Also, problems found with these temporary respite shelters include inadequate safety for the women and children sheltering there, lack of confidentiality regarding the location of safe houses, and while communities want safe houses to "be run by local staff, issues around conflict of interest and safety for the employed local community members have been raised".[46]

Furthermore, remote Indigenous women often have few skills, including literacy or numeracy, few resources and little experience of mainstream living, and little support, making it difficult for them to gain a

---

[43] Flinders Institute for Housing, Urban and Regional Research (FIHURR). *Women, Homelessness and Domestic Violence: A Synthesis Report* (2008).
[44] Ibid., 48.
[45] Days, L. 'Homelessness Family Violence and Homelessness in Aboriginal and Torres Strait Islander Communities' (2011).
[46] FIHURR. (2008), 49.

foothold towards living successfully in an urban environment. A network of supportive, mentoring services and friendships within mainstream Australia, and safety in an affordable home, are critical needs. Without these, longer-term homelessness or a return to a violent home on their remote community are likely:

> Most Indigenous women from regional and rural areas will return to the community from which they came as it is difficult to ask, and expect them to live in a different way – away from family and friends in an almost foreign environment. Leaving your home can make you 'homeless' for two to four years. Whether Aboriginal women stay or leave, choices of longer term housing options are often very limited by discrimination and high costs in the private rental market and the long waiting lists for public housing accommodation.[47]

Indeed, family violence is the major cause of homelessness among Aboriginal Australians. While the Indigenous population is less than 3% of Australia's total population, "(a)lmost a quarter (21%) of women seeking help from a homeless service as a result of domestic violence, are Indigenous women".[48] Clearly, many Aboriginal women are "choosing" to leave a violent relationship despite the hardship of homelessness and other huge impacts of leaving family and country, including retribution against family members.

Another factor brought to my knowledge during fieldwork was that local Aboriginal identity politics could make settling into a new location difficult for Aboriginal people, including women escaping domestic violence. One Aboriginal woman, fleeing a violent relationship from interstate, reported to me that her attempts to be accepted by the town's Indigenous women's group were shunned because she was not a local. Another woman who fled a violent relationship from interstate was

---

[47] Ibid., 48-9.
[48] Homelessness Australia. 'Homelessness and Indigenous Australians' (No date).

denied voting rights at an Indigenous women's workshop on the grounds that she was not a local. Hence, 'local Aboriginal identity' derived from one's traditional or historical belonging to country or place trumping 'Australian Aboriginal identity' is another painful challenge facing Indigenous women fleeing domestic violence, in the already difficult search for a welcome place for themselves and their children.

Australia needs to comprehend the plight of Indigenous women, young people, and 'wrong way' couples fleeing violent punishment and ostracism and too frightened to reside on their community. We need to find better ways to dialogue and work with the communities distressed by losing control over their young people, to assist them to cope with the painful reality of rapid cultural transition. While recognising the positive aspects of Aboriginal culture, we must express intolerance for violence and subjugation of women and young people. We must fulfil our national obligation to meet the critical needs of desperate Indigenous women, young people and couples, in search of a home, safety, and a welcoming, supportive neighbourhood. Above all, we must push aside separatist barriers fostered by years of Coombsian self-determination policies, so that remote Aboriginal people, as integrated citizens, have full access to the individual freedoms, education and employment opportunities of mainstream life, liberated from the punishing yoke of promised marriage and 'correct skin' law.

# 4

# Who Are You to Speak?
# Silencing Aboriginal Dissent[1]

*Kerryn Pholi*

'... *(S)o many irritating dissidents have been described by their enemies as 'self-appointed' ... 'Self-appointed' suits me fine. Nobody asked me to do this and it would not be the same thing I do if they had asked me. I can't be fired any more than I can be promoted ... If I am stupid or on poor form, nobody suffers but me. To the question, Who do you think you are? I can return the calm response: Who wants to know?*'[2]

As a mid-level Aboriginal bureaucrat working in various government and community sector agencies, I had for some time been feeling uneasy about the deference given to my opinions, the leniency around my work standards, and the indulgence of my behaviour that did not extend to my 'non-Aboriginal' colleagues to anywhere near the same degree. In a number of organisations I worked for, I noticed that my non-Aboriginal colleagues were not always free to fully apply their knowledge and expertise to resolving problems in Aboriginal policy and service delivery, as they were required to consult with and defer to the opinions of Aboriginal people such as myself. As a research officer working in Aboriginal statistics, I noticed that while we depended heavily on the guidance of Aboriginal 'key stakeholders', we were disinclined to subject their analysis and opinions to rigorous critical inquiry. I also noticed

---

[1] This chapter is a modified version of an article by Kerryn Pholi published in *Quadrant*, December 2012a, titled 'Silencing Dissent Inside the Aboriginal Industry'. *Quadrant* has given us permission to use the article here for our book.
[2] Hitchens, C., *Letters to a Young Contrarian (Art of Mentoring)* (2001), 81.

that, in following the advice of our Aboriginal steering committees and stakeholders, we did not always collect or report on Aboriginal statistics as accurately as we could have.

In my experiences of working in organisations responsible for direct service provision to Aboriginal people, I noticed that the continued satisfaction of our Aboriginal clients was a primary concern. When funding is allocated and an agency's performance is measured by the number of Aboriginal clients it services, the satisfaction and retention of these clients take precedence over challenging them to make necessary changes in their lives. Rather than risk Aboriginal clients taking their business elsewhere – or worse, complaining about the service's 'cultural insensitivity' – the service provider simply provides whatever the Aboriginal client demands of them.

I began to realise that commodifying Aboriginality – placing a positive value on an individual employee, student, consultant, adviser, or client purely on the basis of their 'race' – was doing little to produce sensible policies and effective programs to solve the problems many Aboriginal people face, and was doing nothing to address the ongoing calamity of daily life in many remote Aboriginal communities. Instead, it was producing divided, fearful, and risk-averse organisations where the subjective happiness of Aboriginal staff, stakeholders, and clients took precedence over the well-being and effective functioning of the organisation overall.

As I read the works of American, Indian, and African-born authors Thomas Sowell, Amartya Sen, and Kwame Anthony Appiah, I realised that there was nothing unique about the mechanisms or the unfortunate effects of Aboriginal race politics in Australia; this was an international problem, a human problem that arises wherever people become emotionally and politically invested in one 'identity' as separate and distinct from the 'identities' of those around them. In Australia, our substantial emotional and economic investment in maintaining a separate Aboriginal identity has created an Aboriginal industry, made up of institutions and agencies with 'expertise' on the distinct needs and wants of Aboriginal people.

In September 2012, the ABC's online opinion website *The Drum* published a short article I had written, which briefly explained my experiences of working in the Aboriginal industry, and the shift I had experienced over time in my own views on race-based preferential treatment for Aboriginal people.[3] I explained my decision to reject such preferential treatment for myself because I could not reconcile myself to racism, and I suggested that other Aboriginal readers consider doing the same. The article generated a substantial number of responses, with a number of commentators expressing support for my views.

Other responses to *The Drum* article provide useful examples of the kinds of suppressing arguments that are centred on the 'legitimacy' and 'authenticity' of the Aboriginal speaker, rather than the quality of the speaker's reasoning and expression. Silencing arguments also point to the speaker's unsavoury character, which is evident through the offensive nature of his or her ideas, as well as through his or her apparent pandering to a 'racist' enemy force. None of these silencing approaches are unique to Aboriginal race politics; they appear in some form wherever the politics of identity take precedence over constructive political debate.

### "You're Not Black"

> *Take a good look at Kerryn and notice how pale she is for an Aboriginal woman that would make her somewhat more acceptable from non-Aboriginals ... you can't ignore the thousands of other Aboriginals who are regularly discriminated against on the grounds of their distinct Aboriginality. ...*
>
> – J: 27 Sep 2012 8:36:03pm

> *Fortunately because of your appearance you would never have*

---

[3] Pholi, K. 'Why I Burned My 'Proof of Aboriginality'' (2012b).

> *had to put up with the stares, abuse, rude offensive behaviour by shop assistants, harassment by the police etc. that is part of everyday life for fullblood Aboriginal people. ...*
>
> **– oneman:** 27 Sep 2012 10:27:41pm

Responses such as these were arguing that if I were a darker-skinned, obviously Aboriginal-looking person, I would probably experience a great deal of racist discrimination and I would therefore appreciate special assistance, support, and compensation for such unfair treatment. They suggested I was unfairly criticising the system from a position of privilege – as an Aboriginal who can 'pass' as non-Aboriginal – while others are not so fortunate.

I agree that my not particularly Aboriginal appearance may render me more acceptable to some, and that I may therefore be treated better in various aspects of daily life than a distinctly Aboriginal looking person may find herself treated. I also agree that I cannot offer an informed view of the degree of discrimination and ill-treatment such a person may experience – how would I know? My argument against race-based preferential treatment is not based in a belief that racism is not a problem; I don't doubt that racism towards Aboriginal people occurs, as it occurs towards people of other 'races' and ethnicities in Australia and elsewhere. Yet how does the provision of special privileges to someone like me – simply because I can claim 'Aboriginality' – ameliorate racist discrimination against other Aboriginal people?

### Can Racism be OK if it Helps Properly Black People?

While there have long been grumblings amongst Aboriginal folk in some quarters that entitlements and concessions intended for 'Aboriginal people' are too frequently claimed by 'white Aborigines' – the grumblers tend to shy away from the obvious solution, which would be to introduce a skin-colour requirement to the assessment process. A chart of Aboriginal skin-colour gradations with a clearly indicated cut-off point would provide much-needed guidance to selection panels for jobs, grants, awards, and other Aboriginal-specific entitlements, ensuring they only go to properly 'black' Aboriginal people. Few would seriously consider such an obnoxious solution – yet even if it were adopted, it would still be merely an administrative adjustment and not a remedy for racism against people of Aboriginal appearance.

A system that responds to racism by implementing special entitlements and assistance for actual or potential Aboriginal victims of racism reflects an incredibly complacent, or perhaps defeatist, attitude to the problem it purports to address. Rather than rejecting racism as a backward belief that has no place in modern Australia, and promoting equal treatment and dignity for all, and enforcing this wherever necessary, our governments simply create an alternative form of racism into which 'vulnerable' Aboriginal people are shepherded for their own safety.

This is a state that has given up on its own citizens as irredeemably backward and ignorant racists, and has given up on Aboriginal citizens as incapable of survival in the nastiness of the world outside the sanctuary of the Aboriginal industry. To genuinely address a problem of racism against Aboriginal people, we must not tolerate racism in any form. Anti-discrimination measures must be clearly expressed and rigorously enforced, and an individual who experiences discrimination or ill-treatment on the basis of his or her race – whatever their 'race' may be – should have the means to seek redress.

Some may counter that a sole reliance on anti-discrimination measures would be insufficient because many Aboriginal people are too oppressed and marginalised to recognise the racism directed towards them, or to take formal action as people of other ethnicities may do when they encounter racism. This then justifies a need for special protective and compensatory measures for Aboriginal people, preferably delivered by other Aboriginal people wherever possible in order to avoid further traumatisation. Yet this is simply further evidence of the complacency and defeatism that pervades Aboriginal affairs – protection and compensation for Aboriginal people is regarded as preferable to the education and empowerment of Aboriginal people to take care of themselves.

### "You're Not Disadvantaged"

*Aboriginal people still do suffer discrimination on all manner of fronts. So, some positive discrimination probably isn't all that bad. You seem to be in a position now where positive discrimination and access to education etc. has given you the opportunities and voice you now enjoy. Others in this time are not so fortunate.*

– **Disagreeable:** 28 Sep 2012 12:26:31am

*Kerryn would appear to have had a good education and agrees that she is equipped to operate on a level playing field and doesn't need to play the "Aboriginal" card. However I think there are some Indigenous people who don't have the same opportunity to reach her level in the community.*

– **Pegaso:** 27 Sep 2012 9:21:03pm

Out of 699 responses to my article on the *Drum* website, not a single apologist for race-based preferential treatment tried to persuade me that I was, as an Aboriginal person, actually quite a disadvantaged individual whether I realised it or not. A number of comments, such as those above, pointed out how disadvantaged *other* Aboriginal people are, and some Aboriginal commentators talked about how disadvantaged they *themselves* were – but no-one contradicted my own fairly obvious lack of disadvantage. If anything, my relative privilege was regarded as further evidence that I didn't know what I was talking about.

Yet if people can readily accept that I am an Aboriginal person who is not particularly disadvantaged, then they must concede that disadvantage must rest in something more than simple 'Aboriginality'. Therefore, bestowing concessions and entitlements simply on the basis of 'Aboriginality' makes no sense as a means to address the problems many – but not all, and not only – Aboriginal people face.

## 'Close the Gap': Aboriginal = Disadvantaged

When we define people by one variable, in this case 'Aboriginal', they become a homogenous collection of indistinguishable, interchangeable units, whose fate is somehow linked. As an Aboriginal person I belong to a statistically disadvantaged Aboriginal population; therefore, I am 'disadvantaged'.

In reality, there is substantial disparity in the Aboriginal population – a 'gap' – between the poorest and most disadvantaged Aboriginal people and those such as myself who are doing quite well. There are disadvantaged Aboriginal people living in circumstances with varying degrees of choices and opportunities, but many individuals do not readily take advantage of these opportunities to alleviate their disadvantage – although opportunities are often vigorously pursued at the collective level, particularly in the form of funding for community organisations. Aboriginal people face powerful disincentives to personal advancement, not least of which is the inextricable association of 'Aboriginality' with 'disadvantage'.

While Aboriginal communities are often socially, emotionally, and often economically invested in maintaining a distinct and separate Aboriginal identity, they exist in a society where Aboriginal 'identity' and 'culture' are increasingly nebulous and changeable concepts. As a consequence, *disadvantage* has become one of the most recognisable and cherished features of the Aboriginal sense of self, and a source of community solidarity. In such an environment, to pursue opportunities to move away from disadvantage is to reject one's Aboriginal identity and one's own family and community.

Then there are the relatively small but rapidly increasing ranks of middle-class Aboriginal 'achievers' such as myself. Some people have suggested that perhaps there would be fewer of us if not for the special opportunities that were made available to us on the basis of our Aboriginality. I suggest that there might be *more* of us if the benefits of education, employment, and a middle-class lifestyle were not anathema to those who treasure their disadvantaged 'Aboriginal' identity.

## Middle-Class Aborigines Are Disadvantaged Too

As I discussed above, one (flawed) rationale behind the offering of race-based entitlements and concessions for Aboriginal people is to serve as a counterbalance to prevailing racism in the broader society. Another rationale is to provide Aboriginal role models, in order to demonstrate to Aboriginal people and to the broader community that is it possible for an Aboriginal person to 'make it'.

The mission of the middle-class role model is to demonstrate to those Aboriginal people lower down the socio-economic ladder that one can take advantage of opportunities to make a more comfortable life for oneself whilst retaining a recognisably Aboriginal identity. Yet at the same time, in order to justify my special Aboriginal role I must reinforce the message that to be Aboriginal is to be disadvantaged – and that only Aboriginal professionals like me have the power to resolve Aboriginal disadvantage. As an Aboriginal role model, I must downplay my own relative privilege and good fortune and instead display my 'authenticity' as a disadvantaged Aboriginal person, despite outward appearances.

To display my 'disadvantaged' credentials, I may do a number of things: I may recount my family's experiences of deprivation, perhaps with anecdotes of unpleasant experiences from my childhood. I may describe my extended family's ongoing disadvantage, complete with examples of my various relatives' health, legal, and financial woes. I may reveal my personal experience of racism, with stories of the offensive remarks, assumptions, and slights that plague my daily existence. Conversely, if I am paler in complexion I can describe the emotional pain I feel when my Aboriginal identity is unrecognised, questioned, or ignored by those around me. If all else fails, I can talk about my personal grief over the suffering of 'my people'. In this manner I can demonstrate that I have 'made it' and bravely continue to 'make it', despite the disadvantages I face daily as an authentically Aboriginal person.

## Perhaps We Could Make Racism Work Better to Fix Aboriginal Disadvantage?

Some of my colleagues in Aboriginal policy have conceded that this blanket approach to resolving Aboriginal disadvantage tends to favour the least disadvantaged Aboriginal people, mirroring Thomas Sowell's findings from affirmative-action policies worldwide.[4] Some have expressed tentative interest in a modified approach, whereby assistance and opportunities are directed more effectively to those Aboriginal people who need it most. However, the practical and ethical considerations of implementing an eligibility criterion of 'disadvantage' are yet to be seriously examined.

An honesty system in which Aboriginal applicants self-assess their eligibility for assistance is unlikely to work, given that even the most prosperous Aboriginal people may still consider themselves to be disadvantaged in some way. Perhaps Aboriginal-specific positions, awards, grants, and scholarships could be subject to means-testing and skills-testing, whereby those Aboriginal people with existing assets, skills, or qualifications may be ineligible to apply or may be ranked lower in order of preference. This solution would, however, make it difficult to hire the best Aboriginal applicant for a job, or award a scholarship or research grant to the most promising and talented Aboriginal candidate. It would also create disincentives for Aboriginal people to develop skills and acquire qualifications and assets, since these would render them ineligible for special assistance. Perhaps Aboriginal candidates from postcodes with lower socio-economic index rankings might be given preferential consideration among the broader pool of Aboriginal candidates. It would, however, be difficult to explain to their equally disadvantaged non-Aboriginal neighbours why the Aboriginal people in their neighbourhood are receiving special assistance from which they themselves are excluded. "Because Aboriginal people are disadvantaged"

---

[4] Sowell, T. *Affirmative Action around the World: An Empirical Study* (2004).

is a rather lame response to give to people who are substantially disadvantaged themselves. "Because the Aboriginal population is more disadvantaged compared to the rest of the population" suggests to our audience that the 'non-Aboriginal' population's relative affluence overall, in which they themselves have very little share, is nonetheless a benefit they enjoy that their Aboriginal neighbours do not. Perhaps we would explain to them that Aboriginal people suffer from the additional burden of racism in ways that other disadvantaged people do not experience. While several in our non-Aboriginal audience could point out that they themselves experience the effects of racism, our entire audience may reasonably ask – "If Aboriginal people are being disadvantaged by racism, why don't you do something about that instead of creating more unfairness for us?".

We know that discrimination on the basis of 'race' is ludicrous and unjust, yet we are afraid to openly challenge preferential policies for Aboriginal people for fear of being regarded as callous, uncaring, ignorant, and of course, racist. Instead, we look for ways to make racist policies 'more effectively targeted', hoping to deliver sufficient benefits to justify our racism as a means to more noble ends. We look forward to reaching a point where such policies are no longer needed, though we have little idea how or when this point will be reached. We try to find ways to make racism 'fairer' – which is even more reprehensible than simple, unreconstructed racism, because we do not have ignorance as an excuse.

### "You Don't Know Your Culture"

> *The genuine traditional Aboriginal people have to put up with people like yourself, who have no experience of traditional custom, language, law or tradition, making public representations on behalf of "Aboriginal people" most of whom they know nothing about and don't even have the basic respect of wanting to find out.*
>
> **– oneman:** 27 Sep 2012 10:27:41pm

*Central questions in court cases dealing with this tricky issue are upbringing and cultural identification. A witness in Eatock v Bolt last year testified about inculturation from early childhood by participating with his grandparents in hunting, fishing and producing the medicines, remedies and tools they needed. Traditional knowledge of sacred sites and stories of his people were passed down to him by relatives and other Elders. He also testified to the racism he suffered growing up within a marginalised community. Was this Kerryn's upbringing also? Or did she choose to identify as Aboriginal later in life, as she later chose not to? This would seem a relevant point.*

– **Alan Austin**: 27 Sep 2012 3:29:22pm

*I am Indigenous, worked in the public service too and never had the problem she mentions, but I think she lacks the type of childhood I had where I was brought up with a strong sense of cultural identity, which acts as a sort of buffer to the issues that appears to plague her. I place this article in the just another "Blame society it's not my fault" rant pile.*

– **Timothy Williams** (Woppaburra): 27 Sep 2012 5:12:01pm

When an Aboriginal person speaks out in criticism of the Aboriginal industry, or speaks in favour of policies that are unpopular with the industry, it is almost inevitable that at some point a venerable Aboriginal spokesperson will declare – more in sorrow than in anger – that the dissident has "lost her culture" or "turned her back on her culture" or is "ignorant of her culture".

This form of silencing suggests that if I had more cultural authenticity I would be disinclined to question or critically reflect on policies that provide preferential treatment to Aboriginal people. I would be less inclined to think independently, less inclined to care about anyone other than myself and my immediate family, and less inclined to voice any opinion that conflicts with those upheld by my 'culture'. If this is the 'culture' that I am supposedly so sadly lacking, then I am glad I missed out on my indoctrination. I feel fortunate that I belong to a modern culture that encourages me to think for myself, speak for myself, to take an interest in ethical and effective public policy, and to have concern for the welfare of those beyond my narrow kinship group or tribe.

### "You're Forgetting Your History"

*I'm not Indigenous but I do believe anyone younger than me (44) shows an amazing amount of historical ignorance sometimes.*

– **Sam of Brisbane**: 27 Sep 2012 3:11:32pm

*When a group is or has been discriminated against it is entirely proper that this group be targeted for redress of the injustice. This is not racism it is remedying racism.*

– **Evan Hadkins**: 27 Sep 2012 6:43:11pm

To the latter comment, I would counter that targeting a present-day 'racial group' for the redress of historical injustice against other people of that 'racial group' is actually racism at its most insidious and contemptible. According to this notion, I am regarded not as an individual with my own personal history, aspirations, and choices, but as a member of a historically mistreated racial group that is now targeted for redress. I have become a representative of all other Aborigines, past and present. This means that if you feel bad about what happened to an Aboriginal person in the past, you can simply compensate me, because we are essentially the same creature.

In reality, some people experienced hardship in the past. I was not one of those people. Why should I benefit from another's hardship, simply because a person who suffered in the past happened to be Aboriginal, and I happened to have an Aboriginal ancestor? It is not as though we consistently embrace this concept of redress for other historically marginalised racial groups in Australia. For example, Chinese immigrants had a particularly hard time during the gold rush eras, yet there are no special benefits extended to Australians of Chinese background today to make up for their historical mistreatment.

## Who to Compensate for Colonisation?

Some Aboriginal advocates for compensation may describe a direct personal link with historical injustice and deprivation (a great-grandfather's unfair treatment on a cattle station; a grandmother of the 'stolen generations'; a parent's experiences of racism in the classroom and subsequent poor self-esteem) as a rationale for race-based concessions as a form of compensation for past wrongs. To this I would ask: "How does awarding entitlements to me make things better for you, your parents, or your grandparents?" The aggrieved party would most likely indignantly respond that such entitlements are not rightfully mine – the redress should go to those people who have been hurt (that is, people like *them*), and people like me should keep our paws out of the compensatory cookie jar.

Given that the compensatory cookie jar is not an endlessly self-replenishing magic pudding, those who feel entitled to compensation for historical injustice would do well to establish some criteria on genuine cases for compensation, to ensure undeserving Aboriginal people like me do not fraudulently benefit. However, as soon as we begin to consider eligibility criteria for compensation for historical injustice, the issue becomes something more than a matter of mere 'Aboriginality', and introduces a greater burden of proof, along with thorny questions of who should have the authority to judge claims and order recompense.

It is understandable that, on further consideration, Aboriginal proponents of compensatory preferential treatment would prefer to maintain a magic-pudding policy, whereby anyone who can claim to be Aboriginal automatically has a *moral* claim to compensation for historical injustice. Although this approach means some Aboriginal people, like myself, might receive more than we deserve, it doesn't really matter so long as there is plenty to go around and nobody makes a fuss about it.

## "You're Hurting People's Feelings"

*I'm amazed that a person with Aboriginal heritage should write such appalling things. This is playing into Andrew Bolt's hands and giving him what he will assume is a licence to continue his racist attitudes towards our first citizens. You should not be proud of your disloyalty to your people.*

– **hammygar**: 27 Sep 2012 3:50:56pm

*As an Aboriginal woman who has worked all my life to get better outcomes and a better quality of life for our people, I find it puzzling why you would write such an article in a major daily newspaper, which most Aboriginal people don't even read! Maybe you want to impress the red-necks. Let's hope such naivety on your part doesn't lead to another ill thought out debate.*

– **Pat Turner**: 27 Sep 2012 11:24:15am

With the decline of recognisably 'Aboriginal' cultural practices and the disconnection of Aboriginal identity with recognisably 'Aboriginal' physical features, the *feelings* of Aboriginal people (or more precisely, the *feeling of being Aboriginal*) has become an increasingly visible concern. In the urban and regional centres where most Aboriginal people live, Aboriginal people may not necessarily appear or behave very differently from the non-Aboriginal people around them, but we are assured that Aboriginal people feel different, and feel differently, and thus require special treatment.

In response to the statistical 'gap' in health and life expectancy for the Aboriginal population, the Aboriginal health sector has increasingly focused on monitoring, reporting, and improving the feelings of the Aboriginal population. This is mainly pursued through the management of others' behaviour towards Aboriginal people rather than through direct dialogue with Aboriginal people about their feelings and how they might manage them. 'Cultural awareness' and 'cultural safety' are important qualities for government agencies and service providers to develop and display towards Aboriginal people, while the broader community is encouraged to demonstrate 'respect for Aboriginal people' by engaging in certain practices (acknowledgements, ceremonies) that help Aboriginal people feel good, and refraining from others (questioning, criticising) that might make Aboriginal people feel bad.

Such expressions of respect for Aboriginal people do not require a clear explanation of precisely what it is that is about Aboriginal people we are meant to be respecting, as qualities that are separate and distinct from other members of the human race. These expressions are a kind of shorthand to indicate that I want Aboriginal people to feel respected, because I care about Aboriginal health and well-being. In contrast, if I speak or behave in ways that are deemed to be disrespectful of Aboriginal people or inconsiderate of their feelings, this indicates that I do not care about Aboriginal health and well-being, and that I accept – or even endorse – ongoing Aboriginal disadvantage. Respect is conceptualised as an active form of caring for Aboriginal people, while disrespect is actively harmful to Aboriginal people – because making Aboriginal people feel bad is bad for their health.

## Be Respectful: The Governance of Sentiment and Policing of Speech

Respect is a sentiment, we either feel respect for something or someone, or we do not. Increased knowledge and understanding may increase our respect for another's particular culture and views – or we may find that our respect for another party diminishes the more we learn about them. As citizens, we should be free to express and explain our feelings of respect or disrespect for each other. These freedoms must include the freedom to express personal feelings of disrespect for Aboriginal cultural values (both traditional and modern), for Aboriginal popular opinion (if there is such a thing), and for the expressed opinions and behaviour of particular Aboriginal people.

Aboriginal people should not be insulated from 'disrespectful' critique and commentary; not only is it infantilising, but it stymies the necessary self-reflection and debate that is a catalyst for change. Aboriginal people should not be afforded special legal protection from being 'hurt' or 'offended' by another's critique of their values or behaviour, as such protection only discourages intelligent people from engaging with and critically examining Aboriginal problems. No Aboriginal individual in public life should be exempt from the scrutiny that others in public life are subject to – particularly those Aboriginal individuals with responsibility for substantial amounts of public funds.

Excessive deference to Aboriginal demands for 'respect' has left many Aboriginal people unskilled in public discourse, with a tendency to conflate contrary opinion with oppression, criticism with abuse, disapproval with racism, and speaking about Aboriginal issues with presumptively speaking for Aboriginal people. Race politics and a minefield of 'cultural sensitivities' have already rendered Aboriginal health, education, and social services professional ghettos, discouraging many – too many – talented and compassionate professionals from pursuing careers in these areas. Excessive restrictions on 'respectful' discourse in Aboriginal policy debate will only create an intellectual ghetto, where only those deemed to be appropriately respectful will be permitted to discuss an increasingly impoverished range of ideas. To attempt to govern and police 'respect' for or amongst Aboriginal people is just another form of tyranny; and as with all tyranny and repression, it is the most vulnerable that suffer from the silencing of debate.

## So, Who Are We to Speak?

In the interests of encouraging free and open debate of Aboriginal issues, the obvious response to the question, "Who are you to speak?" is, "I am a person with a considered opinion and the right to express it. Who are you to stop me?"

When our legitimacy to speak critically is questioned on the basis that we are not dark-skinned enough, not disadvantaged enough, or not sufficiently 'cultural', it can be tempting to respond with proof of our Aboriginal credentials by describing our 'Aboriginal' upbringing and recounting our personal experiences of racism and disadvantage. (Others seeking permission to speak may point to their numerous Aboriginal friends, or describe their experiences of living and working closely with Aboriginal communities).

While it may be momentarily satisfying to prove our legitimacy in this way, leaping through this hoop to demonstrate our credentials does little to encourage others to participate in debate on Aboriginal issues. When we do this, we are perpetuating the convention that only those with an acceptably authentic personal experience of Aboriginality can legitimately participate in discussion. If we want *anyone* with a rational and informed point of view to feel they are able to express it, we would do better to refuse to jump through hoops, and to simply insist on our right to speak on the understanding that our audience will judge our ideas on their merits alone.

Finally, we need to stop talking in terms of 'closing the gap'. There are Aboriginal people whose social and material circumstances are virtually indistinguishable from those of other middle-class Australians, and there are some Aboriginal people who are quite prosperous. Other Aboriginal people, particularly many in remote communities, are living in desperate need, and at present they have limited options and incentives available for them to improve their circumstances. Their circumstances and opportunities – or at least those of their children – *can* be improved, although improvements in material circumstances and integration with the broader community will be necessarily accompanied by some shifts in their beliefs, values, and self-perceptions.

There are other Aboriginal people living with serious – if not quite so desperate – problems and needs. These Aboriginal people have the same choices and opportunities available to them as their non-Aboriginal cohorts, though they face identity-driven social and cultural disincentives to make the choices that would improve their circumstances. Again, improvements in their social and material circumstances may be accompanied by transformations in their current ideal of what it means to be Aboriginal.

The problem is not the 'gap' itself, but the notion of an inherently disadvantaged Aboriginal identity that inhibits Aboriginal people's advancement. Kwame Anthony Appiah notes that the contemporary notion of 'identity' – in which race, ethnicity, sexuality, and other social features are recognised and venerated as the defining elements of one's sense of self – came into being in the social psychology of the 1950s.[5] So up until fairly recently, people managed to function without such 'identities' to tell them who they were and what they needed. Perhaps people of Aboriginal descent will find they too are capable of flourishing in the absence of a narrow and limiting Aboriginal identity. The power of Aboriginal identity politics to suppress Aboriginal people's advancement will diminish the more we challenge and 'disrespect' its many absurdities, and the more we continue to speak about Aboriginal issues as though it is everyone's business to do so.

---

[5] Appiah, K.A. *The Ethics of Identity* (2005).

# 5

# No More Victims

*Anthony Dillon*

*And when people tell you, "You can't get up, you're a victim", that's when you know that it is the devil you're hearing, no one else.*[1]

*Whilst history has no doubt dealt Indigenous people a questionable hand, there is no need to wallow in it such that it cripples us from acting and creating better present and futures for our communities ... It is time we moved beyond the victim, as indeed many have done so already.*[2]

*Getting ahead becomes elusive when you're trained to think like a victim.*[3]

## Introduction

A significant source of the problems facing Aboriginal people today is the status-quo acceptance of the victim status of Aboriginal people. It is one of the elephants in the room. In this chapter I will explore the dynamics of victimhood and why it is so problematic for Aboriginal people.

There is endless debate about how much government can or should do to address health, education, and employment needs of Aboriginal people. However we need to bear in mind how much is already spent – and how effectively. More to the point, these are areas in which Aborigines can and should play a significant role. Focusing on what Aborigines themselves can do is in no way an attempt to absolve governments from their duties, or 'blame the victim'. Rather, it is to empower Aboriginal people, and to achieve the best outcome. I believe that government can

---

[1] Cosby, B. & Poussaint, A. *Come on People* (2007), xv.
[2] Sarra, C. 'Beyond the Victim' (2010), 17.
[3] Elder, L. *What's Race Got to Do with It?* (2009).

only truly be effective when Aboriginal people begin to take greater responsibility for those areas in their lives over which they have direct control. In the words of Eleanor Roosevelt as quoted by Noel Pearson: "There is nothing that government can do for you that you are unwilling to do for yourself".[4] As such, taking responsibility simply means one is ready to embrace a solution. To take responsibility for addressing one's needs, to the degree to which one is capable, is true self-determination.

## The Problem with Victimhood

Some Aboriginal leaders have led many Aboriginal people to believe that many (if not all) of their problems are due to colonisation[5] and/or the white government.[6] Following this view to its logical conclusion, it follows that Aboriginal people are victims, powerless to effect any change in their lives; hence they sit and wait (and die waiting) for the government to fix all their problems. In the words of Amy Wax when discussing race relations in the United States:

> Focusing on the actions of others may sap the determination necessary to achieve difficult internal changes. Deemphasizing or abandoning the elusive quest for racial justice may in fact be a precondition for real progress … The victim must realise that, although others have wronged him, his fate is in his own hands.[7]

In response, some may say something like, "Well, the government should be the ones to solve our problems as they are the ones who …". While it might be highly desirable that the government perform certain actions, the reality is people should not sit and wait for the government

---

[4] Pearson, N. 'Think Big but Start Small: Human Rights, Like Charity, Should be Nurtured in the Home', *The Weekend Australian*, 20, 21 October 2012.

[5] For example, see Smallwood, G. 'Human Rights and First Australians' Well-being' (2011).

[6] For example, see Shaw, W. 'Indigenous 'Solutions' Just Disempower Us Further', *ABC Drum* (2012).

[7] Wax, A. *Race, Wrongs, and Remedies* (2009), 97, 114.

to 'rescue' them. Much like the pedestrian who is hit by a car and the driver drives off, never to return. Yes, the driver should have stopped. But sitting there with a sign saying "I want justice" is not going to help. Aboriginal people who believe they are victims need to ask themselves, "What can I personally do that will make a difference?". Any message or action that focuses on the popular (and politically correct) idea of "What should others [such as the government] do that will make a difference?" is a serious impediment to advancing the well-being and self-determination of Aboriginal people.

## Real Victims and Counterfeit Victims

I fully acknowledge those Aboriginal people in this country who live in environments that are so toxic and impoverished on most dimensions that it is very difficult for them to even survive without significant outside assistance, let alone fix problems. In some parts of Australia where there is little chance of meaningful employment, minimal access to basic services, minimal access to fresh and nutritious food, where alcohol abuse is prevalent, and people have known nothing different, then these people are victims of systems and mindsets that are fundamentally toxic. Some communities are victims of an 'apartheid' government policy: the Commonwealth refusal to allow leases on Aboriginal lands rules out private property and business enterprise and condemns these Aboriginal people to 'welfare poison'.[8]

However, this chapter relates to Aborigines who, generally speaking, can access the same opportunities that most Australians take for granted. Many have learnt to see themselves as victims simply because they have Aboriginal ancestry. Some choose to see themselves as victims for reasons that I would consider relatively minor or trivial, such as failure to acknowledge country, or one's Aboriginality being questioned on the grounds of having minimal ancestry, etc.. I believe these Aboriginal

---

[8] Hughes, H. & Hughes, M. 'The Denial of Private Property Rights to Aborigines' (2012).

people are not victims of colonisation or White Australia, but rather victims of faulty and toxic thinking. Many will claim that they have inherited ancestral trauma (often called 'trans-generational trauma') or other historical baggage, and are therefore victims[9] – more likely they have 'inherited' self-defeating thinking.

## Victimology

Aboriginal people are portrayed as the victims of history (colonisation), racism, and government policies. Inequalities in health and well-being are cited as evidence for victimhood. But these factors alone cannot explain the high degree of dysfunction, disadvantage, and discontent of so many Aboriginal people. The best evidence that these factors are not the ineluctable forces they are made out to be is the Aboriginal people who are doing exceedingly well. This is an inconvenient truth to those who promote the Aboriginal victim syndrome – usually sidelined, or ignored outright, or actually suppressed.

Today's Aboriginal people come from a race of people who adapted to environments which at any time could be very challenging. There can therefore be no doubt that Aboriginal people are very capable when faced with challenges. In contrast to those strong and resourceful Aboriginal people, many Aboriginal people today choose to be easily upset or offended, simply because someone disagrees with them. Apologists portray Aboriginal people now as being so fragile that they need to be showered with special services and programs under the banner of 'cultural safety'. Clearly, people cannot choose their historical circumstances, but anyone can choose their response to their past history and present status. They do not need to be victims. As Spezzano (2001) states:

> Most of us have had traumatic things happen to us. At the time of

---

[9] See for example, Ranzijn, R. McConnochie, K. & Nolan, W. *Psychology and Indigenous Australians* (2009).

the trauma, we have a choice as to what the experience will become for us. Either we choose for this experience to become the thing that wounds us so mortally that it eventually kills us because we never get over it, or we choose for it to become the grain of sand around which we produce a great pearl.[10]

An important point here is that it is not always as simple as just choosing. Feelings of high self-esteem and self-worth are very important factors that influence our decisions. Those with a robust sense of self-worth (that is, those who value their opinion of themselves more than other people's opinion of them, and do not attach conditions to a positive self-evaluation) simply have no need to see themselves as victims. They cope with disasters, mishaps, and undesirable circumstances because they do not see themselves as victims. Take Nick Vujicic as an example. He is a great Aussie who makes his living as an author and speaker. Born with no limbs, he could have easily seen himself as a permanent victim. Yet he has led an amazing life, married a beautiful lady, and they are expecting their first child. He is grateful for what he has, not defeated by what he does not have. I highly recommend you look at Nick on Youtube and listen to what he has to say about life, opportunities, success, and happiness – or read his books.

## Reasons for Adopting the Victim Role

If people can choose not to be victims, then why adopt the victim mindset? Why is it so seductive? What purpose does it serve? In addition to being the easier path to take, Black American author John McWhorter suggests that being a victim feels good.[11] That's right, it feels good. In brief, being a victim feels good because: (1) it enables one to feel special, (2) the victim no longer needs to feel responsible for themselves, and (3) adopting the victim status can be a means of gaining control or power over others.

---

[10] Spezzano, C. *If it Hurts, it isn't Love* (2001), 229.

[11] McWhorter, J. *Losing the Race* (2001).

## *Feeling Special*

Adopting the role of victim, or playing the 'wounded' or 'downtrodden', can enable a person to feel special – and that feels good. There is usually no shortage of people to rally around and give the 'victim' attention. But rewarding attention seeking by people who are perfectly capable of helping themselves is not helpful; and behaviour rewarded is behaviour reinforced, thus reinforcing them in their victim role. Although victimhood can become a badge of honour enabling a person to feel special, there is a downside to the pursuit of feeling special. This pursuit of being special necessitates seeing oneself as different from others, and consequently, separate from others.

The belief that people are separate beings is fundamentally flawed; as Shakespeare knew, no man is an island. Although each of us resides in a separate physical body (obviously), mystics, philosophers, and the spiritually-minded believe that beyond the consciously observable physical and social dimensions of our lives, all of life is interconnected. Many traditional Aboriginal people (and some other groups) do not see themselves as special, and hence different from others (in the spiritual sense), instead they see equality, oneness, and unity of life all originating from one spiritual source.[12] In the words of the Northern Territory's Minister for Indigenous Advancement, Alison Anderson: "I see people. Not categories, divisions, or races".[13] When we see ourselves as spiritually separate from others, we become aware of the observable differences, which leads to comparisons with others, and eventually feelings of being threatened because someone else will always be perceived as better, bigger, stronger, or more deserving. It also leads to the 'us vs. them' mentality which is the basis for not only competition, success etc., but

---

[12] While many new age thinkers and philosophers have been active in promoting the teaching that we are all interconnected, such beliefs were always a part of the traditional Aboriginal belief system. For example, see Vicki Grieves' 2009 discussion on Aboriginal spirituality.

[13] See chapter by Anderson in this volume.

also racism, conflict, fear, and war. So instead of being seen as brothers and sisters, others are seen as opponents and enemies. This mentality, though embraced by activists who are obsessed with Aboriginal identity, as well as the racists (both black and white), who are prisoners of their own fear-driven flawed ethnocentric paradigm, is in stark contrast to the principle of oneness and interconnectedness once embraced by many traditional Aboriginal peoples around the world; a principle that is arguably the basis of what it means to be Aboriginal.

## Abdicating Responsibility

Adopting the role of victim can also provide a ready-made excuse for all failures or any aspect of our lives we don't like – or anyone else mightn't like – and that feels good. According to Zur, "In claiming the status of victim and assigning all the blame to others, a person can achieve moral superiority while simultaneously disowning any responsibility for his or her behaviour and its outcome".[14] Victims are able to tell themselves and others that since their tragic, life-changing event (which may have happened to them personally or even to their ancestors), they are 'emotionally wounded', and therefore can no longer partake in normal life like everyone else, and in fact cannot be expected to be actively involved in finding solutions to their problems. Because of their victim status, they cannot be censured, criticised, or even held responsible for any of their behaviours. Dineen sums it up this way:

> There are many incentives for acquiring, and even for seeking, victim status and, in the short term, there are some pay-offs. The tragedies, the failures, the hardships, the health problems and the disappointments of life become explained, relieving people of at least three of life's natural burdens: dealing with complexity, facing things beyond their control, and accepting personal responsibility for decisions and actions.[15]

---

[14] Zur, O. *The Psychology of Victimhood* (2005), 49.
[15] Dineen, T. *Manufacturing Victims* (2001), 21.

Cosby and Poussaint suggest, "Blaming white people can be a way for some black people to feel good about themselves, but it doesn't pay the electricity bills".[16] Essentially, while blaming others may feel good, the problems continue and the temporary good feelings from blaming others prevent one from realising that problems require solutions to lead fulfilling lives. Even more importantly, the victim status confers a sense of moral innocence and entitlement,[17] and with a sense of entitlement comes a belief that the victims should not have to earn an income, in order to "pay the electricity bills". The victims feel owed and expect that someone else will pay the bills. Such 'moral innocence' and feeling of entitlement can justify any behaviour.

Similarly, in his book for Black Americans, *Man up! Nobody is Coming to Save us*, Black American author Steve Perry states:

> When we blame them [White people], we are expunged of responsibility for the condition of Black people. This allows us to occupy the peculiar position of victim ... It is good for Black folks to know that there are flaws in the assumptions that the root of all Black problems is White people. It is downright freeing to know that we have a hand in perpetuating our current condition. That also means that we can fix it.[18]

I would add that it is 'downright debilitating' for Aboriginal people to deny that they have a hand in perpetuating their current condition. Some will likely interpret Perry's ideas as 'blaming the victim' yet again. A key word here from Perry's advice is 'perpetuating'. We need to examine what perpetuates the problems amongst some Aboriginal people today. I say 'some people' because it is obvious that there are many Aboriginal people who, despite the history of dispossession and discrimination, are doing very well for themselves. Perhaps they have replaced the mindset

---

[16] Cosby, B. & Poussaint, A. op. cit., 40.
[17] Sykes, C. *A Nation of Victims* (1992).
[18] Perry, S. *Man up! Nobody is Coming to Save us* (2005), 5.

of 'The white man is to blame' with 'No more excuses. No more blame. What can I personally do to make a difference in my life?'.

## *Gaining Power*

Being the victim, paradoxically, can place one in a position of power. Few are game to disagree with victims (or their supporters), or question motives, or challenge them in any way for fear of being seen as an uncaring bully. When Aboriginal identity and mandated 'respect' are factored in, questioning victim status will likely be seen as tantamount to racism. Therefore, adopting the victim role (feeling upset, offended, outraged, racially vilified, or whatever) can be a very effective and convenient way of silencing dissent, and inducing feelings of guilt in others. Silencing others provides the 'offended' victim with a sense of power over others – and that feels good. Victims remain unchallenged with their victim status intact and unassailable. Any open debate on the problems facing Aboriginal people is stifled.

### Promoting and Reinforcing the Victim Status

The victim is not a solo performer. There are accomplices who encourage victims to take on the victim role so as they can play the part of helper or rescuer. David Pollard in his 1988 book *Give & Take: The Losing Partnership in Aboriginal Poverty*, suggested:

> The interest of the political parties in maintaining an Aboriginal problem is compounded by the existence of a small group of Aboriginal activists whose vocation is confrontation, who generally derive their own income from governmental sources, either directly or indirectly and who must have poor Aborigines to point to in order to have a raison d'etre themselves.[19]

More recently, Sutton, writing about Aboriginal disadvantage and suffering, argues that some people's careers can depend on the

---

[19] Pollard, D. *Give and Take* (1988), 10.

perpetuation of victimhood.²⁰ There are therefore, people with a vested interest in having Aboriginal people maintain a view of themselves as victims. This has led to the term 'Aboriginal industry' – describing the many positions as 'cultural experts', consultants, advisers, etc., devoted to addressing Aboriginal issues. People in these roles are reluctant to give them up. When trying to argue against those who have a vested interest in viewing Aboriginal people as victims, I am reminded of what Upton Sinclair once said – "It's difficult to get a man to understand something when his salary depends upon his not understanding it".²¹

When some Aboriginal opinion leaders and their non-Aboriginal acolytes continually speak on behalf of Aborigines, it should come as no surprise that self-reliance is eroded and replaced with dependence. Add to the equation a readily available welfare system (aptly described by Noel Pearson as 'welfare poison'²²), and you have the perfect environment for self-doubt and reliance on others. Being the victim pays dividends –and those dividends can be very attractive when the alternatives are so much tougher. It is only natural that people will take 'the path of least difficulty' – even in the face of the fact that, in the long-term, such a path is very difficult indeed!

It is sad that some of the most prominent of those who promote the victim mentality amongst Aboriginal people themselves identify as Aboriginal. This does not seem uncommon within minority groups. In the introduction of The Race Card, the editors write in relation to Martin Luther King Jr:

> But even as King was reaching the apex of his influence ... forces were at work that would undermine this movement of integration and equality. Some of the opposition came from irreconcilables in the white world who had trouble giving up the old ways. But this

---

[20] Sutton, P. *The Politics of Suffering* (2011).
[21] http://en.wikiquote.org/wiki/Upton_Sinclair
[22] For example, see Martin, D. 'An Assessment of Noel Pearson's Proposals for Aboriginal Welfare Reform' (2011).

group was an ever shrinking minority ... A more serious challenge to King came from within the black community itself, where a radical fringe ... developed into a movement for black power – an ideology of separatism addicted to theories of white guilt and "institutional racism," and to demands for reparation for black suffering.[23]

I believe a similar situation is happening here in Australia. Accusing 'whitefellas' of oppressing Aboriginal people is very common, but I believe the most damaging messages for Aboriginal people come from other Aboriginal people, most damaging because these messages are seen as emanating from a trusted source – other Aboriginal people. When non-Aboriginal people are regularly portrayed as the enemy, it is then (wrongly) assumed that Aboriginal people must have the best interests of their people at heart.

## Victims of Racism?

Australia is a great country to live in, but there are some who see it as a racist country. Aboriginal leader Professor Gracelyn Smallwood has stated, "whether we like it or not, Australia is a racist society".[24] Ranzijn et al., have stated, "At a day-to-day level, Indigenous Australians are constantly victims of racism and discrimination".[25] Anthony Mundine has expressed his opinion that Australia is a racist country.[26] The problem with such claims is that the basic assumption of wide-spread racism is largely accepted without any real evaluation of what a 'racist society' means. While those who believe that Australia is a racist country may have personally experienced racism themselves, we need to ask, just how widespread is racism in Australia, and how severe is it?

---

[23] Collier, P. & Horowitz, D. 'Introduction' to *The Race Card* (1997), vii.

[24] Smallwood, G. 'Townsville Professor Blasts Australia over Land Rights and Intervention at International Conference' (2012).

[25] Ranzijn, R. *et al.*, op. cit., 136.

[26] As reported by Jackson, G. 'Man's Apology Turns into Assault on Racism' *Sydney Morning Herald*, 20 October 2012.

Claims of racism are backed up by subjective 'self-report' surveys. For example, in the summary of a survey on racism, Victorian Health state that their survey measures participants' self-reported experiences of racism, yet their findings are worded as if actual verified experiences of racism took place.[27] Such surveys are more likely to be reporting people's feelings that racism exists somewhere, rather than objectively quantifying clearly 'race-based' negative experiences to which they had been subjected. Such surveys are then quoted and used to prove the existence of racism. Little real evidence is proffered and as a result focus is diverted away from the far more serious problems that affect Aboriginal people – education, health, employment, etc.

I am not denying that racism exists in Australia;[28] it does – as it does in any country. Further, quite clearly, the White Australia policy – abolished only in 1972 – defined Australia as White, and was racist by definition.[29] In fact it is impossible to talk about White Australia without talking about racism in the same breath. Anyone born in Australia any time before 1972 grew up, to a greater or lesser extent, in White Australia with all its attitudes, assumptions, values, and prejudices. What I do question is the assertion that racism today is as widespread and as severe as some want to suggest. I further question the widely held assumption that overt racial prejudice is the major cause of the problems that some Aboriginal people experience. I believe it is more accurate to say, not only are most Australians not racist, but many other Australians are sometimes in such fear of being accused of racism that they overcompensate by making ever-increasing allowances for unacceptable Aboriginal behaviour. This naturally leads to an expectation of lower standards of behaviour for Aboriginal people, for example in child protection matters.[30] This, in an

---

[27] Victorian Health, 'Mental Health Impacts of Racial Discrimination in Victorian Aboriginal Communities' (2012).

[28] See Young, Markham, & Doran, in this volume.

[29] Parbury, N. *Survival* (2005).

[30] Sammut, J. 'Is Preventing 'Another Stolen Generation' Racist?' (2012).

anomalous kind of way, becomes racist itself. It's just as racist to expect less of someone on the basis of their race or ethnicity as it is to offer them less – and it is ultimately far more damaging.

Where overt racism exists, it needs to be weeded out and the perpetrators dealt with. However, one of the barriers to weeding out racism is the focus on confected racism. It has become far too easy to make claims of racism when a non-Aboriginal person disagrees with an Aboriginal person. Or a racist motive is assumed (never substantiated, just assumed) when a person of mixed heritage is questioned about why they choose to identify solely as Aboriginal. It is one thing to claim to be victims of racism, but another thing entirely to prove it.

I am not suggesting that overt racism against Aboriginal people has been totally eradicated, but in this century we should be able to look back on and be inspired by the many fine Aboriginal Australians who have tackled racism head on and demonstrated that it need not be a barrier. Rather than just complaining, I suggest it's better to adopt the approach of Aboriginal singer-songwriter Jimmy Little, who said, "Racism has never been a problem for me. I know who I am. If others don't, then that's their problem."

Why wasn't racism a problem for Jimmy? He likely valued his opinion of himself more than he valued some other people's opinions of him. Jimmy did not say he never experienced racism, he just said it has never been a problem for him. I am all for enforcing the law that prohibits individuals from racist acts, such as not hiring Aboriginal people for a job even when they are the best suited. However, for other expressions of racism, such as racial slurs (which, interestingly, some Aboriginal people accept as being okay when spoken by another Aboriginal person), I am suggesting that changing one's response to the slur will be far more empowering than trying to change the person speaking the slur. Rather than taking offence when such slurs are spoken (which is extremely disempowering), perhaps a better response is to laugh. Laughing is not endorsing such racial slurs, but simply communicates, 'I'm a bigger person than you'. Much like when confronted by a flasher, a confident laugh is more likely to deter such behaviour.

## Identity[31]

The previous discussion raises the question, 'Why do some people wish to sometimes see racism where it does not exist?' I offer two answers here, but before I do, consider the story where an Aboriginal Elder (Shane Mortimer) was seeking compensation because he felt offended when Don Aitkin, a former Vice-Chancellor of the University of Canberra, said that Mortimer looked "about as Aboriginal as I do".[32,33] Such statements are neither racist nor offensive, yet some people wish to make them so. So in response to my question on why do some people see racism where it does not exist: Firstly, Black American author Shelby Steele, talks about the belief held by some that the litmus test for being black is to accept racial victimisation not as an occasional event, but as an *ongoing identity*.[34] In other words, he is suggesting that many believe that being the target of frequent racism is necessary 'evidence' of being black. Secondly, Wax, when discussing race relations in the United States, suggests that using ongoing discrimination to explain the existing gaps between Black and White Americans is the "litmus test for dedication to the cause of racial equality";[35] and naturally, most people like to think of themselves as opposing racism and racial inequality, but in order to oppose something, you first need to believe it actually exists. Perhaps some believe that claiming to have experienced racism is proof of being Aboriginal. This is possibly true for those whose Aboriginal ancestry is so minimal that they seek other 'evidence' (such as, 'I'm a victim of racism') to support their claim of being Aboriginal.

---

[31] The topic of Aboriginal identity is discussed at length by Pholi in this volume.

[32] Aitkin, D. quoted by Hair, J. 'Not Fair: Indigenous Identity Back in Court', *The Australian*, 12 November 2012.

[33] In the *Weekend Australian Magazine* of *The Weekend Australian*, 9, 10 March 2012, it reports that "Mortimer had no inkling of his own aboriginality until early middle age", 5.

[34] Steele, S. *White Guilt* (2006).

[35] Wax, A. op. cit., 96.

While this nation takes some pride in including and celebrating Aboriginal culture, the obsession with Aboriginal identity by some (typically by those with the least Aboriginal ancestry) contributes to the divide between Aboriginal Australians and non-Aboriginal Australians, thus leading to a state of separatism. Separatism is the ideology that the interests of Aboriginal people are best served where Aboriginal people, as a collective, function separately from non-Aboriginal people, and hence are assumed to have greater freedom in deciding how they will live. When this happens, there is the potential for Aboriginal people to see themselves and others, primarily in terms of racial/cultural differences, rather than focusing on human commonalities, which far outweigh any differences. It is the human commonalities that unite us and make us one people – this realisation is a prerequisite for reconciliation.

## Where To from Here?

The victim-oppressor relationship can only exist when an individual (or group) sees others as fundamentally different. Separatist views embraced by many people fuel the victim cycle. Abandon these false beliefs and you break the cycle.

Aboriginal and non-Aboriginal people need to begin seeing each other as Australians with common needs and shared interests – not us-vs.-them. This would embrace the spiritual concept of the oneness and connectivity of all life that traditional Aboriginal Australians lived by. Seeing each other as equals in no way denies the past or appalling health and social inequalities. It simply recognises that all people (Aboriginal and non-Aboriginal) have the same fundamental needs, sees oneness and interconnectedness rather than differences and divisions, and serves as a basis for working together.

Let's recognise that current mindsets and policies, which assume Aboriginal people are vastly different from other Australians, do not work. The time has come to re-examine how we deal with Aboriginal affairs if we are to see improvement in the lives of Aboriginal people. It will mean making unpopular decisions, and not being so quick to 'play the victim card'. I am gladdened by what could be our future if we can do away with political correctness and victimology.

Too many are 'sickened to death' because they see no hope. Maybe it is time to promote a new way of seeing to renew psychological and spiritual health as a solid foundation for physical and social health. It is important to continue programs that target physical health and well-being; however, such programs are more effective when they focus on both psychological and physical well-being. This is consistent with the holistic view of life that is both the wellspring of Aboriginality – mental, physical, spiritual, and cultural health seen as inter-related – and surely the key to healthy Aboriginal life in the present and for the future.

# 6
# Indigenous Scholarship and Values-formation

*Brian Roberts*

*Responsible Parents will give their offspring both Roots and Wings.*[1]

## Introduction

This overview attempts to concentrate on trends and generalities, and avoids the personalisation of views which has dogged the Indigenous values debate in recent years. An effort is made to disassociate the ideas presented from a good guy/bad guy conflict which aligns writers with the Sarra, Pearson, Langton, Dodson, Johns, Manne, or Windschuttle choice of philosophical guru. The author's long experience with separatism, his own subjection to forced tuition in another language, and his family's history as settlers and refugees from Apartheid, no doubt colour his reading of the current Australian situation.

This chapter avoids the pedagogical jargon associated with the education debate and is limited to the author's generalised views. No claim is made here that nepotism and closed-shop procedures are the sole preserve of Aboriginal Studies; on the contrary, while some elements of introspection may be somewhat more exaggerated in Indigenous Centres, the quality of research in other discipline areas is far from uniform.

## Background to Indigenous Academe

Indigenous Education has long been accepted by all informed observers as the key to overcoming disadvantage. The public debate on improving

---

[1] This quote is amended from an original by Henry Ward Beecher and is contained in the author's three-part report on overcoming disadvantage. It is available online at: https://sites.google.com/site/brianrobertsreports

primary and secondary school outcomes has raged for two decades and is likely to elicit more and more emotive debate. The concentration of these pre-tertiary curricula on literacy and numeracy supplemented by a selection of social, economic, and biological studies is generally agreed as appropriate.

Since the 1980s there has been a progressive move toward the establishment of University Indigenous Study Centres, followed by the appointment of Indigenous professors and associated teaching and research staff. These Centres have usually been given Indigenous names, often in the language of the region concerned. Their function has been three-fold: to support Indigenous students on campus; to undertake research on Indigenous issues, to be published in appropriate journals; and to act as the voice of their Indigenous community in the broader public arena. These are potentially useful aims. Because of the small base which these Centres have been able to draw on for staff, there has sometimes been a tendency toward the appointment of relatives and close associates. This may have diminished these groups' capacity for self-criticism and serious consideration of alternative views.

## Eligibility of Indigenous Candidates

Indigenous identity as a requirement for financial support may have influenced the selection of candidates for both graduate and post-graduate studies. The self-definition of individuals' claim to Aboriginality passed largely without comment in the early phase of tertiary Indigenous Education. As the benefits of Aboriginality changed from negative to positive over the past two decades, the criteria for eligibility have come under increasing scrutiny. As a result, the principle of using self-selection of race as an adequate and appropriate measure of Aboriginality and its benefits, has been increasingly questioned, with frequent reference to the case of the Tasmanian academic who claims to be only one sixty-fourth Aboriginal but identifies as Aboriginal.[2] Questions arise due to

---

[2] Izzard, J. 'The Trial of Andrew Bolt' (2010). See also article by Caroline Overington, 'Not So Black and White', *Weekend Australian*, 24 March 2012.

the concern of how much financial and other support is potentially available to students if it is based on race identification and not need. As a result, several Aboriginal leaders have in recent times suggested that such assistance should be provided on the basis of economic need, and not racial identity.[3]

There is a clear case for universities to use need rather than race as the measure of eligibility for selective support.[4] Such a move has similarities to means-testing, but includes an ethnic disadvantage element. This encompasses the widespread unspoken recognition of the relationship between the darkness of skin colour and the level of discrimination. Accusations of racism and domination by ethnic invaders do not reduce the validity of this claim. Many academics and administrators now look forward to the Indigenous tick-box being replaced by the income/assets box on applications. This is not reflected in the Behrendt Report (2012) on access and outcomes for Aboriginals in Higher Education.[5] That Report is silent on Aboriginal eligibility criteria and passes the buck in its final recommendation (No. 35: 'That the Australian Government and universities work together to develop a set of standardised words to be used by universities, based on the national census Indigenous identification question, when asking whether a person identifies as Aboriginal or Torres Strait Islander' and to encourage such students 'to identify themselves as such to the university'). It is unfortunate that this expensive report left the Aboriginality question in the 'too hard' basket.

---

[3] Langton, M. *Indigenous Exceptionalism and the Constitutional 'Race Power'* (2012b). See also, http://www.theage.com.au/national/a-case-for-change-20120904-25chg.html

[4] At least one university in America has already ceased its affirmative action process. This change came about through the efforts of a Black American, Ward Connerly. His efforts are described in his 2000 book, appropriately titled, *Creating Equal: My Fight against Race Preferences*. See also http://en.wikipedia.org/wiki/Ward_Connerly

[5] Behrendt, L. *Review of Higher Education Access and Outcomes for Aboriginal and Torres Strait Islander People.* (2012).

## Topics and Aims of Indigenous Research

Understandably, the early thesis topics of Indigenous researchers leaned heavily toward justice and recognition. Many of these studies made significant contributions toward awareness of contemporary inequities and racial gaps in well-being. Most of this work drew heavily on sufferings perceived as the result of what might be grouped into 'colonial traumas'. In the process, these writings strengthened the concept of victimhood and relied on the Guilty Whiteman – Innocent Blackman model.[6] The accumulated historic evidence that was brought by these scholars contributed to the general ethos which holds that the present abysmal level of Indigenous well-being is overwhelmingly due to oppressive government policy, past and present, and discrimination by mainstream employers and services. In more recent years there has been a shift in emphasis toward research topics in education and health, encompassing the role of language in racial pride and the effect of lifestyle and substance abuse on well-being and employment.[7]

Currently the emphasis on racial identity as a major factor in self-respect and acceptance will have to run its course before the real causes of poverty and their alleviation gain the recognition which they deserve. The sooner Indigenous scholars are encouraged to tackle topics of universal humanism and modern societal norms, the sooner they will realise their productive potential. This can be done without losing identity.

## Seeking Clarity on Future Roles in Australian Society

A cursory examination of contemporary writings by Indigenous spokespersons indicates a serious division of opinion on what might be called the Modernism-Traditionalism dichotomy. This lack of agreement on the place and role of Indigenous individuals in the future Open Society of Australia can be expected to affect academics in their answer to the

---

[6] Refer to Johns, G. *Self-determination: The Whiteman's Dream* (2011).
[7] Healthinfonet set up by Edith Cowan University provides a good example of this kind of research. See http://www.healthinfonet.ecu.edu.au/about

question, 'What should we teach?'. The philosophical positioning of individuals along the modern–traditional continuum becomes important both personally and societally when self-motivation is anchored in ethnic pride. This 'Who am I?' question has tended to have an unambiguous answer from the culturally-oriented Indigenous academics and the centres they serve.

For the students, most of whom are motivated self-selecting go-getters seeking greater well-being for their families, the best of Western norms and humanitarian behaviour seem obvious goals. Their concerns are less about political conflict over: integration, assimilation, cultural appropriateness, dualism, separatism, sovereignty, or parallel development etc., than about just being given the tools to become happy, productive contributors to a diverse nation. This group of students probably recognise that separate development in a sovereign 'Aboriginalia' nation will no doubt lead to less tolerance and acceptance of other cultures in this multicultural nation. This realisation is probably a major reason driving their search for change and integration into the 'Open Society'.

## Aboriginal Studies within the Open Society

Analysts of causation of the gap between Indigenous and other Australians have generally fallen into two main categories, i.e., those who choose to blame either the system or the race for current dysfunction. This should be qualified by adding that in recent years several more nuanced commentators, including some from political parties, have supported the view that an individual's well-being is the product of both personal and policy influences. We shall return to this concept later.

For Indigenous academics responsible for guiding the next generation toward becoming positive contributors to the future society, the diversity of views, beliefs, and ideologies has caused a range of responses. Some academics have taken the safe and comfortable route and sought refuge from modern reality in a retreat to separatism in which difference and otherness form the major basis for ethnic pride and sense of belonging.

This has gained them short-term support, declarations of clan loyalty, and martyrism. Unfortunately, academic voices proclaiming a tolerant unifying worldview, where race differences are considered in the context of human commonalities, are largely absent. Why? Because such change agents were never appointed to the Centres. Only a serious reconsideration of the aims of the federally-funded centres and their staff-selection criteria will move these units from self-fulfilling outcomes and the refuge mentality – at least that is what Marcia Langton seems to imply when discussing the need for equal treatment of students to prepare them for a competitive world.[8] In this regard Langton is in serious disagreement with the recommendations of the Behrendt Report (2012) which in turn contradicts the inference that all disadvantaged students be treated on a needs basis as proposed in the Bradley Review (2008),[9] the Indigenous Economic Development Strategy (2011-2018),[10] and the Aboriginal and Torres Strait Islander Education Action Plan (2010-2014).[11]

## Aboriginal Studies and Separatism

The ubiquitous emphasis on pride in difference and on-going discrimination is the norm for Indigenous studies. What this does for the enculturation of tolerant and co-operative future members of the Open Society is uncertain after 200 years of policy which alternated between assumptions that Indigenous and non-Indigenous people are fundamentally similar or different. Integration has built on similarity as humans, while separatism has assumed differences.

Since 1967 Indigenous people have used their full citizenship (= sameness) in a variety of ways. Initiated by Whitlam and encouraged by

---

[8] Langton, M. 'Support Centres Can Hold Back Indigenous Students', *The Australian*, 20 April 2011.
[9] Bradley, D. *Review of Australian Higher Education. Final Report* (2008).
[10] Indigenous Economic Development Strategy 2011-2018. (2011).
[11] Aboriginal and Torres Strait Islander Education Action Plan (2010-2014). *Ministerial Carlton South, Victoria* (2011).

Keating, recognition, respect, and pride have grown to the extent that virtually all Indigenous organisations stress on-going, self-motivating pride in Aboriginality, seemingly above all other attributes and values within the education system. What this contributes to social cohesion is unclear, as is its influence on the ability of young professional job-seekers to accept and work co-operatively in an employment culture different from their own as it is presented to them. Indigenous educators need to ask themselves whether the excessive focus on Aboriginality which they prize is really in the best interests of their charges and genuinely makes provision for individuality. More attention to the attributes which employers seek could be more useful.

## Selection of Indigenous Supervisors and Examiners

The initially small and slow development of tertiary units in Indigenous Studies led predictably to drawing on only a limited pool of well-articulated, knowledge, and experience of Aboriginal worldviews. In an effort to distinguish their ethnic brand, many of the early academics found traction in basing their whole approach to Indigenous Studies on stressing differences – in what they conceptualised as Ways of Knowing, Ways of Learning, and Ways of Doing. Several leading academics became recognised as the drivers of this Different Ways paradigm. This then took over from the earlier emphasis on justice and equity.

It didn't take long for informed observers to ask whether being different was actually an advantage. Put another way, critics examined whether these new (old?) ways were not just different but whether they actually benefited their adherents. In time, the 'So what?' question led at least some proponents of Different Ways to re-consider whether this alternative worldview could successfully prepare future professionals as citizens who could hold their own in modern Australia or whether they would need a sovereign enclave in which to compete.

Unless supervisors and examiners use the universal internationally-accepted measures of rational and evidence-based conclusions in their assessment of student capacity, Indigenous graduates may be largely limited to employment in Indigenous organisations. The present intellectual inbreeding in Indigenous academe requires urgent new blood. This can be done by accepting that both 'radical' Indigenous thinkers and well-informed non-Indigenous scholars could beneficially buck the illogical, inward-looking stance which has captured some Centres.

## Intellectual Rigour and Academic Requirements

All universities have 'written instructions' for post-graduate students and fixed guidelines on expectations for supervisors. In addition, external examiners are provided with detailed criteria by which theses should be assessed, including the recommended changes required to gain thesis approval.

The process by which examiners of Indigenous theses are appointed includes the almost fool-proof exclusion of known critics, contrarians, alternative thinkers, and other nay-sayers known to the supervisor. Because rejection of a thesis reflects on the supervisor's integrity, such unplanned outcomes are to be avoided in favour of meaningful suggestions for cosmetic change – tertiaryspeak for 'Can do better'.

Initially, the intellectual rigour of a thesis is theoretically limited by the research questions agreed on. These are often scrutinised by a staff committee whose job it is to approve the structure and scope of each doctoral candidacy. Later, when the research is complete and the candidate has written up the results and conclusions, an exit seminar is held at which any staff can ask questions and challenge the candidate's methodology and findings. All this happens before the thesis is sent to external examiners, usually two or three approved by the postgraduate panel.

One would expect all these safeguards would guarantee depth, originality, and rigour. Alas, the way the examination procedures work, this is not always the case and goes far beyond Aboriginal Studies.

## Academe's Contribution to Aboriginal Values

The criticism that university Indigenous Centres act as sheltered workshops for individuals who won't face the real job market requires analysis. In essence these centres were established to support transitioning young Aborigines – a noble aim supported by the majority. This development came at a time, mostly in the 1980s, when cultural values and supportive tradition had yet to be properly articulated. It was recognised that statements such as, "I'm a proud Yalanji man" needed to be rationalised by answers to, "What is it that I actually stand for?".

In hindsight, Indigenous academics haven't yet produced a convincing answer to this question, at least not in terms of articulating whether or how their ethnic values and the behavioural norms to which they aspire differ from universal humanitarian values. The truth is that beautiful theory has been trounced by ugly facts. The central fact which characterises the purist view of Aboriginality is a people who have been martyred and as such deserve both empathy and support to gain equity. Essentially the question is "What has happened to us" rather than "What we stand for", which drives not only Aboriginal Centres but activists and apologists generally who demand that they need a hand-up. It is perhaps the strangely comforting feeling of victimhood and disadvantage which binds together the proponents of Aboriginality. The actual values as the sources of pride remain unclear.

Values-formation and its relation to mainstream Australian social norms and cohesion now emerge as important potential challenges to Indigenous Centres. These groups of well-educated Aborigines have the capacity to initiate a much-needed acceptance and tolerance of other cultures, notably the internationally useful English language-based humanitarianism, just as many migrant groups have.

Much of the on-going debate on the compatibility of traditionality and modernity over-values cultural mores at the expense of co-operative tolerance. It is for this reason that the Jews are surprised at how Holocaust sympathy evaporates when inhuman treatment of Palestinians is challenged. In the real world, others do not support the Chosen People or the Disappearing People simply on past hardships. It is for this reason that those privileged with the opportunity to influence young minds in their formative years need to be cognisant of their significant responsibility to take the long view. That view is one in which the real advantages of being culturally different, autonomous, or even sovereign, warrant much more critical examination than has apparently been the case to date. The fact that Different Ways may be useful in designing school curricula doesn't mean that they offer a useful worldview or personal philosophy to future Australian citizens.

## Different Ways of Treating Causality

An important element of Indigenous scholarship has been the way it has handled causality of the gap. As a result of the 'No Excuses' school of thought being bullied out of the debate, the 'Poor fella me' genre has increasingly prevailed. The causality alternatives referred to earlier, in which opposing protagonists largely blame either past and present Indigenous policy, or the lack of initiative and responsibility of Indigenous individuals for their present socio-economic condition are simplistic. Academics push their choice of these chosen causalities at their peril, because in the real world a continuum of both groups of factors has been at work for several decades since comparatively good urban education has been available to the majority. In the longer term, it should be obvious that the 'No Excuses' proponents should be invited back into the tent sooner rather than later.

It is for this reason that the dearth of theses on Individual Responsibility from Indigenous Centres is to be deplored. The over-abundance of Rights theses, while understandable, given injustices of the past, reflects an unhealthy denial of the real reasons why inequity and disadvantage still dog Aboriginal communities. This is not to deny past injustices, but as Marcia Langton points out, "It is not just the historical and continuing exclusion from the economy, or lack of intergeneration capital, or vicious governments, but the practices of Aboriginal people themselves that transform mere poverty into a living hell."[12] Once the holier-than-thou mock innocence of the self-identifying group has been overcome, Indigenous scholars can strongly contribute to their people's well-being. When academics wake up to the fact that an increasing number of young people don't want their lives to be defined by other people's concept of their Aboriginality, the productive process of joining the 'Open Society' might have a chance to flourish.

## Enhancing Respect for Indigenous Studies by De-Racialising Student Support

Just as there is an increasingly strong case to de-racialise government programs supporting those in poverty, there is a growing urgency to base university counselling and study assistance on a non-racial needs basis. How different are the needs of the disadvantaged within the populations of Aboriginal, African, Middle-Eastern, Asian, or Caucasian students? The Indigenous culturists maintain that the above is a non-question for the First Australians who have lost their language and culture to the invaders. However, other battling students have tired of this reverse discrimination, most notably of its perverse financial advantage to their Aboriginal classmates. Is it any wonder they ask why many 'Whites' are 'trying for black' as a result of this racially-based policy. Why, they ask, can't Aboriginals be served by the same counsellors as everyone else, and why can't we all receive means-tested financial support? The answer is long, conflicting, and unconvincing and any opponents quickly tagged and dismissed as racist, right-wing, rednecked, or Hansonite. Such reversion to the 'usual suspects' response reveals a basic lack of logic and reason and won't be carrying the day for much longer as hard-pressed mainstream parents battle to achieve the first graduate in the family.

---

[12] Langton, M. 'Trapped in the Aboriginal Reality Show' (2008).

## Looking Ahead in Indigenous Scholarship

There appears to be a need to distinguish between the future requirements of Indigenous scholarship and Indigenous political aspirations. There are universal scholarship values relating to the integrity and logic which guide the worth of academic studies. These are global and are intellectually determined, without reservation in terms of race, religion, philosophy, or preferred ideologies. The quality of scholarship is determined by the depth of insight, rationality, and evidence-based value judgements.

In Aboriginal scholarship however, there has been an overriding emphasis on the rights of, and justice for, invaded First Peoples. This priority of 'colonial traumas' as a predominant cause of poverty, has replaced rational consideration of individual responsibility as the key to group progress.

Two factors are likely to impede rigorous objectivity in Aboriginal Studies: the definition of eligible Aboriginality and the way in which the Draft Human Rights and Anti-Discrimination Bill (2012) encourages or threatens free speech on racial issues. Several well-credentialed writers have called for an end to legal protection against 'hurtful' public statements. The threat of litigation has been enough to make logical evaluation of Aboriginal issues a non-event since 1975. The similarity of the previous Act (1975) to elements of Islamic fatwas has not gone unnoticed by scholars attempting to inject intellectual honesty into the racial debate.

Similarly, the eligibility of individuals with minimal Indigenous genetic inheritance for education, home, and business loan benefits cannot continue if individuals are to retain self-respect. The select-an-ancestor process, or what Anthony Dillon calls 'ancestral genocide', has passed its use-by date in terms of appropriate and just discriminatory decision-making on funding support policies.[13]

If the current push for Aboriginal Sovereignty succeeds, the call for

---

[13] Dillon, A. 'Too Quick to Take Offence' *The Australian*, 16 November 2012.

an Indigenous University, like the Maori Indigenous University in New Zealand, will surface early in the new triumphalism. The Academic Board of this proud new institution would be faced with the same questions currently facing Aboriginal Centres. Would the Board see merit in Aboriginal ways of knowing and ways of learning, or would they join the rest of society who don't allow ethnicity to define them but keep group identity appropriately recognised. The realities of a self-funded university would soon focus the minds of prospective students on value for money.

Care will need to be taken to ensure that approaches like 'Learn: your way' which emphasise culturally appropriate delivery of courses, are not used as an exemplar for the envisaged university.[14] This is to safeguard against the development of a generation of intolerant students unaware of cultural comparisons. Indigenous Education planners will do well to recognise that self-esteem and motivation can be found in several personal ideologies beside racial pride.[15] It is worth noting that the Bachelor Institute partnered by Charles Darwin University at its new centre aims to provide pathways to build the social, human, economic, and identity capital of Indigenous People across Australia. The approach used is 'to privilege and champion Indigenous identity, knowledges and relational ways of being in ways that empower individuals and communities to enhance cultural security'.[16] This approach "emphasises a 'both ways' approach to developing intercultural communication, decision-making, governance and ways of doing business".[17] These locally noble aspirations need a clear understanding of multicultural

---

[14] See advertisement for the Australian Centre for Indigenous Knowledges & Education in the *National Indigenous Times*, 28 November 2012, 10. See also http://ask.cdu.edu.au/ci/documents/detail/2/2013_s1_ACIKE

[15] For example, Dillon, A. discusses the need *not* to base one's self-esteem on attributes such as Aboriginality as this does not lead to robust self-esteem. See 'Self-esteem (Liking Ourselves)' (2010), 23.

[16] Behrendt, L. op. cit., 226.

[17] Ibid., 227.

tolerance if they are to develop an emerging Indigenous intelligentsia who also benefit from a broader national cohesion. The dangers of producing a separatist 'chosen people' akin to the ultra-kosher Jewry, require attention from Indigenous educators sooner rather than later. The literature offers educationalists a range of successful motivational drivers other than ethnicity and if future Sovereignty students seek competitive openness in their careers, they will steer clear of allowing themselves to be defined by their genetics, especially their ill-defined racial purity. The recently established National Indigenous TV channel could retard the attempts of individuals to become global citizens unconstrained by ethnicity or focus-group expectations, fabricated by committed culture vultures to whom clan pride is everything. Whether NITV encourages mature comparative debate on cultural ideologies will largely determine its relevance and usefulness for its future viewers. It is hoped that transparent discussion and intellectually honest opinion will be given the air-time they deserve.

# 7
# Dispossession – Neo-Liberalism and the Struggle for Aboriginal Land and Rights in the 21st Century

*Jeff McMullen*

*The government has just come in ... and they've really come to disempower Yolngu people. Because they'd rather see Yolngu people not taking over our own affairs, so they can come and mine on our land.*[1]

## Introduction – The Emergence of Neo-Liberalism

Neo-liberalism is shaping the Australian agenda for control of Aboriginal lands and assimilation of Indigenous people. One of the world's foremost social scientists, David Harvey, defines this 21st century strain of capitalism as a system of "accumulation by dispossession".[2] How strikingly applicable this is to the new wave of assimilation and assault on Aboriginal land, rights, and Culture.[3]

Before the Howard years (1996-2007) political scientists and economists usually settled for the term 'Free Market' or possibly 'Late Capitalism' to describe the way the Australian nation did business. In the new millennium 'neo-liberalism' emerged as the popular descriptor of the virulent extreme form of free-market fundamentalism that has

---

[1] Yananymul Mununggurr, Djapu People of East Arnhem Land, from the documentary *Our Generation*, 2010, documentary voicing Aboriginal demands for their right to land and Culture.

[2] Harvey, D. *A Brief History of Neoliberalism* (2005), 159-164.

[3] Culture, in the Aboriginal context, should be acknowledged as carrying for many Aboriginal people the essence of their spirituality, traditional social structures, custodianship of the environment and a philosophical way of seeing. The choice of a capital letter emphasises my own respect and the central importance of Culture to Aboriginal and Torres Strait Islander peoples.

gathered adherents in both major Australian political parties and the support of a handful of highly visible Aboriginal neo-conservatives.

A wise custodianship of the earth's resources and a deep commitment to bio-diversity are important concepts in both the Indigenous knowledge system and modern science. Yet, as I will examine, neo-liberalism asserts a notion of modernism that denies the strongest earth science and is opposed to traditional knowledge, Culture, and custodianship.

Australian Government policy today is heavily influenced by the neo-liberal emphasis on managing access for mining companies to resources on Aboriginal lands. This involves controlling what is still perceived as 'the Aboriginal problem' and forcing a social transition from traditional values and cultural practice to 'mainstream' modernism of a particular brand. It also involves displacing many Aboriginal people from their traditional lands and concentrating them in 'growth towns'.

Transforming the poverty of Indigenous people unquestionably rides on the equitable exploitation and sharing of resources found on their lands. This has never occurred since the arrival of Europeans in Australia. As we will see, the struggle for Aboriginal land and rights is entering a new and critical phase because of the aggressive global marketing of the resources most essential for a fast growing world, including: water, land, food, minerals, and energy.

## Aboriginal Land, Dispossession, and Denialism

Possession Island, off the tip of Cape York, is where James Cook planted the British flag to lay claim to lands owned by Aboriginal people for far longer than European civilisation had existed. After his fateful misadventures and lost opportunities in the east coast encounters, Cook ignored his orders to consult. He looked right through Aboriginal people who appeared along the coast and the lie of terra nullius was born. Then came the invasion, occupation, and near obliteration of a way of life that had continued for longer than anyone knows. Sixty thousand years or was it eighty thousand? It hardly matters to most Australians who live in denial of how this modern nation was created and of the cost to the rightful owners of the land. A strong current of denialism flows through more than two centuries of Australian history. Today the beach on Possession Island is deserted. Just a white monument to the British Captain who stole the land looks down from a hill over the fringing coral reef and green-blue sea. All you hear is the cry of birds in the wetlands. Aboriginal people were cleared off their land here many decades ago. It should have been called Dispossession Island.

"The relationship between black and white Australians, so many of our problems, come down to these few words ... 'it didn't happen'. The country is living in denial."[4] The Jirribal Elder and scholar, Dr Ernie Grant, has devoted much of his life to bringing an Aboriginal way of seeing and the longer timelines of Australian history into the classroom and into our consciousness as a nation. *My Land, My Tracks*,[5] his seminal study of Aboriginal relationships to land, language, Culture, time, and place evolved into the *Holistic Planning and Teaching Framework*[6] championing the value of Indigenous Studies for all Australians. Understanding where we really are, who we are, and how we are shaped by interconnections in our living environment helps us define what it means to be Australian and offers a way of ending the relentless government efforts to assimilate Aboriginal and Torres Strait Islander people. Walking ancient trails in the rainforests of far north Queensland, this eminent custodian of traditional Aboriginal knowledge discussed the future of life on earth, the pattern of global development, and the crushing impact of neo-liberal style growth on Aboriginal lands and communities. Dr Grant emphasised that there are intrinsic links between the holistic Indigenous intellectual system and the most compelling earth science.

---

[4] Grant, E. Interview with Jeff McMullen, Tully, Queensland, 2005.
[5] Grant, E. *My Land, My Tracks* (1998).
[6] Grant, E. *Holistic Planning & Teaching Framework* (2005).

Only through understanding the way Aboriginal people see the world will Australians appreciate how this knowledge is vitally important to us all to manage the health of our country. We have extraordinarily subtle and sophisticated knowledge of this land, its animals and the complexities of the seasons. Our struggle is to get people and Government to understand what it means to be sentient custodians.[7]

Around Australia and in many other parts of the world Indigenous societies, and perhaps the human family as a whole, stand at a crossroads. It is not only the vexing choice of which direction might overcome the current global economic crisis in a world interconnected by extraordinary growth and massive debt. Neo-liberalism, a free-market fundamentalism that worships a particular brand of modernisation, is strikingly hostile to the central tenets of Aboriginal custodianship and to the overwhelming evidence offered by multi-disciplinary scientists that the current pattern of human growth is fuelling chaotic but interconnected threats to the diversity of life on earth. Understanding the big picture allows us to see what is driving the neo-liberal assault on Aboriginal land, rights, and Culture in the 21st century.

## Neo-Liberalism, Earth Science, and Environment

British earth scientist, Norman Myers, has calculated that since World War Two humans have devoured more raw materials than all of our ancestors combined.[8] Travelling the world for over half a century I saw the distinctive pattern of neo-liberal development first emerging in many of the thirty warzones I reported from, especially African nations including: Mozambique, Liberia, Sierra Leone, South Africa, and Rwanda. Rich and powerful nations, responding to the growing market demand for food, water, raw materials, and especially energy,

---

[7] Grant, E. Interview with Jeff McMullen, Echo Creek, Queensland, 2006.
[8] Meyers, N. 'Global Security' (2000).

have swallowed up as much as one third of some African states. "Two-thirds of the land acquired by rich nation investors over the past decade is in Africa, the continent with the greatest food needs. The total acreage transferred to sovereign wealth funds, multinational food producers and even hedge funds could provide food for one billion people," Oxfam says.[9] In Zambia, James Ferguson observed the people of the copper belt pushed by the neo-liberal drive for modernisation into an unsustainable industrial economy and then a staggering, "humiliating expulsion"[10] from the global community. Steven Gregory describes how the neo-liberal modernist project creates widespread social unrest in developing nations such as the Dominican Republic.[11] Through Central America and South America, I witnessed the same pattern. With the global population surging towards eight billion around 2025, it is clear that in the struggle for resources we are at war with one another and with the earth itself. In a world out of kilter, the poorest countries and the poorest communities within rich nations are most vulnerable. We must awake to this clear threat to the long-term survival of our species.

As I warned in *A Life of Extremes, Journeys and Encounters*, there is clear evidence that our world is now in the midst of its sixth period of mass extinction.

> By 2100 one third of all living species may be gone. Watch the birds now on the wing because of the extant 10,000 species, 7,000 are in drastic decline. Take a long walk through a forest and a deep drink on its beauty because up to 50,000 of the world's 250,000 kinds of plants are expected to disappear over the next few decades … As bad as it is now, it can get much worse.[12]

---

[9] Stocking, B. Chief Executive of Oxfam, quoted in *Sydney Morning Herald* and *The Telegraph*, London, 5 October 2012.
[10] Ferguson, J. 'Global Disconnect: Abjection and the Aftermath of Modernism' (2002).
[11] Gregory, S. 'The Devil Behind the Mirror' (2007).
[12] McMullen, J. *A Life of Extremes* (2001).

## Climate Change Denialism and Neo-Liberalism

Climate change is now almost guaranteed to make life worse for millions of people. The political hesitancy and irrational delays by giant industrial economies to respond prudently to this threat, outlined by former American Vice President, Al Gore are heavily influenced by the neo-liberal agenda.[13] "Wealthy right-wing ideologues have joined with the most cynical and irresponsible companies in the oil, coal, and mining industries to contribute large sums of money to finance pseudoscientific front groups that specialise in sowing confusion in the public's mind about global warming. They issue one misleading 'report' after another, pretending that there is significant disagreement in the legitimate scientific community in areas where there is actually a broad-based consensus".[14]

Towards the end of a remarkable scientific life, the brilliant biologist, Edward O. Wilson, described by novelist Tom Wolfe as 'the new Charles Darwin', has issued a passionate call for a new enlightenment and a challenge to the self-interest of neo-liberalism. It is an assertion of our collective responsibility as custodians of the earth, an echo of Ernie Grant's Aboriginal wisdom that holds that every man, woman, and child has some responsibility to ensure the long-term well being of the human family. "Surely one moral precept we can agree on", Wilson writes, "is to stop destroying our birthplace, the only home humanity will ever have. The evidence for climate warming, with industrial pollution as the principal cause, is now overwhelming".[15]

So why, we should ask, is neo-liberalism in denial of this overwhelming scientific evidence? Why is the same ideological mindset so hostile to the concepts of environmental science and to Indigenous Custodianship based not on maximum production or short-term profit but on maximum sustained yield for all generations to come? Why have some prominent Aboriginal people, including Noel Pearson, Marcia Langton, and Warren

---

[13] Gore, A. *The Assault on Reason* (2007), 191.
[14] Ibid., 200.
[15] Wilson, E.O. *The Social Conquest of Earth* (2012).

Mundine, turned their wrath on environmentalists, linked their political and economic strategies to mining companies, echoing unashamedly the neo-liberal cry for free-market capitalism in remote communities?

As Robert Manne has vigorously argued, climate change denialism in Australia "is predominantly a phenomenon of the Right"[16] and is heavily marketed by News Limited newspapers, especially the nation's only national broadsheet, The Australian. "Its style and tone are...unlike that of any other newspaper in the nation's history. The Australian is ruthless in pursuit of those who oppose its worldview... [including] market fundamentalism and minimal action on climate change".[17]

It is no accident that that same Australian mass media outlets amplify the voices of the Culture War warriors who see Aboriginal custodianship, traditional Culture, and attachment to communal living on Aboriginal lands as anachronistic impediments to capitalism. Neo-liberalism connects the agendas of 'modernising' Aboriginal Culture and allowing mining companies to vigorously exploit at minimum cost the mineral treasure on Aboriginal lands.

## How Neo-Liberalism Shapes the Australian Agenda

A close examination of the tenets of neo-liberalism illuminates a great deal of Australian Government policy towards Indigenous people from John Howard to Kevin Rudd and Julia Gillard, or even a change to Tony Abbott.

In *A Brief History of Neoliberalism*, David Harvey[18] identifies four essential features of neo-liberals

1. "privatisation and commodification" of public/community goods,

---

[16] Manne, R.A. 'Dark Victory' (2012).
[17] Manne, R.A. 'Bad News' (2011).
[18] Harvey, D. op. cit., 160-165.

2. "financialisation" to treat good or bad events as opportunities for economic speculation,
3. "management and manipulation of crises" to establish the neo-con agenda, and
4. "state redistribution" of wealth, not to the poor but the rich and powerful.

Harvey presents a convincing argument that neo-liberalism is not 'trickle down economics' but exploitation aimed at upward redistribution of wealth, enriching capital managers: "Redistributive effects and increasing social inequality have in fact been such a persistent feature of neoliberalisation as to be regarded as structural to the whole project."[19] This raises the question of who benefits from neo-liberal style development of Aboriginal lands, whether it be through mining or agriculture?

In her essay, *The Resource Curse*, one of the most prominent Aboriginal neo-liberals, Professor Langton, wrestles with her dilemma of recognising the transformative potential of mining but also its current devastating impact on impoverished Aboriginal communities:

> Australia is a rich first-world nation, largely because of this mineral wealth. Yet the wealth is not evenly distributed, and this has produced economic, social and political problems that are likely to become more acute ... Settler-Australians not working in the resources sector and Aboriginal people in the mining provinces are at the mercy of economic and policy forces that lower their everyday living conditions, and limit their life chances and opportunities. This has the mark of the 'resource curse,' an economic condition that blights many mineral-dependent nations.[20]

The aggressive neo-liberal land grab is dividing whole communities

---

[19] Ibid., 16.
[20] Langton, M. 'The Resource Curse' (2010).

and even brothers. In the Kimberley and Pilbara in Western Australia, across the Northern Territory, on Cape York and in parts of NSW and South Australia, it is disturbing to see the divide-and-conquer tactics of mining companies and governments. Aboriginal Land Councils and even extended family groups engage in costly court battles, arguing bitterly over whether to take the short-term payoff from mining or try to preserve the land and the natural systems that support all life on Earth. Some Aboriginal Elders question whether these choices will ever be compatible but others believe that Traditional Owners and communities must strike the best possible bargain. Geoff Scott of the NSW Aboriginal Land Council advocates active involvement of Aboriginal people in exploring for petroleum on their lands.[21] Lawyer Wayne Bergmann of the Kimberley Land Council made the same argument that Aboriginal communities must unify to reach long-term agreements to transform their poverty.[22]

While the giant machines scrape the red dirt country for bauxite and the foreign ships line up for iron ore, coal, and uranium, so far there is little evidence that mining has eased the disadvantage of Australia's half a million Aboriginal and Torres Strait Islander people. The usual pattern in remote Australia is that local housing and food prices go up and only the fly-in-fly-out workforce can afford the steeper cost of living. In a nation where citizens do not own the sub-soil rights to minerals, Indigenous people are forever denied the genuine control and full value of the most of their lands. In neo-liberal eyes, to grant Aboriginal people such a right would be 'exceptionalism', the concept much targeted by Howard. However, those who believe in the sustainability of Aboriginal communal land ownership, including Professor Jon Altman of the ANU's Centre for Aboriginal Policy Research, contend that a genuine transfer

---

[21] Scott, G. CEO of NSW Aboriginal Land Council, issues statement advocating petroleum exploration licenses on Aboriginal lands, 9 March 2012.
[22] Bergmann, W. Quoted by Jeff McMullen in Address to World Indigenous Business Forum, New York, 4 October 2011. Linked article, McMullen, J. *The Promised Land* (2011b).

of wealth through full mineral rights would be one of the few daring moves that could 'close the gaps' and end Indigenous disadvantage.[23] This is clearly not the plan under the neo-liberal agenda.

It became apparent that with the arrival of various kinds of millennial madness neo-liberalism's distinctive view of growth and modernisation infected Australia's hard-line Cultural War warriors. We frequently heard the demand that Indigenous Culture be 'modernised' from Roger Sandall, Ron Brunton, Keith Windschuttle, Gary Johns, and Helen Hughes. This view was best expressed, however, by anthropologist Peter Sutton, who appeared to be frustrated (like Pearson) by the long period of Aboriginal policy failure and lack of development. Sutton concluded in a landmark essay and later his prize-winning book *The Politics of Suffering*, that Indigenous Cultures must be 'renovated'.[24] The attacks on Aboriginal traditional practice are founded on a narrow and worrying conception of 'modernisation' because very clearly, Sutton's decades of anthropological work, as well as far more reasonable insights from Djinyini Gondarra and Richard Trudgeon,[25] indicate how the 'modern' invasion of the Aboriginal way of life also brought devastating illness, racism, alcohol, and drug abuse, social disruption on the edge of mining communities, the undermining of traditional respect for authority, and a profound sense of pain and confusion. Yet in the relentless portrayal of Top End Australia as a 'failed state', neo-liberals focus their attack on Aboriginal Culture, insisting that the animist attachment to land and communal living is anachronistic. Remote communities are written off as cultural relics, museum pieces, and ghettoes of poverty and pointlessness. Neo-liberalism creates a self-fulfilling prophecy of hopelessness, a wave of dispossession that crushes the spirits of Aboriginal people and leaves them more vulnerable to exploitation of their lands.

---

[23] Altman, J. & Martin, D. *Power, Culture, Economy, Indigenous Australians and Mining* (1993).
[24] Sutton, P. *The Politics of Suffering* (2011).
[25] Trudgeon, R. *Why Warriors Lie Down and Die* (2000).

## Privatisation of Aboriginal Lands

Reflecting Harvey's first tenet of neo-liberalism, 'privatisation' of Aboriginal lands is the neo-liberal spearhead hurled deep into the heart of the traditional Aboriginal way of life. For more than a decade the Howard government waged war on Aboriginal Self-Determination and Land Rights with a vigorous effort to extinguish Native Title, the humiliating dismantling of the Aboriginal and Torres Strait Islander Commission (ATSIC), and a foray against the *Aboriginal Land Rights Act* (1976). Even in the Labor Party, some like Dr Gary Johns and Aboriginal businessman Warren Mundine, then National Vice President of the ALP, jeered at the old 'Nugget Coombs' model of communal Aboriginal society and cheered for private land ownership, arguing that "communal land holding was retarding Aboriginal people".[26] As neo-liberalism began to influence Howard's inner circle of advisers, the bureaucracy in Canberra and some prominent Aboriginal political operators, by far the most influential poison pen was wielded by Professor Helen Hughes.

In the first wave of Australian neo-liberalism in the opening decade of the 21st century, Hughes, a Senior Fellow at the right-wing Centre for Independent Studies, launched her grossly distorted view of the policy of self-determination shaped by the economist and former Reserve Bank head, Nugget Coombs. She decried the "experiment that was to give Aborigines and Torres Strait Islanders a socialist utopia, leading to the establishment of a separate nation".[27] As Robert Manne has noted: "Coombs was not the kind of Rousseauian 'noble savage' dreamer that his ideological enemies on the Right invariably suggest."[28] Coombs advocated autonomy for remote Aboriginal homelands based on traditional Cultural divisions, the kind of Indigenous control that I

---

[26] Mundine, W. Quoted in 'A Way Forward on Aboriginal Welfare', *The Australian*, 11-12 December 2004.

[27] Hughes, F. & Warin, J. *A New Deal for Aborigines and Torres Strait Islanders in Remote Communities* (2005), 2.

[28] Manne, R. *Pearson's Gamble, Stanner's Dream* (2007), 35.

have witnessed bring rapid improvement to the well-being of many First Nations societies in the United States and on the Saami lands of Norway, Finland, and Sweden. The three decades of research by Steven Cornell and Joe Kalt of the Harvard Project on American Indian Economic Development underscores that genuine sovereign control is the key to progress.[29] Like most of the neo-liberal academics in Australia, Hughes ignored this global evidence and instead identified as the first and urgent priority the introduction of an Aboriginal land ownership framework with individual property rights. She proposed 99-year leases of remote communities to allow government to facilitate a switch to private home ownership.[30] Not only was Hughes constructing Harvey's first pillar of neo-liberalism, she was creating for the Howard government the intellectual antecedents to 'justify' the 'shock-and-awe' of the federal government's dramatic and unprecedented Intervention into 73 remote communities in the Northern Territory:

> As children grow into adults (and sometimes even earlier) substance abuse – petrol sniffing, drinking, and smoking tobacco and cannabis – becomes prevalent, following the anomie of lives without schooling that engages children's interest, without interaction with the wider world and without an outlook for employment and income. Child abuse is evident in the high incidence of sexually transmitted diseases.[31]

## Neo-Liberalism and Intervention

We should never forget Harvey's dictum that "management or manipulation of crises" allows neo-liberals to establish their real agendas.[32] The Howard government and the Labor Opposition rushed with obscene haste to pass the Northern Territory Emergency Response

---

[29] Cornell, S. & Kalt, J. (Eds), *What Can Tribes Do?* (1992).
[30] Hughes, F. & Warin, J. op. cit., 1, 4.
[31] Ibid., 11-12.
[32] Harvey, D. op. cit.

Act (2007) because of a manufactured crisis over child sexual abuse. The radicalism of the Intervention was concealed by the government's media manipulation of the scandalising, shaming issue of sexual abuse. Canadian best-selling author Naomi Klein's book, *The Shock Doctrine: The Rise of Disaster Capitalism*,[33] analyses how neo-liberal governments exploit shock therapy in a brazen campaign "of erasing and remaking the world".[34] Like Harvey, Klein examines natural disasters such as Hurricane Katrina in 2005 and shock interventions such as the War in Iraq based on the Big Lie of weapons of mass destruction, to show neo-liberalism in action, manipulating crises to create a new pathway for profit.

In late June 2007, just weeks after the Australian Army and federal police began pouring into the remote communities, I gave a series of public speeches to focus on the real emergency in the heartland of the country in contrast to the manufactured crisis over child sexual abuse:

> The Children of the Sunrise are indeed in danger ... We have had an emergency in the heartland of this country for over twenty years. Syndrome X the doctors call it. This cluster of chronic illnesses, diabetes, renal disease, strokes, hypertension, cancer and heart disease, has reduced the life expectancy of Aboriginal people to seventeen years less than the rest of us. In the remote communities I have worked closely with over many years I rarely meet an Aboriginal man close to my age. Most of the people I knew there twenty years ago are gone. They are dying of totally preventable and treatable illnesses, because the life to which they have been sentenced at birth is barely a life at all. This is our Great Australian Emergency ...We have turned away from the Children of the First Sunrise. Numerous government inquiries, Royal Commissions, State, Territory and Commonwealth agreements, anguished cries from Magistrates, angry authors, endless investigations, PhD studies and shocking media reports have told us for decades that many of this nation's children go hungry, wandering away from

---

[33] Klein, N. *The Shock Doctrine: The Rise of Disaster Capitalism* (2008).
[34] Ibid., 3.

school to look for a scrap of damper or junk food to fill their rumbling bellies, stumbling around with addled brains from petrol sniffing and dope smoking, losing sense of what is healthy and even normal because of this traumatised state, a cross-generational trauma that confuses everything, scrambles all judgement and sees morality surrender, despite the anguish of mothers and fathers who clutch at their children and try to protect them. Too many people, white and black, think it is hopeless. Too many have given up caring. A contagion of sadness and depression sees lives sinking like that big red ball on the horizon … It was this tragic collapse, long ignored despite the pain of the very youngest and the old, that set the stage for the Howard government's dramatic seizure of the remote communities and a vast tract of the Northern Territory.[35]

The ex-Army Captain, Mal Brough, Minister for Indigenous Affairs in the Howard government, clearly shocked the nation by declaring that there were paedophiles in every one of the seized Aboriginal communities.[36] Brough and Howard can be heard building the Australian Government's extraordinary Big Lie in the rapid-cut sequences of the anti-Intervention documentary, *Our Generation*.[37] "Children, children, children …", the words are repeated over and over again but hardly anyone remembers today that after an exhaustive investigation the Australian Crimes Commission reported that there were no paedophile rings as alleged by Brough.[38] It didn't matter, because as Harvey and Klein argue, the shock tactics had established a clear 'reality' in the eyes of the public and the neo-liberals had moved ahead on their real agenda.

While the academic Hughes has been aptly described by Pearson as that most relentless of field-marshals, Mal Brough's role for the neo-liberals,

---

[35] McMullen, J. *The Children of the Sunrise*. Speech at Australian Catholic University, Sydney, 25 June 2007.
[36] Brough, M. Speaking in *Our Generation*, 2010 documentary voicing Aboriginal demands for their right to land and Culture.
[37] Ibid.
[38] Lawler, J. Commissioner of Australian Crimes Commission, quoted in *The Age*, 5 July 2009.

captured in *Our Generation*, was little more than a clumsy corporal barking orders at Aboriginal communities in a military-style campaign replete with jargon about an emergency phase proceeding to normalisation. Unquestionably the neo-liberals' little general in this disastrous season of dispossession was the Napoleonic figure of Pearson. His role was to contribute to tragic divisions in the Northern Territory resistance to the Intervention and enormous moral confusion among white Australians about the government's motives. The Intervention's further extraordinary damage to the Aboriginal sense of control and well-being makes it the gravest policy disaster since the removal of Aboriginal children in the Stolen Generations.

In his first book, a collection of neo-liberal essays entitled *Up From the Mission: Selected Writings*,[39] we get a picture of a 'Labor outsider' deeply depressed by the Aboriginal lack of progress. Pearson's grandly ambitious view of his leadership strengths, as well as his frustrations and contradictions, drove him towards his own version of Klein's 'shock doctrine'. In 2007 Pearson wrote a lengthy letter to the Prime Minister making the case that Howard could win the election late that year by making a bold and uncharacteristic offer to give Constitutional recognition to Aboriginal people in a new preamble to the Constitution. What many Aboriginal people would never forgive him for was Pearson's explicit (although qualified) support for the Northern Territory Intervention because his sway over social conservatives gave enormous authority and momentum to the seizure of 73 remote communities far removed from his traditional sphere of influence.

A skilful polemicist, political power-broker, and big businessman, Pearson captured more attention than any other contemporary Aboriginal Australian during the decade-long ascendance of neo-liberalism in Indigenous policy. The founder of the Cape York Institute was heavily promoted for many years by *The Australian* and ABC television programs like *Australian Story*. Pearson's prolific essay writing made him seem like

---

[39] Pearson, N. *Up From the Mission: Selected Writings* (2009b).

a human printing press, taking obvious delight in manufacturing ideas and slogans such as 'radical hope', 'ending welfare dependency', 'rights and responsibilities', and the intriguing political concept of 'the radical centre'. While this performance from the 'bully pulpit' often dazzled many white Australians, Pearson antagonised a great number of highly respected Aboriginal leaders and has never captured the support of a majority of his own people.

One of Australia's strongest Aboriginal statesmen Patrick Dodson challenged Pearson's neo-liberal forays telling a Yolngu audience in 2008 that Pearson was part of an ideological group including Langton and Mundine that "don't recognise you, they don't recognise your culture."[40]

The Yolngu leader, Reverend Dr. Djiniyini Gondarra, who travelled to Geneva and London to appeal to international human rights authorities to overturn the Northern Territory Intervention, issued repeated pleas to government and fellow Australians, warnings pointedly aimed at Noel Pearson: "Don't listen to these leaders who want to divide and conquer us. You appointed these people as Aboriginal spokesmen, not us. He is not our man, he is your man."[41]

In August, 2007, soon after the launch of the Northern Territory Intervention, *The Monthly* magazine had a cover story with a picture of a confronting, angry man in full rhetorical stride with the headline, *IS PEARSON RIGHT?* It was that well versed analyst of neo-liberalism, Professor Robert Manne, who offered this cogent summation of Pearson's radical political plan to 'remake the world' of Indigenous people:

> Pearson's plan is not merely an audacious (and very expensive) neo-liberal blueprint for the revival of Aboriginal community and

---

[40] Dodson, P. Quoted from Community meeting on Elcho Island, NT, reported by Natasha Robinson in 'Patrick Dodson Lets Fly at Fellow Indigenous Leaders' *The Australian*, 12 December 2008.

[41] Gondarra, Djiniyini. Interview with Jeff McMullen, Darwin 2009. Associated remarks in the documentary, *Our Generation* (2010).

the adaptation of Aboriginal identity to conditions of modernity. It is based on the paradoxical belief that the sticks and carrots of a transformative, interventionist policy of social engineering can create the character of the responsible, acquisitive individual on which the philosophy of neo-liberalism is premised. This is Pearson's gamble.[42]

For all of his eloquence and intellect, there have been wild swings in Pearson's political judgement. During his frustrating battles with conservatives over Native Title he branded them 'racist scum'[43] and yet today he is allied to them and clings to the hope that Tony Abbott will deliver Constitutional recognition and real improvement for Indigenous Australians. When conservative governments were elected in 2012 in both Queensland and the Northern Territory, Pearson still found himself falling into early policy disputes with them, indicating that the 'radical centre' is a distant mirage. The aggression of his political forays has been matched by their disastrous impact.

Pearson's confident but mistaken prediction in 2007 that Howard could triumph and that the conservatives would bring lasting change to Aboriginal society helped persuade another prominent Aboriginal leader, Galarrwuy Yunupingu from Northeast Arnhem Land, to dramatically reverse his original condemnation of the NT Intervention. Just weeks before the federal election of November 2007, Yunupingu switched support to Howard and the Intervention. This stunning political power-play, orchestrated by Pearson and Langton, also a supporter of the NT Intervention,[44] allowed me to witness how desperate the neo-liberals had become for a shock intervention into the Aboriginal way of life. My conversation with Yunupingu in Melbourne that night was telling:

---

[42] Manne, R. op. cit.
[43] Pearson, N. Quoted in Manne, op. cit., 38.
[44] Langton, M. In a discussion chaired by Anglican Archbishop Philip Freier of Melbourne, Langton debates the Intervention with former NT Chief Minister, Clare Martin. Melbourne 2008.

I asked Yunupingu in front of several others that night why he was willing to surrender to the terms of the Intervention. He said Pearson had told him that Howard was going to win the election. A respected Aboriginal scholar, now deceased, asked, 'Jeff, you don't think John Howard is going to win this election?' I replied that I was certain the Howard Government was doomed and that it had been one of the most damaging to the rights and progress of Indigenous people. About two years into the Intervention, Yunupingu changed his mind and again condemned it. He said he was reluctantly persuaded to support the 'rough edges of the Intervention', as he put it, that he had been misled, that it was forced on Aboriginal communities, that it went over the head of the most senior leaders, that it had brought '…no change on the ground, just control of people's lives that is driving us crazy.'[45]

The *Northern Territory Emergency Response Act* (2007) and the *Stronger Futures* legislation (2012) extending the major provisions of the Intervention for another ten years have proven, as Aboriginal advocate, Pat Turner, warned "the Trojan Horse"[46] to control Aboriginal remote communities, a process which ultimately facilitates the exploitation of minerals on these lands. Clearly the Intervention fulfils David Harvey's other key tenets of neo-liberalism. The government is facilitating the redistribution of mineral wealth as well as directing the major development contracts not to Aboriginal communities but to those tycoons heading mining companies and construction alliances. Most of the initial $3 billion of taxpayer's money invested in the Intervention will be absorbed in this fashion with little improvement in Aboriginal life after the first five years of the manufactured 'emergency'. Above all, the new land grab driven by neo-liberalism denies Aboriginal communities the right to shape their own destiny and concentrates extraordinary decision-

---

[45] Yunupingu, G. Conversation at Melbourne Law School, November 2007, quoted by Jeff McMullen in 'The Search for Common Ground' (2012c).
[46] Turner, P. & Watson, N. 'The Trojan Horse' (2007).

making power in Canberra to shape the free-market exploitation and development.

The shadow of the great white protector, Auber Octavius Neville, once more falls across Aboriginal Australians. A century ago Chief Protector Neville insisted that Aboriginal people "have to be protected against themselves whether they like it or not".[47] This is the logic that gave us the Stolen Generations and it is the neo-liberal rationale today for why Aboriginal parents can be judged en masse as being incapable of caring for their children (the false pretext for the Northern Territory Intervention) and it is why Aboriginal parents can be punished by losing welfare payments if a child repeatedly misses school.

"Should we call Jenny ... 'Protector Macklin'? I think perhaps she fits that role at the moment all too well and it's a tragedy."[48] Former Liberal Prime Minister, Malcolm Fraser, with this sharp criticism of current Labor Minister for Indigenous Affairs Jenny Macklin, underscored how neo-liberalism has infected both major political parties in Australia today. It is one of the cutting ironies of contemporary Australian politics that both major parties reached rare bi-partisan agreement to remove Aboriginal people in the 73 prescribed communities from the protection of the Racial Discrimination Act (RDA). This was condemned by United Nations Human Rights authorities but brought no real change of heart in the government's neo-liberal approach. When I complained to the government that it was feigning re-instatement of the RDA but clearly persisting with discriminatory policies only aimed at Aboriginal people the Minister reacted with great indignation. On 21 March 2011, I replied with an open letter to 'Protector' Macklin:

---

[47] Neville, A.O. Testimony before the Moseley Royal Commission. Quoted in Kinnane, S. *Shadow Lines* (2003), 253.
[48] Fraser, M. former Prime Minister of Australia, speaking at a meeting of concerned Australians in Melbourne, March 2012. Quoted by McMullen, J. in 'Protector Macklin's Intervention' (2012b).

## An Open Letter to the Australian Government

"Dear Minister,

The Australian Government has finally admitted that the Northern Territory Emergency Response (the Intervention) was a 'major shock' and a 'serious affront' causing 'anger, fear and distrust' in Aboriginal communities. The government and the Opposition leader Tony Abbott also now admit that there was 'no prior consultation' with Aboriginal people. Mr Abbott adds that 'One of the problems with the Intervention was its 'top-down' nature.'

"Your words to me are strikingly different to those you used when the Howard Government made the first dramatic alterations to the Land Rights Act. You will recall that we both attended the National reconciliation Planning Workshop in Canberra in May 2005, when Prime Minister John Howard declared that Aboriginal land tenure had to be changed. A year later, as traditional owners and communities lost direct control over development and township land, you said in Parliament:

'The Aboriginal Land Rights Act of 1976 was the first and strongest legal recognition of the profound connection Indigenous people have to their country. It recognised the communal nature of land ownership in Aboriginal law and culture through a form of freehold title. The Act, back in 1976, represented the most significant set of rights won by Aboriginal people after two centuries of European settlement.'

"Since you became a minister in the Australian Government, however, we have seen further changes to the Land Rights Act ... Furthermore, you are extending this challenge to Indigenous people's control over their lands by expanding a policy aimed at ending or changing communal ownership of Aboriginal land.

"You bluntly assert that 'economic development on Indigenous lands has traditionally been hampered by the communal ownership of land'. This is an ideological view, easily contested by a wider knowledge of Indigenous history both here and around the world. I would refer you to the work of the Harvard Project on American Indian Economic Development (2008) and research by Nobel laureate economist Elinor Ostrom, who has shattered the myth of the 'tragedy of the common' while producing evidence that, for Indigenous people, communal land ownership is so often a key ingredient of successful development."[49]

## Conclusion

Sadly, neither this letter nor more than 400 public submissions to the Senate's Inquiry on the Stronger Futures extension of the Intervention measures have ended the neo-liberal denialism that prevails in Canberra. There is no real government interest in listening to the voices of Aboriginal leaders such as Djiniyini Gondarra of Elcho Island and Rosalie Kunoth-Monks of Utopia who believe that only a defence of Aboriginal sovereignty and self-determination can ensure the survival of traditional Indigenous Culture on the homelands. Both major political parties deny the global evidence that Indigenous development is best advantaged by self-management. The government denies that it continues to discriminate against Aboriginal people, even as the UN Human Rights Commissioner, Dr Navi Pillay, condemns the ongoing injustice of draconian controls on Aboriginal life in the prescribed communities in the Northern Territory. The government's own national assessment and NT government reports show that the welfare of Aboriginal children has suffered over the first five years of the Intervention, but with Orwellian double-speak Prime Minister Julia Gillard still boasts of a 'stronger future' for Aboriginal people.

At a large gathering of Aboriginal leaders at Maningrida in 2012. Djiniyini Gondarra cried out in anguish: "This legislation is killing us",

---

[49] McMullen, J. 'Correspondence on the Intervention' (2011a).

he said. "We are losing 9 or 10 people every week. People can't live. They have lost their will and all hope."[50]

For Aboriginal Australians, this is the legacy of neo-liberalism.

---

[50] Gondarra, D. Speech at Maningrida Senate Hearings. See McMullen, J., *The New Land Grab* (2012a).

8

# The Problem of Over-Representation of Indigenous Australians within the Western Australian Criminal Justice System: Possible Solutions

*Brian Steels and Dot Goulding*

*There is no indication that anyone comes out of prison better for the experience ... I do not want to simply build another new colonial prison to lock up more Aborigines in the regional parts of Western Australia.*[1]

## Introduction

The over-representation of Aboriginal men and women of all ages in Australia's criminal justice systems has been the topic of many reports, seminars, inquiries, and journal articles.[2,3,4,5,6] The Royal Commission noted, "too many Aboriginal people are in custody too often".[7] Previous research has looked at this complex problem from a range of perspectives:

---

[1] McGinty, J. *Hansard* WA, 22 May 2003, 10 & 30.
[2] Royal Commission into Aboriginal Deaths in Custody (RCADC). (1991).
[3] Blagg, H. *A New Way of Doing Justice Business?* (2005).
[4] Cunneen, C. 'Racism, Discrimination and the Over-Representation of Indigenous People in the Criminal Justice System' (2006).
[5] Steels, B. *Declared Guilty: A Never Ending Story* (2009a).
[6] The Australian National Council on Drugs in 2013 published a report in which it states on page xi, 'Diversion is associated with financial savings as well as improvements in health and mortality ... In monetary terms, these non-financial benefits have been estimated at $92 759 per offender'.
[7] RCADC. op. cit.

- violence, brutality, and the impact of the criminal justice system on individuals, families, and communities as well as victims of crime;[8,9]
- the negative social and emotional impact of extraordinarily high rates of imprisonment upon Aboriginal people;[10,11]
- trends relating to offence, sentencing, and employment and educational background;[12]
- systemic racism within the criminal justice system;[13,14]
- the need to reduce the level of crime and anti-social activity by Aboriginal offenders in order to reduce this over-representation;[15] and
- the extraordinarily high levels of involvement of Indigenous youth in Australia's criminal justice systems.[16]

## The Western Australian Experience

In this chapter we focus on the Western Australian criminal justice system. Australian Bureau of Statistics (ABS) figures for the first quarter of 2012 show that Western Australia had the highest Indigenous imprisonment rate:[17] the national Indigenous imprisonment rate was 14 times higher

---

[8] Goulding, D. *Recapturing Freedom* (2007a).
[9] Steels, B. op. cit.
[10] Blagg, H. op. cit.
[11] Cunneen, C. & McDonald, D. *Keeping Aboriginal and Torres Strait Islander People Out of Custody* (1997).
[12] Walker, J. & McDonald, D. *The Over-Representation of Indigenous People in Custody in Australia* (1995).
[13] Blagg, H. op. cit.
[14] Steels, B. 'Imprisonment of the Many' (2009b).
[15] Weatherburn, D. Fitzgerald, J. & Hua, J. 'Reducing Aboriginal Over- representation in Prison' (2003).
[16] *House of Representatives Standing Committee on Aboriginal and Torres Strait Islander Affairs* (2011).
[17] ABS. *Corrective Services* (no. 4512.0) (2012c).

than the non-Indigenous rate, whereas the Western Australian rate was even more disproportionate at 18 times higher.

## Background

In 2001 the then Western Australian Department of Justice initiated the Aboriginal Over-Representation Project:

> ... because such a high proportion of Western Australia's Aboriginal population is in contact with the Department of Justice at any one time, effective rehabilitation programs or interventions by the Department of Justice can be expected to have a significant impact on the Aboriginal rate of imprisonment and thereby on the overall rate of imprisonment.[18]

However, as with previous projects, little or no change has resulted. Replicating research to illustrate the annual snapshot is one thing but transforming the underpinning Cultures that contribute to such high numbers is another. It goes back to communities and families. Although a response is needed when a crime is committed, it need not always be a prison sentence. If governments were to take the issue of over-representation seriously, and limit prisoner numbers by legislation, or better still, legislate that imprisonment of no one racial or cultural group exceed their percentage of the population, then most prisons in Western Australia would have bed space. If Aboriginal offenders were incarcerated at a legislated percentage, then government would have money to spend on more effective alternatives to imprisonment. This would result in a reduction of up to 36% of Aboriginal men held in prisons and a 20% reduction in the overall prison population. Currently the cost of keeping each adult prisoner in custody in Western Australia is over $100,000 per year, compared to $8,500 per year to monitor offenders in the community. The net cost of prison services for 4,900 prisoners is $609 million per annum.[19] At 39% of the Western Australian

---

[18] MacWilliam, H. *Aboriginal Over-representation Project* (2001).
[19] Department of Corrective Services WA, *Annual Report 2009-2010* (2010).

prison population, the economic cost of Indigenous prisoners per year stands at approximately $237 million.[20] A 20% reduction in the prisoner population would save around $120 million. The consequent availability of monies and policy to effectively reduce victimisation would help many communities in ways which would most likely reduce crime.

When it comes to crime and community safety, Australia's mainstream conversation is to talk 'tough on crime'. This language attracts airtime in the media and apparently gets votes. What 'tough on crime' talk fails to do, however, is to allow smart thinking and effectiveness to rise above the monotonous claims that each political party and commentator makes before and at every election. The consequences can be seen in the building of more prisons rather than developing safer communities. 'Tough on crime' policy has failed to reduce victimisation among Aboriginal women and communities in general. In addition, the discourses of 'fairness and justice' as well as 'equality and human rights' struggle to find traction within this net of social inequity, poor health, and poverty. City based regulators and policy makers continue to roll out culturally inappropriate policy and legislation through the suburbs and into the bush, continually making news with headlines that focus on blame and shame. Consequently, processes such as stigmatic shaming and blaming effectively reduce compliance with the law. It is amongst these conditions that many Aboriginal people are socially excluded. Sadly, this is a journey from birth that places Aboriginal Australians centre stage in the lens of the criminal justice system, as both perpetrators and victims of crime. The 'tough on crime' and 'zero tolerance' policies, combined with over policing in Aboriginal communities, condemn many Aboriginal people to ongoing engagement with the criminal justice system.

Whilst much has been said to counter the over-representation of Aboriginal people within the criminal justice system, little has occurred to effect positive change at grass roots where antisocial behaviour and crime find their feet. The social determinants of crime such as: entrenched

---

[20] Department of Corrective Services WA, *Weekly Offender Statistics*, 16 August 2012.

poverty, high levels of unemployment, poor health outcomes, high levels of alcohol and drug abuse, poor education and general disempowerment help to explain the problem of Indigenous over-representation. Casey notes:

> ... despite 100 years of dedicated Aboriginal affairs agencies, radical shifts in public policy, the continuous review of administrative arrangements by state and federal governments, legislative reform, thousands of recommendations arising from royal commissions and other inquiries, and a surfeit of research findings, the discrepancy between the social and economic well-being of Indigenous and non-Indigenous people could be described as a vast gulf, rather than a 'gap'.[21]

## A Way Forward

The challenge of reducing the over-representation of Aboriginal victims and offenders requires personal, community, and structural transformation. The status quo will be maintained ad infinitum if we continue to modify one and not the others. It is no use having problem-solving courts and restorative encounters throughout the community if the criminal justice system in its entirety from police through the court system to imprisonment fails to increase empathy and concern for others, instead growing its own prison industry complex as a direct result of failing to reduce crime.

Policy makers and legislators have failed for too long to understand that effective rehabilitation cannot take place amongst social chaos and further marginalisation, both in and out of the penal estate. In this way it can be argued that in some instances policy makers can be said to contribute to the problem of crime in communities. We cite the trend of establishing more and more prisons that in turn house more and more Aboriginal offenders. As Findlay *et al.* state:

---

[21] Casey, D. *Report on the Review of the Department of Indigenous Affairs* (2007).

> ... the prison environment requires significant redevelopment, if inmates are not to leave prison more maladjusted than when they went in. Violent, inhuman, unsafe, confrontational and exploitative prison settings will distort social and moral messages that are consistent with crime prevention.[22]

That said, support and guidance ought to be offered outside of the bureaucracy with its passionless offices, business hours, and metro-centric policies.

## Community Policing

This section emanates from our own non-Aboriginal observations of community policing gleaned whilst working within several regional towns and communities with proportionally large Aboriginal populations. The imagery was of a largely frontier mentality more akin to the 'wild west' than contemporary Australia. This of itself has major implications for the individual and the community's attitude to the law or to rule breaking. Research by Tyler clearly shows that people are more likely to comply with lawful requests if they believe that they are being treated fairly and the process is experienced as just.[23] To have local policing policies pushed upon a community with little or no discussion, by policy makers and legislators with poor understanding of crime reduction other than 'being tough' is to plan for continual failure. To further marginalise people who are often both victims and perpetrators of crime is to ignore any opportunities for problem-solving and community reciprocity in crime reduction, as well as providing a space for future conflicts.

The effect of such heightened surveillance among families and communities is often further fear and stress, while adversarial and confrontational practices fail to engender trust, fairness, or participatory processes to reduce harm. Whilst offending behaviours remain forever

---

[22] Findlay, M. *et al.*, *Australian Criminal Justice* (1994).
[23] Tyler, T. 'Restorative Justice and Procedural Justice: Dealing with Rule Breaking' (2006).

under scrutiny and very public, many other members within a household may take on the role of victims in an environment that could at any time become hostile, and yet an environment often unseen and unreported, and in most cases left unresolved. That said, it is often the police who are first on the scene, the most pro-active in time and energy, hopefully providing a calming response, tempered with a degree of support and understanding amid strained relationships with sections of the community. A difficult task made worse by contemporary history and limited dialogue in the public domain.

The Australian New Zealand Policing Advisory Agency's (ANZPAA) Report (2008). identifies community policing as a working partnership with community and key stakeholders that can develop crime prevention and reduction strategies.[24] However, in many instances, 'key stakeholders' do not live within the communities concerned, may not be Aboriginal, may represent a government regulatory agency, and not be trusted to speak on behalf of the local people. Cordner's four dimensions relating to community policing are:[25]

- Philosophical dimensions: The ideas and beliefs found within annual reports, ministerial statements, mission statements, and organisational briefs and aims.
- Strategic dimensions: Strategies that are in turn the link between philosophical notions and their implementation into actions.
- Tactical dimensions: The sum total of philosophical and strategic dimensions that become on the ground responses, behaviours, and programs.
- Organisational dimensions: A whole of service support towards community policing.

---

[24] Australian New Zealand Policing Advisory Agency 2007-2008 Report (2008).
[25] Cordner, G. *Elements of Community Policing* (1999).

These do little to enhance community relationships, or indeed build up crucial relationships throughout communities whereas the traditional Peelian vision includes what Nazemi calls "a relationship with the public that gives reality to the historic tradition that the police are the public and the public are the police".[26] Ramsay suggests that key to Peelian policing was a degree of reciprocity with the community by Peel's officers.[27]

The following nine Peelian policing principles, described here by Nazemi, are useful for this discussion as they highlight what could be a 'relational' approach to Aboriginal community policing: [28]

- The basic mission for which the police exist is to prevent crime and disorder.
- The ability of the police to perform their duties is dependent upon public approval of police actions.
- Police must secure the willing co-operation of the public in voluntary observance of the law to be able to secure and maintain the respect of the public.
- The degree of co-operation of the public that can be secured diminishes proportionately to the necessity of the use of physical force.
- Police seek and preserve public favour not by catering to the public opinion but by constantly demonstrating absolute impartial service to the law.
- Police use physical force to the extent necessary to secure observance of the law or to restore order only when the exercise of persuasion, advice, and warning is found to be insufficient.
- Police, at all times, should maintain a relationship with the public that gives reality to the historic tradition that

---

[26] Nazemi, S. 'The Nine Principles of Peelian Policing' (2009).
[27] Ramsay, A.W. *Sir Robert Peel: Makers of the Nineteenth Century* (1969).
[28] Nazemi, S. op. cit.

the police are the public and the public are the police; the police being only members of the public who are paid to give full-time attention to duties which are incumbent on every citizen in the interests of community welfare and existence.

- Police should always direct their action strictly towards their functions and never appear to usurp the powers of the judiciary.
- The test of police efficiency is the absence of crime and disorder, not the visible evidence of police.

Community policing has failed in Western Australia with not even an overarching aim to build upon community relationships and promote reciprocity. Distrust of police and government services is embedded in many Aboriginal communities, mostly with good reason. Community policing in Australia will remain, at least under current policies, as a localised add-on to traditional method.[29] Colonial policing interventions have left an indelible mark upon the landscape of Aboriginal Australia, underscored by the public tragedy of Aboriginal deaths in custody and the high number of victims of crime within communities.

## The Courts: Problem Solving or Adding to the Problem?

Aboriginal people are often the visible face that attracts the attention of the police at the point of arrest. They are usually interviewed by non-Aboriginal officers, told how serious the charges are, how leniently they are being dealt with, asked to enter a plea of guilty, and told that it is in their interest to 'get it over with and get out' (of prison). Not having full understanding of the language used by interviewing officers is of great concern in terms of just process. Findlay *et al.* suggest that police questioning may involve "elements of unconscionable pressure or even abuse of people suspected of criminal offences"[30] and "interrogation

---

[29] Fleming, J. & O'Reilly, J. *In Search of Progress* (2008).
[30] Findlay, M. *et al.*, op. cit.

of suspects in police custody involves substantial interference with their liberty ... it may, in some circumstances, involve physical or psychological abuse and produce unreliable evidence".[31]

A consequence of 'tough on crime' philosophy is that fewer cautions are imposed. Thus, following an interview the accused generally heads towards the next hearing date. It is here that they may find themselves being shown the charges, often in a language they are not familiar with. At this point the defendant is dependent upon the prevailing political climate, for as Findlay *et al.* note, "the notion of justice which is posited as the hallmark of good sentencing is also very much connected with public opinion".[32] It is this public opinion that relies on punitive measures that has to date targeted Aboriginal people. Particularly in regional Australia, Aboriginal people are required to stand in a local court where the rituals and language are alien, the jargon unpleasant, and the faces of a different colour. Furthermore, they are likely to have seen this often, first as a child when an older relative has been in the dock.

Findlay *et al.* assert that "there are some people who are more prone than others to receiving unjust treatment at the hands of the ... criminal justice system", with factors such as age, gender, race, and class mediating people's "distance from the centres of power in our society which inspire, direct and administer criminal justice".[33] Aboriginal people are most often considered culprits and suspects, labelled the face of crime and characterised as dangerous.

A better way for the courts, the police, and the community is a more therapeutic and problem-solving court approach, whereby harm is minimised. Winick's notion of therapeutic jurisprudence looks to judicial practices that "value psychological health ... strive to avoid imposing anti-therapeutic consequences whenever possible, and when consistent with other values served by law should attempt to bring about healing

---

[31] Ibid.
[32] Ibid.
[33] Ibid.

and wellness".[34] Therapeutic courts are able to question social structures, and ask for community participation in finding solutions to the over-representation of Aboriginal people facing the courts.

Freiberg argues that therapeutic jurisprudence provides a sound and effective alternative to "the sterile, costly and ultimately counter-productive punitive approaches which have resulted in dispirited court and correctional officers and bursting gaols".[35] Making courts and the judiciary and victims' services more effective, participatory, and inclusive is crucial if the rate of Aboriginal over-representation within the criminal justice system is to be significantly reduced. Marchetti and Daly in defence of Aboriginal courts, also claim that the aim of such courts is to:

> make the court system more culturally appropriate, to engender greater trust between Indigenous communities and judicial officers, and to permit a more informal and open exchange of information about defendants and their cases.[36]

Problem-solving courts, therapeutic jurisprudence, and restorative justice linked in a comprehensive and culturally appropriate way, will more likely go to the heart and reduce conflicts than the mainstream adversarial court system. Calma notes:

> the engagement of Indigenous communities in sentencing processes is a very encouraging development, as is the broader acceptance of restorative justice processes and the increased focus on diversionary schemes.[37]

In New Zealand, Judge Fred McElrea states that "criminal justice has been divorced from the community for far too long. Justice has come to be seen as a contest between the state and the defendant".[38] Such

---

[34] Winick, B. 'A Therapeutic Jurisprudence Model for Civil Commitment' (2003).
[35] Freiberg, A. 'Problem Solving Courts' (2001).
[36] Marchetti, E. & Daly, K. 'Indigenous Courts and Justice Practices in Australia' (2004).
[37] Calma, T. 'The Integration of Customary Law into the Australian Legal System' (2006a).
[38] McElrea, F. 'Taking Responsibility in Being Accountable' (1999).

practices make victims of crime invisible and remove the community from solutions.

## Aboriginal Communities and Personal Pressures

Exploring the pressures that some families and communities may be under assists in understanding how these pressures might contribute in structural ways to the over-representation of Aboriginal people in the criminal justice system. Research has demonstrated the many and complex pressures in many Aboriginal communities. Calma notes the invisibility of Aboriginal perspectives in policy formulation, denying the role of Elders, significant cultural events, the complexities of kinship forms and the significance of country to spiritual well-being.[39] Clearly, Aboriginal people must be intricately involved on matters that so clearly affect them.

As families become stressed, illness and death, hospitalisation and incarceration become the norm. The cycle of funerals, medical appointments, and criminal justice appearances becomes part of everyday lived experience for many Aboriginal families. Indeed, quoting *Health infonet* "many more Indigenous people reported stressors like: the death of a family member or friend; alcohol or drug related problem; trouble with police; witness to violence. Almost one in five Indigenous people reported that a member of the family had been sent to jail in the previous 12 months".[40]

It is the entire Aboriginal community that eventually connects to the criminal justice system: culprits, prisoners' visitors, offenders' families, children visiting incarcerated relatives; also the people who are victimised and often remain ever fearful, together with their extended families; plus those who visit courts, legal services, prisons, and parole offices. Aboriginal victims fare worse in terms of service provision. Often, they

---

[39] Calma, T. *Social Justice and Native Title Report* (2006b).
[40] Summary of Australian Indigenous Health. *Health Infoonet* (2012).

are invisible and remain so because Victim Support Services in regional Western Australia fail to provide services and remain at a distance from Aboriginal community structures, most often demonstrating little understanding of their workings. And yet many Aboriginal families have experienced more than their fair share of victimisation. Throughout Australia, pro rata, the number of Aboriginal victims remains well above that of non-Aboriginal people, indicating that current policies are failing to protect Aboriginal communities.[41]

Further, adult victims of crime throughout regional and remote Australia are often forgotten, as most media highlight the plight of young children in reports such as *Little Children are Sacred*.[42]

## Imprisonment: Ensuring the Status Quo Remains

It is pertinent to ask why so many Aboriginal people return to prison following their rehabilitation programs, and discuss various services and their impact on crime and repeat victimisation. Beginning with convictions, it is firstly important to note that the everlasting stigma is often carried with pride by young Aboriginal offenders.[43] Goulding calls for exploration of the way that prior convictions and prison sentences impact upon re-capture and sentencing as a repeat or serial offender and thus deny the right to alternative pathways and diversionary practices.[44]

Findlay *et al.* discuss a range of sentencing options including fines, community work, compensation, and imprisonment, but fail to present the record of conviction as punishment in its own right.[45] A record of conviction evokes consequences well beyond the initial court actions. To the full weight of punishment for Aboriginal offenders is added

---

[41] Ibid.
[42] Wild, R. & Anderson, P. *Little Children are Sacred* (2007).
[43] Beresford, Q. & Omaji, P. *Rites of Passage* (1996).
[44] Goulding, D. 'Violence & Brutality in Prisons' (2007b).
[45] Findlay, M. *et al.* op cit.

collective punishment by association with whole communities being labelled criminal. While a custodial sentence finishes, a record of the conviction for serious crime remains part of the individual's police identification, of their identity, and indelible on their name.[46]

The Australian Institute of Criminology notes that the average prison population in Australia grew by 5% *each year* between 1984 and 2004.[47] An unintended consequence of current 'law and order' debates is that prisons become over-crowded and cost more in both economic and social terms. In turn, this leaves minimal funding and fewer resources to provide local solutions to crime, thus ensuring ineffective 'law and order' cycles.

'Tough on crime' policies with their consequential increase in prison populations do nothing to reduce crime, particularly within Aboriginal communities. The Community Development and Justice Standing Committee report states Aboriginal recidivism rates: male adult – 70%; female adult – 50%; male juvenile – 80%; female juvenile – 64%.[48] Prisons thus produce more crime as a by-product.

## Alternative Sanctions: Policies, Practices, and Philosophies

Many believe that local services should be developed and provided locally among local people and respond to local needs. However, Blagg maintains that community-based regulatory services often:

> simply relocate the service to a community setting, rather than reformulate the fundamental premises upon which the service is constructed. Expressed another way, the community setting becomes a kind of annex to the existing structures of the system.[49]

---

[46] Steels, B. *Declared Guilty: A Never Ending Story* (2009a).
[47] Goulding, D. Hall, G. & Steels, B. 'Restorative Prisons: Toward Radical Prison Reform' (2008).
[48] Community Development and Justice Standing Committee. *Making Our Prisons Work* (2010).

Blagg also notes that "many justice agencies have tended to mistake community based for community-owned", re-colonising and taking leadership and responsibility from local people; policy makers and service planners should, wherever possible develop models of intervention through working within existing community structures and focus "on family violence as a community service, rather than simply a criminal justice problem".[50] Furthermore, in remote areas this "may involve integrating aspects of Customary Law and dispute resolution (including the use of banishment and tribal punishment for offenders)".[51]

Once support rather than punishment is provided, it is possible to find positive ideas that work. Local Aboriginal patrols within many jurisdictions work well at providing immediate shelter for recovery from alcohol binges. This serves to help those affected to avoid being charged with minor offences, reduce fighting, and reduce exposure of anti-social behaviour to the general public. De-criminalisation of street drinking, especially in parks, is unlikely to happen in the short-term so it is important for patrols to assist in removing 'offenders' from the streets. Youth centres and shelters for children, women's shelters, and men's groups are all a part of a larger push to build capacity throughout communities. It is from within communities that solutions will be found. That said, Blagg argues that, "intervention models must provide alternatives to the present system" that are "delivered, as far as possible, by Aboriginal people and organisations; offer culturally relevant support services, respect cultural and family obligations and ties; and assist Aboriginal people in determining longer term solutions".[52]

---

[49] Blagg, H. op. cit.
[50] Ibid.
[51] Ibid.
[52] Ibid.

## Concluding Comments

Twenty years on from the Royal Commission into Aboriginal Deaths in Custody, with millions and millions of dollars spent incarcerating Aboriginal people using the same old racist policies that claim to be 'tough on crime', it is apparent from ABS statistics that the status quo remains.[53] In Western Australia at least, the situation for Aboriginal people has deteriorated as larger numbers face custodial sentences. Tough on crime policies have simply not worked for victims, offenders, or communities. Communities are not safer and fear is still prevalent, with high rates of family violence, Aboriginal-on-Aboriginal violence, and Aboriginal women repeatedly victims of family violence.

If there is to be a reduction in the number of Aboriginal victims of crime and Aboriginal offenders entering the criminal justice system each year, we have to begin to listen to the voices of those most frequently impacted. Aboriginal notions of justice reform should "not be confused with processes simply designed to either extend the reach of the existing justice system or make the existing justice system run more smoothly".[54] Blagg goes on to suggest that they may in fact "challenge some dominant assumptions about the role of law and justice mechanisms" throughout Australia.[55]

It is crucial to reflect on the interconnectedness of individuals and the policies that impact upon them rather than providing a constant knee-jerk response with continuous unintended consequences that recycle victims and perpetrators through the criminal justice system. Future directions to reduce over-representation as victims and offenders throughout Australia's burgeoning criminal justice systems should include communities being "adequately supported to interrupt this perpetuating cycle of personal and collective damage".[56] Ignoring this call for fundamental change, will

---

[53] ABS. *Directory of Family and Domestic Violence Statistics* (no. 4533.0) (2011).
[54] Blagg, H. op. cit.
[55] Ibid.
[56] Steels, B. 'Imprisonment of the Many' (2009b).

"have us witness community demolition, as the path to prison becomes a super-highway, crossing a one-way bridge, taking away many potential community leaders and leaving communities once again in the hands of those who do not live there".[57] The support for a genuine transformation of Aboriginal Australia has to be driven by Aboriginal and Torres Strait Islander people and their communities. However, until they have the resources, motivation, and support to transform and tackle the causes of crime within their communities, they will continue to remain over-represented as both victims and perpetrators of crime.

---

[57] Ibid.

# 9

# On Nudging and Fudging: Paternalism and its Variants in Remote Aboriginal Australia[1]

*Ernest Hunter*

> *Big brown eyes, little dark Australian boy*
> *Playing with a broken toy.*
> *This environment his alone,*
> *This is where a seed is sown.*
> *Can this child at age of three*
> *Rise above this poverty?* [2]

The community of Aurukun on the western coast of Cape York gets a lot of media attention. Much of it has been negative, often portraying a community in perennial crisis. As is the case for a number of other communities across remote Australia, the messages are confusing as there is usually little analysis, a good deal of idealising of some alternative (which may, perhaps, be read as 'authentic') Aboriginal reality, and frequently implicit fatalism and resignation. However, there are also positive depictions of Aurukun, particularly given its prominence as a welfare reform trial community. Education, employment, and enterprise are regularly discussed, notably in Noel Pearson's columns in the *Weekend Australian*.

Indeed, on the front page of the *Weekend Australian* two weeks before writing this piece, in a section by Michael McKenna[3] the work

---

[1] This chapter is an expanded version of an article that appeared in *The Weekend Australian*, 'Inquirer', 24-25 November 2012.
[2] Davis, J. 'Slum Dwelling' (1988), 55.
[3] McKenna, M. 'Return of the Stockmen' *The Australian*, 27 October 2012.

of Bruce Martin in developing Aak Puul Ngantam (APN) Cape York, as a pastoralism and land management enterprise, was profiled. One week later, Ian Mackie, former Principal of the state school in that community and at the time of writing Assistant Director-General of Education in Queensland, described his attempts to utilise the principles of behavioural economics in Aurukun classrooms.[4]

McKenna was stimulated by the work of Richard Thaler and Cass Sunstein whose theories and popular book[5] have been powerfully influential in the UK and the US. By coincidence, just two days before reading his piece I gave a presentation to the health staff in Aurukun on behavioural economics, drawing on that same work. Other key figures whose research and writing is relevant to this area are psychologist and Nobel Laureate in economics, Daniel Kahneman,[6] Dan Ariely,[7] and Paul Bloom.[8] Their work has been driven by economics and the interests, by and large, of the private sector. But it is relevant to health and other social policy and programs, and challenges public sector planners to 'step out of the box' in terms of how to influence individual and group behaviour. As ABC's popular *Gruen Transfer* series should make clear, those of us out to do good in the world have much to learn from those intent on making a buck. That includes not only 'knowing your adversary' and neutralising their advantages (for instance, as we are admirably doing in this country by legislating plain packaging for tobacco products[9]), but also by appropriating their means.

'Teddy bears and robots' was the title of the talk I gave in Aurukun. Across Cape York, Penta-vite chewable vitamins for children is a big

---

[4] Mackie, I. 'Nudge in the Right Direction' *The Australian*, 3 November 2012.
[5] Thaler, R.H. & Sunstein, C.R. *Nudge: Improving Decisions about Health, Wealth and Happiness* (2009).
[6] Kahneman, D. *Thinking Fast and Slow* (2011).
[7] Ariely, D. *Predictably Irrational* (2009).
[8] Bloom, P. *How Pleasure Works* (2011).
[9] Lowe, J.B. Woodward, A. & Daly, J. *The Plain Facts about Tobacco's Future* (2012), 403.

turnover item in community clinics. These ambiguously android-shaped, saccharine-sweetened effigies (teddy bears or robots depending on location and/or gender of recipient) serve as inducements to examination and ease the trauma of injections and procedures. But they are much more, as anyone who has witnessed kids imploring nurses for them will realise. Now, it may be reasonable to ask whether there are real benefits (other than to Bayer Australia), but I'm inclined to believe that there are and that, even if not, those doing the crunching and munching are unlikely to be harmed. However, more interesting questions relate to why this product is so popular and the uses to which it is put. My sense is that the appeal is neither hunger nor opportunism (as 'candy' they are not that good). It certainly involves marketing – thus the kid-friendly shape of the tablet and the colourful, kangaroo-adorned box. It is also about social motivators: across a certain age-band it is cool to get a teddy bear and it can be argued that kids coming to the clinic for no other purpose is a good thing, and supports positive relationships with staff tasked with their health and well-being. That, in turn, increases the persuasive power of those workers to positively influence social and health behaviours.

Thaler and Sunstein[10] would consider this an example of 'libertarian paternalism'; that is, seeking to influence people in their own best interest through mechanisms that do not constrain their rights or their abilities to exercise choice. Governments (and health systems in particular) are inherently paternalistic and when it comes to Indigenous affairs and health in Australia it is paternalism writ large – I know: I'm a well-worn cog in that machine. Paternalism in Indigenous affairs has been and continues to be unsubtle – and not all that successful. From rations, child removal, and prohibition in the past to welfare, child 'protection', and alcohol management now, the shift in Far North Queensland (and much of the rest of remote Aboriginal Australia) is in degree only. So, a bit more libertarianism in the mix may be a good thing.

---

[10] Thaler, R.H. & Sunstein, C.R. op. cit.

Next to Mackie's article in the *Weekend Australian* was one of Noel Pearson's columns which begins with a quote from *The Age*'s Russell Skelton: 'Triumphalism is the enemy of good government, especially a newly elected one driven by an irrational compulsion to replace all the policy furniture – even when it is new'.[11] As this suggests, Pearson's point (if you'll excuse the mixed metaphors) is that as political new brooms sweep clean, there is a risk of throwing the baby out with the bathwater.

The 'baby' in this context is social policy, specifically welfare reform and alcohol management in Cape York. The problems that these initiatives sought to address are massive, longstanding, entwined – and with us still. They were already entrenched and the focus of many commentators a quarter-century ago when I was writing about the Kimberley:

> For Aborigines of remote Australia, the sharp transition from the paternalism of institution life to the paternalism of welfare dependence retarded the development of economic autonomy in communities by obviating the need for independent economic survival in a non-traditional world. Dissonance is further muted by the absence of a subjective reference point of autonomous existence that generates value-derived goals and expectations. It is, perhaps, extinguished by alcohol.
>
> Welfare control also sequesters Aborigines on the peripheries of Australian society. This should not be understood as a rationalisation for a withdrawal of the existing liminal levels of funding (the argument that 'they have to hit bottom before they can find their feet'), but for a redirection. In a system that discourages substantial upward mobility, stifles dissonance, and prevents total collapse, Aborigines, particularly those of remote Australia, are too often suspended, immobile, impotent, and contained.[12]

Decades on, these problems are woven into the social and political

---

[11] Pearson, N. 'Blown by Fickle Winds of Aboriginal Policy' *The Australian*, 3 November 2012.

[12] Hunter, E. *Aboriginal Health and History* (1993), 284.

fabric of remote Aboriginal communities and the long-term negative consequences of the 'enlightened' welfare policies of the 1970s and 1980s on communities such as Aurukun are now well recognised, including by some who were earlier influential proponents.[13] As it is reasonable to assume that the resolution of such problems will be as protracted as they were long in the making; major social policy shifts (in these and other areas) within a generation signal either that the original policies were uninformed and naïve, or that change is expedient, or for its own sake. Which is not to suggest that there is no room for refinement on the basis of experience and 'evidence'. As Pearson notes in the same article: "Getting policies right is like hammering an anvil. Reform policy is the convergence of the right analysis, the right strategy and the right implementation. It is a constant work in progress, where the insights and gains are hard won."[14]

I think this is an apt metaphor; the base metals of welfare dependence and alcohol misuse giving but slowly to the pecks and pounding of policy manipulation on an unyielding anvil, a tough alloy of social disadvantage and political interests. While with the benefit of hindsight both welfare reform and alcohol management in north Queensland might have been better conceptualised and implemented (which, of course, can be said of all policy) they are of already hard-worked metal. In relation to alcohol, well before the alcohol management policy there had been various attempts to address alcohol-related damage by limiting access. Indeed, the harms so caused had been carefully documented in Aurukun in the 1980s[15] and there were extensive consultations to support local controls that were ultimately mired in a web of competing issues and interests.

In more ways than one, Aurukun is the 'battleground' community in these debates. As noted at the outset, the 'good news' stories picked up by the media are often offset (perhaps in clumsy pursuit of 'balanced'

---

[13] Sutton, P. *The Politics of Suffering* (2011).
[14] Pearson, N. op. cit.
[15] Martin, D.F. *Autonomy and Relatedness* (1993).

journalism) by depictions of chaos and danger. I can vouchsafe that these latter are accurate portrayals. But I can also confidently assert from experience that the situation is significantly better in terms of violence and threat by comparison with when I first started visiting some twenty years ago. Furthermore, we need to reflect not only on what the situation is like now compared to 'the past', but what it would be like if alcohol management and welfare reform had not been put in place. A decade ago the situation was heading south rapidly and the outcomes of both policies – driven by Queensland and the Commonwealth respectively – need to be considered in that light.

Indeed, the outcomes so far have been, at best, mixed: sly grog is available for anyone willing to part with their (or someone else's) money, and the most recent annual report of the Family Responsibilities Commission[16] – a key component of the Cape York Welfare Reform Agenda – says more about activity than achievement. As with many other programs and interventions, much rests with the sustained energy of particular individuals, particularly Commissioner David Glasgow who, as Catherine Ford reports, acknowledges in relation to the effort thus far: "Who are we to say that this has been the right way? This is going to take time. Four years is a start."[17]

There is also no doubt that some problems have continued to increase since Welfare Reform and Alcohol Management came into force. For instance, removal or detention of children, incarceration of adults and serious mental illness (which is now at unparalleled levels in Cape York communities).[18,19] Cannabis abuse, which has been around for two decades, is now entrenched and has major health and social

---

[16] Family Responsibilities Commission, *Annual Report: 2011-12* (2012).
[17] Ford, C. 'Great Expectations' (2012), 33.
[18] Hunter, E. *et al.* 'Psychosis and its Correlates in a Remote Indigenous Population' (2011).
[19] Hunter, E. *et al.* 'Psychosis in Indigenous Populations of Cape York and the Torres Strait' (2012).

impacts.[20] For example, research has shown that the average per-capita expenditure on cannabis by users in one Cape community is over $4,000 per year, which translates into an enormous drain on welfare-derived family incomes – cannabis is a huge and increasing problem.[21]

However, as with the other three issues mentioned – child welfare, adult offending behaviour, and mental illness – I am convinced that it is the social context of early family life that is the key mediator, if not the driver. This, then, means foregrounding early life in the analysis of these problems and the policies and programs that result. So far in this chapter I have talked about the Kimberley and Cape York, and in the *Weekend Australian* just one week after Mackie's article about education in Aurukun, two articles appeared, one relating to each region and both relevant to this discussion.

The first, by Nicholas Rothwell,[22] describes the soaring human costs of fetal alcohol exposure and adult suicide in and around Fitzroy Crossing. While there will be consternation and challenges regarding the figures presented by Rothwell, both issues are very real and of concern across remote Aboriginal Australia. There is also no doubt that in relation to the former the consequences have increased – from stunted and syndromic infants, to behaviourally disordered children and adults struggling in communities and prisons.

These adults are, in a sense, the vanguard, part of the first generation within which significant numbers were exposed to alcohol *in utero*, born in the late 1980s and early 1990s when, coincidentally, I was in the Kimberley researching a (then) new problem – suicide – which led directly to thinking about alcohol. At that time, Aboriginal women were less likely to drink alcohol (about half of those aged 15 to 40) than non-Indigenous Australian women, but drank at higher levels, with half

---

[20] Bohanna, I. & Clough, A. *Cannabis Use in Cape York Indigenous Communities* (2012).
[21] Alan Clough, personal communication, July 2012.
[22] Rothwell, N. 'Grog Fight to Beat a Fetal Error' *The Weekend Australian*, 10-11 November 2012.

consuming more than the equivalent of a six pack of full-strength beer on drinking days (thus, much more for some).[23] Of drinkers with children, one quarter admitted to consuming alcohol during their last pregnancy (because of underreporting and the gap between conception and confirmation of pregnancy when women may unknowingly be drinking while pregnant, the proportion of pregnancies exposed was probably higher). Consequently, some of the babies born around that time would have what we now understand to be fetal alcohol spectrum disorder (FASD) which, almost certainly, went unrecognised and unaddressed. They and their unafflicted peers are now men and women in their 20s and many will themselves have young children, some of whom will be identified as having FASD through a proposed study by The George Institute of the prevalence of FASD among children living in the Fitzroy Valley born in 2002 and 2003.[24]

Rothwell also notes soaring rates of suicide in the Fitzroy Valley, the beginnings of which in the Kimberley followed a dramatic increase in deaths from accidents and violence starting in the early 1970s.[25] This occurred in the context of rapid social change, dislocation, entry into a cash (read welfare) economy, and legal access to alcohol. Suicide added to that toll from the late 1980s when the group most at risk were teenage males living in and around towns. These young people were born of the generation that had been rocked by the social changes of the 1970s and grew up in environments in which there was an increasing toll of drinking, accidents, and violence.

At that time I compared the case histories of a group of teenage Aboriginal males who had died by suicide in and around Broome with those of peers who had either died of other causes or been hospitalised. Because completed suicide was associated with intoxication, I wanted

---

[23] Hunter, E. Hall, W. & Spargo, R. *The Distribution and Correlates of Alcohol Consumption in a Remote Aboriginal Population* (1991).
[24] Fitzpatrick, J.P. *et al.* 'The Liliwan Project' (2012).
[25] Hunter, E. *Aboriginal Health and History* (1993).

to see if there were differences in alcohol consumption. There weren't; patterns were similar but what was different was that the suicides were more likely to have had heavy drinking parents. What seemed to be important was what was happening in their homes.[26]

This resonates with findings a decade later in north Queensland from a study on the needs for services to address Indigenous alcohol use across a range of settings, in the course of which pregnant teens were asked about alcohol and pregnancy.[27] What emerged was that while the depth of knowledge was variable, awareness that alcohol was bad for pregnancies was general. But what seemed to have influenced their decisions about ceasing or continuing to drink was not their knowledge per se but levels of parental drinking – again, what was happening in their homes.

Which brings me back to families and early development. In the same issue of the *Weekend Australian* as Rothwell's article was another by Noel Pearson regarding Cape York Welfare Reform, which ended: "the self-interest of families desiring a better life for themselves and their children is the strongest driver of development and the road out of poverty."[28] I agree with this position but the journey presents enormous obstacles, including an issue foregrounded by Rothwell – the mounting burden of disability. For instance, among the young adult Aboriginal residents of Cape York the prevalence of serious mental illness (psychosis) is extremely high. Of those so affected, some 40% have functional intellectual impairment, much more than among patients with psychosis in the adjoining Torres Strait or elsewhere.[29] While we do not know how common intellectual disability is in the general population of these Cape

---

[26] Ibid.
[27] Hunter, E. Brady, M. & Hall, W. *Services Relating to Alcohol in Indigenous Ccommunities* (1998).
[28] Pearson, N. 'Reform without Principles of Empowerment Will Never Lead to Meaningful Social Change' *The Weekend Australian*, 10, 11 November, 2012.
[29] Hunter, E. *et al.* 'Psychosis in Indigenous Populations of Cape York and the Torres Strait' (2012).

York communities, the levels are almost certainly high. Though alcohol was not the sole causal factor, it was probably the major contributor, if not through fetal exposure then through its consequences in terms of violence and stress during pregnancy, and diversion of sustenance incomes (for nutrition in pregnancy and infancy) resulting in small babies and stunted infants – well known to compromise brain development.

Sadly, in these remote communities the proportion of residents so disabled is increasing and their circumstances compounded by the paucity or lack of services – despite escalating pressures from privatised 'employment' agencies to shift residents from unemployment to disability payments. Further, while the brightest and most capable youth are benefiting from access to prestigious boarding schools and will make significant contributions to Aboriginal affairs nationally that may benefit Cape York, my guess is that few will spend their professional lives there. In parallel with this 'capacity leakage', overwhelmed child protection services are pressing to relocate disturbed and disabled youth to (or back to) remote settings where child dependency ratios are twice that of Australia as a whole, and where existing caregivers are often exhausted.

So, while "the self-interest of families desiring a better life for themselves" as noted above by Pearson may lead those who can to seek stability and opportunities elsewhere before circumstances change locally, that is not an option for all – particularly the disabled. If these settings are to be other than incubators of disadvantage, disability, and discontent where, as Aboriginal poet Jack Davis wrote in the late 1980s as these tragedies were beginning, "*a seed is sown*", much must change – especially the environments of pregnancy and early childhood.[30] While the debates will intensify and there will be increasing invocation of 'rights', the voices (and rights) of the most vulnerable – the disabled and unborn – will not be heard. Even so, their interests should be represented and we might ask (paraphrasing Pearson) – Whose responsibilities are their rights?

---

[30] Davis, J. op. cit., 55.

Neither welfare reform nor alcohol management is without shortcomings, but the alternatives are not good. In the face of the chaos associated with sly grog coming into remote communities in Cape York, those who will argue for the repeal of alcohol management legislation should answer how the children of young adults who are struggling in their parental roles now because their own childhoods were blighted by others' drinking, will be advantaged by having more and cheaper alcohol available. If the rationalisations are economic they should present their forward costings for caring for the disabled versus preventing disability. Unfortunately, given the current Queensland government's dismantling of preventive social and public health capacity, that analysis is unlikely to be considered. Ironically, it is probable that the same 'libertarian' rationalisations that were deployed by the Bjelke-Petersen era ancestors of this government (notably Russ Hinze) – that is, promoting and enabling local sale of alcohol in Cape York communities – will be dusted off in the service of bringing it back.

I am not the first (non-Indigenous) professional who after several decades working in Indigenous affairs, has relinquished comfortable certainties from an earlier career phase. For me, some disappeared without trace while others linger despite uncertainty and ambivalence. For instance, the tension between beneficence and autonomy; I would not have imagined two decades ago that I would one day be making a case in support of 'coercive' paternalism. But that is, in fact, what I am doing in relation to these particular issues in Cape York – at least for the foreseeable future. While it can be argued that paternalism (beneficence) which has as its ultimate goal supporting Aboriginal control over lives and livelihoods is a different beast to that which undermines autonomy, paternalism it remains.[31] That acknowledged, to the extent that this can be shifted to more libertarian paternalism, it should be.

What about ventures like APN Cape York near Aurukun, mentioned at the beginning of this chapter? I believe they should be commended and

---

[31] Hunter, E. *Back to Redfern* (2006).

supported. But while such approaches can potentially be an important part of wider solutions – they will be a small part. As the National Food Plan green paper reported: "In 1971, 24% of Aboriginal and Torres Strait Islander people were employed in agriculture, fisheries and forestry but by 2006 this had fallen to only 3%".[32] The days of Aboriginal preeminence as workers in the cattle industry have gone – economics and technology (aerial mustering, fencing, road transportation, etc.) have seen to that. But as with other initiatives, such as community-based horticulture projects, of which there have been many but largely unsustainable,[33] there are other and very good reasons for enterprises to be supported in the long-term even if they do not become 'economically' viable. Activity, competence, pride, nutrition – and models of expertise and responsibility – are powerful outcomes in their own right. Money so allocated that would otherwise be paid through welfare entitlements and the additional costs of child protection, policing, and health – is well invested. That's nudging – libertarian paternalism in action.

So, remote Aboriginal communities will continue to be subject to paternalistic policies and programs. In the short-term, coercive paternalism will dominate and, despite their onerous nature, shifts in major policy areas such as welfare reform and alcohol management should be informed by a historical perspective and careful analysis. Encouraging libertarian 'nudges' and policies informed by behavioural economics should be welcomed. Let's also look critically at the analyses and evaluations, and reflect on the language used. In terms of the former, correlation is not the same as causation; cross-sectional associations in the present miss the importance of historical and (child) developmental causal factors. Regarding language, beware rationalisations based on simple correlations and couched in terms of choice and liberties (such as we are currently hearing from Queensland's politicians and bureaucrats) – fudging. If it looks like a rationalisation, and smells and waddles like one – it probably is one.

---

[32] Australian Government. *National Food Plan Green Paper* (2012), 158.
[33] Hunter, E. Onnis, L.-a, & Pritchard, J. *Gardens of Discontent: Health and Horticulture in Remote Aboriginal Australia* (in press).

# 10
# A Life Remote: My Own Cultural Journey

*Patricia Shadforth*

*I have no doubt that individuals from remote Australia can be empowered such that they can exercise the same choices and have the same degree of control over their destinies as metropolitan Australians.*[1]

### Introduction

On a memorable night in 1970, I sat in the lounge of the nurses' quarters of a small country hospital in South Australia and made the decision that was to change my life forever. A colleague and I made the momentous decision that we would both attend the Olympic Games in Munich in 1972. In 1970, nurses really were paid a pittance, so even with all the overtime we worked, we accepted that financing our dream needed some serious decision-making. Our best option was to work in a remote area, particularly in the north of Australia, where not only were higher wages offered but bonuses were paid at the completion of contracts. Eventually my friend decided to go to Papua New Guinea, I settled on the Kimberley. We made plans, organised communication methods, and agreed to reunite 12 to 18 months later, cash in hand, ready to go. I never made it to Munich. Forty-two years later I am still in the north, the matriarchal head of a large Aboriginal family and have yet to attend any Olympic event. In this chapter I would like to share with you some of my experiences from the early '70s living with Aboriginal people.

---

[1] Hunter, E. 'Where Choice is an Aspiration, Not Real', *The Weekend Australian*, 14, 15 May 2011.

## The Kimberley (A Step Back in Time)

Even today, with all the modern methods of communication, the Kimberley is about as remote as you can get in Australia. In the '70s it was like stepping out of the plane and into another country. No amount of planning can prepare you for the actual reality of the sheer size and emptiness of the area, or the beauty. From the air I witnessed an endless panorama of thick bush bisected by shadowy gorges and winding rivers, the edges melding into mudflats etched with the tracery of tidal streams. The latter was an incredible sight that was totally forgotten the moment I stepped out of the plane. I arrived in late October, probably the worst part of the year, weatherwise. The heat and humidity were unbelievable, way beyond anything I had expected. Stepping out of the air-conditioned plane onto the airstrip was like walking into a hot, wet blanket, an almost physical weight. Even now, after more than forty years, I still find the wet season very difficult. Back then, it was unimaginably hard. The hospital I was assigned to was small, basic, and only partially air-conditioned. Fortunately the nurses' accommodation was fully air-conditioned, so we, at least, got some relief from the heat.

Apart from a vague idea of mission-run settlements, I had few preconceptions about Aboriginal people before my arrival. In my ignorance I had anticipated a population of Blacks and Whites. In actual fact, although most of the hospital patients were traditional Aboriginal people it came as quite a surprise to find the majority of the population were actually a mixture of Aboriginal, White, Asian, Afghan, and Islander, all intermarried, with an incredible cuisine and a language, Kimberley Kriol that was spoken throughout the whole region. The pearling industry in Broome had attracted divers and lugger crew from various parts of Asia, whilst Afghan camel drivers had been imported along with the camels introduced into the north to help solve the problem of transporting goods over such vast distances with few roads. These men, alone in a foreign land, had taken as partners the only women available to them, the full- and part-Aboriginal women of the north. White stockmen with the same problem completed the exotic mix. The result was a rich race of physically attractive, hardworking people with a unique culture found only in the Kimberley and through to Darwin. These people self-identified as: White, Asian, Black (Aboriginal), or Coloured, where 'Coloured' meant having Aboriginal ancestry.

At the time, Aboriginal people in the Kimberley had no citizenship rights, which in essence meant they could not drink alcohol and most presumed they were not entitled to vote, although I did learn years later that this was in fact not true – they were actually allowed to vote from the early '60s. An exemption to the alcohol restriction could be obtained by application to the Honourable Minister in Charge of Native Affairs, but most of the locals refused to apply, referring to the permit as a 'dog tag'. Many self-identified as Asian to avoid this indignity. Compounding this lack of rights was the stance taken by the local police, that any Aboriginal person who moved into town had to find employment within a week or risk arrest for vagrancy. In effect, this meant that almost all Aboriginal people were employed. Despite the total lack of any form of assistance or support for Aboriginal people in terms of Aboriginal-specific services or programs, the local coloured and Aboriginal population provided the bulk of labour in the area. They worked at the local hospital, the school, main roads department, public works department, and local shops and businesses. A few were qualified as teachers and nurses. Many of the men were expert machine operators, others were tradesmen. They were hard working, reliable, and literate. They were the backbone of the workforce of the Kimberley. One of them was an Aboriginal man, named Percy, who was to become my husband and father of our four children.

## I Am One of 'Them' Now

Despite the reservations of some of my family, my marriage into this community was not a disaster. In the '70s communication with the rest of Australia was basically by letter or telegram. There was no television, the computer age had yet to evolve, and few people even had house phones.

As all my family were thousands of kilometres away I came to depend on my new extended family for support and companionship, especially once I became relatively housebound with small children. Percy's family became my family and in time I came to realise that, for all practical purposes they were really no different from mainstream Australians. All they really wanted was secure employment, good health and educational services, and perhaps the chance to fulfil their dream of home ownership. In contrast with current assertions that all Indigenous people are the same, regardless of colour or culture, back in the '70s the part-Aboriginal (Coloured) people did not identify with being black. They referred to the full-blood traditional people as 'natives' with even the hospital having a 'Native Only' toilet. Part-Aboriginal people then lived very similar lifestyles to Europeans, with similar aspirations and ambitions. They did not speak any traditional languages, attend traditional ceremonies, nor even interact with their traditional relatives. Spiritually, they were strict Catholics and the church frowned on the so-called 'primitive' activities of the remote Indigenous people. Priests actively discouraged any interest their flock might express in exploring their cultural roots. The part-Aboriginal congregation was encouraged to embrace their non-Aboriginal heritage rather than explore their Indigenous roots. Naturally this led to a strong degree of assimilation with the Europeans and Asians in the area, based upon similar cultural and ethical values. The three main cultural groups, White, Asian, and Coloured integrated well, with only the traditional people left on the fringes of society.

Naturally there were some cultural differences (for example, funeral ceremonies, large numbers of family members arriving without advance warning) but nothing that couldn't be ignored by all involved, and I must say, that after some initial wariness on both sides, I was made to feel very welcome and accepted by my new in-laws – and there were literally thousands of them!

The early years of our marriage were fairly conventional, by Kimberley standards. We had four children in five years, Percy worked and I was a stay-at-home mother. Because of the immense size of Percy's family our social life was dominated by family events that kept everyone in touch and up-to-date with current gossip. Life on the whole was good, with the normal ups and downs experienced in any marriage and the expectation was that our circumstances would basically follow the same prescribed path of most of the family.

## Return to the Mission

Eleven years into our marriage Percy made the surprise decision to return to his home community of Djarindjin (200km north of Broome). There was a Catholic mission at Djarindjin. During the intervening years he had made regular visits to Djarindjin that had been the home of his mother's family for many years and was situated within the area of their tribal origins. The vast majority of the inhabitants were close or extended family. For reasons of pregnancy and multiple small children, I had been unable to accompany him on these trips so I was totally unprepared for the situation I encountered there. In our discussions prior to moving, Percy hadn't thought to warn me of the major cultural differences between his urban family and the relatives who had never left the mission, but perhaps it was rather he simply didn't appreciate the immensity of that difference due to familiarity with both cultures. Whatever the reason, I was soon in for a rude shock. Djarindjin community was totally run down to say the least, but more about that shortly.

The mission had previously been almost self-sufficient. There had been a bakery, a small poultry farm, goats providing milk and cheese, a large vegetable garden supervised by Percy's grandfather, and a small herd of beef cattle. The local women helped in the communal kitchen and made clothes. On the mission, the men were employed within all the various enterprises. As with similar missions throughout the north, the lay brothers and nuns had endeavoured to teach skills that would endure whilst promoting a degree of independence from the wider community. Though I knew that many of these activities no longer existed, I had somehow imagined the underlying knowledge and motivation to work still remained. Nothing could have been further from the reality.

The community was divided into two parts, separated by a fence. To one side lay the church, school, store, and health clinic with housing for those workers, plus one Aboriginal family – Percy's. On the other side of the fence lived the rest of the Aboriginal community in the area known then, and still today, as 'the camp'. Within the camp, housing ranged from derelict, almost unliveable huts to new 3-bedroom houses, but all were neglected, mostly unfurnished, with yards consisting mainly of dirt and weeds, the whole overlayed by a patina of litter. Tick- and flea-ridden starving dogs roamed everywhere. Most days and nights a card game was in progress under a tree or on someone's veranda. Unless they were fishing, the rest of the population were either engaged in make-work in the Community Development Employment Program (CDEP), which was not meaningful work, or sitting aimlessly around endlessly watching for sources of gossip.

After my initial feeling of shock dissipated a little, I began to wonder why the people in the camp, who were the siblings, cousins, and extended family of the in-laws I had become attached to in towns such as Derby and Broome, had such different standards of living and apparently no ambitions beyond winning at cards. Here were families sharing the same past and origins as those I had met in the towns, yet the differences were amazing. Why was this? I wanted to know.

Percy had a theory about this seeming anomaly. He genuinely believed that paternalism had retarded the development of the residents of remote communities. Those family members with independent functioning lives in townships and cities had been the original, or the descendants, of those teenagers selected from the mission dormitories, and sent into neighbouring towns to work as house servants, apprentices, labourers, or lugger crew. Percy had started working on a pearling lugger at the age of 14. Once in town, they had no choice but to adapt to the same work ethics and habits as their employers.

There were no special considerations given to cultural differences, no allowances for language barriers, no departments created to 'close the gap', no affirmative action regarding employment, education, or housing. They were expected to not only understand the law of the land, but to obey it. They understood that if their children missed school, the local priest would be knocking on their door wanting to know why. If they didn't work, they didn't eat. They learnt to evolve and function at an advanced level, yet still managed to create a unique culture distinctly their own. As they married and raised families, they passed on this adaptive behaviour to their children. This was the unique coloured culture that existed in the Kimberley then.

What I saw in the '70s is similar to what I see today. I cannot help but think that many of the policies designed to eliminate Aboriginal disadvantage, with their emphasis on 'cultural differences' and 'impact of colonisation', are not helping Aboriginal people. Certainly there are some differences between Aboriginal and non-Aboriginal people, but my experiences have taught me that we all have far much more in common. We need to recognise these commonalities.

The family members who were not sent to neighbouring towns to work moved back into the adults' camp and spent the rest of their lives being sheltered, enabled, and treated like children. As an example, the attitude of the resident nurse was that the Aboriginal people couldn't be trusted to look after themselves. She openly nurtured them, to the extent of walking around the camp four times a day to give antibiotics to those children who had been prescribed them, because she didn't believe the mothers were capable of doing it themselves. I well remember when Percy banned her from this practice. She came to me in tears, begging me to get him to change his mind, dreading the health outcome of sick children who didn't receive their medication, convinced some child would die. To placate her, Percy gathered up all the women under the mango tree that served as an informal meeting place and advised them of the new policy, adding that if children became sick or even died because their mothers had not followed the instructions of the nurse then the blame would lie with the mother, not the nurse. Harsh words perhaps, but no child ever did die, and today the mothers there give the medications themselves to their children.

## Met with Resistance

Percy wanted for his extended family what he had. He knew it was possible. Given his stated intention of dragging his people into the twentieth century, he was not popular with the authorities in place at the time: thus the only house we were allowed to live in was an indescribably disgusting, old native welfare house in the camp that had been rejected by everyone else. Percy scavenged the rubbish dumps of neighbouring communities for building materials, which we topped up with purchases of goods like bags of cement from our savings and we set to work. It took us two months of hard labour to clean, renovate, and furnish that dwelling to a standard we were happy with. The final product was a clean, comfortable home, fully furnished with a beautiful yard that was producing fruit within two years and a functioning vegetable garden. The locals sat on their verandas and watched with interest as we transformed the unliveable into the best house in the place. We hoped that our example would inspire some sense of purpose in others to improve their own homes, but despite our offers to teach basic skills like house painting, simple plumbing or gardening, no one showed any interest.

Initially, Percy worked as a general CDEP hand whilst I taught our children via Distance Education, having decided the local school syllabus was far too basic for the level our children were already at. Between housework, teaching, and gardening, I had no spare time. But I soon realised that the other women in the community had far too much time on their hands, most of them, if not playing cards, out sitting on their verandas, watching and gossiping. Nothing private or secret ever happened in the camp. Your business was everybody's business and gossip was rife. It didn't take me long to realise that the women desperately needed occupations or some form of outlet to engage their hands and minds, but none showed any interest in housework or gardening or any other activity apart from fishing or gambling. Hence they remained bored, frustrated, and looking for trouble to bring some excitement into their lives. At one stage a screen printing course held most of the women's interest for several months but, as usually happened, as soon as the instructor left, the project was abandoned.

## Community Governance and Empowerment

Like all communities, they had a council and held meetings. The meeting was held on the mission lawn and run by the mission administrator, with little acknowledgement of the elected council. Decisions were announced, then people were asked if they had any questions or objections. Only a few people spoke. There was no real debate despite the mutterings and muted grumblings I could hear around me, leaving the decisions unchallenged and passed into rulings. Walking back to the camp I listened to the women complaining about the content and outcome of the meeting, but when I asked why no one spoke up, all I received in response were shrugs and hung heads.

The following year, Percy became chairman and instituted many reforms, but even before then he changed the whole tenor of community meetings. He taught a few of his more educated relatives the basics of meeting procedures. This was revolutionary stuff back then and caused a ripple of shock through the establishment, but most people soon got the idea and quickly learnt they had the right to a point of view. By the time we left, these meetings were very robust, vocal, and at times bordered on the physical, but at least there was none of the apathy that was present on our arrival.

At that time all males of working age were employed under the CDEP scheme. As the mission ran a small cattle operation some men were used as stockmen and fencers. A married couple ran an old wood-fired bakery that produced incredible bread, but the remainder of the men simply whiled away their time doing very little around an old workshop. Percy, having good mechanical skills, concentrated on getting the few old community vehicles up and running.

During his time as chairman of the Djarindjin Aboriginal Corporation, Percy tried to implement work programs that actually had visible outcomes, thus giving the men some sense of achievement, even if the money was small. In addition he tried to instil the understanding that, as this was Aboriginal land, everything that was done was for themselves and their family, regardless of how much money was involved. The entire time we lived in the community Percy only ever received CDEP wages. I eventually had to take over the bookkeeping when the existing employee resigned so for the last three years I received the normal bookkeeping award wage.

One of the first projects Percy initiated was the resurrection of the gas stoves. Each house came with a gas stove installed but as few people ever cleaned them, most had blocked gas jets from years of ingrained grease and food. He selected a small crew of men and taught them how to dismantle a stove, soak the parts in a weak acid solution to strip back the grime, scrub clean then reassemble and reinstall the stove. He then appointed a foreman for the group and set them to work in the camp. It took a couple of days to do each stove but the residents were overjoyed to have functioning cookers again. Each household also received a lecture on stove cleaning along with the service but that was far less successful. Naturally, the work crew did their own houses first but eventually the renewal of every stove was complete.

Other projects included the purchase of a lawnmower and the appointment of one worker to mow the lawns for any pensioner who had a lawn. Any community member could borrow the lawnmower for a small fee, which went towards fuel and depreciation. Artefact making was another area that was successful. One group of men (the non-artistic ones) took a Toyota and chainsaw out into the bush to cut timbers suitable for shields and boomerangs which they brought back to the group who did the carving. This last venture was actually too successful. Instead of allowing the finished artefacts to accumulate before being sold to tourist outlets in Broome, then receiving a payout to top up their low wages, the artisans would smuggle their products into town to be sold cheaply on the streets for grog money. However, despite the financial failure of this venture it was one of the favourite activities, following fishing.

## Jobs for the Locals?

The issue of jobs that pay real money (award wages) in remote communities is problematic. The populations are too small to support any but the smallest of capitalistic ventures and even then family ties make obtaining a profit almost impossible. Whilst people still cling to cultural habits like kinship obligations, it is not possible for a community member to run a profitable private enterprise, even if the population was large enough to support one. The well paid jobs currently available in these places are available to any community member as long as they are prepared to invest the time and effort into obtaining the relevant qualifications. Nurses, accountants, teachers, and builders can all be community members rather than outside imports, but to date very few people had shown enough initiative or had the necessary support from family to obtain the educational level required. Mining companies currently provide training and opportunities for many, but even so these jobs are no sinecures and Aboriginal people have to be prepared to perform at the same level as non-Aboriginal people if they wish to benefit from these offers. Tourism, artefact making, meat production, and other forms of income are possible, but it has to be accepted that these types of operations will probably never provide enough employment opportunities nor will they provide high wages. In the end, it comes down to a choice of moving away from the community to an area that provides better job choices, or remain on traditional land and accept that whilst conditions can be improved by the residents, their income will remain low.

## Self-Determination

In our community we found a strong need for a source of income to provide what we considered either essential goods or desirable activities. For instance, few possessed a fridge or washing machine, which impacted upon the health of the people. As we were not able to use government money for any type of loan venture an alternative was required. Percy, myself, and a distant relative of Percy's thought of forming a social club which would consist of people volunteering labour to help raise money to be used for social benefit. At that time, the store was owned and managed by the church and was not open for business on weekends. We decided to open the community office on Saturday and Sunday mornings, manned by voluntary labour, to sell goods such as cool drinks, cigarettes, recycled clothes, and video hire. The initial start-up money came from our own pay packets, to be replaced once a profit was made.

Despite only having only a small number of volunteers, the social club was a huge success and we soon found we had several thousand dollars in the account. At this point we introduced the social club interest-free loan. People who wanted an item of household goods, such as fridges, freezers, washing machines, etc., could apply for the loan. They were required to sign a loan repayment agreement, in which they agreed to repay one tenth of the value of the goods each payday. No money ever changed hands. Each time my husband took the community truck into town he would use social club money to purchase the required goods, load them on the truck and transport them back to the community. When the goods were delivered the owner would receive the invoice and a copy of the repayment schedule. This way everyone could see that no interest was charged or profit made. The payments were then automatically deducted from the purchasers' CDEP pay each week. By the time we left the community almost every house had a fridge and washing machine.

Even with these financial demands upon the social club funds we still had money left over so one year we held the first ever Christmas party that the locals had experienced. The social club paid for the food, cool drinks, enough beer for each drinker to have four cans, a Santa suit, and bags of lollies for the children. The local band played (badly), one of the men played Santa and handed out bags of lollies and simultaneously created a public scandal by kissing one of the women. I will never forget the squeals of laughter and shock from the children when this happened. They never did see past his disguise and realise it was his own wife he was kissing! It became an annual tradition whilst we were there.

## Learning from My Elders

We spent six years amongst my husband's people at Djarindjin and looking back, I feel a great deal of affection for them. While living there, I was the only white woman in the camp, whilst on the mission side there were two teaching nuns and a nurse. Often when my husband was away I would spend time talking to the old women about many things. I had a good relationship with them and wish I had talked longer and learnt more of what has now been lost. Too many of the old stories have been rewritten for the sake of cultural sensitivity and political correctness. Although I did learn a great deal, there was so much more I could have discovered and passed on to my descendants.

My time with the women was the highlight of my time in the community, especially those days I had time to sit in on the card game, not to gamble, but simply to listen and laugh at some of the incredibly funny comments. Traditional women have a very 'biological' sense of humour, sex being the main topic, combined with a wicked imagination and a very descriptive turn of phrase. I laughed a lot during the card games. Despite the huge differences in colour and culture I was always made to feel welcome by the women, the older ones especially, regardless of the tensions that frequently occurred over local politics.

I spent time talking to the old women about the early days of the mission when they were young, before modern society had intruded upon their lives. Following white settlement, children raised in Catholic

Missions were removed from their parents' care at the age of seven and placed in dormitories. They would see their parents working around the mission on a daily basis, but according to a few of the old people I spoke to, the children only had actual visitation with their families for brief periods on Sundays. I am not suggesting that removing the children from their parents was a good thing, but that is what did happen. It did ensure that all children went to school daily, which is probably why I found the people of my husband's age and older to have far better literacy skills than today's children. One old uncle, in fact, would pester me for paperbacks to read. As he preferred westerns, I had to make a special effort for him whenever I was able to get into town to a book exchange, as I would never willingly read one myself.

## Law and Initiation

The old women taught me my role as the mother of initiates and demanded I be treated with respect as the mother of young lawmen. Law time was my favourite part of the year – the only time I felt truly content. At this time feuds and grudges were temporarily held in abeyance and everyone in the place understood their role and how to perform it, which gave them a sense of purpose and left no time for mischief making. The success of a series of traditional ceremonies was dependent upon communal co-operation and organisation, and gave everyone a sense of purpose that translated into a happy, non-violent, and uplifted population. Violence and disputes were actually forbidden by the Elders as it was thought to bring bad luck and even death to one or more of the initiates. Law season was the only time (apart from Christmas parties) I saw evidence that a tribe comprised of distinct family groups could work together toward a specific goal to the benefit of all and achieve a positive outcome.

Our sons asked to be allowed to go through traditional initiation. Both my husband and I were hesitant about this, especially considering the risks of infection and deformity. As a nurse myself (and naturally as a mother also), I had strong reservations, but the boys were very insistent. Initiation was a rite of passage for all the boys and without it our sons would be denied access to some parts of traditional life. In the end we agreed and my husband did everything in his power to ensure the procedure was as clean and safe as he could make it. We never regretted our decision. My sons tell me now that much of the law has been lost or misconstrued since their time.

## Escaping the Inertia

At the time of our departure, my main feeling was one of frustration. I could see what needed doing to improve lives, and to me, it seemed so uncomplicated. It simply required some physical work and a degree of communal co-operation. At that time I didn't see the effect of cultural influences or the impact of Christian paternalism. All I could see was a group of people who had given up any hope of a positive future and who were distrustful of everyone to the point of paranoia. In addition, Percy had met with a lot of opposition to his effort to promote self-management. Not everyone wants independent, informed Aboriginal people running communities. Many people (and not all are non-Aboriginal) had, and still have, vested interests in maintaining the status quo and we were met with a fairly relentless campaign to try and persuade us to leave. Eventually we gave up, especially me. It was difficult to help the people when we could not convince the community members to stand up and fight for themselves. We finally accepted defeat and decided it was in the best interests of our children to relocate back to a town.

## Conclusion

All of the programs my husband initiated dissolved when he left. Two years later my husband died from a heart attack. No one had enough confidence to take over the leadership, which led to the collapse of all he had built. I have been asked to return many times by the older people who remember me, but you cannot go back, and you cannot help people who will not help themselves. I understand that fear was one of the underlying factors behind the lack of involvement; fear of change and retribution, fear of failure and ridicule. But I believe that if people fully understand their rights and responsibilities as community members and can begin to understand that they, themselves, are the only ones who can truly bring improvement to their lives, then there is hope that one day, remote communities can evolve into less violent, more productive societies. It will take strong, impartial leadership and a lot of goodwill on all sides, but it is achievable as long as people's expectations are kept realistic.

Before his death my husband spent years trying to promote self-respect allied with self-sufficiency. His mantra was that Aboriginal people would never be equal until they were treated equally, and whilst they had been granted equal rights, no one had imposed equal responsibility. To his mind, his countrymen would never achieve their potential until they accepted responsibility for their own destiny.

I dedicate this chapter to his memory and his belief that Aboriginal people would eventually achieve that destiny. I am encouraged to see that around this country, many Aboriginal people are achieving their potential. However, there are still many more to join. We are at the crossroads – let's continue the journey together.

# 11
# Politics of Difference

*Sara Hudson*

*[Indigenous Australians] will overcome the burdens of history and recent welfare dependence and dysfunction to become a prosperous yet distinctly Indigenous people whose children can walk in two worlds and enjoy the best of both.*[1]

## Introduction

At its extreme, discussion on Aboriginal people in Australia is polarised into two camps: those who argue that Aboriginal people need to live separate lives in order to retain their unique cultural identity; and those who view Aboriginal culture as a corrosive influence that needs to be left behind if Indigenous Australians are to move forward.[2] The problem with these two extremes of thought is that Aboriginal culture and modernity are viewed as irreconcilable. Those who see cultural preservation as being of primary importance often vilify proponents of mainstream education, as if by advocating for this basic right, they are guilty of committing a form of cultural genocide.

> The school is stealing all our kids ... its assimilation policies. But in a 'nice' quiet way. Make our children's [sic] all coconuts, that's what the school is doing. Yapa with a white man inside. We won't think Yapa way anymore – nothing.[3]

---

[1] Pearson, N. http://www.cyp.org.au/
[2] Two books released in 2010 epitomised these extreme positions. *Culture Crisis: Anthropology and Politics in Aboriginal Australia*, edited by Jon Altman and Melinda Hinkson, and Gary Johns' *Aboriginal Self-Determination: The Whiteman's Dream*.
[3] Independent Media Centre, Australia. (April 15, 2011).

While those who see Aboriginal culture as a negative influence think Aboriginal people should simply abandon the old ways and move off their traditional lands:

> Aboriginal leaders may have to do what white southerners would not: lead their people away from the Promised Land.[4]

But as with many things, the truth lies somewhere in the middle. Culture cannot be separated from who we are and put in a box never to be touched again. Culture is more than what anthropologists describe as 'high culture' – language, dance, painting, and music – it is the sum of our lived experiences and worldviews. At the same time, every culture has to adapt when it encounters another. To not adapt is to stagnate and die. Culture is dynamic, not static. The belief that Aboriginal culture could avoid this characteristic and be 'preserved and frozen in time' has contributed to the disadvantage and dysfunction experienced by remote Indigenous Australians and hindered their participation in the modern world.

Expecting Aboriginal people to adapt and participate in Australian society should not be equated with assimilation. There is a big difference between assimilation and the concept of integration. Assimilation requires people to give up or lose a part of their identity in order to become something else. Integration on the other hand recognises people's differences and does not expect them to abandon their personal beliefs and practices in order to gain the skills needed to participate in society. Assimilation policies of the past, which prohibited Aboriginal children from speaking their language while at school, or removed them from their homes to raise them as 'white' and train them as domestic servants or labourers, did not show much appreciation of, or value, Aboriginal culture. But arguably things are different today. Few people expect Aboriginal people to cease speaking their own languages or

---

[4] Johns, G. 'Bess Price Must Lead Her People from Promised Land', *The Australian*, 30 August 2012.

identifying as Aboriginal. The concept of integration recognises people's right to their own cultural identity. Yet to take their place in the world and be successful and self-reliant, Aboriginal people need the right tools – specifically English literacy and numeracy.

## Cultural Relativism and Separatism

The fallout from the cultural relativist and separatist approach in Indigenous affairs has become increasingly apparent. One of the first people to identify its failings was anthropologist Peter Sutton in 2000 when he gave the Inaugural Berndt Foundation Biennial Lecture 'Politics of Suffering' and later in his book *The Politics of Suffering: Indigenous Australians and the End of the Liberal Consensus*.[5] Sutton exposed the failure of the progressive rights-oriented view of Indigenous policy by pointing out the 'downwards spiral' in Indigenous communities since the 1970s. In brief, the liberal consensus view was: communities should be self-managed and free from government control; traditional culture should be encouraged not discouraged; pressures to assimilate to a Euro-Australian way of life were racist and should be curtailed; liberation, not training, would lift people's self-respect and pride; and communal land rights, collective decision-making, and Aboriginal run organisations would lead to a new era in which the quality of Indigenous people's lives would improve.[6]

Unfortunately, many residents of remote communities lacked the education needed for self-management and floundered when the missions and government managers left. The withdrawal of formal controls coincided with the advent of welfare and a downturn in employment opportunities. In 1968, the Conciliation and Arbitration Commission's ruling on equal wages in the cattle industry came into force, and rather than paying Aboriginal stockmen higher wages many station owners ceased employing them. Unemployment was also exacerbated by the

---

[5] Sutton, P. *The Politics of Suffering* (2011).
[6] Ibid., 17.

increasing mechanisation of farm work, with bulldozers and cattle trains replacing farm hands and drovers.[7,8]

In late 1960s and 1970s, under the principle of Indigenous self-determination, land rights were enacted and the federal government gave money to allow people to return and settle in their traditional lands (homeland communities).[9] There is no doubt traditional land has deep spiritual meaning to many Aboriginal people, and when given the chance by the federal government, many embraced the opportunity to return to their homelands. However, the fear that Aboriginal people would lose their culture if they became too westernised led to communal ownership of Indigenous land and the ghettoisation of Aboriginal people in remote outstations. Well intended as land transfers were, communal ownership failed to identify individual landowners. This effectively denied Aboriginal people on Indigenous lands the private property rights that all other Australians enjoy, and prevented the development of businesses and a real economy on Indigenous lands. As many have said, remote Aboriginal people are land rich but dirt poor.[10] Government policies made the return to country a one-way ticket and helped create the crisis now facing homeland communities. The permit system under Aboriginal land rights legislation keeps travellers and the general population out, while poor education delivered by remote homelands 'schools'[11] has locked Aboriginal residents in.

---

[7] Discrimination Commissioner, *Alcohol Report: Racial Discrimination Act 1975 Race Discrimination, Human Rights and the Distribution of Alcohol* (1995).

[8] Broome, R. *Aboriginal Australians* (1983).

[9] Hudson, S. *From Rhetoric to Reality* (2009).

[10] Peatling, S. 'Black Dilemma: Land Rich Dirt Poor' *The Sydney Morning Herald*, 24 February 2005.

[11] The Northern Territory government appears to recognise that Homeland Learning Centres are not proper schools. See Hughes, H. & Hughes, M. (2012b).

## Separatist Education

The creation of distinct education facilities for remote Indigenous people (such as the 39 Homeland Learning Centres in the Northern Territory) was based on the notion that mainstream education has no place in Indigenous communities and Aboriginal children should be taught from separate curricula.[12] This view is exemplified in the following quote by Professor Jon Altman, the former director of the Centre for Aboriginal Economic Policy Research at the Australian National University.

> Too much emphasis is being placed in the current debate on providing opportunity for indigenous kids in very remote Australia for imagined futures as 'lawyers, doctors, and plumbers' (as suggested by Amanda Vanstone) and too little for futures as artists, land managers and hunters living on the land they own ... rather than just seek mainstream education ... we should develop curricula relevant to local settings.[13]

This belief in 'culturally appropriate' education has led to remote Indigenous schools failing to teach remote Indigenous students literacy and numeracy in any language, let alone English. In many remote communities, only a handful of older people educated in missions, or those lucky enough to attend boarding schools, are literate and numerate.

With no real education in remote communities, the principle of self-determination fought for throughout the 1960s and '70s has become a farce. A vast bureaucracy now supports Indigenous people on Indigenous lands. But most of the positions are filled by non-Indigenous people or Indigenous people from the south (NSW and Victoria). Because of their poor education, only assistant positions are given to local Indigenous people. The culture of separatism has created a second tier of employment, where Aboriginal people are channelled into segregated Aboriginal career-stream positions like Aboriginal Teaching Assistants,

---

[12] Ibid.
[13] Altman, J. 'Letter to the Editor' *The Australian*, 2 June 2006.

Aboriginal Health Workers, Aboriginal Community Police Officers, and even Indigenous Ranger programs. Rather than empowering people with the benefits of employment, these positions reinforce the perception that Aboriginal people cannot cope in a mainstream job.

The Aboriginal Health Worker program established in the Northern Territory in the 1970s demonstrates the consequences of having separatist 'race-based' policies. The goal of this program was to have Aboriginal people take over responsibility for all primary (or first contact) health care in their communities. To facilitate this the Northern Territory government began a program of withdrawing nursing sisters from the smaller settlements (communities) and encouraging Aboriginal people to consult with Aboriginal Health Workers before they saw a nurse in the larger settlements. In line with the principle of self-determination, Aboriginal Health Workers were selected by their communities, whose primary concern tended to be the maturity and standing of the person in the community not their education level. As a result a number of non-literate health workers were employed, particularly in the Southern region of the Northern Territory where (at one time) one out of every three health workers was illiterate.[14]

Despite Aboriginal Health Workers themselves requesting that the Aboriginal Health Worker program contain a literacy and numeracy component so that they could read medicine labels, count pulses, and write up medical records there was a general belief that too much western education risked alienating Aboriginal Health Workers from their communities. At that time it was believed that the poor health of Aboriginal people was a political problem not a technical (lack of skills) problem, and that the solution lay in providing Aboriginal people with more authority and responsibility, not more training. According to Susan Rifkin, author of *Politics of Barefoot Medicine,* all that was needed for Indigenous Health Workers to undertake a wider variety of medical

---

[14] Willis, E. *Has the Primary Health Worker Program Been Successfully Exported to the Northern Territory?* (1984), 13.

tasks than previously was a change in attitude from supervisors and nurses to give health workers more responsibility and respect: "Better health is not a question to [sic] training. It is a question of authority and responsibility ... The answer is health care workers who can mobilise their own communities to improve their own health."[15]

Unfortunately, instead of improving, the health status of remote Indigenous Australians has declined in the last 30-40 years. Unconditional welfare and increased access to alcohol have wrought havoc on remote communities and many residents do not live past their 40s.[16] The failure of the Aboriginal Health Worker program to achieve its goals is because community control and culturally appropriate approaches were favoured over western education and literacy. Without education, and with few incentives to work (such as home ownership for those who work hard and save), most residents in remote communities rely on welfare or Community Development Employment Projects (CDEP) payments. CDEP is a work-for-the-dole and training initiative for Aboriginal people, but has been woefully inadequate in preparing and training people for work, with some people getting paid for doing home duties, or for nothing at all.[17] The limited hours that people are required to 'work' under CDEP has also created plenty of spare time for people to engage in problematic pursuits such as gambling and excessive drinking.

Historically, Aboriginal and Torres Strait Islanders were prohibited from drinking alcohol, though many non-Indigenous people made a profit supplying them with alcohol illegally. The lifting of alcohol restrictions for Indigenous people led to the introduction of alcohol canteens in Aboriginal communities. Canteens in Queensland were owned and operated by local councils. The revenue from the sale of alcohol in these canteens created perverse incentives for councils to increase the sale of

---

[15] Devansesen, D. & Briscoe, J. 'The Health Worker Training Program in Central Australia' (1980).

[16] Hope, A.N. 'Record of Investigation into 22 Deaths in the Kimberly'(2008).

[17] Hudson, S. *CDEP: Help or Hindrance? The Community Development Employment Program and Its Impact on Indigenous Australians* (2008).

alcohol rather than address the harm caused by excessive consumption.[18] Few canteens practised responsible serving of alcohol and would serve people until they became severely intoxicated, with dire results. Prior to the introduction of a canteen in 1985, Aurukun was described as a 'liveable and vibrant community.' However, following the introduction of a regular supply of alcohol with no controls on its use, levels of violence, abuse, and neglect skyrocketed. In 2000, the town's homicide rate was estimated to be 120 times the state average.[19]

As the above paragraphs illustrate, treating Aboriginal people differently has had many unintended consequences. The belief that Aboriginal people could have self-determination without formal education is like giving a car to someone without teaching them how to drive. Education should not be viewed as assimilationist but as a liberator and vehicle for freedom. The sooner this is recognised, the sooner more Aboriginal people will have the opportunity for real self-determination.

## Romanticised Notions of Traditional Culture

In seeking to retain Aboriginal people's traditional culture, advocates of the culturally relativist and separatist approach have painted a rosy picture of traditional Aboriginal life, with many refusing to accept historical evidence that Aboriginal people's traditional lives were often harsh and brutal. An example of this myopic blindness is Mick Gooda's assertion that in traditional Aboriginal society, "physical violence was very rarely used".[20] Early historical records of the first European explorers to Australia documented considerable violence towards Aboriginal women. For example, in Voyage de Decouvertes aux Terres Australes, the zoologist Francois Peron wrote: "nearly all [women]

---

[18] Chikritzhs, T. Gray, D. Lyons, Z. & Saggers, S. *Restrictions on the Sale and Supply of Alcohol: Evidence and Outcomes* (2007), 76.

[19] Sutton, P. op. cit., 1, 54.

[20] Chikritzhs, T. Gray, D. Lyons, Z. & Saggers, S. *Restrictions on the Sale and Supply of Alcohol: Evidence and Outcomes* (2007), 76.

were covered in scars, shameful evidence of the ill-treatment of their ferocious spouses."[21]

Although European colonisers introduced many diseases, which had a devastating effect on the Aboriginal population, disease and sickness were also present before white men came. For example, Yaws, a bacterial infection that leads to physical deformity and death was probably introduced by the Macassans, thousands of years before the arrival of Captain Cook. Dr Phillip Playford, a former Director-General of the Geological Survey of Western Australia, visited the remote Kimberley region of Western Australian in 1959 as a young government geologist and encountered Aboriginal people living totally nomadic lives, with little to no experience of, or influence from, Western society. Many of the Aboriginal people suffered from Yaws, easily cured by penicillin but fatal if left untreated. One of the Aboriginal men, probably in his 30s, died of his long-term Yaws infection a few weeks after Playford's encounter with him.[22]

People with a romantic view of traditional Aboriginal culture often hold a negative view of Western culture, as evident in the following extract from the National Aboriginal Health Strategy published in 1989 and reprinted in 1996:

> Aboriginal culture is the very antithesis of Western ideology. The accent on individual commitment, the concept of linear time, the emphasis on possession ... the rape of the environment and, above all the devaluing of relationships between people ... are totally at variance with the fundamental belief system of Aboriginal people.[23]

---

[21] Quote in Nowra, L. *Bad Dreaming: Aboriginal Men's Violence against Women and Children* (2007), 12.
[22] Playford, P. 'Report on Native Title Welfare Expedition to the Gibson and Great Sandy Desert' (1964).
[23] National Health Strategy Working Party. *A National Aboriginal Health Strategy* Reprint (March 1996), ix.

The view that Aboriginal people are fundamentally different to non-Indigenous people, has led to the acceptance of harmful or negligent practices on the basis of assumed cultural difference. In the past, before the Northern Territory Intervention banned criminal courts from considering customary laws as mitigating factors in offending, there were many instances where Aboriginal culture was used as an excuse for offenders to receive lesser sentences, for example the case of a 14-year-old Aboriginal girl who had been promised in marriage to an older man when she was four. When she decided she would rather have a boyfriend her own age than marry a man more than 40 years her senior, the prospective groom, with the co-operation of the girl's grandmother, 'beat the girl with a boomerang, then locked her in a room for four days during which time he repeatedly forced her to have anal sex'.[24] Brian Martin, the chief justice of the NT Supreme Court, imposed a remarkably lenient penalty – a suspended sentence of two years, with only one month to be served – when the maximum penalty for the crime is 16 years. When the NT government appealed the sentence, Martin acknowledged that he had placed too much emphasis on customary law and the offender's ignorance of the Northern Territory's law.[25] This example shows the danger in making too much of Aboriginal difference. Although every effort should be made to ensure Aboriginal people have interpreters in court and understand the processes, the different treatment should end there.

Similar instances have occurred in the child protection arena. Under the 'Aboriginal Placement Principle' Indigenous children needing to be removed from the custody of their parents should be placed firstly with their extended family, next within the local community, and third with an Aboriginal and Torres Strait Islander family. Although it makes sense to maintain a child's family and cultural ties as much as possible, the safety of the child should be paramount. Unfortunately, this has not

---

[24] Hughes, H. *Lands of Shame* (2007), 27.
[25] Ibid., 28.

always been the case. The 2010 Bath Report into child protection in the Northern Territory found that the application of the Aboriginal Placement Principle had justified "Aboriginal children in care receiving a lesser standard of care than non-Aboriginal children".[26]

The belief in maintaining a traditional Aboriginal life at all cost ignores the fact that though Aboriginal people may be living on their traditional land they are not living traditional lives. The door to a traditional life was well and truly shut when Aboriginal people started receiving welfare and buying televisions. Nowadays remote residents who hunt and fish do so primarily for recreation. Access to media has made Aboriginal people distinctly aware of their relative deprivation, leading to frequent calls from them and activists for government to provide more funding to address Indigenous disadvantage. Yet there are inherent contradictions with this approach, on the one hand Aboriginal activists say: "Aboriginal people will not assimilate." While on the other hand they say: "Aboriginal people need employment, housing, education, from the government."[27]

Since the 1970s, the emphasis has been on government responsibility not personal responsibility. Traditionally, Aboriginal people had to be self-reliant. If you didn't hunt and play an active role in the community, you starved. Colonisation and successive government policies have effectively 'stolen' Aboriginal people's independence.[28] Universal welfare without any compulsory work requirements has taken away Aboriginal people's self-reliance and sense of responsibility. Left to itself, without government influence (such as the homelands policies) Aboriginal culture could have evolved differently. An example is the renaissance of Maori culture in New Zealand. Following World War II, many Maori chose to move from their tribal and rural communities to find work in the cities. Not all traditional practices were lost as some Maori established

---

[26] Sammut, J. 'Custody for Indigenous Kids More Than Black and White' (2011).
[27] Shaw, W. 'Indigenous 'Solutions' Just Disempower Us Further' (2012).
[28] "They Have Stolen Our Responsibilities." – Lajamanu Elder from Hughes, H. & Hughes, M. (2012a).

traditional institutions such as urban maraes (meeting houses/villages) in the cities. As urban-based Maori became educated, they established a Maori-language education system and started industry initiatives such as fishing, aquaculture, and farming. The Maori people have demonstrated an amazing ability to adapt, drawing on elements of Western culture while retaining their unique identity.[29]

## Adaption: Integration not Assimilation

Like all cultures, Aboriginal culture has not remained static. But the absence of the conditions and norms experienced in mainstream Australia in remote communities has meant the changes have been more maladaptive than adaptive. The lack of education, skills, and work ethic needed for employment in today's society has contributed to alcoholism and a reframing of cultural values so that positive Indigenous values such as the responsibility to share with relatives have been corrupted by alcohol abuse and transformed into negative traits of exploitation and manipulation.[30,31]

Adaptation, particularly for those who have only recently emerged from nomadic lifestyles, is a difficult and painful process but every culture has to adapt when it encounters another. To not adapt is to stagnate and die. Ideally, in making the journey towards integration, it would be best if remote Aboriginal people themselves decided which aspects of their traditional culture to retain and which to discard. Real change has to come from within. There are, however, several problems with this approach. As Bess Price says, "When Aboriginal people follow their own law, they break 'white fella' law; when they follow 'white fella' law, they break their own laws".[32] Many remote Aboriginal people are caught between these two world views and can see little way of reconciling them.

---

[29] Royal, T.A.C. 'Māori—Urbanisation and Renaissance' *Te Ara—the Encyclopaedia of New Zealand* (3 March 2009).
[30] Pearson, N. 'Outline of a Grog and Drugs (And Therefore Violence) Strategy' (2001), 11.
[31] Jajirdi Consultatnts. 'Should Customary Law Be Recognized by the Courts?' (2009).
[32] Hudson, S. 'Straddling Black-fella and White-fella Laws' (2011).

Remote Aboriginal people have two choices — adapt or continue to live in a no-man's land. Living on government welfare means they are not living traditional lives – even if they were willing to forgo government entitlements to welfare, health, and housing, outside influences (such as television and store-bought food) will continue to affect them. There can be no return to a romanticised past (particularly as it never existed in the first place), only courageous steps forward.

To make an informed choice, Aboriginal people need the right tools. The absence of decent schooling on Indigenous land has kept many residents largely ignorant of Western society. The following story of an Aboriginal man from Central Australia highlights the vast gaps between what we in mainstream society know and what many Aboriginal people know. This Aboriginal man had no idea what tax was, when it was explained to him that everyone who works pays a portion of their wages as taxes to government, and that government uses that money to pay for social welfare, the man went quiet for a while. Eventually, he said: "So that's why all those white fellas don't like us – they're paying for our welfare." Arguments for cultural relativism have tended to be one-sided, with non-Indigenous people expected to appreciate where Aboriginal people are coming from by being more 'culturally respectful' or 'culturally appropriate'. The same attention has not been paid to explaining Western culture to Aboriginal people in a way they can comprehend. Too often, it is assumed that Aboriginal people understand what we are saying, but deeper questioning often reveals they do not.

## Why Education is Important

Past practices, for example, when Aboriginal people were punished for speaking their language at school, have tainted many Aboriginal people's views about Western education. Today, being well educated needn't equate with the loss of one's cultural identity. Indeed, it is unlikely that Aboriginal university graduates somehow feel less 'Aboriginal' after graduating. Yet, many believe that as Aboriginal people become more educated and 'westernised' all that will remain of their Aboriginality is their family tree.

Many Aboriginal people have internalised negative perceptions of what it means to be Aboriginal, and see successful, hardworking, and Aboriginal as mutually exclusive terms. They accuse those Aboriginal people who have achieved success in mainstream society of being 'too flash' or a 'coconut' (black on the outside and white on the inside). However, embracing education and modernity does not mean discarding Aboriginal culture. There are many Indigenous Australians who are successfully living in two worlds, such as Noel Pearson, Tania Major, June Oscar, Alison Anderson, and others too numerous to mention. Many of them have come from remote communities and gone to boarding school. Though they are sometimes derided by other Aboriginal people as being a bit 'toffee nosed', they have retained a strong connection with their family and community and still speak one or several Aboriginal languages. Pearson embodied his ability to live in two worlds in a speech on identity when he translated a section of Shakespeare's *Richard III* into Guugu Yimithirr (his Aboriginal language).[33]

Sadly, despite the existence of a few bilingual schools, few Aboriginal children are able to translate English into their own Aboriginal language or vice versa. Children living in remote communities may be able to speak several Aboriginal languages but cannot read or write English very well because of appalling schooling. Conversely, while Indigenous children living in cities and towns speak English, many do not know their traditional languages. As Major pointed out in an article in the *Sydney Morning Herald*:

> The tragedy is that too many of our young people today have no such sense of their own identity or place ... They don't know who they are or where they belong. They don't know their own language and all too many can't even speak standard Australian English.[34]

If bilingual education for Aboriginal students was truly bilingual then

---

[33] Pearson, N. 'Layered Identities and Peace' (2006).
[34] Major, T. 'Why has Indigenous Policy Failed' *The Sydney Morning Herald*, 28 July 2010.

this might be a way of bridging two worlds. However, the problem with the bilingual schools in the Northern Territory is that they tended to view the teaching of English as assimilationist and delayed teaching in English until students were in Year 4. Waiting until students are 10 before they learn to read and write in English goes against all research in this area. It is common knowledge that the younger children are when they learn another language, the better.[35]

The failure of Aboriginal students to meet national benchmarks in literacy and numeracy saw the former NT Education Minister Marion Scrymgour announce that all schools in the territory would have to teach in English for the first four hours of the day.[36] Traditional language is important for maintaining a distinct cultural identity and should not be devalued. At the same time, it should not be taught at the expense of a mainstream secular education.

Pearson has written: 'Our hope is dependent upon education. Our hope depends on how serious we become about the education of our people.'[37] Getting more serious about education involves not only ensuring that kids go to school but also that Aboriginal language and culture is passed on to the next generation. Key to the maintenance of a cultural or ethnic identity is the passing on of cultural knowledge and fostering a positive self image among the next generation. However, the passing on of cultural knowledge should not be the responsibility of government. Government cannot be expected to maintain a culture's distinct identity. Government's primary goal is to ensure every child in Australia receives the same standards in education, no matter who they are or where they live. It is up to Aboriginal people themselves to decide how to continue to keep their culture alive.

---

[35] Lang, S. 'Learning a Second Language Is Good Childhood Mind Medicine, Studies Find' (2009).
[36] Toohey, P. 'Northern Territory Kids Get Four Hours A Day in English' *The Australian*, 15 October 2008.
[37] Pearson, N. 'Radical Hope: Education and Equality in Australia' (2009a).

Depending on the background and location of students, different strategies to deliver education and cultural knowledge will need to be used. In those remote communities where children learn numerous Indigenous languages from birth, the teaching of Aboriginal language will have less relevance and government should ensure children are immersed in English language instruction and taught English as a second language as other foreign language students are. In urban areas where many Aboriginal children have little knowledge of their traditional language it could be that a Board of Aboriginal Education is established which promotes the teaching of Aboriginal languages in schools as the Board of Jewish Education has done with Hebrew. Such a board would need to be established by Aboriginal people themselves with members of the community deciding which Aboriginal language or languages are taught in particular schools based on the background of the majority of Aboriginal students. Although somewhat tokenistic in the time allowed, Aboriginal spirituality could be taught to Aboriginal children in public schools during scripture classes. Aboriginal people should not wait hoping that the government will implement policies to preserve and maintain their culture, but do it themselves (as some already are).[38]

The challenge of learning about and perpetuating the richness of their cultural heritage to the young could be a source of pride and self-worth to Indigenous people. Instead of remote Indigenous communities being seen as places of dysfunction, they could become the spiritual hub – the centre of Aboriginal culture and tradition. Places of learning that provide a connection to land and culture for those Aboriginal people living in larger towns and cities to return to and visit as rural maraes in New Zealand are for many Maori people. This is Noel Pearson's vision for his people in Cape York.[39]

---

[38] For example the Yiriman Project in Fitzroy Crossing. Australian Government, 'Fitzroy Crossing: Looking to the Future' *Indigenous Newslines* (September- November 2009), 5.

[39] Pearson, N. 'Aborigines Can Learn from Jews How to Preserve Culture and Prosper' *The Australian*, 15 February 2010.

## Conclusion

Indigenous Australians have always been treated differently. First, they were subject to discriminatory laws which prevented them from living where they chose, voting, drinking, and even being counted in the Census. When these discriminatory laws were abolished, they were replaced by equally damaging 'positive discrimination' measures. Maintenance of a distinct cultural identity should not be the role of the state. Despite the best of intentions, state sanctioned difference has always had unfortunate consequences. As Marcia Langton describes, the exceptionalist initiatives have isolated many Aboriginal people from the economic and social life of Australia. She argues treating Indigenous people as the exotic 'other' has meant they are not required to be normal and attend school regularly.[40] Langton is also highly critical of teachers who treat Aboriginal children differently from other students and modify curriculum to make lessons culturally sensitive, stating that it is "just a bunch of racist codswallop".[41] The belief that Aboriginal people should be treated differently and receive 'culturally appropriate' education has prevented many Aboriginal people from having the opportunity to choose a life that they value. Without proper education, the choice has effectively been made for them. However, if Aboriginal people were taught both mainstream education and aspects of their Aboriginal culture then they would be able to make an informed choice. The irony is that Western education will give Aboriginal people the skills and wherewithal to introduce initiatives (as the Maori have done) to maintain their culture and language. Rather than leading to a loss of culture, Western education will enable people to participate in the world according to their own interests, passions, and beliefs.[42,43,44] It is time to put to bed the mistaken

---

[40] Langton, M. *Indigenous Exceptionalism and the Constitutional 'Race Power'* (2012b).
[41] Short, M. 'A Case for Change' *The Sydney Morning Herald*, 5 September 2012.
[42] Pearson, N. op. cit.
[43] Pearson, N. 'Adam Smith and Closing the Gap' *The Australian*, 24 July 2010.
[44] Pearson, N. 'Conservatism, too, is relevant to our culture' *The Australian*, 31 July 2010.

notion that Aboriginal culture and modernity are irreconcilable. As the Northern Territory Minister for Indigenous Advancement said recently: "We need to show our fellow Australians we want to be normal. We want the right to be just like them and keep our identity, but to live fully in the 21st century."[45]

---

[45] See chapter by Anderson in this volume.

# 12

# Good Culture – Bad Culture, Where Do We Go From Here?

*Dave Price and Bess Price*

*Settlement may seem natural to us, but it requires a set of wrenching adjustments for hunter-gatherers. They must abandon the freedom to move away from danger or from the people they don't get along with. They must yield their firmly egalitarian way of life for a hateful social order of superior and inferior, rife with rules and priests and officials.*[1]

*Cynics have observed that those who have benefited most from "progress" – the citizens of the First World – are the people most inclined to disdain it. The privileged few who eat better, lead longer and more stimulating lives because of modern agriculture, medicine, education, mass communication, and travel, and are most cushioned from physical discomfort and inconvenience by industrial technology are the most nostalgic about the primitive world.*[2]

## Romanticised Culture

Whitefellas used to demonise Indigenous cultures and sanctify their own. The people who lived them were savages. Blackfellas couldn't do anything right, whitefellas nothing wrong. The natives had to be civilised whether they liked it or not. All this is now reversed. Whitefellas are incorrigibly racist, imperialist, homophobic, and misogynist and can't do anything right. Excepted are those who are deeply apologetic, self-loathing, or can be defined as 'victims'. If Blackfellas murder and rape their own, steal or self-destruct it's justified as resistance or blamed on 'the Whitefella'.

'Culture' is fetishised. We have refused to discuss 'difference' – afraid of encouraging racism. The superficial moral relativism of the West

---

[1] Wade, N. *Before the Dawn, Recovering the Lost History of Our Ancestors* (2006), 101.
[2] Keeley, L.H. *War before Civilization: The Myth of the Peaceful Savage* (1996), 169.

deems all cultures equal in value though Indigenous peoples can't live without theirs, and whitefellas are urgently obliged to radically change their own. Attempts to change other peoples' cultures are condemned as 'cultural genocide', an extremely odd, if not an outright oxymoronic term. Bess' culture is revered. Dave's is condemned. When a young white man working for an Aboriginal organisation in Alice Springs was reminded of the incredibly high levels of homicide and assault perpetrated by Aboriginal men on their own women his reaction was predictable, typical, and irrational: "Aboriginal men have been gutted by invasion and racism". Aboriginal women, particularly the young, are lambs on the altar of culture, sacrificed to assuage white guilt.

Contemporary Australians are busy re-mythologising. We are all wont to invent a past for our people that gives us a sense of identity and pride. We have a strong urge to identify with a culture older than a mere two centuries that we can cherish, with none of the taints of colonialism and racism or what is seen as conservative and anti-progressive. So we lie to ourselves. It is an inherently problematic process. The manufactured identities of the 'born to rule' make them a definite problem for those they want to continue ruling even as they take on all the blame and all responsibility. That of the 'ruled' leads to a glorification of victim status and a tendency to self-destruction blamed on 'the oppressor'.

Around one-third of the population of the Northern Territory is Indigenous. The problems faced by one-third of us face us all. We cannot solve them without calmly and rationally debating the issues and identifying that which is preventing us from dealing with them properly. There must be open debate and a willingness to find some truths worth expressing and defending. We have to rid ourselves of both racism and political correctness – neither of which is interested in truth. They are two sides of the same coin.

We believe that we belong to not only different cultures, but literally the most different on Earth, or at least our parents did. We have both adapted enough to keep our marriage together for more than three decades. That has been a mighty but very worthwhile struggle. Bess has adapted enough to acquire a bachelor degree and to be elected to the Territory Parliament. Thanks to modern genetics and evolutionary psychology, we know that racism based on physical difference is so irrational as to be a form of mental illness. We need not be afraid. However, the cultural differences that form our world-views, challenge us almost every day of our lives. What we look like doesn't matter at all, what we think and value matters critically.

The great majority of Australians who currently identify as 'Indigenous' speak English, live in suburbs, and produce children with Australians who do not identify as Indigenous. Around eighty percent of their children also identify as Indigenous, usually exclusively. Many of them do quite well in the mainstream economy and society, supplying Indigenous Australia with its middle class and the majority of its spokespeople. They are regularly asked by journalists to define the 'Indigenous View' on any issue. Unless they have studied anthropology and linguistics, their understanding of traditional law and culture will come from the half-remembered musings of aged relatives, themselves several generations removed from the traditional life. Yet their opinions are accepted as unquestionable truth.

## Silenced Voices

A substantial minority, around 12%, of Indigenous Australians live in remote Australia, speaking traditional languages, and are trying to hold onto the fast disappearing shreds of traditional culture. They are largely alienated from the mainstream economy and culture, die at a young age, fill the jails and hospitals of Northern Australia, and are rarely asked by journalists for their opinion on anything. Among them are still living individuals who were born and raised in a traditional culture, speaking traditional languages, and surviving the realities of brutal frontier violence. They are fast reaching the end of their drama – and pain-filled lives. Many of their children are self-destructing and many of their grandchildren live a nightmare. Cultural fantasising in the southern cities helps to keep them trapped in that nightmare.

Discussion around issues relevant to the nightmare is highly emotive and rarely rational or commonsensical. The strident obsession with racism and political correctness permeating the academy and media, and a profound ignorance of our history mean that practically useful publicly available analysis of the issues is rare and endangered. The voices of the dispossessed, the most marginalised, those who suffer most are routinely ignored in the clamour – in fact, often deliberately and systematically excluded by those who have appointed themselves as spokespeople.

Too many of our loved ones are among the most marginalised and most dispossessed. We have spent a lot of time in courts, hospitals, gaols, and cemeteries. We have buried too many of our dead well before their time. Life-threatening crises are frighteningly common in our lives. We are interested in pragmatic solutions, not in the advancement of ideologies or the quest for soul-soothing esoterica for the comfortable urban middle class. So we offer the following based on our reading and our two lifetimes of pondering the problems we and our loved ones face on a daily basis. Our purpose is simple. We want our loved ones to prosper and to live in peace. We want our kids to survive, to be properly educated, to be proud of who they are based on knowledge of the cultures that constitute their heritages and an ability to benefit from the wonderful, open, tolerant society we live in and to be able to influence that society to change it for the better. That is our kids' birthright.

## Different Cultures Meeting at the Crossroads

All we humans started off pretty much the same. All of our ancestors were foragers and this way of life is not that far behind any of us. We haven't changed much physically and neurologically:

> These ways of knowing and core intuitions are suitable for the lifestyle of small groups of illiterate, stateless people who live off

the land, survive by their wits and, depend on what they can carry. Our ancestors left this lifestyle for a settled existence only a few millennia ago, too recently for evolution to have done much, if anything, to our brains.[3]

In one lifetime Bess' people have experienced forces and processes that Dave's people have had millennia to adapt to. They didn't progress peacefully, happily and lineally to contemporary civilisation. It has been a long drawn out saga of war, genocide, persecution, and savagery as much as anything positive you could say about it all. However, all Australians of all backgrounds, including Indigenous, have produced one of the freest, most tolerant, and most open societies our species has so far managed to create. That should make us feel proud, positive, and confident. Let's get on with it.

Bess' people are in turmoil. Their ancient culture worked brilliantly for tens of millennia. Now everything has changed. They have inherited very few cultural tools needed to cope with the devastating problems they now face. They are asking for help. Governments have not yet found ways to effectively help. One thing we all can do is help to identify those elements of the two clashing cultures that hinder problem-solving. We have been keen to criticise the whitefella side of the ledger but have never properly attempted to carry out this urgently needed exercise on the other side in any rational way. Aboriginal people can achieve change for themselves only with the help and support of the rest of us. It is encouraging that many have already achieved positive change, or are in the process of achieving it.

Below we consider some elements of traditional culture that we believe need to be discarded if there is to be hope for the future of the residents of remote communities. We include the town camps of Northern Australia in this. They are not geographically remote from the urban centres but are in every other way – economically, socially,

---

[3] Pinker, S. *The Blank Slate* (2002), 220.

culturally, and psychologically. We have personally witnessed many of the incidents discussed or they have been related to us by those close to us who were directly involved. We have tried to preserve their privacy. We have no wish to betray confidences or shame or anger those we hold dear.

## Humbug – Demand/Share

Domesticated animals can only be raised by people who are committed morally and ethically to watching their families go hungry rather than letting them eat the breeding stock. Seed grain and breeding stock must be saved, not eaten, or there will be no crop and no calves the next year. Foragers generally value immediate sharing and generosity over miserly saving for the future, so the shift to keeping breeding stock was a moral as well as an economic one.[4]

### Scenario 1

*A Warlpiri man knocks at his white 'father's' door. He has been drinking but isn't drunk:*

- A  *'Jangala, you're my father and I love you'* – *the usual style of greeting preceding a request for financial assistance.*
- D  *'Jampijinpa, you're my son and I love you'* – *an appropriate, but in this case, slightly cynical, response.*
- A  *'I love you that's why I'm going to ask you for $100'* – *a perfectly appropriate way to make a request for money from a kinsman in this man's culture.*
- D  *'What do you want money for?'*
- A  *'Hey I thought you were my father!'* – *by asking what he wants to do with the money the father has broken his son's Law and has thus shamed both of them.*

---

[4] Anthony, D.W. *The Horse, the Wheel and Language* (2007), 155.

D   *'I know that your way I shouldn't ask but in my Law that's what a father does. If you call me 'father' then you're stuck with a kardiya (whitefella) father and I think you want money for grog. I'm not giving you a cent for grog.'*

A   *'Well make it $50 then.'*

D   *'Good try – same problem'!*

*A turns to a young woman present, the biological daughter of D.*

A   *'Sis, can you help me out?'*

D   *'Hey my daughter is a single mum with three kids – she needs her money more than you do.'*

A   *'I'm talking to my sister, keep out of it' – again in terms of this man's Law a father has no right to interfere in a transaction between his own adult children.*

D   *'I know my daughter hasn't got any spare cash. Even if she did, and wanted to give it to you I wouldn't let her. In my Law I can do that.'*

A   *'You're a hard man Jangala, like my grandfather' – A's grandfather, now deceased, was D's father-in-law. A does not mean that D follows his Warlpiri grandfather's Law but that he does strictly follow a strong Law. This tendency is admired by Warlpiri men.*

## Scenario 2

*A teacher with over thirty years' experience retired. She had accumulated $111,000 in superannuation. She gave away $110,000 within twenty minutes to her close family. Each of three sons were given $20,000 which they used to buy second hand cars. One of those sons was asking for money from kin to fill his fuel tank to get him home within a week. The retired teacher, who'd kept $1,000 only for herself, was asking for money for food from close family within two weeks of the generous disbursement of her liquid assets.*

## Scenario 3

*An old man undertook management training because of the senior position he occupied in his community and his involvement in the joint management of a National Park. He kept complaining that although he had several sources of income he never had enough money. His income was analysed with his permission. He was earning annually about the same as the Prime Minister. He acted like a financial funnel. In his culture an extended family grows in proportion to the income received by an individual. Authority within a restricted domain, influence and popularity grows with an individual's generosity. The more he gave away, the more influential he became. He wanted more money so that he could give even more away. He kept none for himself over the long-term. He continues to live in poverty despite his income.*

Society in the central Australian deserts survived with one of the world's lowest population densities, with no permanent housing or furniture, cooking utensils, vehicles, domestic animals, clothes, hats, shoes or bedding, and of course, no money. In material terms they owned almost nothing. The only shelter came from nature or temporary constructions made from local materials that could be quickly abandoned when there was a need to move. They had to be physically and mentally tough. Population size remained static. Death was an ever-present possibility.

There were family and land and nothing else, so these are the twin obsessions at the core of desert Aboriginal culture. Society is based on an extremely elaborate and complex kinship system. Everybody relates to everybody else on the basis of kinship. A stranger is an actual or potential enemy and is made a friend by being drawn into the kinship system.

Food could not be transported or preserved in large amounts. It was immediately consumed. The demand/share economy made sure that everybody in the group received a share. There were complex rules relating to distribution depending on the age, sex, and status of the recipients of the hunter's bounty. Distant kin could not be helped. Those who asked, received. If there was no request for food, the assumption was that it wasn't wanted. However a request could not be refused. These rules are now applied to money, clothing, housing, and transport. Distribution is based on the strict rules based on kinship. It has nothing to do with an abstract concept of fairness – and now it is an economic disaster.

Even those anthropologists, the majority, who turn themselves and their arguments inside out in order to 'confirm' Indigenous culture and its worldview, sometimes grudgingly acknowledge the contemporary negative consequences of the demand-share economy:

> Sometimes beleaguered women, however conscientious, could not prevent malnourishment in kids, due to insufficient cash. This circumstance was exacerbated by failures at the level of relatedness, community, and the state. Relatives were often irresponsible, especially with gambling and alcohol consumption. The individuating power of cash has made reciprocal relations more variable and tenuous.[5]

The principles of the demand-share economy are very deeply ingrained, taught from the beginning of life. Conforming to the rules is deeply emotionally satisfying but completely rules out the ability to budget, or to plan, and invest in the future. Refusing to conform to the rules in order to maintain personal or familial solvency can lead to verbal or physical assault. The much greater acceptance of interpersonal violence in small-scale societies leads to ferocious attacks on wives in particular and to 'granny bashing', the young assaulting the old to obtain the means to finance addictions to alcohol, ganja, or gambling. Every family has this problem to some degree. Many Aboriginal families have found ways to cope. Many are very generous to close kin and retain pride in their identity but also budget and plan to the degree that they feed and house their families. Most in the remote communities are trapped in poverty as a result of their unquestioning loyalty to this traditional moral system.

---

[5] Austin-Broos, D. *Arrernte Present, Arrernte Past* (2009), 147.

## Violence

Peaceful prestate societies were very rare; warfare between them was very frequent, and most adult men in such groups saw combat repeatedly in a lifetime ...

A typical tribal society lost about .5 percent of its population in combat each year. Applying this casualty rate to the earth's twentieth-century populations predicts more than two billion war deaths since 1900.[6]

Scenario 1

*A drunk young man drives his car around a town camp in Alice Springs in an erratic and dangerous manner putting the lives and safety of children and the aged at risk. His older sister calls out to him in an aggressive tone to get him to stop. He stops the car comes up behind his sister, who is standing talking to her female cousin, and hits her on the head with a hammer. She collapses requiring major surgery including the insertion of a metal plate in her head. He is charged and serves a short gaol term. They are reconciled within days.*

Scenario 2

*A middle aged female teacher recounts an incident during a major feud in her community to her cousin's white husband.*

N   Our family were really strong. They were all there on the football oval. When the others saw them standing there they all ran away.

D   Did anyone get hurt?

N   No they ran too fast, oh, except for one old lady. She couldn't run fast enough. Some of the young ones caught her and gave her a hiding, wiyarrpa (poor thing). But no, she deserved it. She doesn't fight but she is one of the 'generals'. She tells all the young people to fight, so she deserved it.

---

[6] Keeley, L. H. op. cit., 25, 93.

## Scenario 3

*During an eight year feud sparked by a jealous fight between teenage girls, one octogenarian great grandmother hit another great grandmother from an opposed family over the head with a kuturru (heavy fighting stick made of mulga wood). The victim was medivaced to Alice Springs. The perpetrator felt sorry for her within hours. They were classificatory sisters. She sent her daughter to visit her in hospital to apologise. No charges were laid.*

Those living in small-scale societies tend to have a very strong emphasis on formal politeness and complex rules, based on kinship relationships, of interpersonal interaction. Breaking of the rules can produce seriously violent outcomes. There is no institution above the family. There are no defence services, police or courts, no 'Leviathan' that the citizens of a state can rely on to protect their families from violence. There is only family. Therefore every family must defend itself. Every individual has the right to resort to violence when that is seen as appropriate and then accept punishment for using violence when that is also seen as appropriate.

Everybody is taught to fight but men are more likely to use weapons now – knives, machetes, tyre levers, star pickets, anything that comes to hand, as well as traditional weapons. Grievous bodily harm and homicide are depressingly common and regularly excused in traditional terms. Girls are taught to 'put up with' rape if it is inflicted by a man from the kin groups that supply potential husbands. A woman has no right to deny sex to a promised or actual husband.

There is a strong emphasis on maintaining balance. Small groups cannot survive without that overarching emphasis. The problem for the physically weak and vulnerable, especially women and girls, is that balance is often achieved at their expense:

> "The law as far as the Aboriginal law stands, violence on an Aboriginal woman is not really terrible but a mild one," Wali

Wunungmurra told the court. "You can work around it."[7]
... it's against our law for people like that breaking the law, they shouldn't be there. Aboriginal ladies, they're not allowed to go anywhere near that. if they had been caught, a woman, Aboriginal lady got caught she (would) be killed. Simple as that.[8]

These statements represent the honest attempts of men who know their traditions to explain aspects of the status of women in traditional societies. They come as no shock to those of us who have lived and worked in remote communities or for their residents. They do shock those who have invented a fantasy-world culture for their own purposes, political or psychological, and so they are simply ignored by them. They produced no response whatsoever from those who see themselves as actively progressive in relation to the mainstream culture. They clearly show that the individual human rights of Aboriginal women, as understood by western conservatives and progressives alike, are routinely ignored by traditional Aboriginal Law.

Balance is traditionally achieved by the brutal beating of widows following the death of husbands and of mothers at the death of their children. Blame has to be laid and the one blamed must accept punishment to ensure that balance is achieved. The achieving of balance after a disturbing event is sometimes at the expense of women's lives. Deborah Bird Rose gives to us two disturbing examples of balance restoring. In one a wife murderer is eventually exonerated of his crime in an attempt to return relations between several Aboriginal groups to harmonious balance. The whitefella court is convinced to give him a minimal sentence (two years) to demonstrate the legitimacy of Customary Law. He serves his sentence, only to acquire and then murder another wife.

The other concerns a 13-year-old girl, Annie, sexually harassed by her paternal uncle (classificatory father). Balance is eventually achieved

---

[7] Wali Wunungmurra, quoted by Robinson, N. 'Bashing Women 'Not Terrible' in Aboriginal Law' *The Australian,* 6 October 2010.

[8] Jajirdi Consultants. 'Should Customary Law Be Recognized by the Courts?' (2009).

by all of the adults involved in the drunken fighting that accompanied the harassment laying blame for it all at the feet of the child victim of the harassment. She is the most vulnerable and the weakest. She cannot defend herself. So she is blamed, balance is restored and everybody, except the victim, is satisfied.[9] In our experience such cases are not uncommon. The shocking prevalence of violence now is exacerbated by the stresses and effects of colonisation, alcohol, and illegal drugs. It is not caused by the precepts of Traditional Law; however, they are part of the complex of contributing causes and not a solution as some would maintain.

Some Aboriginal men are aware of the injustice of all this. In July 2008 over 300 met at Ross River near Alice Springs and issued a media release apologising to their women and children for:

> ... the hurt, pain and suffering caused by Aboriginal males to our wives, to our children, to our mothers, to our grandmothers, to our granddaughters, to our aunties, to our nieces and to our sisters.[10]

This courageous apology was virtually ignored by the media, activists, social commentators, academics, and Aboriginal organisations across the country. These decent men received no offers of funding support for ongoing programs to reduce male violence. None of their recommendations were accepted by governments. We owe it to Aboriginal women and girls, as Australian and world citizens, to defend their rights in relation to their own culture as well as that of the mainstream. We owe their apologetic menfolk at least the support they need to act on their apology. Anything else is intolerably hypocritical and grossly immoral.

## Sorcery

Witchcraft is one of the most common motives for revenge among hunter-gatherers and tribal societies. In their theory of causation, there is no such thing as a natural death. Any fatality that cannot be

---

[9] Rose, D.B. *Dingo Makes Us Human* (2000).
[10] Central Australian Aboriginal Congress Inc. *Aboriginal Male Health Summit 2008* (2008).

explained by an observable cause is explained by an unobservable one, namely sorcery.[11]

Scenario 1

*A young child, a girl, playing with a ball accidentally shattered a car windscreen. Fearing punishment, she hid. Family members heard the noise and came out to investigate. Seeing no human agent present they assume that the windscreen was shattered by 'yarda' directed at a person but hitting the car's windscreen accidentally.*

Scenario 2

*An architect suggests to a family in a remote community that an outside toilet would suit their needs better than an inside one. Their house is used by large numbers of visitors and the toilet often clogs and backs up with raw sewerage flowing into the house. The family responded with a firm 'no'. The country they live in is dangerous: having to leave the safety of the house at night puts them in danger of 'yarda' aimed at others but entering their bodies by mistake.*

Scenario 3

*A Warlpiri man rings his young mother (mother's young sister) from a community in the country of another language group. He is very ill and it is obvious to him that he has been 'boned'. It takes a great deal of heated argument from his mother to get him up from his bed to go to the community clinic to seek treatment. He had spent several months prior to the illness drinking and carousing in the town camps of Alice Springs. He looked for the cause of his illness in sorcery, she in his aberrant behavior in town. He has worked as a health worker for decades and has chaired the management committee of an independent health service.*

In small-scale societies living a very precarious life in an extreme environment, belief in supernatural forces that can be manipulated by human agents is universal. All premature death or life-threatening disease is caused by a human agent using supernatural means or a supernatural agent and blame must be laid. Customary Law is based on 'fear and favour';

---

[11] Pinker, S. op. cit., 137.

kinsmen are favoured, and violence and supernatural forces or powers wielded by human agents are feared. Terror is used as a social control.

In 2003, a report on the Aboriginal Kurdiji Law and Justice Committee meeting at Alekerange identified 'yarda', the spirit world and malevolent curses as common causes of violence, sickness, and death.[12] The meeting reported that there were eight different, mostly malevolent, spirits active around communities. Apart from these there are the ever present yardalyungku (men who know how to use jarnpa – sorcery) to introduce yarda – sticks and bones – into the bodies of their victims to make them ill or to die. The Kurdiji Committee estimated that as many as 50% of adults on some communities are affected by 'yarda' at any given time. In their eyes it is an epidemic.

After a death, unless it was obviously caused by advanced old age or is that of an infant, families will meet to hold an inquest into the cause to try to identify the culprit. This is done far more regularly after the death of a man than that of a woman. Recent dreams related by the deceased of close relatives will be examined for evidence. The Dreaming totem of the family of the guilty sorcerer will often appear in such dreams. Other portentous events, like apparitions, the odd behavior of birds or animals, will also be discussed. Sometimes the most knowledgeable old men will be blamed since they obviously have the required skills. Accusations arising from such inquests will deflect blame from the family of the deceased onto others therefore reinforcing solidarity and 'balance' within the family while destabilising the wider community – possibly leading to ongoing violent feuding, homicide, grievous bodily harm, and the wanton destruction of property. We could be much more specific about particular incidences but we would risk making already dangerous and delicate situations worse by publicly discussing them.

The sorcery theory of causation can also lead to a refusal to seek or accept conventional treatment, leading to avoidable morbidity and death.

---

[12] Refer to Federal Court of Australia's Indigenous Dispute Resolution & Conflict Management Case Study Project. *Solid Work You Mob Are Doing* (2009), 84.

We know of many such incidents involving very close relatives, again too delicate to discuss. It can also lead to a refusal to accept responsibility for criminal acts.

Scenario 4

*A driver crashes into a tree while drinking. The floor of the car is littered with empty beer cans. Another man sitting in the front passenger seat is killed. The driver is charged, convicted, and sentenced. On release he is not remorseful and accepts no responsibility. He is convinced that a sorcerer had killed the victim and arranged the incident to appear that the driver was at fault. The community accepts this explanation.*

Positive change is possible. We have witnessed it in our own lives. Bess's father was 10 or 11 years old when he first laid eyes on a whitefella, a terrifying experience for him. He was a Warlpiri Law Man in the real meaning of that term. He also called himself a Christian with a deep loyalty to the Baptist Church. He knew that human behaviour needed to be law governed. Bess' promised husband was also such a man. They were taught to follow and implement a strict traditional Law and took an active and central role in ceremonial life. They were also philosophers who knew the difference between the spirit and the letter of the old Law they could see was breaking down. At the age of 13 Bess was expected to join her sister's husband's camp as his second wife. She refused. Rather than beat her senseless, as the Law allowed and as was routinely done, they agreed to allow her to finish her whitefella education first. Later they agreed to her marrying a kardiya to escape a violent relationship.

Whitefellas accepting all the blame when things go wrong is another perverse kind of racism. They still want to be masters of the universe. We are all vulnerable and fallible and we're all in this together. We need to be humble enough to learn and confident enough to teach. There has never been a society easier to adapt to than ours with all of its problems and unresolved issues. Bess's people will be in a position to most benefit from its economy and its institutions if they are prepared and able to choose to leave behind those elements of their culture that no longer work for them. They are free to keep those elements that give them pride and confidence. They are also free to reject the negative and destructive elements of the mainstream culture while accepting those best suited to satisfy their needs and solve the problems now facing them.

To proudly claim that we have in Australia the remnants of a culture that is the longest surviving living culture in the world and then insist that, in the celebration of this fact, we do whatever we can to keep what's left of it intact is to condemn its practitioners to poverty, violence, and ignorance of the rest of the world. For that political stance to be taken by those who benefit directly from the most deliberately and rapidly changing culture our species has yet produced is monumentally hypocritical and profoundly immoral. What worked brilliantly millennia ago can only get you into a world of trouble in the twenty-first century.

# 13
# 'You *are* Boss for Me!' A Case Study in the Erosion of Indigenous Self-Determination in Education[1]

R.G. (Jerry) Schwab

*Indigenous peoples have the right to self-determination. By virtue of that right they freely determine their political status and freely pursue their economic, social and cultural development.*[2]

On a summer afternoon in 1814, His Excellency the Governor of New South Wales, Lachlan Macquarie, met with small number of Aboriginal families in Parramatta to persuade them of the advantages of enrolling their children in the soon to be established 'Native Institution'. The aim of that institution was to "effect the Civilization of the Aborigines and to render their habits more domesticated and industrious" through a school for native children.[3] Governor Macquarie pointed out "in an affable and familiar way the advantages they would necessarily derive from a change of manners, and an application to moderate industry". Apparently suspicious that their children would be forcibly taken, most Aboriginal people in the area stayed clear of this meeting.[4] Yet following

---
[1] The title of this chapter is an inversion and a play on the phrase 'you're not boss for me' which Indigenous kids across the country use with various degrees of indignity, disdain and delight. The phrase 'you *are* boss for me' refers to the frustrating realisation among many Indigenous people today that they no longer have the ability they once had to shape education and community programs at the local level.
[2] United Nations Declaration on the Rights of Indigenous Peoples. (2008), to which Australia is a signatory.
[3] Government of New South Wales. (1814).
[4] *Sydney Gazette*. (1814).

a "fine dinner of roast beef ...and a cheering jug of ale", some appeared convinced and "three children were yielded up to the benevolent purposes of the institution".[5,6]

Ultimately, the Native Institution lasted only a few years and failed to make appreciable advances in 'civilising' the locals. The historical record suggests that many parents were probably coerced and deceived into enrolling their children in this boarding school and most children either ran away or were taken back by their parents.[7] In contemporary terms one would argue that the policy goal was assimilation and within a very short time the local Aboriginal people began to remove their children from the school when they realised that its aim was to distance the children from their families, communities, and culture. That summer in many ways signalled the beginning of government Indigenous Education policy in Australia and, perhaps, the first occurrence of Indigenous self-determination.

While self-determination is not a straightforward concept, its place in the recent history of Indigenous Education is fundamental. As I will show, self-determination has been a cornerstone of Commonwealth education policy in Australia and an aspiration for many Indigenous people who have come to believe they have a right to participate in decisions related to the shape of educational programs in their communities. In this chapter I set out to accomplish four aims: to consider recent discussions of the concept of self-determination in Indigenous affairs in general; to trace its conceptual evolution in the context of Commonwealth education

---

[5] Ibid.

[6] The notion of autonomy among Indigenous people is often a feature of discussions about why Western systems (in particular, education) are seemingly so often and effectively resisted. See, for example, Schwab, R. 'That School Gotta Recognise *Our* Policy! (2001); Burbank, V. 'From Bedtime to on Time' (2006); and Myers, F. *Pintupi Country, Pintupi Self* (1986).

[7] See, for example, Brook, J. & Kohen, J.L. *The Parramatta Native Institution and the Black Town* (1991); Cruickshank, J. "To Exercise a Beneficial Influence over a Man" (2008); and Read, P. 'Shelley's Mistake' (2006).

policy; to explore the manifestation of that policy on a programmatic level through a case study tracing changes in a hallmark program, the Aboriginal Student Support and Parent Awareness (ASSPA) program; and finally to demonstrate through that case study the nature of the erosion of Indigenous Educational self-determination at the federal level.

## Self-Determination in Indigenous Affairs

The notion of self-determination in Indigenous affairs is fraught, to say the least. At one extreme end of a continuum is a notion of self-determination as a sort of political independence and exclusivity that Indigenous Australians should, could, or would return to. Its adherents are few, and though a handful were vocal in the 1970s, they are rarely heard from today. At the other end is a more realistic understanding of the possibilities of self-determination in which Indigenous Australians play an active role in shaping policy, and programs and allocating funding. This end of the continuum, I would argue, is what most Indigenous and non-Indigenous people assume self-determination involves. Yet even in this position, views polarise: on one hand, some argue, the policy of self-determination for Indigenous people was delusional and led to a "bureaucratic, political, and financial cocooning of Indigenous Australia",[8] and on the other hand some claim self-determination is a logical extension of basic human rights that act to enfranchise Indigenous people and ensure free choice.[9]

This notion of self-determination might most usefully be thought of as allegorical, but based on recognition of the unique status of Australia's Indigenous cultures within the nation state.[10] While I would argue that

---

[8] Sutton, P. *The Politics of Suffering* (2011), 56.
[9] Rowse, T. *Indigenous Futures* (2002). See also *Traditions for Health* (1996) and Rowse's discussion of the three levels of self-determination: the individual/person/citizen, the family/household and the organised communal agency.
[10] Sanders, W. *Towards an Indigenous Order of Australian Government* (2002).

this has always been the predominant model, there are many, especially in politics, who have found that the first unlikely extreme has some political traction if played to the right audience. In 1998, Alexander Downer, then Minister for Foreign Affairs, argued that the draft United Nations declaration on the rights of Indigenous peoples should not include the term 'self-determination' because it could create the impression that the Australian Government was open to the idea of a separate Aboriginal state.[11] Pauline Hanson, leader of the One Nation Party, labelled the UN declaration a "treacherous sell out" and a "precursor to the establishment of a taxpayer-funded Aboriginal state".[12]

While criticism of 'self-determination' was predictable, particularly from conservative columnists and in opinion pieces published by conservative 'think tanks', a quantum increase in critique of Indigenous self-determination and enabling government policy was reignited with the fuel of moral outrage that resulted from the *Little Children are Sacred* report.[13] That report, alleging widespread child sexual abuse within Indigenous communities in the Northern Territory, has continued to be wielded with vigour as proof that Indigenous self-determination not only does not work, but has been damaging.

For example, in her recent 2012 Boyer Lectures, Aboriginal academic Marcia Langton attacked the "vaporous dream of self-determination", setting up a straw person of "Aboriginal sovereignty" and denouncing the notion as nothing more than a slogan, an "absurd political ideology", held by "a small but powerful group of Aboriginal people". But that small group is faceless and itself vaporous, because the reality is such extreme

---

[11] Forbes, M. 'Downer Fears Phrase Will Split Australia' *Melbourne Age*, 22 August 1998.
[12] Ibid.
[13] Wild, R. & Anderson, P. *Little Children Are Scared* (2007).

notions have never been more than fantasy in Australia.[14] Ironically, while she stops short of referring to educational self-determination, she points to Indigenous-led education initiatives promoted by her colleague Noel Pearson as a model of inspiring and transformative education which mainstream education has been unable to provide.

## What is Indigenous Self-Determination in Education?

In the 50 or so years following that summer picnic in Parramatta in 1814, formal Indigenous Education in the colony was virtually nonexistent and few if any Aboriginal children attended school; when education was offered it was usually part of the Christianising efforts of various groups. The Public Instruction Act of 1880 in New South Wales made education compulsory for all children up to the age of 12. This, coupled with an easing of relations between colonists and local Aboriginal groups and desires among Aboriginal parents that their children attend school, led to rising levels of participation in school. In more remote areas, typically on and near missions where large numbers of Aboriginal people lived, schools were by default segregated, but where there was no other option but for Aboriginal children to attend with white students, novel policies were developed. Aboriginal children were initially accepted into white schools provided they were 'clean, clad and courteous' but as numbers increased and white parents began to object, a policy was established whereby Aboriginal children could be denied access simply because white parents complained.[15] This policy was effectively in place as late as 1972 when "the NSW Director General of Education approved the elimination of the section of the Teacher's Handbook which dealt with the Principal's right to refuse enrolment to Aboriginal children because

---

[14] Langton, M. *Counting Our Victories* (2012a). In the context of all five of the Boyer lectures it is abundantly clear that her critique is part of a political project in which she attempts to corral those unnamed villains with 'anthropologists', 'romantics', 'new age mystics', 'old racists', 'lefties', 'bureaucratic monsters' and 'environmentalists' who, she argues, are blocking the economic advancement of Indigenous Australians.

[15] Fletcher, J. *Clean, Clad and Courteous* (1989).

of home conditions or substantial opposition from the community".[16] But in the late 1960s and early 1970s some important events helped shift the direction of Commonwealth Indigenous Education policy.

## The 1967 Referendum

The 1967 Referendum, now considered a landmark in Australian history, asked whether two references in the Australian Constitution, which discriminated against Aboriginal people, should be removed:

> 51. The Parliament shall, subject to this Constitution, have power to make laws for the peace, order, and good government of the Commonwealth with respect to:- ...(xxvi) The people of any race, other than the aboriginal [sic] people in any State, for whom it is necessary to make special laws.
>
> 127. In reckoning the numbers of the people of the Commonwealth, or of a State or other part of the Commonwealth, aboriginal natives should not be counted.

The referendum saw the highest YES vote ever recorded in a Federal referendum, with 90.77% voting for change. What is so important about this is that the 1967 Referendum gave the Commonwealth constitutional powers related to Indigenous Australians, enabling legislation to be drawn up specific to them. In the education arena that meant special national policies and programs could be introduced. The 1967 Referendum signalled an emerging moral view that as the most disadvantaged Australians, Aboriginal people deserved social justice, support, and opportunity.

## The National Review of Education for Aboriginal and Torres Strait Islander People

With the arrival of the Whitlam government in 1972, a new policy framework of self-determination for Indigenous people emerged; this framework quickly extended to the arena of Indigenous education

---

[16] Cook, T. cited in Reynolds, R. '"Clean, Clad and Courteous" Revisited' (2009), 89.

policy. Over the course of the next 15 years, various reviews were commissioned, consultations carried out, and task forces organised. Of particular significance was the Aboriginal Education Policy Task Force, an all-Aboriginal body that recommended in 1988 the adoption of a national policy for the education of Aboriginal and Torres Strait Islander people; the landmark National Aboriginal and Torres Strait Islander Education Policy (known as the AEP) was endorsed by all governments and came into effect on 1 January, 1990.

Five years later, a National Review was conducted that identified 21 long-term goals under four themes: involvement, access, participation, and outcomes.[17] Importantly the review emphasised Indigenous self-determination. Indeed, the second recommendation of the review states explicitly that all bodies developing policy and providing programs or services that impact on Aboriginal and Torres Strait Islander peoples should be based on (among others) the principle of self-determination in education.[18]

Ultimately, the term 'self-determination' was not included in the policy (it was replaced by softer words like 'involvement' and 'participation'), but the principle that local communities should shape local education remained. The policy was a crucial advance: for the first time, the states and territories were able to identify and unanimously support a series of national goals for Indigenous education; the policy facilitated many new initiatives that created a national focus on Indigenous education; the policy was based on a triennial funding model enabling, for the first time, longer term planning for programs; and the national policy included a supplementary funding program, the Aboriginal Education Strategic

---

[17] Yunupingu, M. *National Review of Education for Aboriginal and Torres Strait Islander Peoples* (1995), 11.
[18] Ibid., 27.

Initiatives Scheme, to initiate and support new programs not provided by the states and territories.[19]

## Self-Determination in Education: A Working Definition

Though the phrase is absent from recent and current Commonwealth Indigenous education policy, the desire of many Indigenous people remains to have some degree of self-determination over the educational policies and programs that affect them. Historically, many of the programs developed and deployed under the policy suggest and perhaps even provide some degree of self-determination. In the absence of an official definition, and in order to frame the discussion to come, I want to propose a working definition of self-determination in education that I believe many Indigenous people would accept:

> the process whereby Indigenous people enact their own decisions about the shape and focus of education in order to attain greater equity and opportunity and to address local needs and issues and enhance various outcomes including community, parental, and student engagement with education.

But how does this definition fit with the realities of Commonwealth Indigenous education polity and programs? As I have shown, the phrase

---

[19] It is instructive to search for occurrences of the phrase 'self-determination' in Commonwealth and national education policy documents and web pages. A search of the Department of Education, Employment and Workplace Relations website in late 2012 showed 'no result' for the phrase 'self-determination'. A similar search in 2011 revealed three 'hits': one identified the phrase in a speech by Julia Gillard to the Australia-Israel Leadership Forum in 2009 where she said: 'Australia supports Israel's right to self defence and its right to self determination', while two more 'hits' identified Government statements in 2008 where the government affirmed its belief in the value and potential of self-determination (for people living with disability or mental illness). The Commonwealth foundation policy document, the National Aboriginal and Torres Strait Islander Education Policy – that emerged from the 1989 Review and remains valid today – does not contain the phrase. Similarly, neither the National Strategy for the education of Aboriginal and Torres Strait Islander Peoples 1996-2002 nor the Aboriginal and Torres Strait Islander Action Plan 2010-2014 make mention of self-determination.

'self-determination' never gained traction in policy, but as a principle, one could argue, it continues today. Or does it? There is a range of different programs, funded primarily by Commonwealth education dollars, that might represent Indigenous self-determination in practice if not in name.

## Cape York Aboriginal Australian Academy

The Cape York Aboriginal Australian Academy (CYAAA), for example, is a high profile program in far North Queensland led by prominent Aboriginal leader Noel Pearson. Established in 2010 with a grant from the Commonwealth and Queensland governments of about $7.7 million, the Academy includes schools in the Aboriginal communities of Arukun, Coen, and Hope Vale. The Academy is based on an unusual arrangement in which these three state schools, while still mostly government funded, operate outside the state education system with governance through an independent board chaired by Pearson. Established with much fanfare – and the implicit promise that the schools would close the academic achievement gap and attain improved educational outcomes – the CYAAA is built around the US-imported Direct Instruction methods combined with a structured program incorporating Indigenous culture, art, and sport. Though no external evaluation of the program has been carried out, the Commonwealth announced in November 2012 that it would cease funding following disappointing results in the national literacy and numeracy tests.

Certainly one could argue that CYAAA represents one form of Indigenous self-determination in education. Pearson has written at length about his vision for education.[20] But one of the features of the CYAAA is its links to the umbrella institution, the Cape York Partnerships, a conglomeration of Indigenous, government, and industry interests. The CYAAA is inextricably linked to government funding of a range of conservative social and political reforms in the region, including the well publicised welfare reform trial, part of which involves cuts to welfare

---

[20] Pearson, N. *Radical Hope* (2011).

payments for parents who fail to ensure their children attend school. To the degree that it represents self-determination, it is a 'top down' rather than 'bottom up' version significantly shaped by institutions outside the Indigenous community.

## Indigenous Education Consultative Bodies

Another possible form of Indigenous self-determination in education, funded by the Commonwealth, takes the form of the various state and territory Indigenous Education Consultative Bodies (IECBs). Indigenous Education consultative groups had been established in every state and territory by the late 1970s. Charged with advising the Commonwealth on the educational needs of Indigenous people and providing assistance with program monitoring and development, these groups were envisaged as conduits for community views and structures for engagement and decision-making. In an external review by the Department of Education, Science, and Training in 2003, IECBs were described as 'symbols of self-determination and self management in the provision of independent advice on education issues to governments at the state, territory and national level'. According to that review, the IECBs are variably constructed across the states/territories (e.g., some bodies elected, others appointed by government; some independent organisations, some contained within state bureaucracies).[21] Most significantly, however, they have been variably effective.

The degree to which IECBs represent Indigenous self-determination is questionable, and it is impossible to know to what degree problems in the 2003 review have been resolved since there has been no publicly released follow-up review. A more recent description of the role of IECBs acknowledges their continuing advisory and advocacy role, but states that "IECBs provide indirect assistance to Aboriginal and Torres Strait Islander students by effectively supporting the priorities of

---

[21] Commonwealth of Australia. *Review of Indigenous Education Consultative Bodies* (2003), 11.

government".[22] If a body is established to provide advice but doesn't, or if it has no real power to frame policy, is that a form of self-determination? If those bodies are charged with supporting the priorities of government, to what degree is that reflective of self-determination? I would suggest IECBs are probably not very effective instruments of self-determination, but given the current government lack of interest in the issue, IECBs are probably doing the work they are currently designed to do.

## Aboriginal Student Support and Parent Awareness Program

There is, however, a very good example of a Commonwealth education program that fits with the notion of Indigenous self-determination as I have defined it. The Aboriginal Student Support and Parent Awareness program (ASSPA) was established in 1990 and then abolished in 2004/5. It was designed to support educational opportunities for students and engage parents and community members in education at the local level. Historically, ASSPA was one of the most direct ways in which parents and community members have been able to access and employ Commonwealth education dollars to identify and enact their ideas about Indigenous education. When it was abolished, a new program, the Parent School Partnership Initiative (PSPI) took its place; subsequently it too was abolished and replaced by the Parent and Community Engagement Program (PaCE). In this series of programs, I will argue, it is possible to see a gradual and calculated erosion of Indigenous self-determination in education. I will provide more details below, but to provide some context it is necessary to examine the recent history of Commonwealth funding support for schools.

## Commonwealth School Funding

Figure 13.1 portrays Commonwealth funding for schools over the ten year period 2001-11. Note that this figure does not show the total of DEEWR funding, just the portion aimed at School education.

---

[22] Commonwealth of Australia. *Indigenous Education (Targeted Assistance) Act* (2009), 37.

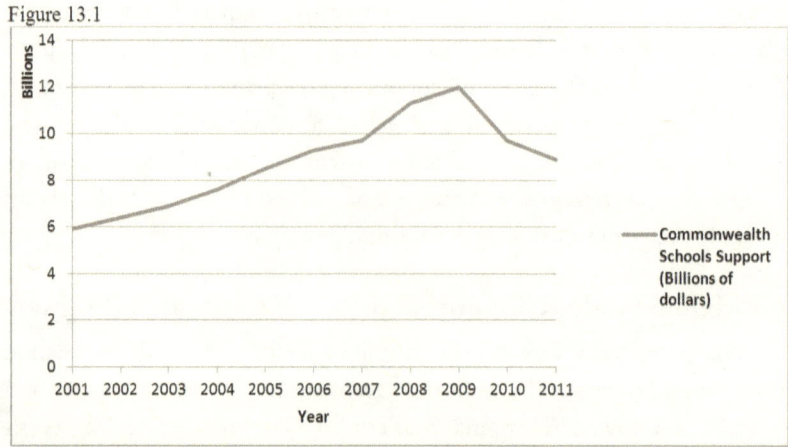

Figure 13.1. Commonwealth Schools Support, 2001-11.
Source: Australian Government Budget Statements DETYA, DEST, DEEWR.[23]

As shown, school support funding doubled from $6 billion in 2001 to $12 billion in 2009; the Indigenous specific component of this tracks roughly in tandem though it is obviously only a fraction of this amount. The drop after 2009 is a function of a reconfiguration in funding and policy through the National Reform Agreements, including the National Indigenous Reform Agreement (known also as 'Closing the Gap', a policy subject to the Intergovernmental Agreement on Federal Financial Relations). Essentially, National Reform Agreements represent a new arrangement whereby the Commonwealth turned over significant amounts of funding to the states and territories.

---

[23] School support figures are derived from the annual budget statements of the Australian Government Departments of Education, Training and Youth Affairs (2001/2), Education, Science and Training (2002/3 to 2007/8), Education, Employment and Workplace Relations (2008/9 to 2010/11).

## Commonwealth School Funding to Parent and Community Engagement Programs

Figure 13.2 compares trends in School funding to funding of the various parent and community engagement programs funded by the Commonwealth over the past 20 or more years.

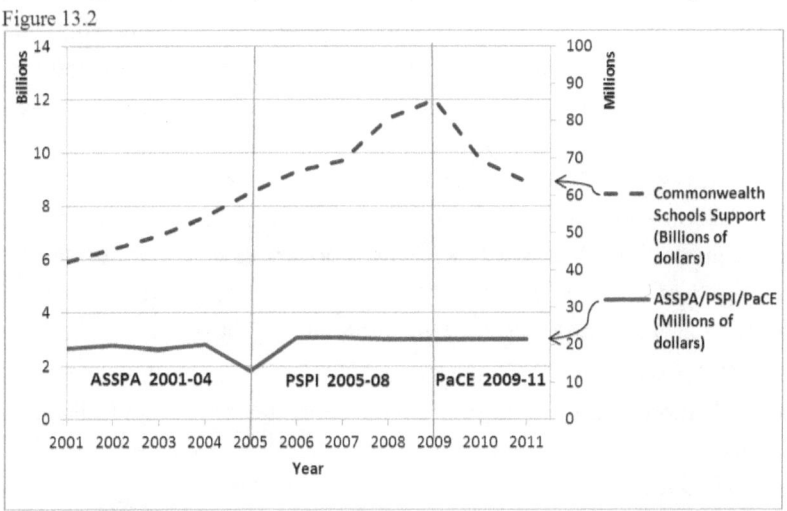

Figure 13.2 Commonwealth School funding compared to funding for successive Indigenous Engagement programs, 2001-11.[24]

Source: Australian Government Budget Statements DETYA, DEST, DEEWR.[25]

ASSPA, the first in the series of programs, shown here over the period 2001-2004, was the widely regarded as a very effective way to engage parents and communities in education. Applications for funding

---

[24] Note there are two distinct axes of the graph. The left axis relates to school support and refers to billions of dollars; the right axis relates to funding for three successive parent and community engagement programs and those figures refer to millions of dollars.

[25] Indigenous engagement program figures are derived from the annual budget statements of the Australian Government Departments of Education, Training and Youth Affairs (2001/2), Education, Science and Training (2002/3 to 2007/8), Education, Employment and Workplace Relations (2008/9 to 2010/11).

were channelled through locally formed committees comprising parents and often a school Principal.[26] At its peak there were nearly 4000 local ASSPA committees scattered across the country. Significantly, over 90% of all Indigenous pre-school and school students attended schools with ASSPA committees. The funds were awarded on a per capita basis and were administered by local ASSPA committees. The monies were essentially in the hands and under the direction and control of the Indigenous parent and community committees. ASSPA funds typically supported a wide range of programs (e.g., nutrition programs, swimming classes, excursions, NAIDOC activities, art, music, and other cultural programs). Overall Commonwealth funding for ASSPA averaged about $20 million a year for the last several years of its life. Grants to ASSPA committees ranged from a few hundred dollars to several thousand; the average was about $5000. In 1999, 22% of committees received under $500 while about 10% received greater than $10,000.

ASSPA was formally evaluated in 1997 and again in 2000 as part of an evaluation of the larger program of which it is a part (the Indigenous Education Direct Assistance Program). The first evaluation was never publicly released but the second found ASSPA was:

> effective in addressing and improving educational outcomes for Indigenous students, according to both the evaluation of the programme, consultations and through anecdotal evidence.[27]

## Parent School Partnership Initiative

But effectiveness does not ensure the survival of Commonwealth programs. ASSPA was replaced by the Parent School Partnership Initiative (PSPI) in 2005. PSPI was a very different program. Where

---

[26] While it is sometimes said that some school Principals, often non-Indigenous, shaped and ultimately determined the allocation of funds, in my experience and in the many conversations with Indigenous parents I have met over my twenty years working in this field, there is no doubt that in most places ASSPA was seen to be locally controlled.

[27] Commonwealth of Australia. *Review of the Indigenous Education Direct Assistance Programme* (2000), 18.

ASSPA funding was based on a funding formula model, PSPI was a competitive, complicated application-based program, where schools had to compete with one another for funds.

The program dramatically changed the nature of Indigenous parent and community engagement in education. Where ASSPA had allowed parents to identify local needs and enact local solutions, PSPI was aimed at more global issues and required 'strategic interventions' addressing attendance, nutrition, incentive and awards, community liaisons, and literacy and numeracy.

The Senate Employment, Workplace Relations and Education References Committee undertook a review of Indigenous education funding (published in 2005) and remarked that the abolition of ASSPA was "the most contentious issue faced by the committee at its meetings with Indigenous communities". Specifically, those community members expressed frustrations that:

- eliminating ASSPA signalled a retreat from a government commitment to self-determination and was widely regarded as an indication of lack trust in the good sense of Indigenous representatives; and
- the end of the program greatly reduced funding to support educational programs, particularly in student welfare and attendance support and in covering extra-curricular activities.[28]

While funding levels remained similar to ASSPA (roughly $21.5 million per year), there were fewer grants given and thus fewer communities supported by these funds. For example the average PSPI grant was $25,000.

The process of application was more stringent and clearly many applying organisations were not up to the task. In 2006, for example, there were 805 applications of which 547 were approved. The problem

---

[28] Australian Senate Employment, Workplace Relations and Education References Committee *Indigenous Education Funding* (2005), 13.

was especially acute in remote areas: in the Northern Territory in 2006 there were 197 applications of which only 102 were funded (Senate Estimates).

The program also included more stringent accountability guidelines; to this end application for PSPI funds had to be made through legal entities (the school, business, or community organisation). In most cases the program funds were under the control of school Principals, few of whom were Indigenous. Consequently, there was a reduction of Indigenous involvement in decision-making. In addition, the delegation of decision-making in funding to state and territory offices meant there was wide variation in what was funded.

Application numbers declined over time. The Australian National Audit Office (ANAO) found that a DEEWR regional office fielded 27 PSPI applications in 2005, 15 in 2006, and two in the first round of 2007.[29] Both the Senate Committee and ANAO were critical of the program with the ANAO noting that "the department has found it difficult to measure the program's effectiveness and contribution to the achievement of outcomes from the Indigenous Education Program".[30]

## Parental and Community Engagement Program

In the policy arena, things seldom stand still. In 2009, PSPI was replaced by the Parental and Community Engagement (PaCE) program. PaCE is intended to enhance the capacity of Indigenous families and communities to engage in school and education, including in educational decision-making, and to establish school and community partnerships. PaCE was funded at $84 million for the 2009-2012 quadrennium (essentially the same amount of $20 million over four years as allocated to the two preceding programs).

Unlike the earlier programs, PaCE funding goes to state and territory DEEWR offices and local staff allocate the program funds. The

---

[29] Commonwealth of Australia. *Parent School Partnerships Initiative* (2008), 19.
[30] Ibid., 16.

program catch phrase is to support the capacity of families to 'reach-in' to schools, participate in local school decision-making, and reciprocate school outreach activities. The stated focus is on:

- Supporting improved educational outcomes.
- Build strong leadership that supports high expectations of Indigenous student educational outcomes.
- School community partnerships.
- Support and reinforce learning at home.

Again, unlike the earlier programs, PaCE funding is by negotiation. It is not application based. Like PSPI, schools communities compete against one another. Similarly, funding must go to a legal entity and that means that a group of parents who wanted to apply for funding would need to work through an auspicing body; only under exceptional circumstances can this be a school. Consequently, business has entered the arena.

As of September 2011 there were about 400 projects around the country. That would average about $50,000 per project (in contrast, ASSPA projects averaged $5000 and PSI $25,000). Obviously, demand far exceeds available funds (some estimates are that the demand is 4 times that of supply).

Examples of funded projects include:

- Parent education.
- Community school fun day.
- Parental cultural awareness and identity training courses. Interestingly, these courses involve content on conflict resolution; and numeracy, literacy, and communication in the workplace (including job interview techniques and resume building, computer courses with the opportunity to obtain certificates).

- A $575,000 project over two years with the Newcastle Knights, a National Rugby League team (in partnership with Coal & Allied [Rio Tinto], to provide industry-based mentoring, field trips, and work experience).

By any measure these last two projects are a far stretch from the earlier programs and reflect less a desire for parent and community engagement than a focus on employment as an outcome.

## Community Engagement Over Time

One of the most significant changes over time as ASSPA was replaced by PSPI and then PaCE, can be seen in the drop in the number of communities that received funding from the programs. Figure 13.3 provides a rough depiction of the number of communities engaged by these programs. Clearly, the outreach has diminished dramatically (from

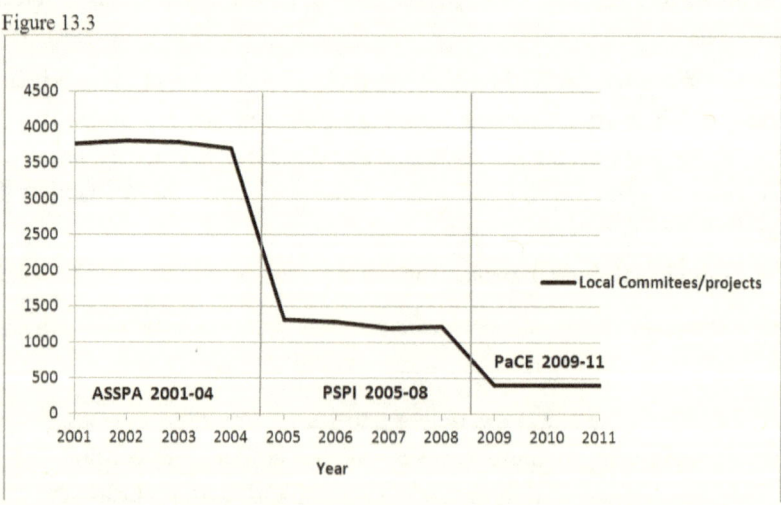

Figure 13.3

Figure 13.3 Number of communities receiving funding through parent and community engagement programs (ASSPA, PSPI and PaCE), 2001-2011.

Source: Commonwealth of Australia *National Reports to Parliament* (2001-2009) and Department of Education, Employment and Workplace Relations.

about 4000 ASSPA committees – remember that 90% of Indigenous school children attended schools receiving ASSPA funds – to only about 400 PaCE projects funded across the country.

## Conclusion: The Erosion of Self-Determination in Indigenous Education

While ASSPA was but one of many Indigenous-specific education programs funded by the Commonwealth since the era of self-determination, it is important in the tale its history tells. Over time:

- Commonwealth funding for parent and community engagement in Indigenous education has declined in real terms;
- the numbers of parents and communities who have access to these funds has dramatically declined;
- local needs and solutions are being replaced by regionally and nationally defined needs and solutions, especially those defined by the Closing the Gap targets established by the Council of Australian Governments;
- funded programs increasingly emphasise literacy and numeracy, school attendance, parent education, and employment;
- success has been increasingly measured in terms of meeting standardised, measureable outcomes;[31]
- hands-on parental and community control of program funds is disappearing;
- the emphasis on accountability has decreased flexibility in who is eligible to apply and what is eligible for funding;
- per capita direct assistance has been replaced by competitive, application-based (and later negotiated) funding;

---

[31] Schwab, R.G. 'Indigenous Early School Leavers' (2012).

- the process of applying for funding has become increasingly complex and lengthy; and
- education and community engagement has been increasingly 'outsourced' to business, NGOs, and other 'anything but the school' organisations.

Together these changes mirror the evolution of Commonwealth Indigenous policies more generally. Indigenous people are still invited to the table, but the rules have changed. The notion of self-determination has been eroded, corrupted, and recast as divisive. Its allegorical and inspirational value denied. It has been effectively erased from current policy and replaced by softer notions of engagement and participation or the harder realities of coercion and punishment. Programs and policies now focus on 'mainstreaming', accountability, and ultimately employment.

ASSPA was specifically, and perhaps uniquely, a program with the clear aim of empowering Indigenous people in educational engagement and decision-making at the local level. A visit to any Indigenous community today will yield puzzlement and frustration that the program no longer exists. Its impact was not only symbolic, but practical as well. ASSPA committees held purse strings and committee members made decisions and allocated funds according to local interests and needs. While one cannot deny there were and are some very good outcomes from the successors of ASSPA, Commonwealth parent and community education engagement programs and policies are moving further and further away from any notion of Indigenous self-determination. And that is a loss to all Australians.

# 14
# A Short Critique of Indigenous Education Research

*Geoffrey Partington*

*Whether Australians of Aboriginal origin are to live together with other Australians or apart from them; are they to have the same opportunities or different opportunities; are they to bear the same responsibilities and be subject to the same laws or are they to be regarded as a 'lesser breed' from whom less should be required? Is Australia to have one society or two societies?* [1]

*The ability of the Aboriginal people to transmit their traditional culture to future generations has been and continues to be undermined by the imposition of a normative 'European' view of the nature of social and economic relationships which is external to the standards, expectations and practices of traditional Aboriginal culture.* [2]

This chapter examines some recent articles in The *Australian Journal of Indigenous Education (AJIE)*.[3] Although about two-thirds of children classified as Indigenous live in towns and cities and attend similar schools to all other children, *the AJIE* concentrates on the third in schools that provide specifically Aboriginal education, many in remote areas. As such, for whatever reason, most theorists and practitioners hone in on what is different in Aboriginal students and virtually suppress what they have in common with other Australian children. In 2000, I carried out an

---

[1] Hasluck, *Mucking About* (1994), 226, 227.
[2] Coombs *et al. A Certain Heritage* (1983), 147.
[3] Formerly The Aboriginal Child at School, the name change in accord with its remote focus.

extensive review of late 1990s issues of the *AJIE*[4] published in *AJIE* and at greater length in the *National Observer*.[5] Here I have concentrated on only a few articles.

I was born in England but have now lived half my life in Australia and admire much in its people and institutions. As a historian and teacher, I was confronted almost immediately with the failure of my countrymen to establish good relationships with Australia's Indigenous peoples. Yet I came to the opinion that British officials in London and in Britain's Australian colonies, made sincere efforts to share what they thought the best their country had incrementally built: representative government, the rule of law, and a fair degree of religious tolerance. I adopted the viewpoint of Sir Paul Hasluck that public policy should build on aspirations shared by both Indigenous and non-Indigenous cultural commonalities, rather than focus on what divided them.

In 2000 there was wide consensus that Aboriginal education as a whole was in a very unsatisfactory condition. A decade later, the situation seems even worse. As to the causes of malfunction there are two completely opposed positions. The first, held by Dr H.C. Coombs, was that colonisation, racism, and oppression had critically disrupted a once vibrant intellectual tradition. Therefore the first task in Aboriginal education is to use curriculum and teaching methods to rebuild and then sustain traditional Aboriginal culture. The alternative view, advanced by Sir Paul Hasluck, is that schools should give priority to literacy, numeracy, and technical and scientific knowledge. Without these Aboriginal people will be almost permanently at a disadvantage in the workforce. Families and communities or 'out-of-school' activities will be able to sustain traditional culture if it is viable. If they cannot, that will demonstrate the frailty of that culture, so there is no point in expecting a rescue operation from non-Indigenous teachers.

---

[4] Partington, G. 'Non-Indigenous Australians and Indigenous Autonomy' (2000), 15-19.
[5] Partington, G. 'Current Orthodoxy in Aboriginal Education' (2001), 2.

## Sir Paul Hasluck

Hasluck wrote that by the 1930s in Western Australia most mixed-race people lived apart from Aboriginal people and shared the popular belief that they should live in the 'white community'. However, as a group mixed-race people were rejected by Aboriginal people as not being true Aborigines at all and were moving away from the Aboriginal side of their ancestry, some already in the white community, almost all the rest on the fringes.[6] He cited a press report of a March 1928 deputation to the Premier of Western Australia led by William Harris, a part-Aboriginal, 'speaking in perfect English' and showing 'no small signs of erudition'. A decade later, the *Abo Call* was about Aboriginal people "wanting to be absorbed into the Nation of Australia … on equal terms".[7]

These Aboriginal assimilationists were not ashamed of their ancestors or of Aborigines still living in traditional ways, but wished to advance to modernity to be equal in society. Hasluck saw assimilation[8] as an anti-racist policy that was especially needed in times of eugenics and the ascendancy of fascism. The hope was that:

> all persons of aboriginal blood or mixed-blood in Australia will live in the same manner as white Australians do … they will have full citizenship and … will, of their own desire, participate in all the activities of the Australian community. Full assimilation will mean that the aboriginal shares the hopes, the fears, the ambitions and the loyalties of all other Australians and draws from the Australian community all his social needs, spiritual as well as material.[9]

For Hasluck the basic questions were:

> Whether Australians of Aboriginal origin are to live together with

---

[6] McGregor, R. (1993). 'Protest and Progress' (1993).
[7] Abo Call, no. 1, April 1938, page 2, cited in McGregor, op. cit., 561.
[8] Although referred to as 'assimilation' by Hasluck, in today's language, 'integration' would be the equivalent expression.
[9] Hasluck, P. 'The Future of the Australian Aborigines' (cited in Porter, R. 1993, 197).

other Australians or apart from them; are they to have the same opportunities or different opportunities; are they to bear the same responsibilities and be subject to the same laws or are they to be regarded as a 'lesser breed' from whom less should be required? Is Australia to have one society or two societies?[10]

Each Aboriginal child should be 'given a chance' as an individual person rather than as an anonymous figure in a social group; the first priority was to transfer children who gave promise of benefiting from the experience or who faced severe cultural disadvantages, particularly an uncaring family environment, to places where they could gain something like the same education received by other Australian children.

### Dr H. C. ('Nugget') Coombs

Coombs's central idea was that Aboriginal education should strengthen 'Aboriginal identity': being and identifying, the Dreaming, being related to the land and environment, "knowing the pervading moulding character of all these in matters Aboriginal".[11] He commended Marcia Langton's claim that all Aborigines have a "world view derived from the Dreaming and irreconcilable with the demands of a modern industrialised market economy".[12] Aborigines should have "unquestioned authority ... without veto by any agency outside their own community' over matters which affected their welfare".[13]

Despite earlier criticism of taking Aboriginal children from camps to centres where there were qualified teachers, in 1976 Coombs denounced the new policy of taking the teachers to the children; Aboriginal children were now being "taught by teachers on short term assignments who know next to nothing of the people whose children they are to teach or

---

[10] Hasluck, P. *Shades of Darkness: Aboriginal Affairs 1923-1965* (1988), 143, 144.
[11] Coombs *et al.* op. cit., 34.
[12] Coombs, H. C. *Aboriginal Autonomy* (1994), 173.
[13] Ibid.

the country they live in".¹⁴ Surely the teacher's job was not to teach about environment or culture, but knowledge that could not be acquired from the local community.

Coombs had no time for missions and their schools:

> When different groups were brought together in missions and settlements their internal authority structure was encroached upon by white authority ... Similarly, the nurturing and education of children became significantly a function of white institutions. These changes were invariably destructive. Aboriginal responsibility was impaired, if not wholly destroyed, law and order became difficult to sustain and vandalism and delinquency became characteristic of Aboriginal child and youth behaviour.¹⁵

What really happened was that demoralisation and violence followed the end of the missions.

## A Review of Selected Articles in *AJIE*

Now let me discuss some *AJIE* contributions with a view to how they contribute to Aboriginal education.

Jan Stewart relates that she:

> had often discussed with Indigenous academics and students the frustrations and implications of inappropriate research being conducted by non-Indigenous researchers with Indigenous individuals and communities ...¹⁶

However, the outcome of these conversations was very satisfactory for Stewart because, although she herself is non-Indigenous, her Indigenous interlocutors:

> constantly reminded me that it was not always necessarily a matter of non-Indigenous individuals and communities being ignorant of

---
[14] Ibid., 173.
[15] Ibid., 47.
[16] Stewart, J. 'Grounded Theory and Focus Groups' (2007), 32.

or insensitive to Indigenous methodologies, but rather an ingrained attitude that placed Western-based methodologies as the only valid and rigorous approach to research.[17]

It is a common and misleading error to contrast Indigenous and 'Western' methodologies. For 'Western' read 'modern' or simply 'knowledge', since Western methodologies have been utilised in many parts of the world, including non-Western China and Japan, not to mention the 'Middle East'. Next, why do Stewart and so many other non-Indigenous academics so frequently accuse people like themselves (though not themselves, being among the 'elect') as ignorant and inappropriate in their dealings with Aborigines – whereas the use of such words as ignorant or insensitive to describe any Indigenous people would be met with storms of protest against racism and stereotyping?

The abstract of an article by Steve Dillon begins with:

> This paper examines the idea of embedding indigenous perspectives drawing upon a metaphor for designing an environment that nurtures indigenous cultural identity and relationships. This paper constitutes a teacher's personal way of emerging understandings of Indigenous Standpoint Theory and pedagogy, which began with embedding indigenous perspectives within a tertiary music and sound curriculum.[18]

The stated emphasis is on the differences between two cultures, but in practice special attention is given to the writer's personal ability to transcend barriers and combine the best of both cultures in a way most people cannot. Another fragment from Dillon in this vein:

> I am not suggesting that the songs I have written are equivalent to the level of knowledge and significance of cultural meaning that an Indigenous song line holds, nor to reduce the sacred nature of

---

[17] Ibid.
[18] Dillon, S. 'Maybe We Can find Some Common Ground' (2007), 59.

Indigenous song and knowledge, but it does help me experience and privilege an embodied relational understanding.[19]

Australians were in the past frequently accused of kow-towing to British and European culture, but the cringe now by members of the 'elect' to: Aboriginal uniqueness, spirituality, and sensitivity to nature is often so exaggerated that the recipients must grasp its hollowness? It can seem also that, despite the stated aim of "finding common ground", the effort of cultural understanding is to be one-way rather than reciprocal.

Pretentiousness of language is particularly unfortunate when writers claim to want to improve communications between educators and Indigenous students, families and communities; likewise obscurity of language. Stewart writes:

> This paper captures an ideological moment in time in which I contemplated the methodological approach I was embarking upon ... I chose focus groups set within the qualitative process or grounded theory. This paper explores the meaning, usefulness and persistence of grounded theory, how it juxtaposes with focus groups, and the implications for the reciprocal integrity of the research for the Aboriginal and Torres Strait Islander students and me ... I see possibility in the complementary use of grounded theory and focus groups that creates dialogic relationships between the students as both narrators and audience.[20]

Cat Kutay, a specialist in Information and Communication Technology, complains that "Indigenous people have been for a long time deprived of financial benefit from their knowledge";[21] this misappropriation continues today and sinister forces have apparently stolen from Indigenous Australians both traditional and cutting-edge knowledge. In her view, the non-Indigenous need the technical expertise

---

[19] Ibid., 61, 62.
[20] Stewart, J. op. cit.
[21] Kutay, C. 'Knowledge Management as Enterprise' (2007), 137.

of the Indigenous far more than the other way around. Yet Indigenous people who want now to enter the world of scientific technology evidently suffer from a "lack of background skills".[22]

Verbal trickery can secure the condemnation of virtually any principle or policy. Provision of modern knowledge is often attacked as a further intrusion into traditional beliefs and ways of life, and by some as a form of cultural genocide, but failure to provide Indigenous children with the same curriculum as non-Indigenous children can be castigated as unfair discrimination. Such tactics do not help Indigenous children but they provide fuel for unending indictments of Australian governments and society.

Jonathan Makuwira condemns international capitalism, imperialism *et al.* for taking advantage of the vulnerability of the ever victimised Indigenous peoples of the world. He cites Ajalu's definition of "capacity-building" as "an acknowledgment of powerlessness, weakness, helplessness, vulnerability, acquiescence, marginalisation, oppression, domination, dehumanisation, culture of silence, passivity, fatalism, dependency, exploitation and susceptibility of those considered helpless or poor".[23] Charges of indifference and neglect follow when international cartels and big businesses fail to increase capacity in Third and Fourth World countries.[24]

Materialistic considerations undermine traditional values and, according to Sachs in whom Makuwira appears to have complete confidence, "The idea of development stands like a ruin in the landscape ... in practice did not work".[25] To be sure, some projects and developmental plans are ill conceived, some that are well planned still fail, and some people make a mess of whatever project. On the other hand, many plans for increasing capacity in different fields achieve great

---

[22] Ibid., 138.
[23] Makuwira, J. 'The Politics of Community Capacity Building' (2007), 131, 132.
[24] That day has not yet arrived, but 'cuts' are often anticipated.
[25] Sachs, W. 'Introduction' to *The Development Dictionary* (1992), 6-25.

success. Like many *AJIE* contributors, Makuwira generalises too often and too broadly.

Many *AJIE* articles begin with praise for 'communities' and 'parents', but so often the ideal community with which they long to co-operate exists only in their minds – reality lets them down. Libby Lee and Andrew Thompson,[26] when quoting Zubric *et al.*, write of "re-engaging Aboriginal parents and caregivers as educators of their children in the first five years of life".[27] They do not explain how and why the disengagement took place. Were they pointing to long past injustices, or to errors made recently by teachers and administrators?

Lee and Thompson call for greater authority and power to be invested in Indigenous parents and the 'community', but they clearly believe that non-Indigenous persons like themselves will have to take the initiative. In this they will often be proved right, since many Indigenous parents find the formal atmosphere of parent-teacher and other school functions somewhat intimidating and fear ridicule if they do not know the latest education-speak language.

They cite Zubrick *et al.* that "many Aboriginal children feel they have to sacrifice or compromise their own culture in order to survive or be successful in western education",[28] but do not discuss what they must regard as an absurd idea. Yet it may be true that much of 'the culture' must be abandoned by young Indigenous people in order to become heart surgeons, dress designers, aircraft pilots, or plumbers.[29] This is frequently so among non-Indigenous groups: the 'First Year Syndrome' in grammar school, university, or at the Bar is a familiar feature of education history and family lore. This is not to suggest that the 'critical transition' into a new milieu is not typically more difficult for many Indigenous Australians, but one wonders whether exceptionalism – the

---

[26] Lee, L. & Thompson, A. 'Working Productively with Indigenous Communities' (2007).
[27] Zubrick, S.R. *et al. The Western Australian Aboriginal Child Health Survey* (2006), vii
[28] Ibid., xxxiv.
[29] Ibid.

notion that Aboriginal students are fundamentally different – helps or holds back their education.

Lee and Thompson attribute the failure of past initiatives to substantially improve educational outcomes to "a failure of schools to work in partnership with communities" and "acknowledge the critical role played by parents in their children's education".[30] How do they want 'communities' to help? As Noel Pearson argued, the word 'community' is used to soften the images of bloated bureaucracies and among Aborigines to give an attractive colour to very unattractive realities.[31]

Many of the parents on whom Lee and Thompson apparently rely to ensure high educational achievement for their children are the very parents they described as needing to be "re-engaged". Many parents "want their children to succeed in mainstream education and have the same employment as other Australian children whilst retaining their cultural integrity",[32] but the key issue here is whether parents and children, are prepared to sacrifice present enjoyment for future betterment. Further, excessive praise may make some parents ignore pleas for greater efforts, since they seem already to be very satisfactory in the eyes of the schools.

Apparently to condemn capitalism, imperialism, colonialism, and racism some contributors understate more obvious reasons for educational failure within dysfunctional families and communities, such as child abuse, broken homes, filth and rubbish left to rot, alcoholism, drugs, petrol sniffing, and truancy. Jenny Adermann and Marilyn Campbell discovered deep suicidal anxiety is much more common among Aboriginal than non-Aboriginal children. They attribute some of the blame to "Western psychotherapy when applied to indigenous populations".[33] Surveys they cite, such as a 2005 Western Australian

---

[30] Education Queensland (2000), 19, cited in Lee, L. & Thompson, A. op. cit., 34.
[31] Pearson, Noel, 'The Aboriginal 'community' amounts to a dangerous myth for some and an alibi for others', *The Australian*, 8 December 2012.
[32] Zubrick, S.R., *et al.* op. cit., vii.
[33] Vicary & Bishop (2005) cited in Adermann, A. & Campbell, C. 'Big Worry' (2007), 75.

Aboriginal child health inquiry, list as basic causes of depression and suicidal tendencies in young people: "poorly functioning families and poor quality of parenting, being in the care of a sole parent or people other than their original parents and having lived in five or more homes", together with "physical health of the child and carers, speech impairment; severe otitis media, vision problems, carer access of mental health services, and smoking and marijuana use".[34] Yet Adermann and Campbell added, "being subjected to racism in the past six months" and "disruption, forceful removal ... social isolation, and cultural identity and racism".[35]

How many depressed students had actually been subjected in the previous six months to disruption, forceful removal, substance abuse, social isolation, and cultural identity and racism? Or are we dealing with folk memory? However one may regard the assimilation policies of the 1950s and 1960s, they simply do not compare with the dreadful experiences of many other peoples during the twentieth century, whose descendants in Australia are among the most productive people in the world.

Loretta De Plevitz wrote on the four major social justice themes identified by the National Task Force on Indigenous Education in 1988. The first is "involvement of Indigenous people in educational decision-making".[36] Are today's Indigenous parents less involved than other parents? De Plevitz provided no evidence. If it is true that many are not involved and that this poses serious barriers to effective education of their children, surely the matter should be pursued further? Is the root cause lack of interest or feelings of impotence or alienating procedures or other things? It would be worth further investigation.

The second principle is "equality of access to educational services".[37] Even allowing for the fact that 'equality' softened to 'equity' in the

---

[34] Zubric, S.R. *et al.* op. cit.
[35] Adermann, A. & Campbell, C. op. cit.
[36] De Plevitz, L. 'Testing the Social Justice Goals of Education' (2007), 98.
[37] Ibid.

National Policy, is it possible for children, Indigenous or otherwise, who live in the middle of the Simpson Desert to have equality of access with children who live in Metropolitan Sydney? The same goes for Principle Three: "Equality of educational participation, commensurate with all Australians".[38] Although relevant statistics are not available, clearly there are Aboriginal students who have access to education but do not participate and often truant from school. Some reasons for this lie outside the power of schools to change, but some are open to educational influence. For example, the frequent denial that schools can and often do make a huge difference to a person's path in life: to give students the impression that much of knowledge is irrelevant to them and, worse, that they might be unable to cope with it even if it is relevant, is to put unnecessary obstacles in their path.

De Plevitz expressed concern about the "endemic effects of dominant power on mainstream education".[39] She must spend time in different schools from the ones I have known – students and their teachers are subjected to very little coercion by agents of dominant power. In how many jurisdictions in Australia can state power end truancy among Indigenous children?

Students or teachers can rarely do as they please, but it is often very difficult to cope with students who are determined to disobey. Suspension from school as punishment is unlikely to deter tough disrupters. Inability to control turbulent classrooms vies with isolation in reasons for the massive turnover of young teachers in 'Aboriginal' schools. And it can be difficult for school authorities to discipline recalcitrant teachers. That goes for outlandish conduct in and out of school.

To achieve anything like equity of educational participation, draconian powers would have to be conferred on the state apparatus. Massive coercion would be needed to achieve even a relatively small and

---

[38] Ibid.
[39] Ibid.

simple target such as truancy rates. Many families look after their children very well and thus give them a significant advantage in education and subsequent employment; other families either cannot exercise adequate control or, if they can, will not.

An accusation 'welfare' academics are determined to avoid is to have blamed the victim. This presumes a victim status for all Indigenous persons unless they have clearly shown themselves to be otherwise. To appear to criticise the "community" is tantamount to blaming the victims collectively.

Barry Osborne stated bluntly, "there is little evidence of intellectual quality, relevance or recognition of difference" in the range of Queensland schools he had come across, but he attributes this to insufficient "equitable multiculturalism" in the schools.[40] However, Osborne was comforted by the 1966 findings of Coleman *et al.* in the United States that schools made very little difference to students' progress or lack of it – it all depends on families and social environment.[41] Osborne evidently did not know that Coleman and his colleagues almost totally repudiated those earlier findings and instead identified several critical factors in student achievement, even after every background and contextual factor had been allowed for. Among key features of effective schools were that they:

- demanded regular school attendance;
- set high standards of personal conduct;
- maintained strong and consistent discipline;
- offered a rigorous and demanding curriculum;
- assigned regular homework (in the case of secondary

---

[40] Osborne, B. 'Preparing Preservice Teachers' Minds, Hearts and Actions' (2003), 17, 18.
[41] Ibid.

schools) and ensured that it was marked regularly.⁴²

Osborne wanted us to accept "knowledge as socially constructed and open to challenge" but knowledge is far from being "only" socially constructed.⁴³ That is one important reason why some societies failed to survive: what they believed to be knowledge was plain wrong. Osborne also thinks that "culturally relevant pedagogy involves personal warmth towards, respect for and demandingness of students".⁴⁴ However, cool objectivity often serves as well as personal warmth. There is more than one type of good teacher.

## Confused History

Jennifer Houston considers that "a significant need exists for Indigenous people to conduct and present research in a manner respectful of Indigenous ways of understanding and reflective of the ways in which Indigenous peoples wish to be framed and understood".⁴⁵ This requires her to "challenge the imperial basis of Western knowledge and the images of the Indigenous 'Other'".⁴⁶

Those who worked in this field before her are accused as having "fed racist ideologies and stereotypes and created distorted images that were fed back to Indigenous people".⁴⁷ Other unnamed persons engaged in "research practices that have devalued their peoples and subjugated their knowledge." Evidently none of those teachers and research workers before her time was "free from the constraints and biases of imperialist colonialism".⁴⁸

John Maynard has "prioritised" his work to "concentrate on aspects

---

⁴² Coleman, J. *et al. High School achievement* (1982).
⁴³ Ibid.
⁴⁴ Ibid., 19.
⁴⁵ Houston, J. 'Indigenous Autoethnography' (2007), 45.
⁴⁶ Ibid., I think Houston meant 'imperial' and not 'empirical'.
⁴⁷ Ibid.
⁴⁸ Ibid.

and issues of Aboriginal history that are either unknown or not recognised".[49] Maynard believes: "There is a general misconception that history belongs to the Western and Europe thought and that its interpretation and preservation is bound by the rigid guidelines they see fit to impose upon it".[50] One may wonder who expressed that "general misconception" where and when.

Maynard considers that, "History from the Western perspective is largely confined to the Rankean model of inquiry and practice: diligent archival research cementing documentary evidence as fact", with everything else "regarded as not real history". He thinks "academic historians have lost the art and history is being strangled by analysis and theoretical interpretation". It must be conceded that in the study of pre-literate societies, little or no archival evidence will be available, but R.G. Collingwood, a great prehistorian as well as a philosopher of history, advised, "If you can enter the mind of Neolithic man and make his thoughts your own you can then write his history, but not otherwise".[51] It may well be that an Indigenous historian will have an edge in understanding, but surely this cannot be simply assumed.

The late Professor Kenneth Maddock collected six Aboriginal stories about the visit of James Cook to Australia.[52] In a Victoria River myth, the first white arrival in Australia was Ned Kelly. Ned was kind and gave the Aborigines horses and bullocks, but then Captain Cook came along, killed Ned and despoiled the Aborigines. The remaining five myths are equally inaccurate but it seems the Aboriginal informants considered those manifestly mistaken accounts of relatively recent events to be historically true. Maynard may well be among those who consider those "Captain Cook" myths to be psychologically true, but surely those who

---

[49] Maynard, J. 'Circles in the Sand' (2007), 117.
[50] Ibid.
[51] Collingwood, R.G. *The Idea of History* (1962), 214, 283.
[52] Maddock, K. 'Myth, History and a Sense of Oneself' (1988).

cannot distinguish between historical fact and fiction should find pursuits other than history.

After telling us that "History is about finding the voices from many different perspectives and identifying the layers", Maynard goes on to claim that:

> generations of Australians including Aboriginal people have been fed histories that were based on fabrication and distortion of the truth. This fabricated history glorified the imperial conquerors, administrators, discoverers and settlers.[53]

Maynard protests, "We are at a great disadvantage if we do not have access to our history".[54] But who are "we"? It is hard to see what point there would be in the study of history if all accounts were regarded as equally true. A good test would be to read about twenty pages of each of the two accounts that Procopius wrote of the joint reign of Byzantine rulers Justinian and Theodora: in the official histories he praises them fulsomely and extravagantly, but in his *Secret History* he denounces them as vicious and among the vilest of rulers.[55] Both accounts cannot be right; historians surely must distinguish between levels of authenticity, not accept all "stories" as much of a muchness on the grounds that the roots of "history" and "story" are identical.

## Conclusion

Whilst reading those journal articles I came to the conclusion that resentment and hostility towards the post-1788 Australian past and our present institutions are growing stronger. I hope, but with little confidence, that educators will work towards harmony rather than hatred – focus on what unites us rather than what divides us: a united Australia rather than separatism till the end of time.

---

[53] Maynard, J. op. cit., 118.
[54] Ibid.
[55] Procopius. *The Secret History* (2007).

For many thousands of years up to and largely including the present the human race lived by what Sir Walter Scott called the 'good old rule' of history: 'The simple plan/That they should take who have the power/And they should keep who can'. All of us have now in Australia the opportunity to live in peace and to replace power by reason and persuasion.

We should reject any who seek to increase difference, separatism and enmity between any peoples who now dwell in this great continent. Most of all, we should seek closer understanding between Indigenous Australians and all who came here after them.

# 15

# Indigenous Education – Policy, Pedagogy, and Place

*Bill Fogarty*

*"Education is the kindling of a flame, not the filling of a vessel."*
— Socrates

There are 168,803 Indigenous students in Australia, diverse in geography, socio-economic status, and culture.[1,2] With educators, parents, communities, policy-makers, and politicians, they make up something referred to broadly as 'Indigenous education'. Given this diversity of stakeholders, it is perhaps not surprising that Indigenous education in Australia is a highly politicised field of endeavour, long marked by policy contestation. This chapter concentrates on one part of this larger field – remote Indigenous education – where it seems we are stuck at the 'crossroads'. Nearly a decade of policy-making has had a firm focus on remote Indigenous education, with a policy paradigm dominated by statistical representation of educational outcomes. The poor outcomes of Indigenous students in the Northern Territory have driven a policy remedy based on 'closing the gap' and literacy and numeracy scores from standardised tests have become the key measure of progress. Unfortunately, this not-so-new order in remote Indigenous education has increasingly cast Indigenous perspectives in learning as detrimental to educational achievement, and as dialectically opposed to pathways into further learning and work. This has happened both as an unintended

---

[1] These are primary and secondary school-aged students.
[2] ABS. *Schools Australia 2011* (no. 4221.0) (2012d).

consequence of the 'Intervention'[3] and its proliferation of a wider deficit discourse,[4,5] as well as global shifts in educational ideology driven by the rise of neo-liberalism. The contemporary evidence suggests that this 'back to basics' policy approach is not working for remote Indigenous students.

This chapter examines three key issues. First, an analysis of the current situation of Indigenous education in Australia, with an emphasis on discrete remote communities in the Northern Territory. Then a history of what I see as a symbiotic relationship between national policy and pedagogy in remote Indigenous education. Remote Indigenous education has long been characterised by dichotomies that mirror the discourses of Indigenous affairs at a national level, and consequently, there is a dramatic tension between what people want from education locally and the goals of policy nationally. My final point is the importance of local 'pedagogies of place' in ameliorating tensions and providing critical opportunities for engagement.

## The Current Situation

Indigenous education, as a distinct pedagogic field, can be characterised in modern policy terms as either an attempt to attain statistical equality with non-Indigenous Australians, or the pursuit of cultural imperatives through self-determined educational development.[6] The degree to which policy emphasis has concentrated on educational equity, as opposed to more self-determined forms of education, has shifted

---

[3] The 'Intervention' refers to the suite of measures passed into law by the Northern Territory Emergency Response (NTER) Bill in 2007. The NTER finished in 2012 and has been replaced by the *Stronger Futures Act*, which keeps some of the key elements of the NTER. Importantly for education, the *Stronger Futures Act* introduces 'Improving School Enrolment and Attendance through Welfare Reform Measure (SEAM) which focuses on penalising parents whose children do not attend school.

[4] Macoun, A. 'Aboriginality and the Northern Territory Intervention' (2012).

[5] McCallum, K. 'Journalism and Indigenous Health Policy' (2011).

[6] See Rowse, T. *Indigenous Futures* (2002).

as policy has shifted in Indigenous affairs at a national level. These sometimes dichotomous positions in policy are set against an unresolved historical legacy of institutionalised racism, systemic underfunding, and assimilation's ideals that have dominated educational provision for Indigenous students in Australia. This is most starkly evident in the paucity of opportunities remote Indigenous students have had to attend high-school in their own communities, to study in their own languages, and in schooling disengagement and non-attendance by many remote Indigenous students.[7,8]

Increasingly, though, contemporary policy has paid less attention to these structural, historical, and social determinants of educational achievement. Instead, policy is increasingly focused on the roles and responsibilities of parents and schools, coupled with 'carrot and stick' programs such as the Improving School Enrolment and Attendance through Welfare Reform Measure (SEAM) and formulaic testing regimes, best evidenced in NAPLAN. Unfortunately after over 10 years of these approaches, the constants in Indigenous education continue to be poor attendance, low retention, and literacy and numeracy outcomes well below those of other groups within Australian society.[9]

## Year 12 Retention

Over the last decade or more, Australia has experienced a sustained period of resource-driven economic growth, yet most indicators show that the relative economic position of Indigenous Australians has not improved.[10] More positively, there have been some small gains for Indigenous Australians in education and training outcomes. Figure 15.1 shows a small but steady increase in the number of Indigenous students completing Year 12 over the last three inter-censual periods.

---

[7] Commonwealth of Australia. *Our Land Our Languages* (2012).
[8] Fogarty, B. 'Country as Classroom' (2012), 82.
[9] Altman, J. & Fogarty, B. 'Indigenous Australians as 'No Gaps' Subjects' (2010), 112.
[10] Altman, J. & Hunter, B. 'Evaluating Indigenous Socioeconomic Outcomes' (2003); Altman, J. *et al.* 'How Realistic Are the Prospects' (2008).

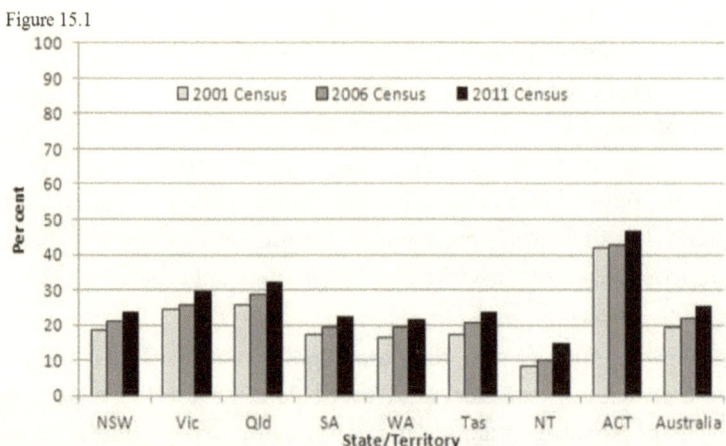

Figure 15.1 Per cent of Indigenous population who have completed Year 12 (or equivalent) in 2001, 2006 and 2011 Censuses.[11]

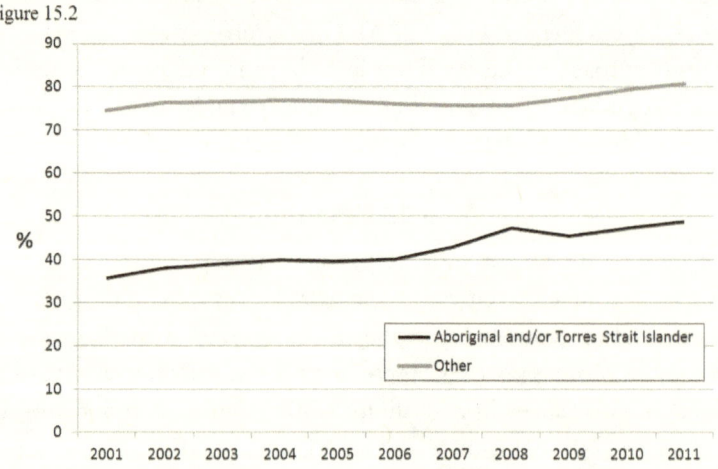

Figure 15.2 Apparent retention rates 2001–2011 for full-time students by Indigenous status, Year 7/8 to 12 ("Other" includes non-Indigenous students and 'not stated').[12]

---

[11] Biddle, N. 'Australian Census' (2012).
[12] Original data: ABS. *Schools Australia 2011* (no. 4221.0) (2012d), 29.

However, as Figure 15.2 demonstrates, these small gains have not kept pace with other Australians and disparity continues to be a dominant feature of the Indigenous education landscape. Between 2000 and 2010, for example, the apparent retention rate 'gap' has stubbornly oscillated between 28 and 39% and shows no significant sign of diminishing (see Figure 15.2).

The continuing relative educational disadvantage of Indigenous people is most pronounced in the very remote parts of the country where the likelihood of students speaking languages other than English is highest and the availability of education and training services and infrastructure is lowest. One obvious explanation for this pattern is that few Indigenous students in remote country have secondary schools in their communities. Not surprisingly, distance to a secondary school has a strong effect on school attendance and completion of studies by individuals.[13]

## School Attendance

Poor retention to Year 12 is compounded by poor school attendance. Over the last 50 years, a litany of research has detailed the poor attendance at school by Indigenous students in Australia.[14] Figure 15.3 shows the attendance of students in schools in the Northern Territory in 2011 and 2012. Average attendance at school for Indigenous students is just 68%, while in very remote areas the average is as low as 59%. This compares to a national school attendance rate of approximately 97%.

---

[13] Fordham, A. *et al.* 'Knowledge Foundations' (2010).
[14] See, for example, Watts, B.H. & Gallacher, J.D. *Report on An Investigation into the Curriculum and Teaching Methods* (1969); Parish, D.F.G. *Minj Kabirridi* (1990); Lasorsa, T. 'Bilingual Programs' (2011); Baarda, W. 'The Impact of the Bilingual Program' (1994), 204; Groome, H. & Hamilton, A. *Meeting the Educational Needs* (2005); Kays, M. & Romaszko, J. *Away Yesterday and Today* (1995); Taylor, J. 'Demography as Destiny' (2010); Fogarty, B. & Schwab, J. 'Indigenous Education' (2012).

Figure 15.3

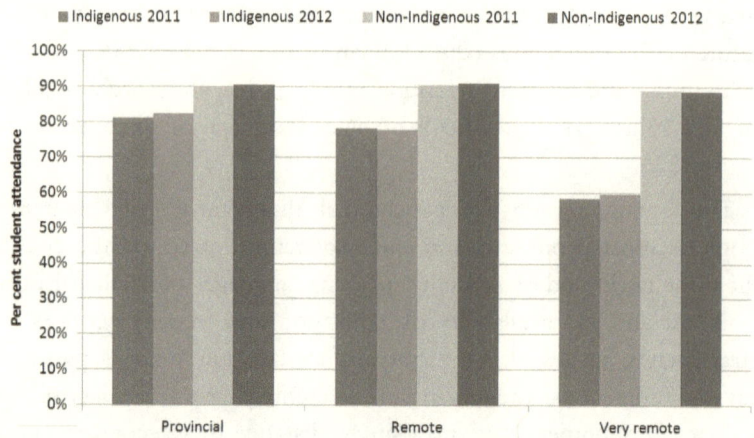

Figure 15.3 Student attendance, Term 2, 2011 & 2012, NT.[15]

At a national level, the enormity of Indigenous non-attendance is somewhat softened by better attendance patterns in urban areas. Most pronounced is the low number of students in their middle and later teens choosing to engage in education in remote areas – highly conspicuous in their absence.[16]

The lack of engagement of a significant proportion of Indigenous youth in remote areas is, understandably, presented in the literature as a 'problem'. However, this view is also challenged. Schwab, for example, in discussing success and failure in education, finds that traditional performance measures such as student attendance, retention, and national test results ignore the fact that Indigenous people may use education to fit their specific needs.[17] Similarly, Devlin argues that the 'value' of an education program should be:

---

[15] Original data: Northern Territory Department of Education and Training. *Enrolment and Attendance Statistics* (2012).

[16] Ministerial Council for Education, Early Childhood Development and Youth Affairs (MCEECDYA). (2011).

[17] Schwab, R. G. 'Kids, Skidoos and Caribou' (2006).

... considered from a human, quality-of-life perspective. People's views count every bit as much as the wants of government politicians which are inevitably swayed by short-term considerations, and arguably more so, for it is the people that the government serves. People know what they want and care about, and so they sign petitions, write letters to put their views and vent their frustrations. While it may come as a surprise to mainstream Australia and to the NT government, Indigenous people in remote settlements know what they value.[18]

Rhetorically, however, all from Ministers and administrators to parents and, sometimes, students themselves, openly and consistently represent non-attendance and poor outcomes as an issue.[19]

As noted, the discourse of Indigenous education policy has seen chronic non-attendance as a consistently prominent problem for well over fifty years. Unfortunately, the spectre of 'intractable' looms over an ever-mounting pile of discarded programs designed to 'combat the problem'.

## Education Outcomes

In the same vein as retention rates and school attendance, patterns of poor outcomes for Indigenous students are replicated nationwide and are especially poor in remote and very remote areas of the Northern Territory. Indigenous outcomes have increasingly come to be represented as literacy and numeracy outcomes only, as the pre-eminent measure of performance in contemporary policy is the NAPLAN test.[20]

---

[18] Devlin, B. 'Bilingual Education in the Northern Territory' (2009), 14.
[19] MCEECDYA. op. cit.
[20] NAPLAN results are reported using five national achievement scales, one for each of the NAPLAN assessment domains of Reading, Writing, Spelling, Grammar and Punctuation, and Numeracy. In 2011, results for Writing are reported on the Persuasive Writing scale. Each scale consists of ten bands, which represent the increasing complexity of the skills and understandings assessed by NAPLAN from Years 3 to 9. Six of these bands are used for reporting student performance in each Year level. Student raw scores on tests are converted to NAPLAN scale scores so that the scores can be located on the national domain scales. For more details, see ACARA, *National Assessment Program* (2012).

## NAPLAN

Figure 15.4 shows the percentage of students nationally, both Indigenous and non-Indigenous, who have reached national benchmarks in selected literacy and numeracy outcomes, according to 2011 NAPLAN data.[21] The gap in these selected NAPLAN outcomes shows that across the reading and writing spectrum, Indigenous students perform significantly worse in the NAPLAN tests. These results, with some minor variations, have been reasonably consistent since national NAPLAN testing data first became available in 2008.[22]

|        |          | Indigenous, Australia (%) | Non-Indigenous, Australia (%) | Gap in percentage |
|--------|----------|---------------------------|-------------------------------|-------------------|
| Year 3 | Reading  | 75.1 | 94.9 | 19.8 |
|        | Writing  | 79   | 96.2 | 17.2 |
|        | Numeracy | 76.6 | 96.4 | 19.8 |
| Year 5 | Reading  | 66.2 | 92.6 | 26.4 |
|        | Writing  | 70.5 | 93.9 | 23.4 |
|        | Numeracy | 71.4 | 95.5 | 24.1 |
| Year 7 | Reading  | 76.6 | 95.7 | 19.1 |
|        | Writing  | 69.8 | 92.6 | 22.8 |
|        | Numeracy | 77.0 | 95.5 | 18.5 |
| Year 9 | Reading  | 64.2 | 93.5 | 29.3 |
|        | Writing  | 59.0 | 86.4 | 27.4 |
|        | Numeracy | 70.5 | 94.1 | 23.6 |

Figure 15.4 Achievement of benchmarks by students, by Indigenous and non-Indigenous status for all Australia, as assessed by NAPLAN 2011.[23]

The NAPLAN results have also been instrumental in showing that Indigenous students in remote and very remote areas are performing markedly worse against these benchmarks than their Indigenous peers

---

[21] 2012 results for NAPLAN were yet to be fully released at the time of writing.
[22] See ACARA. op. cit.
[23] Original data: ACARA. Ibid.

in the rest of Australia. Figure 15.5 shows a massive disparity across the selected literacy and numeracy outcomes as measured by the 2011 tests, with the resultant gap in outcomes across all key areas of testing increasing in concert with geographic remoteness: the more remote the cohort, the fewer students achieve the benchmark.[24]

|  |  | Indigenous, very remote NT (%) | Non-Indigenous, Australia (%) | Gap in percentage |
|---|---|---|---|---|
| Year 3 | Reading | 25.2 | 94.9 | 69.7 |
|  | Writing | 26.2 | 96.2 | 70.0 |
|  | Numeracy | 48.5 | 96.4 | 47.9 |
| Year 5 | Reading | 10.8 | 92.6 | 81.8 |
|  | Writing | 11.4 | 93.9 | 82.5 |
|  | Numeracy | 29.9 | 95.5 | 65.6 |
| Year 7 | Reading | 24.8 | 95.7 | 70.9 |
|  | Writing | 7.8 | 92.6 | 84.8 |
|  | Numeracy | 25.2 | 95.5 | 70.3 |
| Year 9 | Reading | 13.4 | 93.5 | 80.1 |
|  | Writing | 6.7 | 86.4 | 79.7 |
|  | Numeracy | 20.3 | 94.1 | 73.8 |

Figure 15.5 Achievement of benchmarks by students, by Indigenous status & geo-location, as assessed by NAPLAN 2011.[25]

Data presented in Figures 15.4 and 15.5 leave little doubt that Indigenous students are doing far worse than their non-Indigenous peers on these tests. However, education researchers have consistently and vehemently cautioned against the use of such data as an acme of educational measurement.[26] Jerry Schwab and I have also written extensively about the propensity of such tests to narrow the curriculum and to shrink the space for Indigenous perspectives.[27] Devaluing

---

[24] See also Taylor, J. 'Demography as Destiny' (2010).
[25] Original data: ACARA, op. cit.
[26] Sarra, C. *NAPLAN Data, 2009* (2009); Dulfer, N. 'Testing the Test' (2012).
[27] Fogarty, B. & Schwab, J. 'Indigenous Education' (2012).

Indigenous perspectives in curriculum in turn leads to disengagement by Indigenous students.[28]

There are serious questions as to what such benchmarks actually test. Cultural and economic bias in standardised testing is well noted in both international and Australian research literature.[29] For these reasons, over 100 education researchers and academics from around Australia recently signed a petition against the Federal government's use of NAPLAN.[30] Furthermore, the use of testing regimes as the indicator of educational 'success' can perpetuate stigmatising of minorities in the wider community and lead to students or teachers being blamed for poor outcomes. For example, Heath,[31] writing about education in the USA, warns that notions of equity narrowed to everyone reaching a level in standardised tests, the idea of an 'achievement gap' took root, descriptors trapped young people in ghettoes, and the ideals of equal opportunity vanished.

Heath's analysis resonates strongly with contemporary policy in Australian Indigenous education where the focus is firmly on 'Closing the Gap' in literacy and numeracy skills, and redress stubbornly focuses on test score equity.

## Breaking the Mould

Considering the evidence of apparent retention, school attendance, and NAPLAN results at face value, it is clear that the current national policy approach is showing no signs of ameliorating the vast disparities between Indigenous and non-Indigenous students. Similarly, the international and national research base clearly suggests that the continued pursuit of a test-based education policy agenda will lead to increasingly reductionist

---

[28] See Carstairs J.R. *et al.* 'Influence of Language Background' (2006); Hambleton, R. & Rodgers, J.H. 'Item Bias Review' (1995). See also Amrein A.L. & Berliner, D.C. 'High-stakes Testing' (2002); Wright, W.E. 'The Effects of High Stakes Testing' (2002) for Similar Findings of Research in the USA.

[29] Altman, J. & Fogarty, B. op. cit.

[30] Holderhead, S. 'Protest Against NAPLAN Tests by Academics' (2012).

[31] Heath, S.B. 'Family Literacy or Community Learning?' (2010), 9.

pedagogy and 'teaching to the test' at the chalkface. This in turn will result in an increasingly narrowed curriculum: less able to be inclusive of Indigenous perspectives and consequently less likely to (re)engage poorly attending Indigenous students. Yet it seems that the policy settings that arguably found a louder voice as a result of the Intervention and are now ensconced in the Stronger Futures Act will continue to permeate pedagogy in the remote classrooms of the Northern Territory. Unfortunately, this detrimental relationship between policy and pedagogy is far from new in Indigenous education; in fact, it is de rigueur. Changing this relationship is key to the development of new policy settings that are driven by localism and learning, rather than by political expedience at the national level. A first step in this requires an understanding of the historically complex relationship between national Indigenous affairs policy and pedagogic practice in Indigenous education.

## Policy History

Indigenous education's historical beginnings were in a paradigm of colonial dispossession, coupled with the protectionist and paternalistic practice of both secular and non-secular education. A tool of repression, education policy aimed at disenfranchising the cultural fabric of Indigenous communities dominated much of last century. Key components of cultural production such as language and cosmology were deliberately subverted. This is best evidenced through the common practice of banning children from speaking their own languages in school.[32] Such practices occurred against a policy landscape of protectionism and later assimilation which dominated governance until 1970.[33] In Queensland, Western Australia and Northern Territory, Education departments deliberately adopted pedagogic frameworks

---

[32] Commonwealth of Australia. *Our Land Our Languages* (2012).
[33] Sanders, W. *Towards an Indigenous order of Australian Government* (2002).

which denied 'cultural difference' of Indigenous students.[34] Coupled with a relative paucity of resourcing, particularly in remote settings, this denied equitable access to education. Concurrently, non-Indigenous students were denied, except in the most basic terms, the opportunity to engage with Indigenous history and culture.[35] While the effects of this practice could, in part at least, be represented in the quantification of poor educational outcomes for Indigenous students relative to the rest of the Australian population,[36] its individual and collective effects on the educative process are much more ambiguous. At the very least, the possibility that the assimilation era created cultural misrecognition between Indigenous and non-Indigenous educational communities must be entertained. Indeed, a number of submissions to the inquiry into the 'Stolen Generations' drew attention to the relationship between past practices in education which excluded or marginalised Indigenous children, and contemporary low secondary school retention rates and low participation rates in tertiary education.[37] As such, the symbiotic linkages of policy and pedagogy cannot be underestimated.[38]

In the early 1970s,[39] the advent of self-determination as an ideological framework for governance saw a profound shift in educational policy for Indigenous people. The rise of a distinctly Indigenous sector of

---

[34] In 1970, there were only 2,000 Indigenous identified children enrolled in secondary schools throughout Australia (Hughes, P. *Report of the Aboriginal Education Policy Task Force* (1988), 8). At the same time, at the post-compulsory level, there were fewer than 100 Indigenous people enrolled anywhere in Australia (Ibid., 11).

[35] School Council NBEET, *Aboriginal and Torres Strait Islander Education in the Early Years* (1992).

[36] Hunter, B.H. & Schwab, J. 'Practical Reconciliation' (2003).

[37] Commonwealth of Australia. *Bringing Them Home* (1997).

[38] To return briefly to Indigenous education's metaphorical scar, the rawness of assimilation's injury and the need to account for it can be evidenced in Indigenous education communities' reactions to the Northern Territory government's controversial move to cut bilingual education programs in 1998.

[39] Sometime between April 1971 and January 1973 (see Rowse, T. op. cit.).

governance[40] saw the creation of many publicly funded organisations at state and national levels, while at local levels, particularly in remote communities, constructs of 'community government' developed.[41] With the rise of this sector came issues of representation and tensions in the strategic fit between democratic notions of governance on one hand and self-determined expressions of Indigeneity on the other. These tensions also permeated all areas of service delivery, and the need to be inclusive saw the development of a distinctly 'Aboriginal' field of education. Indigenous education branches were created in all states and territories during the 1980s, and the Commonwealth Aboriginal Education Policy (AEP) was officially born. As with other areas of Indigenous service delivery, the idea of self-determination began education's search for 'public policy arrangements which recognised the distinct minority nationalism of Indigenous people, while also drawing them into a single nation state'.[42]

During this time, much effort went into 'Aboriginalising'[43] education for high numbers of Indigenous students: parental committees, representation on school boards, Indigenous faculties in universities, 'consultative' decision-making, and training and employment of Indigenous staff in schools. Ideologically, education underwent a fundamental shift from the assimilation policy era, where pedagogy had been an instrument of acculturation. The process and style of educational delivery became paramount while outcomes took a decidedly back seat. The underlying ethos was Indigenous people would control the nature, pace, and delivery of education. In reality, however, many remote communities lacked the capacity for this to occur within education's

---

[40] Ibid.
[41] Sanders, W. 'Local Governments and Indigenous Australians' (1996).
[42] Sanders, W. *Towards an Indigenous Order of Australian Government* (2002), 16.
[43] The concept of 'Aboriginalisation' dominated remote Indigenous education in communities in WA and NT during the 1990s. This was seen as a key component in self-determined education.

often rigid institutions,[44] and power and control remained very much in the hands of government.

Self-determination policy provided the environment for pedagogic change. Notions of 'cultural appropriateness' and 'Indigenous learning styles',[45] coupled with English as a Second Language (ESL) strategies based on communication theories of writers such as,[46] Vygotski[47] and Halliday[48] began to dominate the pedagogic landscape. Simultaneously, deconstructionist theory and critical literacy approaches emerged as a major development in educational theory. Pedagogically, this emphasised the difference, or otherness, of Indigenous students and proposed curriculum and content design based on 'culture'. However, pedagogic development was still firmly mainstream, with implementation distinctly top-down.

One of the key educational developments in the NT during this time was the bilingual education program, where students' first language is used as a basis for instruction and teaching while students simultaneously learn to use English.[49] Bilingual education was adopted in remote communities during the 1970s and early 1980s, yet by the mid-1980s funding became scarce. In 1998, the then-NT government chose to phase out bilingual education. This was met with strong resistance by remote communities, and the program was eventually rebranded to become the 'two-way learning' program.[50] More recently, in October 2008, the NT

---

[44] Schwab R.G. & Sutherland, D. 'Indigenous Learning Communities' (2003).
[45] Christie, M. 'Constructing a Galtha Curriculum' (1993); Harris, S. *Culture and Learning* (1980); Harris, S. *Two-way Aboriginal Schooling* (1990).
[46] Chomsky, N. *Chomsky on Democracy and Education* (2002).
[47] Vygotsky, L.S. *Mind in Society* (1978).
[48] Halliday, M.A.K. 'Language and the Reshaping of Human Experience' (1995).
[49] Devlin, B. 'Bilingual Education in the Northern Territory' (2009), 14.
[50] Ibid., 6. Many remote communities demonstrated against the cut to bilingual education programs, using the slogan 'Don't cut off our tongues'. In Maningrida NT, where I was teaching at the time, a large community meeting was organised and hundreds of cardboard tongues were plastered across the school in symbolic protest to the decision.

government[51] announced that 'two-way learning' programs would be superseded by 'English only' instruction for the first four hours of every day.[52] The program was re-instated in 2011.[53] The history of bilingual education policy[54] in the NT provides a clear example of the tensions between local pedagogic wants and the control over pedagogy exerted by the state.

With the advent of 'Practical Reconciliation' under the Howard government Indigenous education once again experienced a distinct ideological shift. Concepts of 'mutual responsibility'[55] combined with a global shift in education theory and economic rationalism,[56] created a shift towards demonstrable outcomes in education, seen in national and state benchmarking of educational performance. The reasons for this benchmarking can be seen as twofold. Firstly, measurement: agreed educational benchmarks allows for homogeneous reporting and increased monitoring and evaluation of state education. Teaching and learning becomes subject to 'outcomes' – more easily controlled by centralised systems. Secondly, on the corporate model inputs and outputs are measured as a function of value. Increasing commodification of education, driven by economic rationalism, makes outcomes paramount and learning increasingly forced to fit the demands of the labour market.

Outcome frameworks and testing data allow for the mapping of performance trends, but they also disaggregate key areas of literacy development (e.g., reading, writing, listening, speaking, and numeracy). However, homogenising educational approaches also privileges Western

---

[51] Scrymgour, M. *Education Restructure* (2008).
[52] See Simpson, J. *et al.* 'Gaps in Australia's Indigenous Language Policy' (2009) for full discussion. See also 'Chronology: The Bilingual Education Policy in the Northern Territory' ABC *Four Corners* (no date).
[53] See Commonwealth of Australia. *Our Land Our Languages* (2012).
[54] Simpson, J. *et al.* op. cit.
[55] For critique of this see Rowse, T. op. cit.
[56] Greening, T. *Pedagogically Sound Responses* (2000).

knowledge, elevates English literacy and numeracy above all other learning, and subverts local control.

The outcome era of Indigenous education, which has dominated the last decade, exacerbated an already historically and socially complex relationship between policy, governance, and pedagogy at the local level. On the one hand, ideals of Indigenous control of education have fostered pedagogy based around context-specific, culturally appropriate development, while on the other, external governance structures, poor resourcing, and an increased focus on narrow educational outcomes have made it difficult to realise these ideals. The potential of locally developed pedagogy has consequently been subverted. This has in turn resulted in compromised curriculum and teaching practice, and an increasing disconnect between school and remote Indigenous students' lived experiences and the reality of remote labour markets.[57]

## The Case for Place

Given the demonstrated propensity of historical policy settings to disrupt and dictate pedagogic approaches at the local level – generating concomitantly poor outcomes – future policy approaches to remote Indigenous education need to avoid doing more of the same. One way is to create policy frameworks that encourage 'place-based' educational approaches. A plethora of research on Indigenous education shows that the best results in engagement and outcomes arise when learning is linked to local community aspirations and values, respects Indigenous languages and perspectives, and involves local people in its development.[58]

Similarly, a recent review for the 'Closing the Gap Clearinghouse'[59]

---

[57] Kral, I. *Writing Words – Right Way!* (2007).
[58] McRae, D. *et al. What Works?* (2000); Miller, C. *Aspects of Training that Meet Indigenous Australians' Aspirations* (2005); Catts, R. & Gelade, S. 'Rhetorics and Realities' (2002); Gelade, S. & Stehlik, T. 'Exploring Locality' (2004).
[59] Australian Institute of Health & Welfare, and Australian Institute of Family Studies. (no date).

evaluated which programs work to increase Indigenous attendance or retention and found:

> A common feature of successful educational programs was that of a creative collaboration, which builds bridges between public agencies and the community, often by engaging parents or community-based organisations.[60]

In 2012, National Curriculum Services analysed 11 schools in remote regions that were considered to be improving. They listed seven key factors of success that work:[61]

- Leadership – this is critical.
- Making learning content engaging, accessible, and culturally responsive.
- A school culture built on high expectations for all students.
- Empowering, supporting, and engaging Aboriginal and Torres Strait Islander students to enhance their learning capacity.
- Building and sustaining teacher capacity to deliver whole-school practice.
- Coherent whole-school approaches to evidence-based literacy and numeracy teaching.
- Profound understanding of the importance of school-community partnerships.

Yet current policy approaches seem consistently unable to support such creative collaborations. Conversely, 'place-based' pedagogic approaches link schools with local development and/or social activity and use this as a platform for learning about wider concepts. Without a full analysis of place-based education,[62] it is finding out what people

---

[60] Purdie, N. & Buckley, S. 'School Attendance and Retention of Indigenous Australian Students' (2010).
[61] National Curriculum Services. *What Works. The Work Program* (2012).
[62] Fogarty, B. & Schwab, J. op. cit.; Gruenewald, D.A. 'Why Place Matters' (2006); Gruenewald, D.A. 'Place-Based Education' (2008), 137.

want and need to learn in the place where they live and tailoring their education accordingly. The resulting education is both relevant and engaging to the local community while simultaneously able to incorporate local Indigenous aspirations and perspectives, as well as embed literacy and numeracy learning in real activity.

## Pedagogy in Place

In conclusion, I turn briefly to an emergent type of place-based education program in remote Indigenous Australia that is challenging the reductionist approaches of current policy, albeit in a very pragmatic and somewhat unknowing sense.

Over the last decade or so there has been an exponential growth in Indigenous land and sea management programs, Indigenous Ranger programs, and natural resource management programs. This is hardly surprising given that the Indigenous estate is now over 20% of Australia. These programs deliberately combine Western scientific and local Indigenous knowledge to manage environmental threats such as feral animals, wildfires, and weeds while also pursuing economic development in carbon offsets, sustainable wildlife harvesting, and fee-for-service coastal security and biodiversity work.[63]

Schools and education programs in remote areas of the NT – and in other Australian states – have begun to recognise that these land and sea management programs provide a live opportunity for experiential learning. Such programs are able to engage students and – importantly – the wider community, in learning that recognises and values the importance of Indigenous cosmologies, connections to 'country', and customary practices while also providing a concrete reason to learn literacy, numeracy, and scientific knowledge. Furthermore, being a Ranger or working with boats, crocodiles, four-wheel-drives, and guns is seen by students as 'cool', and Rangers become local role models, providing an added incentive to learning that standard school programs may not. An

---

[63] See Kerins, this volume.

increasing number of junior Ranger programs, environmental education programs, back-to-country programs, and school- and community-based science projects are engaging students and teachers in education that connects Indigenous land and sea management with more formal education programs and curricula, particularly in middle and senior school.

Over the last few years, I have spent time in eight remote locations researching these types of programs, which I call "learning through country".[64] Generally, these programs and others like them are disparate in their development, often unsupported at systemic level, and characterised by peaks and troughs as key teaching personalities come and go in settings renowned for their teacher 'churning'. Despite this, the programs are durable, they engage students and the wider community in schooling in a practical sense, and they have the ability to fulfil the dual purpose of intergenerational transfer of Indigenous knowledge on country and achieving mainstream educational outcomes. This is no mean feat in some of the most difficult educational contexts imaginable. In this regard, these and other small, localised 'pedagogies of place' may hold some very important lessons for the highly politicised relationship between policy and pedagogy in remote Indigenous education.

## Conclusion

Pedagogic practice in Indigenous education has too long been influenced by the political to and fro of the national Indigenous affairs discourse. The latest example of this is manifest in policy settings that are built around measurement and high-stakes tests like NAPLAN. The evidence shows that these approaches are not working. The key task ahead is to find ways to ensure a better educational future for Indigenous students. One thing I am sure of is that the formulation of a new relationship between policy, pedagogy, and place at the 'crossroads' of Indigenous education would certainly be a welcome and fruitful start.

---

[64] Fogarty, B. 'Country as Classroom' (2012), 82.

# 16
# Whatever the Problem, Education is the Key: The Scots College Experience

*Jonny Samengo*

*"What do you mean, you don't know any Aboriginal people? Call yourself an Australian?"*
(Mia Samengo, author's nine-year-old daughter, talking to one of her school friends.)

I was born and brought up in typical upper-middle class privilege in England. We had a comfortable home, a family holiday house in Italy in the '70s when few people went 'on the continent' for holidays, and I went to a private boarding school. My family prided itself on being of Italian descent. It meant we were interesting, lively, sophisticated, and knew about good food, wine, and sunshine. Englishness seemed very dull in comparison. Certainly most English people seemed to think so.

I came to Sydney in my 20s at the tail end of the '80s and found it very different here. Early on, a new friend said to me: "Mate, you shouldn't tell people you are part-Italian, they will look down on you; that's very working class, you know. Just say you are English. Why the hell would you admit to being Italian? That's all concrete garden, statues of Mary and tomato plants."

Apparently, it wasn't just immigrants that were looked down upon in Australia. I also enquired where the Aboriginal people were, as I hadn't come across any. Funnily enough, virtually no one I spoke to had met an Aboriginal person either, but that didn't stop everyone having a very firm opinion on them and it wasn't a good one.

Unlike most of them, I was fascinated by the fact that Australia's

Indigenous people had lived for 40,000 years without the need to build anything or own anything. They had lived with the land, not off it and they had stood the test of time in spectacular fashion. Success indeed as I saw it. However, in our myopic western world, success was all about GDP, possessions, construction, and economic growth, rather than happiness, relationships, and sustainability. I remember trying to get my father to understand my non-materialistic, Indigenous definition of success. He just told me not to be such a stupid cretin.

I mentally compared a crowded Sydney street with its thundering buses and tut-tut people looking at their watches with the opposite – being in native bushland, surrounded by the shrieking and yacking exuberance of birdsong, looking through fleshy angophoras to craggy outcrops of sandstone and twinkling ocean beyond. I realised I wasn't a cretin afterall.

Fast forward 23 years. I married a beautiful and vivacious Aussie girl and we had twins in 2000. My son was at Scots College, in Sydney's Bellevue Hill. A school very like the one I was at in England: proud and traditional. I was at a dinner at Scots to raise money for their Indigenous program. A Year 9 Indigenous boy by the name of Kyol Blakeney took to the podium. He was dignified, handsome, and articulate. He spoke of the need to educate Indigenous young people as the key to their futures. It was a light-bulb moment for me. A turning point. From that moment onwards my life was going to change direction in a way I wouldn't have thought possible. I turned to Bee, my wife, and said: "I want to help. This is it. It's all about education. This is what Aboriginal people need: a hand up, not a handout". Bee looked at me, suggested I had yet another beer and my altruistic outburst would be doused.

She was right about almost everything, but not this. Even without the liquid inspiration the next day, I still felt just as driven to help. I went to the school the following Monday to offer help. Within 12 months, I had left my career as a strategic planner in advertising and was working full-time running the Indigenous program at Scots, with a wife who was extremely supportive and encouraging of this life change. Now *that's* progress.

Our Indigenous Program has now grown from five boys to almost 20. Boys from as far as Nhulunbuy on the coast of Arnhem Land to as close as La Perouse, which is a short drive away in Sydney's East. My dream is to build the best Indigenous program of its kind in Australia, backed by a corpus of $10 million which will allow Scots to educate Indigenous boys forever. With the help of the wonderful community at Scots and its spirit and generosity, I think we will achieve both.

Programs like ours are sometimes criticised as being tokenistic and self-serving. Let's address these negatives before we get onto the positives. Eight per cent of our boarding community are now Indigenous, compared to under three per cent in Australia, so it's certainly not tokenistic. One of the main reasons to have the Indigenous Program is for the benefit of all the non-Indigenous boys at the school. For them to live shoulder to shoulder with Aboriginal young men, learn from them and appreciate and understand their culture, law, and traditions. If that is self-serving, then guilty as charged.

We make a point of taking on boys whose lives we can make a profound change to. We don't want a Scots education to be a 'nice to have' for a near middle-class boy with a distant Indigenous connection. We want this education to be transformational for Indigenous boys with limited opportunities and uncertain futures. As such, we look for boys with a degree of vulnerability, whether this be through contact with isolation, poverty, neglect, incarceration, drugs, alcohol abuse, or lack of positive male role models. Most of our boys have been affected by at least one of these, some by many, and at least one by all of them. We plan for our boys to break the cycle and lead lives with direction, meaning, compassion, connectedness, and personal success. Hopefully their experience will influence other family members along the way, giving their education a ripple effect on to those close to them.

A wise person once said, '*It doesn't matter what the problem is, education is the solution*'. I completely agree when it comes to Indigenous issues.

Drink, unemployment, violence – all these things can be alleviated in a generation with the right education. By that, I don't just mean schools like Scots. I mean a raft of different education solutions to meet a raft of different situations. In fact, programs like ours are probably only suitable for a minority of Indigenous kids. Many don't want to leave home and many benefit from staying close to extended family. However, being in a boarding environment can be the best solution for some. Allowing them to concentrate on their education, far away from the temptations at home. Close to positive role models and far away from the negative ones.

One yardstick of success for our boys is how much they feel they truly belong as Scots boys. Of the 15 we have here this year (2012), I think 13 would identify strongly as Scots boys, in the same manner as any boy at the College would. They belong equally at home in their communities as well. These boys have demonstrated that they can successfully embrace a 'westernised' education system, and still maintain their Aboriginal identity. Here at Scots, what we aim to do with these Aboriginal boys is create an environment where their natural innate desire to learn can flourish. We celebrate both worlds and very much encourage the Indigenous boys' parents and families to feel part of the Scots community as well. This spirit of belonging transcends barriers of culture, race, and economy. It is what unifies us. Importantly, the boys' families are every bit a part of this journey as the boys themselves are. We are all in it together.

Last year I was at an Indigenous education conference in Darwin. I met some wonderful people and was inspired by many of the Indigenous speakers and I learned a great deal. However, I reflected at the time that there was too much talk about the issues and too little about new ideas and initiatives to solve them. Too much reliance on governments to solve the problems and too little focus on new avenues and partners to move forward with. Often we are too outcomes-driven, always wanting to know the end result, the end benefit (very much the white man's way, I suspect, management-think). It would have been great to have discussed ideas that could have lead to journeys of discovery. A *'Let's try that see where that can lead'* approach. Hopefully, books like this will help move towards this. Certainly young organisations such as Yalari and the AIEF (Australian Indigenous Education Fund) are blazing a trail in demonstrating that independent organisations with financial backing from the business and commercial world can have a big impact on the lives of Indigenous kids. Waverley Stanley and Andrew Penfold, the respective founders of Yalari and the AIEF, are pioneers in this area and I have huge admiration and respect for them both.

I expect some of the Indigenous boys from The Scots College will become the thought leaders in the Indigenous world in years to come. I can certainly see some excellent leaders in the making. As far as their education is concerned, our involvement doesn't stop at the end of Year 12. We aim to continue mentoring, guidance, and support for many years after they have taken off the blue and gold uniform. In many ways, we hope they are Scots boys forever.

However, for these boys, fitting into Scots is not always a bed of roses. Homesickness is a big factor early on. In some cases this can last as much as a year. Boys have so much change to cope with. It can be exhausting and disorientating. A new world of tight routine, pressure, deadlines, new friendships, and an overall culture which is alien to most of them. The boys' mums and families feel this separation as acutely just as the boys do. My approach is to spend as much time as possible letting parents know how their boys are doing and helping them feel part of the experience. Encouraging them to fight the good fight and remind their boys about the benefits of staying when they are missing family, feeling the pressure of study, and just want the warm hug of Mum back home.

From experience, I find that by their second year, they come back from the long summer break having missed their new friends; and their burgeoning identity as Scots boys gives them a sense that Scots, too, is their home in many ways.

Their education will lead them into many directions. Whether a boy ends up a proud plumber or a principled Prime Minister, our aim is for each boy to reach his full potential, for all to have a deep understanding of themselves and how to lead a happy, fulfilling life that they are proud of. Afterall, a good education isn't just about the academic results. It's about self belief, self assurance, care for others, and leadership.

I am not sure if the world is a better place than it was in 1989, but Australia certainly is in my view. We have a long, long way to go, but we have a society that celebrates diversity and is looking for ways to learn from and understand about different cultures. We help this transformation in a small but significant way.

I encourage every Australian to heed my daughter's words: only call yourself a true Australian when the circle of people you love and respect includes the ones most deserving of our respect, our brothers and sisters that have spent 40,000 years refining how to live at one with this large brown land. Impressive stuff, in anyone's language.

To give you a further insight into the experience for the boys here at Scots, I thought I would let them speak for themselves. Let me introduce you to Thanasi and Curtley.

## Thanasi (Year 8)

Hi, my name is Thanasi from the Gurindji mob. I have been at Scots College for nearly one term and I already feel at home. All the students and staff are very friendly. Everyone at Scots just has a great presence about them. I like the fact that you can shake the hand of one the Scots boys, or staff member, and just get that safe feeling like you've known them for years.

I left my friends and family back in Darwin when I moved to Sydney; every now and then I get homesick – but only because I worry about my grandmother being at home alone – what if something was to happen to her and I wasn't there to help her. I really can't begin to imagine what would happen to me if I lost her. I would probably crash and burn. But I have been told not to be sad that they are no more, but be happy that they once were, and to remember them for all the good and not the bad. I stay through the homesickness because I know my grandmother is happy I am in boarding school, and I know I will make her proud by staying here.

All my life I have been surrounded by drugs and alcohol, and very few of my immediate family have actually finished school. My uncle and grandfather work all day in the hot sun and don't get much money, but this is only because they did not get a good education. I want to finish school and get a good education to make my family and friends proud of me but also so that some day I can make a difference in the world. I will start off small like donating as much money as I can to a cancer foundation, then I'll hopefully be able to buy food and water for the families in Africa who are dying of hunger and thirst. In order to do those things I'll need lots of money so mostly I want an education so I can get a good job with a good income. My family are always telling me that education is the key to life, because education is knowledge and knowledge is power – but with great power comes great responsibility. One of the great things about Scots is that you learn responsibility. The staff help as much as they can but it is up to you to get the work done; it will get hard but a wise man once said, "Don't pray for an easier life, but pray to be a stronger man."

When I was five my Mum asked what do I want to be when I'm older. I said, a fireman. When I was nine my Mum passed away and I just fell to pieces; my whole world came crashing down. I didn't let it show – I was trying to hold my sisters together. Even now I fall to pieces every time I remember her lying there in the coffin cold and lifeless. I remember her for all the good things and still I cry. While I'm typing this I am fighting back the tears. One can't change the past but we can change the future. If someone was to ask me what do I want to be when I grow up my first answer would be lawyer; but I would probably say that I don't really know – depends what I find interesting. I might want to become an actor or architect, but I do know I will try my best to get somewhere good in life. Life is just a big ride: in the end we are all going to end up in the same place but it is our choice if the ride is good or not. It's our choice what path we take; there is always a choice in life. All you have to do is make that choice and don't let anyone change your mind.

## Curtley (Year 10)

I am Curtley from Temora. Education is very important to my family and me. It helps to build character, to create leaders, and to boost an individual's stature within their community. An education, whether it be an elaborate one or a basic one, is helpful to the individual and the community. This is why my parents have always wanted me to try my hardest in school, and this is why I have always wanted to try my hardest in school. I know that it will not only help me, but it provides the opportunity to help me help the people around me. This is important to me. This school has made me who I am. I not only have learnt valuable knowledge about science, math, and English, but also knowledge about life and how to be a better person.

Being at Scots has been a major part of my life so far. There has been both good and bad times but I know that I am always becoming a better person throughout my time here. Scots has provided many opportunities to me, and I have taken as many as I can. I have tried to learn the bagpipes, been involved in the Cadets, and been overseas on a school tour. I have also received a fine education. This education has helped me to become the type of person I used to look up to.

I know that I can do whatever I want to when I finish school. This is a belief that Scots has instilled in me. The Scots College Indigenous Program doesn't just care about the present but also the future of the students. They provide the education as a base for the future, and this is part of the reason I have stayed at Scots through the tough times. I have been homesick on numerous occasions but I wouldn't be able to leave knowing that I have left behind the opportunities that have been provided to me. Also leaving behind all of the friends that I have made at Scots wouldn't be smart, either. Completing my time at Scots is important to me. I have a future I am looking forward to living.

# 17
# Gambling Spaces and the Paradox of Aboriginal Social Inclusion

*Martin Young, Francis Markham, and Bruce Doran*

*The separation of public works from the state, and their migration into the domain of the works undertaken by capital itself, indicates the degree to which the real community has constituted itself in the form of capital.*[1]

## Introduction

Australia's Northern Territory (NT) is home to both a relatively affluent white population and a marginalised 'fourth-world' Aboriginal one. Aboriginal people are relatively less involved in economic activity in ways that are visible to the state compared to the rest of the population, and are commonly characterised in public discourse as 'welfare dependent'.[2] Racialised policing of public places in the NT's remote towns represents a further spatial marginalisation of Aboriginal people; their occupation of sites of consumption such as public shopping malls is highly regulated and subject to discriminatory policing.[3] In this context, commercial gambling spaces (i.e., pubs, clubs, and casinos) have emerged as one of the few quasi-public spaces for Aboriginal social inclusion.[4] Yet at the same time, these spaces represent sites of material exploitation that efficiently redistribute resources from the poorest in society to sites of

---
[1] Marx, K. *The Grundrisse* (1993 [1857]), 531.
[2] Lawrence, R. 'Governing Warlpiri Subjects' (2005).
[3] Lea, T. *et al.* 'Being Moved (On)' (2012).
[4] Young, M., Doran, B. & Markham, F., 'Gambling Spaces and the Racial Dialectics of Social Inclusion' (in press).

centralised white power.⁵ In this Chapter, we ask if there is a resolution to this apparent contradiction. We argue that rather than reproducing the discourse of pathology that is routinely deployed not only to describe Aboriginal people in public space⁶ but also to inform harm-minimisation strategies and other government policies, gambling spaces may actually offer insights into how a more equitable politics of public space may be approached. To build this case we approach gambling spaces as both uniquely inclusive and extraordinarily economically exploitative configurations within the context of racially-policed remote towns. We argue for a revision of the political economy of gambling spaces to afford Aboriginal groups greater ownership and control of the spaces that they support financially. We compare gambling spaces in the NT with examples of Indigenous-controlled gambling spaces overseas to identify possible directions for the management of gambling venues in remote Australia. While the differences are stark, we propose a possible direction in the development of locally-controlled Aboriginal gambling venues.

## From Cards to Pokies

Aboriginal card gambling has formed a part of Aboriginal social relations in the NT for at least two-hundred years.⁷ Card gambling usually takes place in large groups of up to a dozen people, often kin, playing in public areas or private dwellings.⁸ Because such games are non-commercial in nature, stakes gambled tend to be redistributed among the players involved.⁹ On one hand, card gambling can serve specific positive social ends, such as the reduction of financial inequality and the creation

---

⁵ Young, M., Lamb, D. & Doran, B. 'Gambling, Resource Distribution, and Racial Economy' (2011).
⁶ Lea, T. *Bureaucrats and Bleeding Hearts* (2008).
⁷ Brady, M. *Regulating Social Problems* (2004).
⁸ Goodale, J.C. 'Gambling Is Hard Work' (1987).
⁹ Although there are certainly exceptions to this rule, with an established 'house' taking a cut of wagers, e.g., Robinson, M. & Yu, P. 'A Note on Kuns' (1975).

of resource pools for large purchases.[10,11,12] On the other, it has been associated with negative social consequences stemming largely from the time and money lost during games and the sometimes disproportionate expenditure of winnings on alcohol.[13,14]

The introduction of electronic gaming machines (EGMs, or 'pokies' in the vernacular) into the NT's two casinos in 1981, and subsequently into its network of clubs and hotels in 1996, reconfigured the political economy of Aboriginal gambling. While card gambling continues to be practised in the NT, Aboriginal people have increasingly taken up EGM gambling in the towns where it is available.[15,16] While EGM gambling arguably assists in the reproduction of Aboriginal social relations,[17] the political economy of Aboriginal EGM gambling is vastly different to that of card gambling. To the authors' knowledge, all EGMs in the NT are owned by non-Aboriginal commercial interests, which may even be located internationally as in the case of the two casinos. Their use involves the transfer of cash from already impoverished Aboriginal people to venue owners and governments,[18] a redistributory dynamic identified as problematic in the NT by Aboriginal people themselves.[19,20]

Coinciding with the introduction of EGMs in the NT was a shift in the discourse surrounding Aboriginal gambling. In recent years,

---

[10] Altman, J. 'Gambling as a Mode of Redistributing and Accumulating Cash among Aborigines' (1985).
[11] Altman, J. *Hunter-gatherers Today* (1987).
[12] Goodale, J.C. op. cit.
[13] See, for example, Martin, D. 'Autonomy and Relatedness' (1993).
[14] McKnight, D. *From Hunting to Drinking* (2002).
[15] Foote, R.J. *Aboriginal Gambling* (1996).
[16] Young, M. Lamb, D. & Doran, B. op. cit.
[17] Young, M. Doran, B. & Markham, F. op. cit.
[18] Young, M. Lamb, D. & Doran, B. op. cit.
[19] Christie *et al. Regulated Gambling and Problem Gambling Among Aborigines from Remote Northern Territory Communities* (2009).
[20] Nagel, T. *et al.* 'Yarning about Gambling in Indigenous Communities' (2011).

Aboriginal gambling has become visible to the academy largely through the disciplinary apparatus of the 'psy' sciences.[21] Such research has tended to investigate individual harms and the convenient, discrete category of pathological gamblers, rather than investigating the social uses of gambling or its political economy.[22] Pathology and Aboriginal gambling are similarly synonymous in public policy discourse. As a case in point, gambling was specifically identified by the Federal Northern Territory Emergency Response (NTER) in 2007 as one of the four goods and services on which income-managed funds may not be spent, the implication being that gambling consumption is harmful, wasteful, and tied to a range of social ills that require paternalistic intervention by the state.[23] Indeed, the NTER represented just one example of a continuous series of place-based government policies designed to discipline problematic Aboriginal gamblers.[24]

## Policing of Public Space

The spatial, social, and economic marginalisation of Aboriginal people in the NT is clearly revealed in official statistics. In 2011, Indigenous people comprised an estimated 68,901 individuals or 29% of the total NT population.[25] The majority of the Indigenous population (63%) live outside the Territory's five largest towns of: Darwin, Alice Springs, Katherine, Nhulunbuy, and Tennant Creek where 94% of the non-Indigenous population reside.26 This remote Aboriginal population is

---

[21] For the definition of the 'psy' sciences, see Rose, N. *Inventing Our Selves* (1996).
[22] For example, Breen, H. 'Risk and Protective Factors Associated with Gambling Products and Services' (2012); Hunter, E. *Aboriginal Health and History* (1993); Stevens, M. & Young, M. 'Betting on the Evidence' (2009); Stevens, M. and Young, M. 'Independent Correlates of Reported Gambling Problems Amongst Indigenous Australians' (2010).
[23] Lamb, D. & Young, M. 'Pushing Buttons' (2011).
[24] Lea, T. 'When Looking for Anarchy, Look to the State' (2012).
[25] ABS. *Australian Demographic Statistics, Mar 2012* (2012b).
[26] ABS. *Aboriginal and Torres Strait Islander Peoples (Indigenous) Profiles Datapack, First Release* (2012a).

also the most acutely poverty stricken in the country.[27] For example, less than 50% of Aboriginal adults aged 15-64, are in paid employment compared to 84% of the non-Aboriginal population.[28] Furthermore, colonisation and marginalisation have had devastating effects on Aboriginal health, with Indigenous life-expectancy in the NT 14 years lower for men and 12 years lower for women compared to their non-Indigenous counterparts.[29]

This macro-level segregation and marginalisation is reproduced locally in the racialised bio-politics of public space in the NT's urban centres.[30] While broader government policy aims to centralise Aboriginal populations in 'Growth Towns' and service centres,[31] neo-colonial practices such as 'moving on' make Aboriginal occupation of urban public space problematic. To select but one example from a raft of measures, the Alice Springs Management of Public Spaces By-laws 2009 empower council rangers to disperse groups of Aboriginal people congregating in council controlled areas. Other more standard prohibitions such as those against public loitering or drinking are disproportionately enforced against Aboriginal people. Aboriginal people respond to such intensive policing by remaining in motion in public places and finding refuge in the marginal areas of the remote towns.[32] Inclusionary public spaces are rare.

It is in this context of spatio-racial policing that gambling spaces appear to be fulfilling an important role. While in times past Aboriginal card games on public lawns were often condoned if not explicitly

---

[27] ABS. *National Aboriginal and Torres Strait Islander Social Survey, Northern Territory, 2002* (2004).
[28] ABS. *Population Characteristics, Aboriginal and Torres Strait Islander Australians, Northern Territory, 2006* (2010b).
[29] Australian Institute of Health and Welfare, *Life Expectancy and Mortality of Aboriginal and Torres Strait Islander People* (2011).
[30] Lea, T. *et al.* 'Being Moved (On)' (2012).
[31] Taylor, 'Postcolonial Transformation of the Australian Indigenous Population' (2001).
[32] Lea, T. *et al.* op. cit.

sanctioned, the redevelopment of open spaces and heightened policing has displaced such social gambling gatherings into commercial gambling premises. Increasingly, casinos offer one of the few spaces for Aboriginal social inclusion.[33] Surprisingly, EGM gambling itself facilitates this, at least in part. In interviews the authors conducted with Aboriginal residents of Alice Springs and its hinterland in 2010, our participants indicated that EGM gambling in the casino is a largely pro-social activity. Individualistically-orientated EGM technology is reappropriated by Aboriginal gamblers in Alice Springs to constitute a complex social practice. Aboriginal gamblers tend to use the machines in groups, either with a single gambler playing an EGM and others standing and watching or with a group of associates playing adjacent machines. According to our participants, the distribution of winnings and stakes that inevitably takes place in this context serves to reproduce rather than erode networks of kin relations and obligations.

Thus, while the system of EGM spaces in the NT amounts to an extremely efficient form of capital accumulation,[34] they offer more than just economic exploitation insofar as Aboriginal consumers utilise the space for their own ends and appear to recognise its ideology.[35] EGM venues serve specific cultural and social needs by providing a social space in which cash and co-presence can be appropriated within Aboriginal systems of sharing and obligation.[36] This is reflected in the popularity, in particular, of the NT's casinos. The Darwin casino was noted to accommodate around fifty Aboriginal gamblers daily in 1996, most of whom played EGMs,[37] a number which has anecdotally increased in the intervening decades. The irony is that in the NT's racially managed settlements, one of the key inclusionary spaces are EGM venues,

---

[33] Young, M. Doran, B. & Markham, F. op. cit.
[34] Young, M. Lamb, D. & Doran, B. op. cit.
[35] Young, M. Doran, B. & Markham, F. op. cit.
[36] cf. Sansom, B. *The Camp at Wallaby Cross* (1980).
[37] Foote, R.J. op. cit.

configured as a primary point of social engagement for an otherwise disenfranchised population.

## Towards a New Resolution of the Inclusion-Exploitation Contradiction?

There is a clear tension between the gambling spaces' racialised political-economy and the ways in which Aboriginal social systems transform and re-appropriate them. This produces EGM venues as a contradiction – one that exploits while simultaneously providing a major local space of Aboriginal social inclusion. To this extent the EGM venue, as a cultural form of late capitalism has, at least in surface appearance, achieved something that the public sector has failed to do across remote Australia. However, while the casino offers the consumer palace, the grandest experience white society can offer, it remains costly in terms of Aboriginal economy.[38]

Is there an alternative radical resolution of this contradiction, a reconfiguration of space that will produce social inclusion for Aboriginal people from Central Australia that is not economically exploitative? We suggest that gambling spaces themselves offer great possibility for synthesis of the exploitation-inclusion dialectic. North America furnishes an example of how casinos can economically support Indigenous nations, rather than furthering their impoverishment. After a 1987 Supreme Court case established that Indian reservations are exempt from states' gambling regulations, casinos proliferated on reservations, providing a transfer of wealth from outside the region to support tribal activities.[39] In the United States in 2010-2011, over 200 Indian nations owned 421 casinos, raising more than USD27 billion annually in

---

[38] No reliable data on Aboriginal expenditure in any Australian casino exists. While high-levels of use have been documented in Darwin by Foote, we cannot disregard the possibility that Aboriginal people are merely occupying the casino space while minimising expenditure through small bets. Nevertheless, resource loss remains a concern given the low income levels among this population.

[39] Wenz, M. 'Matching Estimation, Casino Gambling and the Quality of Life' (2007).

revenue.⁴⁰ Gambling in these casinos is generally most popular amongst among older and more affluent white people rather than the Indigenous groups.⁴¹ In an example that is perhaps more pertinent, First Nations in Canada are not exempt from provincial gambling regulation, but instead must be granted a license by provincial authorities prior to establishing a casino. Despite this impediment, the US example led First Nations to lobby for licenses to establish casinos on reserve land. Timed to coincide with the liberalisation of casino licensing in Canada in the 1990s, the First Nations' lobbying efforts were highly effective and profitable First Nations casinos have subsequently been established in almost every Canadian province.⁴²

While concerns have been expressed regarding the Indian and First Nations' casinos potential to increase gambling-harm, little is known about the extent of casinos' negative impacts on residents of reservations.⁴³ Anecdotal evidence suggests increased gambling problems on reservations with casinos,⁴⁴ while an increase in crime rates is also associated with the presence of an on-reservation casino.⁴⁵ In general however, rather than redistributing funds away from Indigenous communities, as is the case in Australia, the development of 'tribal casinos' has arguably been the most successful form of Indigenous economic development in the United States.⁴⁶ Profits from casinos have benefited community development, as they are administered by Indian nations themselves.⁴⁷ Indeed, for the Seminole tribe of Florida, casino gambling has given economic substance to political sovereignty, with

---

[40] National Indian Gaming Commission, *NIGC Tribal Gaming Revenues* (2012).
[41] Rephann, T.J. *et al.* 'Casino Gambling as an Economic Development Strategy' (1997).
[42] Belanger, Y.D. *Gambling with the Future* (2006).
[43] Ibid.
[44] See, for example, Belanger, Y.D. *et al.* 'Casinos and Economic Well-being' (2011).
[45] Evans, W. & Topoleski, J.H. *The Social and Economic Impact of Native American Casinos* (2002).
[46] Cornell, S. 'The Political Economy of American Indian Gaming' (2008).
[47] Ibid.

federal funding of tribal activities falling from 90% to less than 5% with the introduction of a casino.[48]

However, as Nicoll points out, the "situation in Australia could not be more different ... Indigenous people are rarely imagined as potential owners or as direct beneficiaries of gambling revenue and the issues raised by gambling businesses are almost always considered in relation to consumption."[49] The politics of Indigenous economic development and the casino licensing regime in Australia are markedly different to those in North America. As in Canada, Indigenous groups in Australia cannot develop casinos on their own land without state government consent. However, such consent is unlikely to be granted in Australia unless the discourse surrounding Indigenous gambling can be shifted from one of pathology to economic opportunity. Furthermore, given that Australian Indigenous estate covers mostly the remote and sparsely populated parts of the continent,[50] any casino development in the Northern Territory would be unlikely to thrive given the distance to large urban markets, although Aboriginal land holders in New South Wales may be better situated in this regard.[51]

While not providing for the same level of economic development, local ownership and control of Aboriginal EGM gambling venues in the Northern Territory may provide a feasible opportunity to mitigate the regressive political economy of Aboriginal EGM gambling.[52] Local ownership and control might minimise economic expropriation while retaining the attractive features of EGM venues — that is, their ability to provide welcoming and comfortable quasi-public spaces in towns with few alternatives. Given that Aboriginal people already support EGMs

---

[48] Ibid.
[49] Nicoll, F. 'On Talking About Indigenous Gambling and Economic Development in Australia, the US and Canada', (2009), 56.
[50] Pollack, *Indigenous Land in Australia* (2001).
[51] Markham, F. *et al.* 'Estimating the Spatial Extent of Casino Catchments in Australia Using a Trade-area Model' (in press).
[52] Christie, M. & Young, M. 'The Public Problem of "Aboriginal Gambling"' (2011).

venues financially but realise none of the profits, a change in ownership would do little other than to return funds to the communities from which they were extracted. We would suggest that current governance models that remit funds for community development such as those administered by various Land Councils might provide a suitable method for disbursing profits. In addition, an Aboriginal EGM venue might be able to offer other services to its patrons, beyond ameliorating the problem of an Aboriginal public space. For example, sporting facilities might be offered as in other non-Aboriginal clubs.

To be clear, an Aboriginal gambling venue would not be a silver bullet to eliminate all the negative consequences of EGMs for Aboriginal people. For individual gamblers, it would be associated with the same harms associated with existing EGM venues. However, what an Aboriginal-controlled gambling venue would provide is some measure of local control over the use of gambling losses, and the ability to institute harm-minimisation measures that are culturally appropriate to Aboriginal ways of gambling. Essentially, we are arguing here for a transfer of responsibility for gambling to local groups, both in terms of its financial benefits and associated harms. The alternative, simply doing nothing, will continue to see gambling funds removed from Aboriginal control.

Of course, the idea of an Aboriginal-controlled club in the NT is not a new one. While funding was set aside for an Indigenous Sports and Social Club in Darwin, the club was never constructed due to difficulties in accessing suitable land for development.[53] In Alice Springs, the Tyeweretye Social Club was established in 1993 to provide a safe and pleasant environment for Aboriginal congregation and drinking.[54] The club, whose business model revolved around alcohol sales, proved unviable in the absence of a takeaway alcohol license and defaulted on

---

[53] Yilli Rreung Regional Council, *Annual Report, 2000-2001* (2001).
[54] Brady, M. *The Grog Book* (1998).

its start-up loan in March 2005.⁵⁵ Such financial difficulties may be less likely to impede an Aboriginal-owned EGM venue given that the EGM revenue would make it self-sustaining.

Such a venue would undeniably face many challenges. First of all, garnering support for its establishment may prove difficult in an era in which the discourse of Aboriginal gambling is dominated by pathologisation. Second, such a venue would need to ensure that culturally appropriate harm minimisation measures were designed and implemented by Aboriginal members themselves, as it seems unlikely that measures proposed for the general population would be suitable for Aboriginal gamblers in the NT given their unique economic and cultural circumstances. Third, it seems likely that such a venue would also enable non-commercial gambling to take place, which might put at risk the EGM revenues that would fund its operation.

## Conclusion

Gambling spaces are sites of racial contestation over public space in remote Australian towns, itself part of a broader politics of dispossession and neo-colonialism.⁵⁶ Their potential reconfiguration opens a role for the state to supports local policies of self-determination that allow Aboriginal people to appropriate and use public space as they see fit. This agenda would involve free access to public space, the sharing of the right to the city, and the tackling of race relations, public space, and alcohol consumption in a participatory manner as opposed to the current reactive forms of policing currently in place. We stress local here as, while we argue a role for state intervention, the evidence from the Northern Territory is that Aboriginal people have been buffeted by continuous and self-reproducing wheels of macro-policy intervention with no sign of abatement or consequent improvement in living conditions.⁵⁷ This

---

⁵⁵ Thomson, G. 'Former Social Club Set for Bush Camp' (2006).
⁵⁶ Lea, T. *et al.* op. cit.
⁵⁷ Lea, T. 'When Looking for Anarchy, Look to the State' (2012).

would indeed be a radical proposal, in part reversing over 100 years of government prohibition, segregation and moving-on of Indigenous people in Alice Springs. The promise for a radical transformation may lie in the mimicry by the state of the actions of capital. A strange synthesis indeed, perhaps a hopeful one, yet nonetheless revolutionary in remote Australia.

# 18
# A Key Role for Indigenous Peoples in Australia's Sustainable Future

*Seán Kerins*

*Once the government cleared us off our lands by shooting us and putting chains around our necks and dragging us off. Then, long time later, they said "Here's your land back, we don't need it". That tall man he poured the sand through that old man's hands. That made us real happy and we began to move back home. Government gave us a bit of help to get back and set ourselves up. But you know what? They never really took those chains off from round our necks, 'cos now they slowly pullin' on them. They pullin' us off our lands again and yardin' us up like cattle in town. They pullin' us off our land by not giving us schooling, health and housing services on our homelands. They not helpin' us. They sayin' to the parents if you don't send your kids to school we gonna stop your money and send you to prison. But there aren't no schools, so the parents have to move off their country to live like white man in town with no culture.* (Interview, Jack Green, 17 April 2012).

There are about 1,200 small discrete Indigenous communities scattered over Indigenous owned lands throughout the remote regions of Australia, with a total population of about 100,000 people, or about 20% of the total estimated Indigenous population of Australia. A small number of these communities have a population of over 500, while nearly 1,000 have a population of less than 100 each. The larger communities are townships, established during the colonial period as government settlements and missions. The tiny communities are generally referred to as outstations or homelands, or are community living areas on pastoral stations and within some National Parks.[1] Many of the Indigenous peoples living in these

---

[1] Altman, J. 'People on Country as Alternate Development' (2012).

remote regions are providing a variety of environmental services. This work is in the national interest and vital to all our lives, yet their efforts and achievements get little recognition in the media or in government policy. This may be due, in part, to the fact that Australia has one of the most urbanised populations in the world, with about 8 in 10 people living in cities. Many of us who live in Australia's cities pay little attention to what is occurring across the vast remote regions of the continent. It's a place that many of us fly over on our way to somewhere else; a place where our minerals come from and where workers 'fly-in-and-fly-out', rarely settling. Those who do pass through often do so later in life, driving air-conditioned four-wheel-drive vehicles, pulling caravans along the arterial highways or the single-lane beef-roads, staring out at the remoteness waiting for the next settlement to appear. It's almost another country, so different from our periodically parched urban environments and very distant from our busy city lives. Yet, these vast remote regions are intimately tied to our well-being, both in the present and the future.

No matter where we live, we all benefit from the multitude of natural resources and processes that are supplied to us by the ecosystems located within the remote regions of the continent. Together, these benefits are known as ecosystem services.[2] They include things so fundamental to our lives that we often overlook how they function: clean drinking water, carbon sequestration and climate regulation, waste decomposition and detoxification, and crop pollination. Our energy, minerals, food, and pharmaceuticals are all products of ecosystem services. Many of us also draw cultural, intellectual, and spiritual inspiration from the remote regions; they feature in Australian art, stories, songs, and poems with the 'outback' woven through the collective Australian identity.

Crucial to the protection and maintenance of the ecosystem services are the lands of Indigenous Australians. The Indigenous estate comprises between 20 and 30% of the continent, representing as much

---

[2] Millennium Ecosystem Assessment. *Ecosystems and Human Well-being: Biodiversity Synthesis* (2005).

as two million square kilometres of land held under a variety of tenures. Over the last 40 years this land has been returned to its original owners through land rights and native title legislation. Not all of Australia's Indigenous peoples were lucky enough to get back some, or all, of their ancestral land, or have full control of it. Land that had high mainstream economic value in the 18th, 19th, and 20th centuries tended to have been appropriated permanently via free-holding. In New South Wales, the state with the highest Indigenous population, less than one per cent of the land is in Aboriginal ownership. Most of the land returned is in regions where it had little or no commercial value for a variety of reasons such as climate, poor soils, or distance from markets.

For nearly fifty years researchers have documented the limits to sustainable development in remote regions, especially northern Australia and examined the reasons why European Australian attempts at agricultural and industrial development have failed.[3] A study of forestry, agriculture, pastoralism, and mining developments in the Northern Territory found that many European Australian attempts at large-scale development were spectacular failures. That is, they had such a degrading impact on the environment or benefited so few individuals that they could not be seen as successful, with un-costed public and intergenerational costs greatly exceeding even private benefits.[4]

Land returned to Indigenous peoples included places like the Aboriginal Reserves in Arnhem Land, where pastoralism never gained a foothold, and the arid regions of central Australia, long considered the dead-heart by European Australians. This Reserve land was returned without the need for claim. Indigenous peoples outside the reserves managed to get some of their land back by claiming unalienated Crown land and then demonstrating authenticity of attachment, or, when pastoral leases came on to the market purchasing the leases, usually through Aboriginals Benefits Account grant monies, before turning them

---

[3] Davidson, B.R. *The Northern Myth* (1965).
[4] Woinarski, J. & Dawson, F. 'Limitless Land and Limited Knowledge' (2001).

into inalienable freehold property under the Aboriginal Land Rights (Northern Territory) Act 1976. These lands represent places where capitalism never succeeded, or spectacularly crashed and burned through inappropriate large-scale development and a lack of environmental knowledge.[5]

Today, however, these landscapes are of vital importance. This can be clearly demonstrated by overlaying a template of Indigenous-owned lands on to resource atlas maps of Australia illustrating priority regions of high biodiversity value, mean annual water run-off, and the extent of land and river disturbance. This demonstrates Indigenous-owned lands contain significant areas of very high biodiversity significance – essential for developing an adequate and representative system of protected areas within the National Reserve System – along with vast areas of low land disturbance where there remains significant coverage of native forests, scrublands, heathlands, and grasslands.[6] Indigenous lands also contain river systems that are virtually untouched by human development, uninterrupted from their headwaters to their mouths with intact riparian margins. It's not only the high biodiversity value of the land, or, its vast size that is important but also its connectivity, which plays a vital role in providing essential corridors for native animals to freely move about their ranges to various breeding and feeding habitats.[7]

These enormously rich ecosystems, from the monsoonal tropics in the north to the arid lands in the centre, are under threat from species decline, the invasion of exotic species (feral animals and weeds), changed fire regimes, and mining activity. There's a great need to be vigilant, especially at a fine-scale. Ecologists tell us that species are relatively specialised in their roles within ecosystems and their ability to compensate for the specialised activities of another species at its extinction is not always

---

[5] Ibid.
[6] Altman, J. C. Buchanan, G. & Larsen, L. *The Environmental Significance of the Indigenous Estate* (2007).
[7] Woinarski, J. Mackey, B. Nix, H. & Traill, B. *The Nature of Northern Australia* (2007).

optimal, sometimes escalating ecosystem disturbance.[8] The downstream effect of individual species loss and the impact on ecosystem function has been described using an analogy of rivets on an aeroplane wing. If only one species becomes extinct, the loss of the ecosystem's efficiency as a whole is relatively minor. However, when several species disappear, the whole ecosystem may collapse in much the same way as the wing of the aeroplane does after popping dozens of rivets.[9] With Australia having one of the highest global extinction rates of native wildlife there is an urgent need to halt this decline before the downstream catastrophe affects us all, imposing unprecedented economic and social costs.

Significantly, it's not only at the fine-scale with the loss of individual species that Australia's ecosystems are beginning to unravel, but also at a much broader scale where vast regions of diverse ecosystems and habitats are being rapidly degraded. One of the most significant drivers of change on a massive scale is altered fire regimes. This is especially so in regions where Indigenous Australians have been forced off their ancestral lands and moved into townships. Unmanaged landscapes have become characterised by frequent extensive wildfires, occurring in the late dry season and typically under parched, hot weather conditions. The effects can be catastrophic. In places, wildfires annually burn thousands of square kilometres of land. The long-term result of uncontrolled hot fires is evident in many places across Australia where vast areas have lost vegetation. The loss of this vegetation means the loss of feeding and breeding habitats for many species, and has a particularly harsh impact on vulnerable or critically endangered species. Vegetation loss exposes skeletal soils to erosion by monsoonal rains. Furthermore, hot late-season fires emit hundreds of thousands of tonnes of greenhouse gases (methane, nitrous oxide, and carbon dioxide) into the atmosphere, exacerbating global warming.

---

[8] Lawton, J.H. 'What Do Species Do in Ecosystems?' (1994). Naeem, S. 'Species Redundancy and Ecosystem Reliability' (1998).

[9] Ehrlich P.R. & Ehrlich, A.H. *Extinction, The Causes and Consequences of the Disappearance of Species* (1981).

Combine these fine and broad-scale changes with climate change and the future of the ecosystems we all depend on looks bleak. These environmental threats are recently confirmed by the Australia: State of the Environment 2011 report, placing Australia at the crossroads in its journey towards a sustainable future.[10] In choosing which direction to move forward it is important to look at the evidence of what is working to halt or mitigate some of these environmental changes.

## Caring for Country — It's in the National Interest

Just as many of us know little about the ecology of remote Australia, many of us know even less about the Indigenous peoples whose homelands are situated throughout the remote regions. Few Australians can name even one or two Indigenous peoples by way of language group. Instead, Aborigines tend to be perceived as a homogenous population characterised by poverty, ill health, lack of skills, poor education, unemployment, drug and alcohol dependency, inadequate housing and dysfunctional communities, or else living in cultural museums practising a way of life that inhibits their assimilation into mainstream Australian life with its imagined benefits. Such a view fails to take into account numerous successful community-based initiatives across many areas of remote and regional Australia that are providing social, economic, and environmental benefits to Indigenous peoples and, importantly, contributing to the national interest through ecosystem maintenance.[11]

For the past 20 years many of Australia's Indigenous peoples have been playing an essential role working to halt or mitigate drastic environmental degradation through a variety of cultural and natural resource management projects, or what Indigenous Australians term 'caring for country'.[12] Numerous Indigenous community-based initiatives

---
[10] State of the Environment Committee. *Australia: State of the Environment 2011* (2011).
[11] Altman, J. & Kerins, S. (Eds.). *People on Country, Vital Landscapes, Indigenous Futures* (2012).
[12] Kerins, S. 'Caring for Country to Working on Country' (2012).

provide excellent case studies of the sort of caring for country activities which make a valuable contribution to a potentially more sustainable future. I provide brief summaries of such initiatives before turning to a more substantial case study of an Aboriginal community-based development in the highly challenging southwest Gulf of Carpentaria region of the Northern Territory. While these examples are all drawn from the 'Top End', it is important to note there are other caring for country projects similarly providing significant environmental and social benefits in the southern states.[13]

Warddeken Land Management Limited is a company established by Bininj people, charged by customary land owners and managers to protect and manage the cultural and natural resources of the sandstone country of the west Arnhem Land Plateau. It manages the Warddeken Indigenous Protected Area, a region of international biodiversity and cultural significance encompassing over 13,000 square kilometres of land. Warddeken, along with Indigenous and non-Indigenous partners, was instrumental in developing the West Arnhem Land Fire Abatement project. This intercultural project is contracted to abate at least 100,000 tonnes of carbon equivalent greenhouse gases per year for the 17 year life of a liquefied natural gas plant based in Darwin and operated by ConocoPhillips. From 2006 ConocoPhillips have contributed about $1.2 million per year to off-set emissions from their plant. This project has exceeded the initial target of abating 100,000 tonnes of carbon equivalent greenhouse gases per year – since 2006 abating an average 140,000 tonnes. The Indigenous partners are currently working to reshape this project from the original agreement to one recognised under the Australian Government's Carbon Farming Initiative, which would create tradeable carbon credits from abatement. The West Arnhem Land

---

[13] Hunt, J. 'North to South' (2012).

Fire Abatement project won the inaugural Eureka Prize for Innovative Solutions to Climate Change.[14]

Other successful initiatives include Dhimurru Aboriginal Corporation, established by Yolngu people on the Gove Peninsula in northeast Arnhem Land. For the last 20 years Dhimurru has been trail-blazing in 'both-ways' management; using Yolngu (local Aboriginal) and western scientific knowledge systems in combination to deal with ecological threats such as the highly invasive and ecologically destructive Yellow Crazy Ant. Dhimurru won the 2010 Origin Gold Banksia Award for its success and innovation in managing this pest.[15]

There's the Yirralka Rangers who manage 15,000 square kilometres of land and sea country and are at the coalface of ecosystem decline. Established by Yolngu whose lands sit within the Laynhapuy Indigenous Protected Area, they are witnessing localised dying-off of paperbark trees, a freshwater species, and the growth of saltwater mangroves in their place, most likely due to the impacts of feral animals, such as buffalo and pigs.[16]

In west Arnhem Land are the Djelk Rangers — established by Bininj and Yol peoples in the early 1990s. The Djelk Rangers play a key role in the West Arnhem Land Fire Abatement project, along with undertaking coastal surveillance and biosecurity protection. Operating successfully for over 20 years, the Djelk Rangers manage the Djelk Indigenous Protected Area of 6,672 square kilometres.[17]

---

[14] See Cooke, P. 'A Long Walk Home to the Warddewardde' (2012); Russell-Smith, J. Whitehead, P. & Cooke, P. (Eds.). *Culture, Ecology, and Economy of Fire Management in North Australian Savannas* (2009).

[15] Marika, M. & Roeger, S. 'Dhimurru Wind Bringing Change' (2012).

[16] Marika, B. Munyarryun, B. Munyarryun, B. Marawili, N. & Marika, W. facilitated by Kerins, S. 'Ranger Djäma? Manymak!' (2012).

[17] Rostron, V. Campion, W. & Namarnyilk, I. facilitated by Fogarty, B. 'Countrymen Standing Together' (2012).

## The Garawa and Waanyi Peoples' Development Approach

The Garawa and Waanyi are two closely related neighbouring peoples situated in the south-west Gulf of Carpentaria. They lost all their land beginning in the 1880s during development of the pastoral industry. Those who resisted were shot.[18] Development could be measured by the dramatic increase in the stocking rates, which corresponded to the dramatic decrease in the Indigenous population across the region.[19] To survive, once their land and resources were usurped, some Garawa and Waanyi people were forced to provide their labour for rations and later meagre wages, while others endured life in the mission at Doomadgee, described as "a history of infantilising surveillance underpinned by Australian law".[20] The development of pastoralism in this region was a failure. Its decline is attributed to a number of fundamental barriers to production such as poor grasses, infertile soils, remoteness, lack of infrastructure, low occupancy, and low inputs of capital.[21] This failure provided an opportunity for Garawa and Waanyi peoples to claim some of their land as expired pastoral leases through the Aboriginal Land Rights (Northern Territory) Act 1976. In 1984 they claimed the Nicholson (Waanyi/Garawa Aboriginal Land Trust), and in 1990, Robinson River (Garawa Aboriginal Land Trust). These land trust areas cover some 20,000 square kilometres (see Figure 18.1).

When the land was returned it was in a degraded state. Heavy grazing had, in places, removed vegetation, exposing skeletal soils, and increasing erosion. Feral animals and invasive weeds were also spreading, damaging sensitive habitats and competing with native flora and fauna. No compensation was paid for the damage to the land or for the cost of restoring the land by removing feral animals and weeds. This meant

---

[18] Roberts, T. *Frontier Justice, A History of the Gulf Country to 1900* (2005).
[19] Roberts, T. *Black-White Relations in the Gulf Country to 1950* (2009).
[20] Trigger, D. & Asche, W. 'Christianity, Cultural Change and the Negotiation of Rights in Land and Sea' (2010).
[21] Holmes, J. 'The Multifunctional Transition in Australia's Tropical Savannas' (2010).

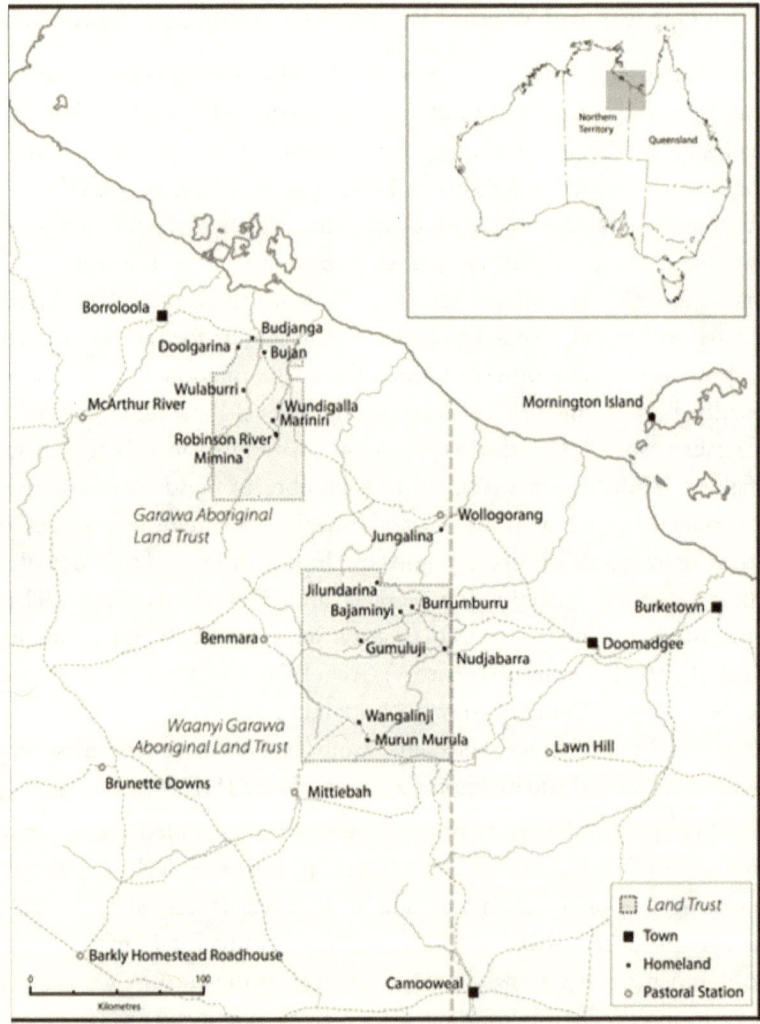

Figure 18.1 South-west Gulf of Carpentaria (Courtesy: S. Kerins & J. Hughes).

that when Garawa and Waanyi families returned to their land they had degraded natural capital, no financial capital and, in some cases, little social capital after decades of mission life, making their development aspirations extremely difficult to achieve.

The families who moved back on to the Nicholson from the mission in Doomadgee and other places where they felt corralled tried to make a living, but it was tough. Supported by the Australian Government Community Development Employment Program (CDEP), they were running small herds of cattle for domestic consumption, keeping gardens, and hunting and fishing. The CDEP scheme provided the equivalent of participants' unemployment benefits as a block grant to community-controlled organisations, which used these funds according to local decisions for community development and employment. At first, they were receiving health, education, and housing services through the Burramana Resource Centre based in Tennant Creek, some 600 kilometres to the west. For a number of reasons service delivery started to break down in the mid-1990s. Without basic services, families were again forced to move off their country.[22]

As the people moved back to regional townships and over-crowded housing, the region began to experience destructive late dry season wildfires; some fires were extending over 16,000 square kilometres – further degrading habitats, emitting carbon, and placing increased pressure on native species. The wildfires were also burning out feed on neighbouring pastoral properties, making marginal properties' economic existence even more difficult. Tensions between residents of the southwest Gulf were further exacerbated by claims that Indigenous people had lit the fires.

In 2004 the region was declared a fire natural disaster area by the Australian Government, and senior Garawa and Waanyi saw an opportunity to convert this major environmental threat to their benefit. In 2005, working with the Northern Land Council, land owners and managers began a series of community-based planning meetings, which are still occurring across the region as projects progress and in-depth consultation continues. These meetings can involve dozens of families

---

[22] Green, J. & Morrison, J. facilitated by Kerins, S. 'No More Yardin' Us Up Like Cattle' (2012).

and almost always have the right 'owners' (Minggirringi) and 'managers' (Junggayi) for specific estates. They are often held on country away from the stress of township life and where people can see the changes occurring to their country from environmental threats, or associated absence of customary practices. These types of meetings are important. They provide opportunities for wider kin groups to reconnect and make decisions about managing their property held under a regime where land is not individually titled but held as common property. At the meetings people work out ways of protecting their country and its biodiversity, and in the process create employment opportunities and accrue benefits to themselves and their communities. Meetings help affirm customary decision making processes and build consensus. They provide an important opportunity for people to take control of their future development. Importantly, they also introduce children to country and facilitate the passing of cultural and ecological knowledge between generations.

These community-based projects are also attempts to resist government domination of Aboriginal lives. As Green and Morrison say:

> The government sees our future in the towns, living like white people, speaking English with no culture and no law. This is the way ahead they say. But we don't see it. It's our culture and law that give us strength to move into the future the way we want to. This region is our home; this is where we are from, where we were created. Our roots are deep; they go a long, long way back to the Dreaming. We don't want to be pulled up inside the town like a tin of sardines. The government has to stop dragging us off our homelands and back into town, yardin' us up like cattle.[23]

Community-based planning, in addition to helping land owners take ownership and set the direction of their own projects, introduce people to new knowledge and information systems, such as remote sensing

---

[23] Ibid.

technology that plays an important role in managing vast areas of land with high biodiversity and cultural values. In using these new knowledge and information systems, in combination with their own knowledge systems, land owners are able to make some decisions about how they would go about replacing this destructive pattern of wildfire with their own customary early dry season patchy-burn fire regime.

These community-based projects are cross-cultural collaborations, building relationships with a variety of agencies such as philanthropic organisations, research institutions, and some government agencies. One important collaborative partnership is Bushfires Northern Territory and the Tropical Savannas Co-operative Research Centre (1996-2010), who, working with land owners, placed over 50 monitoring sites on Aboriginal lands to measure greenhouse gas emissions. These fuel load monitoring sites provide valuable data for future carbon trading initiatives.

In 2006, Garawa and Waanyi peoples won competitive Australian Government natural resource management funding, first through the Natural Heritage Trust and then the Caring for our Country program. This provided vital financial resources to establish two ranger groups – Garawa Rangers and Waanyi/Garawa Rangers – and implement their own land management plans, resulting in significant change to the destructive fire regime across the region and creating meaningful employment for some of their people. Prior to the mid-1990s Aboriginal landowners had little success in obtaining land management funding because mainstream programs were targeted mainly to highly degraded agricultural land in long-settled areas, and a clientele of commercial operators. Little Aboriginal land was located in these target areas and the types of degradation found on Aboriginal land and their remedies differed.[24]

Garawa and Waanyi peoples in the last five years have dramatically altered the destructive fire regimes of the south-west Gulf, something

---

[24] Young, E. Ross, H. Johnson, J. & Kesteven, J. *Caring for Country* (1991).

that Bushfires Northern Territory working alone had failed to do for over a decade. In its place they have implemented an early dry season mosaic-burn fire regime, which is significantly more beneficial to flora and fauna fecundity and importantly emits far less greenhouse gases. Data from the monitoring sites indicates that there has been a 32% reduction in greenhouse gas emissions since this fire abatement project began.[25] This is a significant breakthrough, almost matching the 34% reduction achieved by the highly successful West Arnhem Land Fire Abatement project and opening up commercial opportunities for carbon trading and income generation.

Garawa and Waanyi peoples are building on their success by developing an Indigenous Protected Area plan of management for Nicholson River, which may see some of their land included within Australia's National Reserve System, further generating income and employment opportunities. This plan is beginning to detail aspirations for small-scale enterprises, such as feral animal management and cultural and environmental tourism, along with environmental monitoring projects. Discussions have also recently begun between neighbouring language groups in the southwest Gulf to develop a land management company to facilitate regional decision-making for sound environmental governance, employ people, hold funds, and importantly to invest income from land management activities back into community development.

It is through community-based projects, which recognise and build on cultural knowledge, reinforce kin relationships and customary law, create employment, and introduce new knowledge and skills, while also protecting the environment, that some Garawa and Waanyi leaders see themselves as empowered to take control of their own futures in a manner they define and control and in a way that has meaning to themselves.

Green and Morrison outline some fundamental reasons for project successes to date:

---

[25] Cameron Yates, Bushfires NT, personal communication e-mail, 18 October 2012.

The way we started the caring for country projects, making sure that all the right people, the owners and managers, were at the meetings, was important as it laid the foundation for how we do business, Aboriginal way. It's because of this that the program has wide community support. The land owners see the rangers as working for them, under their direction and with their permission. It sounds simple, but it never happens when government works with us. They overrule us, tell us what should happen and choose who to talk to. They don't seem to know that we are different peoples, they just see us as all the same, poor and black.[26]

## Some Lessons and Future Directions

Some valuable lessons can be learnt from Indigenous caring for country. The most significant is that when Indigenous peoples' aspirations, knowledge, cultures, and skills are given priority in project development they often succeed. In addition, where outsiders participate in these Indigenous-led projects instead of making Indigenous peoples participate in externally defined, top-down government programs, as is the dominant practice, both Indigenous socio-economic circumstances and biodiversity outcomes can improve.

While the environmental work of remote-living Indigenous peoples is in the national interest, it remains on the margins of debates about climate change, biodiversity loss, changes in water availability, and resource depletion. Government spends billions on plans it dreams up for Indigenous affairs. Yet so much flows into the excessive architecture of top-down government 'development' programs that have demonstrated little success, with only a trickle flowing via the Commonwealth Environment Department into these successful Indigenous community-based development initiatives.

Surely, it's time to start looking at the evidence of what's working for many Indigenous peoples and their communities, to understand

---

[26] Green, J. & Morrison, J. facilitated by Kerins, S. op. cit.

why it's working, and then begin developing policy frameworks to build on this success: creating broader opportunities for public and private investment, intercultural collaborations and problem-solving towards a more sustainable future. It is, afterall, in all our interests: black, white, local, national, and global.

# 19
# The Social Benefits and Costs of Indigenous Employment

*Nicholas Biddle and Kirrily Jordan*

## Introduction

One contested issue in Indigenous affairs is how far increased participation in mainstream employment is necessary to overcome disadvantage and what government should (or should not) do to encourage more Indigenous people into paid work. In the dominant discourse, engagement with the mainstream labour market is the primary means to improving Indigenous lives; a 'responsible' adult earns income through paid work or enterprise rather than relying on the welfare safety net.[1] Benefits of paid employment include: increased income and economic independence; skills development; expanded social networks; and improved self-esteem. It is not surprising that high-profile advocates argue strongly for increased Indigenous participation in paid work. However, there may also be costs associated with paid employment. For example, recent research suggests there might be particular tensions between the daily demands of paid work and some cultural and kinship obligations. Furthermore, even where employment does have a net non-economic benefit, certain types of work might deliver this more reliably than others. This chapter seeks a 'middle ground' in the debate about Indigenous employment. We suggest building on emerging research that explores ways in which Indigenous well-being and paid employment

---
[1] Anderson and Mundine each have spoken about the importance of employment in this volume.

may conflict and identifies the kinds of work – and work practices – that might better match diverse Indigenous attitudes, experiences, and aspirations.

## A Snapshot of Indigenous Employment

While there is considerable variation amongst the Indigenous population in terms of employment status, one of the defining characteristics is that in almost all parts of the country, an Indigenous person is less likely to be employed than a non-Indigenous person.[2] However, while Indigenous Australians are overrepresented among those out of work and living on low incomes, there is a recognition that Indigenous people are increasingly entering the professions. This is noted in debates about an emerging (predominantly urban) Indigenous 'middle class'.[3]

Data in Figure 19.1 clearly show that employed Indigenous Australians are more likely to be at the upper half of the income distribution compared to those who are not. This difference is especially pronounced for males. Median weekly income in 2011 for the total Australian population was around $577. A standard poverty line in Australia is half the median, meaning that all those with an income below the $300-399 income group could be classed as having an income low enough to potentially be in relative poverty. Using this cut-off, 72.3% of Indigenous males who were not employed had a low income, compared to 13.0% of those who were employed. For females, about 58.2% of the population not employed had a low income compared to 16.7% of those who were employed.

---

[2] However, such general statistics can obscure rather than illuminate the varied experience of the Indigenous population. Indeed, just as public discussion of socio-economic disadvantage can reinforce the misconception that most Indigenous Australians live remotely, so too can it reinforce the false notion that all Indigenous people are equally likely unemployed.

[3] Lahn, J. 'Aboriginal Urban Professionals and 'Middle Classness'' (in press).

Figure 19.1

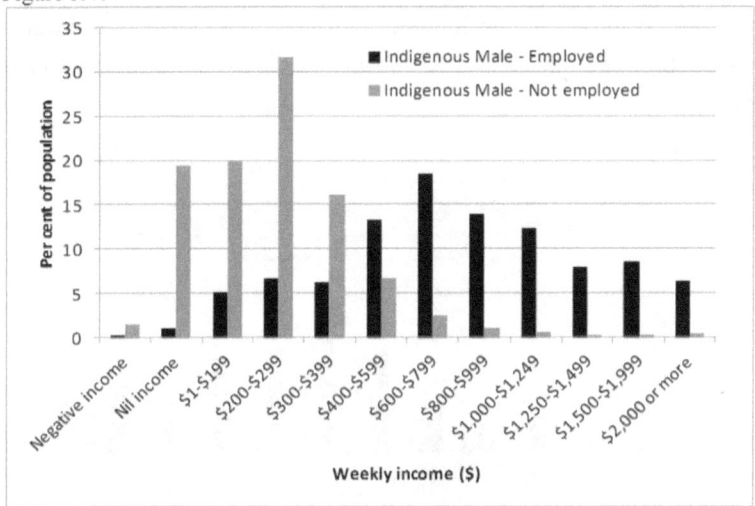

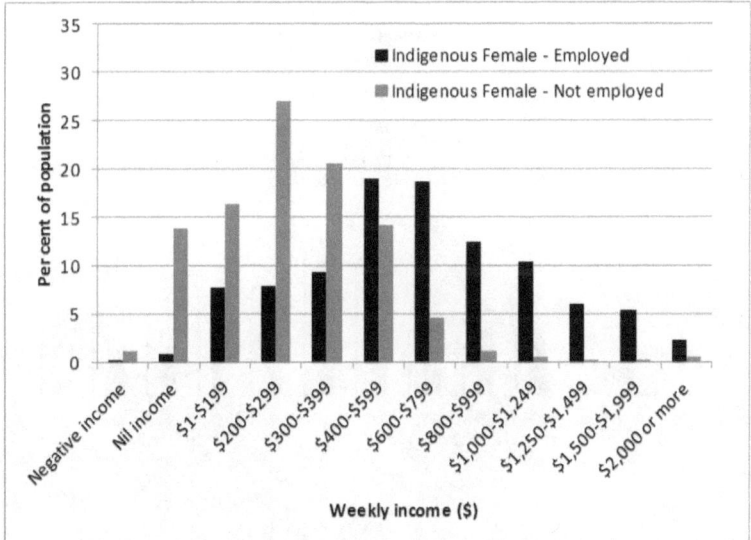

Figure 19.1 Proportion of population by income and employment, 2011.
Source: Customised calculations based on the 2011 Census.

However, it is also true that an employed Indigenous Australian will tend to have a lower income than an employed non-Indigenous Australian. This is demonstrated in Figure 19.2. Just as there was a larger difference in income by employment for Indigenous males, there is also

Figure 19.2

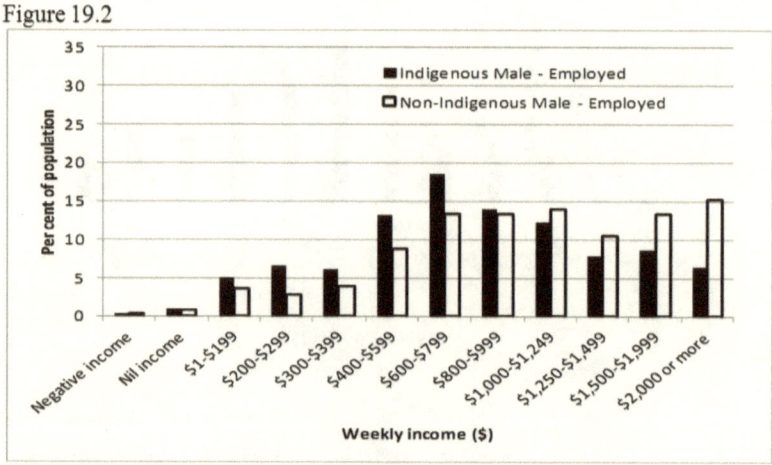

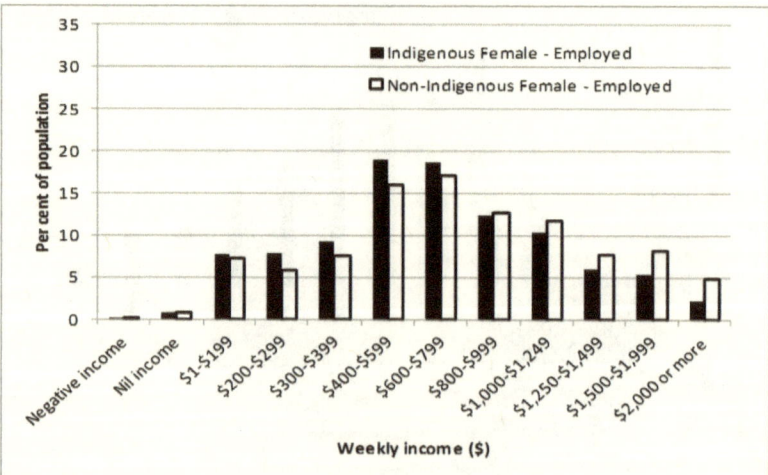

Figure 19.2 Proportion of employed population by income and Indigenous status, 2011.

Source: Customised calculations based on the 2011 Census.

a larger difference in income between an employed Indigenous male and an employed non-Indigenous male compared to employed Indigenous and non-Indigenous females. Focussing on the upper-end of the income distribution, 28.6% of employed non-Indigenous males have an income of $1,500 or more per week, nearly twice the rate of employed Indigenous males (15.0%). Having such high incomes is less common for Indigenous and non-Indigenous females (7.5% and 13.1% respectively).

While income is important for accessing financial resources (either for an individual or their family/kinship networks), it is only one aspect of a person's well-being. Further, well-being is conceptualised differently by different people, depending on factors such as upbringing and cultural background. While increasing employment and income for disadvantaged Aboriginal people has appeal, it should be explored carefully.

## The Relationship Between Employment and Indigenous Well-Being

The ABS defines well-being as a "state of health or sufficiency in all aspects of life".[4] Well-being is a broader concept than socioeconomic status and is notoriously difficult to include in academic analysis because it can be understood in so many ways. It is often deemed to include both 'objective' and 'subjective' well-being. Gasper describes these simply as 'non-feeling aspects' (such as income or longevity) versus 'feeling aspects' of well-being.[5]

Income is often considered an 'objective' measure of well-being, with well-being research also emphasising broader indicators of 'subjective' well-being. The mainstream social and behavioural sciences literature tends to rely predominantly on two main notions of subjective well-being.[6] These are the balance between a person's positive and negative

---

[4] ABS. *Measuring Wellbeing* (2001).
[5] Gasper, D. 'Human Well-being: Concepts and Conceptualizations' (2004).
[6] Kahneman, D. & Krueger, A.B. 'Developments in the Measurement of Subjective Well-Being' (2006).

feelings over a particular point in time (emotional well-being), as well as how they feel about their life and the extent to which it has met and is meeting their expectations (life evaluation).

It is often argued, that there are particular aspects of well-being relevant to Indigenous peoples that are not readily apparent in non-Indigenous people. According to the United Nations Permanent Forum on Indigenous Issues, these include "control of territories, lands and natural resources", "promotion of Indigenous languages", the "inclusion of hunting and gathering practices in modern economic systems (economic pluralism)", and the "percentage of Indigenous economy generated through traditional subsistence activities".[7] In developing these indicators, the aim was to question dominant approaches to socio-economic development and make international leaders "more culturally sensitive and responsive" to Indigenous peoples' diverse realities and aspirations.[8] This approach draws attention to the fact that measures of well-being are often contentious because they must always prioritise some indicators of well-being over others. A policy or program that improves well-being for one individual or group of individuals might have no effect, or even a negative effect, for others.

Employment has the potential to impact not only on objective well-being but also on broader aspects of subjective well-being. However, the assumption that employment will necessarily improve subjective well-being where deficits exist, should not be taken for granted. To gain an insight into the interplay between employment, cultural norms, and well-being, this section uses available data from the 2008 National Aboriginal and Torres Strait Islander Social Survey (NATSISS) to explore some measures of self-reported well-being among Indigenous Australians by employment status.

The NATSISS was conducted from August 2008 to April 2009, with

---

[7] Jordan, K. Bulloch, H. & Buchanan, G. 'Statistical Equality and Cultural Difference in Indigenous Wellbeing Frameworks' (2010).

[8] Tebtebba Foundation. *Indicators Relevant for Indigenous Peoples* (2008).

broad information collected across a range of demographic, social, health, and economic indicators. Importantly, a number of well-being measures collected were developed specifically for the Indigenous population. The survey has a reasonably large sample size (7,823 Indigenous adults participated in the survey), spread across the geographic hierarchy.[9] Within this adult sample, there were 5,188 Indigenous Australians living in non-remote parts of the country (major cities and regional areas) alongside 2,635 Indigenous Australians living in remote areas (33.7% of the sample).

The well-being measures from the NATSISS used in this chapter (which span some aspects of Indigenous and non-Indigenous notions of well-being) are as follows:

- Happiness – feeling happy in the past four weeks all or most of the time.
- Sadness – feeling so sad that nothing could cheer one up at least a little bit of the time in the past four weeks.
- Cultural – being involved in cultural events, ceremonies, or organisations in the previous 12 months.
- Have a say – feeling that one is able to have a say within the community on important issues all or most of the time.
- Raise $2k – feeling that household members could raise $2,000 in an emergency within a week.
- Discrimination – reporting that in the past 12 months a person was treated unfairly because they were Indigenous.

While this list obviously does not capture all of the potential costs and benefits of employment identified earlier, it is useful because it provides a limited amount of survey data with which we can compare responses

---

[9] The survey was administered via Computer-Assisted Interviewing (CAI) and went through extensive pre-testing and field-testing.

by employment status. Specific measures designed to capture elements of Indigenous well-being include questions on cultural participation and experiences of discrimination due to a person's Indigenous status. The focus on cultural participation goes some way to addressing questions of "work-family conflict",[10] at least in the sense that employment commitments may sometimes compete with other cultural obligations in the allocation of people's time. Discrimination, as reported here, is not necessarily restricted to discrimination either in a job or while looking for work, but the data do allow analysis of the relative experience of discrimination by employment status. While firm conclusions cannot be drawn, the more general indicators, such as happiness or sadness, may capture some of the additional concerns such as whether participation in paid work adds to or detracts from feelings of purpose or self-esteem.

Findings from the NATSISS are that those who are employed are more likely to report higher levels of well-being than those who are not employed. This includes:

- A higher probability of reporting that they were a happy person all or most of the time.
- A lower probability of reporting that they were so sad that nothing could cheer them up.
- A higher probability of being able to have a say within the community.
- A higher probability of being able to raise $2,000 within a week in an emergency.
- A lower probability of being treated unfairly in the past 12 months (compared to those who were unemployed).

While these results may be expected, they do not, of course, prove that employment causes higher levels of well-being, even as it is measured by the variables available in the NATSISS. There may be other observable or

---

[10] This topic is discussed later in this chapter.

unobservable characteristics that influence both employment and well-being. However, the results do show that from a predictive point of view, those who were unemployed or not in the labour force were most likely to report lower levels of well-being on these measures. At least some of this difference is likely to be causal. However, an interesting finding is that the type of employment matters. Those in CDEP employment had significantly higher levels of self-reported happiness and cultural participation than those in non-CDEP employment. They were also significantly more likely to report being able to have a say within the community on important issues than those in part-time, non-CDEP employment. For two of the other variables (self-reported sadness and financial security), it was those in full-time, non-CDEP employment that had the most favourable outcomes.

If one focuses only on financial security, the results give qualified support for the notion that well-being could be improved if people moved to non-CDEP employment. However, there is also evidence that there will be potential costs in terms of lower cultural participation and self-reported happiness. Consideration should be given to ensuring that positive aspects of CDEP employment are maintained or strengthened in the mainstream labour market.

## Employment, Unemployment, and Their Social Consequences

Paid work clearly has financial benefits, such as promoting economic independence and the ability to meet basic material needs. However, a large number of studies have also sought to identify non-financial benefits associated with employment. Social psychologist Marie Jahoda, has identified five 'categories of experience' facilitated by employment and sees these categories of experience as 'required' psychologically; that is, as basic and potentially universal human needs.[11] The five categories are:

---

[11] Jahoda, M. *Employment and Unemployment* (1982).

- the imposition of a time structure;
- the enlargement of scope of social experience beyond the family;
- participation in a collective purpose or effort;
- the assignment of status and identity; and
- the requirement of regular activity.

In psychology, sociology, and economics it is widely accepted that paid work can contribute to a range of benefits including: expanded social networks, a sense of collective purpose, improved status and self-esteem, positive identity, and a sense of satisfaction from regular participation in productive activity. Conversely, being out of paid work (especially for long periods) can be associated with reduced mental and physical health, increased financial stress and social disconnection.[12] The notion that employment has broad social benefits, and the associated idea that unemployment is likely to produce social ills, has clearly been influential in Australian policy debates. Many researchers have identified long-term unemployment as being especially detrimental to well-being. One school of thought about long-term, and especially intergenerational, unemployment draws on the work of Mead, who argues that long-term unemployment becomes self-perpetuating through successive generations, with children of unemployed parents being socialised into a non-working environment; a 'culture of poverty' – lack of commitment to consistent employment, and relying on welfare payments – all but condemns younger generations to a disadvantaged future.[13]

In Australia, the culture of poverty argument has found traction in concerns about 'welfare dependency', particularly in Indigenous affairs. While this concept is rarely explicitly defined, it embodies the idea that

---

[12] Harris, E. & Morrow, M. 'Unemployment is a Health Hazard' (2001); McClelland, A. 'Long-Term Unemployment' (1993); Warr, P. *Work, Unemployment and Mental Health* (1987); Winkelmann, L. & Winkelmann, R. 'Why are the Unemployed So Unhappy?' (1998).

[13] Mead, L. 'Welfare Reform and the Family' (2012).

unless unemployed welfare recipients are required to do active work in return for their payments, they become conditioned to idleness and dependence on the state. For well over a decade, both major political parties have represented themselves as supporting active welfare policies that seek to propel more people into paid work.

Noel Pearson argues that "passive welfare dependency" is the primary obstacle to overcoming Aboriginal disadvantage in Cape York: where income support is paid without the requirement that able-bodied recipients undertake productive activity in return, it undermines people's sense of personal responsibility and induces disempowerment and passivity.[14] While income support can help ease the financial strain of unemployment, it will tend to exacerbate its more intrinsic effects on self-esteem and self-confidence by sending recipients the message that "there's something about you that means you have to have extra assistance".[15] For Pearson, the implications of passive welfare dependency are so profound that unless it is reversed "it will inevitably cause the disintegration of our communities and the annihilation of our culture".[16]

To encourage personal responsibility, Pearson argues that economic, social, and cultural development in Cape York Aboriginal communities must be achieved through engagement with the "real economy". This is effectively defined as the market economy, "real" jobs in the mainstream labour market and private asset accumulation.[17]

## Can Paid Work be Detrimental?

It is certainly true that many remote Aboriginal communities are faced with serious social pathologies, and there is widespread recognition – including from many Aboriginal people – that passive welfare – "sit-

---

[14] Pearson, N. 'Our Right to Take Responsibility' (2000a).
[15] Cape York Institute for Policy and Leadership (CYI). 'Freedom, Capabilities and the Cape York Reform Agenda' (2005).
[16] Pearson, N. 'Passive Welfare' (2000b).
[17] CYI. op. cit., 4, 11.

down money" — is a major contributor. However, there are a number of reasons why many Indigenous people might experience particular tensions between some kinds of paid work and other roles.

While the dominant political discourse emphasises the benefits of paid work, there is a substantial body of academic literature that questions whether all kinds of work have positive effects. Several studies have suggested that 'inadequate' work — whether it is intermittent, poorly paid or insecure — as well as excessive or unsatisfying work can actually be damaging for mental and physical health.[18]

Jahoda has argued that although employment tends to be better for mental and physical well-being than unemployment, paid work under some circumstances can be problematic and even 'inhumane'. This includes employment at very low wages not sufficient to extricate people from poverty, and working conditions that create 'psychological burdens' of their own kind. If the labour market is a reflection of the dominate culture in which it resides, then cultural differences should be considered when dealing with groups whose practices and world views (or aspects of it at least) differ from the dominant culture. For example, consider the problem of 'work-family conflict'.[19] Prominent among organisational researchers and psychologists, this means 'the extent to which experiences in work and family are mutually incompatible'.[20] Work-family conflict occurs when commitments in one role inhibit performance in the other. This may be due not only to competing claims on a person's time but also to the transference of stress between roles or application of a behaviour useful in one role to the other where it is counterproductive.[21] A growing

---

[18] Faragher, E.B. et al. 'The Relationship between Job Satisfaction and Health' (2005); Prause, J. & Dooley, D. 'Effect of Underemployment on School-leavers' Self-esteem' (1997); Sparks, K. et al. 'The Effects of Hours of Work on Health' (1997); Wooden, M. et al. 'Working Time Mismatch and Subjective Well-being' (2009).

[19] Bellavia, G.M. & Frone, M.R. 'Work-family Conflict' (2005).

[20] Greenhaus, J.H. et al. 'Health Consequences of Work-family Conflict' (2006).

[21] Greenhaus, J.H. & Beutell, N.J. 'Sources of Conflict between Work and Family Roles' (1985).

body of work points to the potential for negative impacts of work-life conflict on physical and psychological health.[22]

Much of the literature on work-family conflict focuses on 'Western' nuclear families, which some believe has limited relevance to non-western peoples, including many Indigenous Australians. Morphy argues that Indigenous people in much of remote Australia operate in "extensive, overlapping kinship networks" rather than relatively contained nuclear households.[23] While the "tide of history" has of course altered understandings of "kinship ties" and their meanings, their importance for Indigenous Australians in urban areas may be no less profound. Demographic research also shows that Indigenous households tend to be relatively large.

On the one hand, having responsibilities to larger households or kinship networks may increase the demands on individuals in their domestic roles. On the other hand, it is also possible that larger kinship networks may reduce time pressures by sharing responsibilities for domestic and caring work. Some added considerations are the relatively young age profile of the Indigenous population – which translates into a larger average number of dependent children per adult – and the overrepresentation of Indigenous people among those with disabilities and chronic illnesses. While it is impossible to be definitive about whether these factors are offset by any tendency to share caring work among larger family networks, one study suggests that, on balance, Indigenous Australians are overrepresented among those caring for others.[24]

Perhaps more importantly though, responsibilities to extended kinship networks may also take on a qualitatively different character to those experienced by non-Indigenous Australians. This brings us to a key concern: the influences of culture and socialisation on Indigenous attitudes to, and experiences of, paid work. Some of the literature on

---

[22] Bellavia, G.M. & Frone, M.R. op. cit.; Greenhaus, J.H. *et al.* op. cit.
[23] Morphy, F. 'Uncontained Subjects' (2007), 165.
[24] Edwards, B. et al. *The Tyranny of Distance* (2009), 6.

the costs and benefits of employment does identify the significance of cultural factors. While Jahoda has been criticised for failing to adequately acknowledge that her analysis is culturally contingent, she does recognise that basic psychological needs can also be met in other ways.[25] While these needs are most often met in modern industrialised societies through paid work, in other societies religious and social rituals may meet them:

> the psychological functions of employment are met by rituals, religious and community practices, which provide the time experiences appropriate to that society, sharing of experience, recognition of collective purposes, a clear identity and the need for some activity.[26]

Employment, or the experience of looking for work, can also expose a person to a range of potential negative experiences including discrimination and harassment. While the effects of discrimination on labour supply are somewhat ambiguous, a meta-review by Pascoe and Smart Richman[27] found strong evidence for there being a negative effect of discrimination on physical and mental health; this "may occur through the mechanisms of stress responses and health behaviours".[28]

Drawing on Hofstede's cultural theory, Liu and Spector have argued that a key difference in how people relate to work stems from being in either a collectivist or individualist culture.[29] People from collectivist cultures see adherence to cultural norms as more important than maximising their individual interests. From this perspective the "primary task ... is to fit in, to engage, to belong or to become part of the relevant social relationships".[30] So, particular work-family tensions arise for 'collectivist' employees if their cultural norms are a poor fit with

---

[25] Jahoda, M. op. cit.
[26] Ibid., 59.
[27] Pascoe, E.A. & Richman, L.S. 'Perceived Discrimination and Health' (2009).
[28] Goldsmith, *et al.* 'The Labor Supply Consequences of Perceptions' (2004), 547.
[29] Liu, C. & Spector, P.E. *International Issues* (2005), 496.
[30] Ibid.

workplace practices or expectations, and they will be more likely to put their cultural commitments first.

A number of recent Australian studies identify tensions between the demands of paid work and Indigenous patterns of relatedness and social obligation:[31,32] the real 'work' for many Indigenous people is the ongoing negotiation, mediation, maintenance, and affirmation of social and cultural relationships. McRae-Williams and Gerritsen argue that, among Aboriginal people in the remote Northern Territory community of Ngukurr, these processes take considerable time and energy and are usually prioritised over employment commitments. This reflects the 'Ngukurr Aboriginal world view': work "primarily managing social relatedness and autonomy ... reaffirming ties is equally if not more important than attendance at the formal workplace".[33]

Gibson has examined attitudes to paid work among Aboriginal people in Wilcannia in regional New South Wales.[34] Here, too, paid work and its benefits 'sit uneasily' with the demands of relatedness and sociality, so that while many people recognise that wages would increase their access to desired material items, few are prepared to make paid work their day-to-day priority if it means forfeiting "other culturally perceived and culturally attributed values, social obligations and desires". To meet one's social and moral obligations in Wilcannia, as in Ngukurr, one must productively 'work' outside the sphere of paid employment: taking a grandmother to the doctor or an aunt shopping; attending a funeral; or staying with relatives to prevent an argument or just because they need you to be there.[35] There appears to be "a take it or leave it attitude to employment as well as a prioritisation of other things".[36]

---

[31] Austin-Broos, D. '"Working for" and "Working" among Western Arrernte in Central Australia' (2006).
[32] McRae-Williams, E. & Gerritsen, R. 'Mutual Incomprehension' (2010).
[33] Ibid., 18.
[34] Gibson, L. 'Making a Life' (2010).
[35] Ibid.
[36] Ibid., 148.

Such attitudes are very deeply ingrained. According to Gibson, not only do they reflect the centrality of relatedness in Aboriginal personhood but, at least in the Wilcannia context, they have also become a 'companion' of Aboriginal identity. Here, "asserting blackness often means positioning oneself against whiteness", including against "white ways of working".[37] For most, then, the notion of being regularly employed "as a particular way of looking at life" is "at once peripheral to, irrelevant to, and resistant to the 'business' at hand: that is, the 'business' of being Aboriginal".[38]

Burbank has suggested that ways of being that collide with western work practices may be ingrained not only socially, but also neurologically.[39] Drawing on recent research that brings together ethnography and neuroscience, he points to the observation that early learning – such as the socialisation that occurs in families – is "instantiated in patterns of the brain's synapses" and becomes both "enduring and highly motivating". Since Aboriginal children are less likely than Western children to be socialised to set aside personal feelings or familial needs in order to yield to enforced schedules, there is an incompatibility between the Aboriginal cultural self and regimented Western institutions like school and paid work.[40]

## Aboriginal and Non-Aboriginal at the Crossroads

A key point, then, is that notions of 'correct behaviour' and 'achievement' are socially constructed. It is useful here to reflect on the long inculcation of the value of paid work in Western societies, with the idea that paid employment is a 'rational' use of our time a product of particular historical circumstances.[41] As Kral has noted in an Australian context, for

---

[37] Ibid., 155.
[38] Ibid., 148.
[39] Burbank, V. 'From Bedtime to on Time' (2006).
[40] Ibid., 4.
[41] Edgell, S. *The Sociology of Work* (2006), Chapter 1.

some Indigenous people the 'normative logic' of a sequenced pathway involving the individual pursuit of educational credentials and subsequent entry into paid employment is a notion introduced only in very recent generations.[42] It should not be surprising, then, if for many people the much more longstanding adherence to cultural systems in which value and meaning derive from kin-based obligations remains dominant.

Differing Indigenous and non-Indigenous attitudes to paid work clearly give rise to much misunderstanding, if not animosity. It may be difficult for non-Indigenous people to fully grasp the depth of meaning and expectation that Aboriginal systems of relatedness entail in practice.[43] Activities that Aboriginal people perceive as highly productive – especially leaving work to attend to familial needs – may be perceived by non-Indigenous work managers as indulgent. In addition, because the demands of relatedness cannot be left at the door when an employee enters the workplace, it may be 'rational' for them to display what others perceive as unproductive behaviours at work – such as disobedience or disengagement – to position oneself in the ongoing negotiation of kin relations.[44] These can be seen as examples of 'family interference in work', in which behaviours learnt in the family (or non-work) environment inhibit performance in the work role. On the other hand, for many Indigenous people, 'work interference in family' can be particularly intense. Putting work commitments ahead of kinship obligations can sometimes result in strong criticisms that one has abandoned Aboriginality and 'gone whitefella way'[45] and even in being 'disowned' – either temporarily or permanently – by a kinship group. Clearly, in these circumstances, participation in regular paid work may not be a straightforward route to feelings of personal pride, self-worth

---

[42] Kral, I. 'Generational Change, Learning and Remote Australian Indigenous Youth' (2010).
[43] It can even be difficult for some Indigenous people to understand such systems given the diversity of beliefs and experiences of Indigenous people.
[44] McRae-Williams, E. & Gerritsen, R. op. cit.
[45] Gibson, L. op. cit., 150.

and self-esteem. Indeed, where work commitments compromise the ability to support kin in expected ways, a predictable emotional response may instead be one of shame.[46]

## Conclusion

Arguments that high rates of unemployment and welfare dependency are a principal cause of Indigenous social pathologies have had considerable influence on many policy decisions. Most recently, these include the introduction of income management among some groups of welfare recipients since 2007, the removal of CDEP from urban and regional areas between 2007 and 2009, and the series of recent changes to remote CDEP that will culminate in its reformulation as the Remote Jobs and Communities Program (RJCP) in 2013. As this chapter showed, there are advantageous of being employed. The 2008 NATSISS reported that those who were unemployed had substantially lower levels of subjective well-being than those who were employed. In contemporary Australia then, it would appear that the kinds of things that employment offers are valued by Indigenous Australians.[47] However, it was also shown that employment may not always have its intended benefits for some Indigenous Australians. Without wanting to generalise or stereotype, for many Indigenous people, the westernised concept of paid employment may not always be an optimal solution for addressing Indigenous social pathologies. We are at the crossroads.

---

[46] McRae-Williams, E. & Gerritsen, R. op. cit.
[47] Jahoda, M. op. cit.

# 20

# The Rose that Grew from Concrete[1]

*Thomas Draper*

*Did you hear about the rose that grew from a crack in the concrete?*
*Proving nature's laws wrong it learned to walk without having feet.*
*Funny it seems, but by keeping its dreams it learned to breathe fresh air,*
*Long live the rose that grew from concrete when no one else ever cared.*
*You see you would not ask why the rose that grew from concrete had damaged petals,*
*On the contrary, we would all celebrate its tenacity.*
*We would love its will to reach the sun.*
*Well we are the roses, this is the concrete and these are my damaged petals.*
*Don't ask me why, thank god ask me how.*
Tupac Shakur[2]

My name is Thomas Draper – or 'Drapes' as most of my mates know me. I'm a construction supervisor with Arrow Energy and I'm here to talk a little bit about how I got my role at Arrow – and I guess mostly about where I've come from and how I got from there to here.

I was born in Moree in northwest NSW. I grew up on a mission just outside of town in a community riddled with drugs, alcohol, crime, and violence. Growing up on that mission I saw and experienced things that no kid should ever have to! But I'm not here to ramble on about how bad it was – because for as much as I hated that place I have just as much love for it as well. I still have family there. It will always be my home, and

---

[1] This chapter is based on speeches given by Thomas Draper at functions conducted by 'Former Origin Greats'.
[2] Shakur, T. *The Rose that Grew From Concrete* (1999).

beginning to learn my forefathers' language has only strengthened my connection with my land, but it was hard growing up in an environment that was built solely for killing dreams. Those sorts of places trap kids everyday and I guess one reason that I'm not on the dole or living in a prison cell or rotting in a box like so many of my friends that I grew up with can be traced back to one man, my Dad. His name is Peter Draper and that's the reason why I get called Peter as well because I am my father's son. He taught me from a young age the true value of hard work. He told me that in life some people succeed because they are destined to but most people succeed because they are determined to. He told me that if I wanted anything in life I had to get off my butt and work for it. We stayed in everything from a tin shed to a house on that mission and even though my Dad didn't have a proper education or any work skills, he still worked two jobs to make sure we always had what we needed.

He showed me a great work ethic so at the age of eight I started my first job as a newspaper boy. Now because I had to pay for the papers myself just to sell them I was only working for tips, but I used to make around twenty bucks every morning and for an eight-year-old kid that was a lot. It was the first time in my life that I saw the rewards of working, but on the mission and in that environment people didn't like to see others doing well for themselves. They didn't like to see a rose grow from concrete. So for almost two years I got the crap kicked out of me. But then I took up boxing, trained hard and five Australian boxing titles later no one picked on me since.

Dad told me the only thing that Kooris and Murris should be fighting for is better education, to take advantage of an opportunity that his generation never had. So I worked hard, did all my homework and really applied myself and the rewards came. I graduated primary school not only as school captain but as the first Indigenous kid to finish top of the class. I was the first black dux of my region. That's an accomplishment I will always hold high. Especially given the fact that no more than thirty years before that my uncle was the first Indigenous kid in northwest

NSW to attend a public school. As a kid he endured one of the ugliest sides of mankind – he was escorted to class by police. He along with others paved a way for what I could achieve; they paved a way for what you should achieve. The truth is, there was a lot of blood spilt for you to be able to sit in class and get an education or to attend events and openly talk about securing an apprenticeship or a traineeship. If you don't believe me, ask some of the older people around you – they'll tell you exactly what the score is.

When I finished primary school I left there with all these hopes and dreams of becoming a doctor or a lawyer and moving out of the mission to Toowoomba. But when I hit my teenage years I faced the same problem that all teenage kids face, both black and white – the need to feel accepted. I lost my way in a big way. I started hanging around the wrong crowd and doing things I never dreamed of. I know the buck stops with me. I refuse to blame my cousins or my family and friends. It was my problem with drugs and alcohol that I let become an addiction. It was my fists covered in blood because I let violence rule my life. It was my choices that led me to break into people's homes and steal their cars and their belongings. It was my behaviours that I let develop that led me to be on my last strike with authorities. It was only a matter of time before I ended up in jail with so many of my family and friends. It was a life that I felt trapped in; it was like quicksand if you know what I mean. It was a life that I wanted desperately to change but I didn't know how. Until one day a complete stranger pointed me back in the right direction and became the second reason for who I am today.

I remember I was sitting at the front of Village Fair, or Garden Town as it is now known, out front having a smoke, you know, trying my best to look cool, like all the tryhards you see at the front of Grand Central or hanging downtown after dark. This lady walked up and sat next to me. She was an older lady in her late fifties-early sixties and she asked if she could bum a smoke. Now I've never had a problem with sharing so I handed her a smoke and I lit it up and we got to talking. At first it was normal stuff in general and then she hit me with a brick. She looked at me and said, "You were in a car crash weren't you?"

Now to this day I have no idea if she had talked to someone who knew me or if she had heard about me, but the fact is that I was in a car crash. About three weeks before I met her I was lying in an Ipswich hospital with my stomach cut open and pieces of my intestines and body taken out. Because some mates and I, we were drunk and we were high, we decided to go for a drive to Brisbane at 2 o'clock in the morning. We made it down to Brisbane and naturally everything was closed – it was a Tuesday night. So we piled back in the car and headed home. On the way back we all fell asleep, including the driver. I woke up as we were heading off the road at 120 kilometres an hour. We clipped a telephone pole and the car started to roll. I reckon we flipped about 4 or 5 times before the car smashed into a concrete culvert. Thankfully, no one died but we all suffered pretty serious injuries. So I looked at this lady and I said I was in a car crash and I asked how she knew that. Then she looked into me and said, "Have you figured out why God has kept you alive yet?". I remember a chill went up my spine and the hairs on the back of my neck standing up. I said that I'd never thought about it and then immediately as if to change the topic she looked me up and down and said, "You know what? You're a pretty good looking bloke; you should be a model" – and that was when I lost it. I remember laughing, saying that the only woman who thought I was good looking was my mum and she only said that because she was my mum. But she looked at me and said, "Just think about it", and stood up, crushed out her cigarette and walked away.

I remember looking at her as she walked off thinking that that was the weirdest conversation I ever had and thinking that she was nuts. But you know what? I did exactly what she said. I thought about it. I thought about what she had said and her words haunted me. I would spend most of my days and nights thinking about it until it finally dawned on me. Now I don't know whether she was an angel or not but she definitely was a messenger of some sort on behalf of the Big Marn himself to let me know that he wanted me to be a model – and not the kind you see in magazines or on billboards but the kind you see in life. He wanted me to be a role model and that struck deep with me because I was at a point in my life where I didn't need anybody to tell me that I was a loser. But here was someone that wasn't looking at the kid I was; but looking at the man I could become.

Take a good look at the people here today, especially the teachers. I'm guessing that they look at you guys in exactly the same way and they wouldn't like to hear it, but in a way they are angels and they might not be aware of this but they are playing a part in a much bigger picture. You know, of all the places in the world where they could be there is a reason why they are here today. They're not afraid to invest their emotions or their time in you because where others see a lost cause they see everything that you could be. But to get there you will have to make a choice to make change. I decided to change my life. I made a decision to never use the colour of my skin or the circumstances of my life as an excuse to not at least try and succeed.

I graduated high school, just. No honours, no distinctions. Only a deep regret for a wasted education, but I wasn't going to let that stop me. So while most of my school mates were on schoolies walking the beaches of Surfers Paradise, I was walking from business to business, jobsite to jobsite, asking anybody if they needed any workers or a labourer. I picked up work here and there with employers and when the work dried up I kept walking. I came to this one site and the carpenter came out to meet me. I asked him if he needed a worker and I can still remember the look in his eyes. I could tell he was impressed to see a young black kid get off his arse and look for work. He told me that he wasn't looking for a labourer but he was looking for an apprentice if I wanted it. So I jumped at the chance.

Now I'll be honest. I grew up on a mission and it was pretty hard but those four years of my apprenticeship were the hardest years of my life. I put up with a lot of racism from other workers, and I put up with a boss that ripped me off every way he could, and there were days that I didn't want to get out bed. But every time I made myself see the big picture. I kept telling myself, it's only four years and then I'll have a trade; then three years; then two; only one year, only one week and finally the day came when I got my Trade Papers. I remember sitting down at home and holding them in my hands and almost breaking down because I knew how much effort was poured into them.

The next day one of the electricians that usually gave me stick came up to share the latest 'black joke'. I grabbed him by the shirt and told him I was a qualified tradesman and if he came to me with that crap again I would punch a hole clean through him. Needless to say no one ever gave me crap again, at least not to my face. I quit the job and started working for other builders. I've worked for many, many builders and most of them still ring me up to do work for them because they were so pleased with my work ethic and the way I handle myself. I have helped build over two hundred homes, including four of my own. With the help of my wife, we have built and sold three homes together. We are living in our fourth one now at Westbrook with our daughter and niece – and let me tell you when I go home every day and put a key into a door that leads into a house that I own and built with my own two hands, it gives me a sense of pride that is out of this world. It's hard to explain to you, but it feels exactly the way I felt as an eight-year-old kid holding twenty bucks worth of change in my hand and knowing how hard I worked for it.

Do you want to know what the best thing about having a trade is? I can work anywhere in the world. So my wife and I moved to England for two years. I signed with a Rugby League team just outside of Manchester and before I left I stated my terms: along with match payments I wanted a car, a house, and some work as a carpenter. They got back to me within a couple of weeks and told me that it was all organised and to jump on a plane. So we headed over. I played with a team called Rochedale Mayfield in the winter amateur comp and a team called East Lancashire in the summer professional comp. Now, because I took a chance and worked hard no matter what, I've been lucky enough to see more of this world than a kid from a mission could ever dream.

I've sat in the Colosseum in Rome. I've walked where gladiators have walked. I've looked up in the Sistine Chapel and marvelled at Michelangelo's paintings. I've floated through the streets of Venice and watched the sun setting over the ocean from the Greek island of Santorini. I've looked out at Paris from the top of the Eiffel Tower and searched for the Loch Ness Monster in Scotland. I've sailed around the Caribbean. I've been to America, Canada, Thailand, and I have seen so much of this great country of ours that sometimes I think I need to pinch myself – but the one thing that grounds me in reality is knowing how much hard work and sweat I have poured into achieving the things I have. So I guess the question I want to ask is, "If I can do it why can't you?" I'll be brutally honest again. I think that for some kids, both black and white, you are just lazy. You'll always expect everything to be done for you and I can promise you that you'll grow old and bitter because things won't get done for you. But for most of you the reason's a little less obvious. My best guess is that just like I was, you're scared, scared of failing. You're scared of putting in the hard yards and getting knocked back. You're afraid of giving it everything only to be told you don't cut it. Well, I'm here to tell you that there is nothing wrong with that. My dad used to tell me to aim high in life, to always aim for the sky and the worst I'll ever do is end up sitting in a tree. In other words, he meant that if you wanted to be an astronaut and you worked hard at it, gave it everything you had and failed, the worst you'll ever do is end up becoming an airline pilot for Qantas or Singapore Airlines and that's a really good job. Do you understand what I mean? Be more afraid of not even trying because regret is something you will carry till you die.

You know, before I got this job with Arrow I applied for many jobs online. For over a year I came home from work and filled out online expressions of interest and uploaded my resume to a lot of companies. I spent a lot of time on the phone ringing companies asking for a job and for over a year I kept getting knocked back but I didn't let it stop me. I wasn't going to wait and expect for something to come to me.

Early this year I had a rainy day at work and had to go home early. So I rang up my wife and asked if she wanted to go down to Logan to a Careers Expo. So we loaded up the car and went. I remember going to almost every stall and pleading for a job in the coal and gas industry. I told them that I wasn't looking for anything flash, I was just looking to get my foot in the door and I was willing to do anything – making coffees, cleaning toilets, or any kind of labouring. Most stalls except for Arrow and a few others gave me a card and told me to apply online which I had already done. Rachel who worked in Human Resources was at the stall for Arrow Energy and she told me my best option would be to apply for an entry level job as a field assistant. So I applied along with others and she rang me back not long after to tell me a phone interview had been arranged, so how things went from there was now in my hands. So a call came one lunch hour for an interview and I talked to some people at the Moranbah office and basically stated my case and they were really impressed. They asked me if we could meet for a face-to-face interview and when was the best time for them to come down to meet. I told them not to come down and that I would drive up to see them. So I arranged an interview a week later so that I could organise a day's work doing an insurance job in Moranbah to pay for my fuel up. I drove 10 hours up and did the insurance work. I then went to the interview after work and told them everything I had said on the phone and then I just threw it on the line and told them the truth. I told them that I didn't drive 10 hours not to get a job. I basically said that I wasn't going to leave Moranbah empty-handed and that if they didn't have a job for me I was going to leave their office and approach every single company in town and on the way home. I told them that I wasn't cocky but that I just had a lot of confidence in my own abilities. The guys looked at each other and then looked at me and said that they could find a spot for me, no worries.

So I left Moranbah with my foot in the door and I knew my work ethic would only push me higher and it happened before I even started. Rachel rang me back and wanted to know what I had said to the Moranbah office. She said that the guys were surprised and really impressed with the interview. She told me that they wanted to change the job I had from a Field Assistant to an Assistant Construction Supervisor. I was over the moon.

Now most people would say I'm lucky and even I think that at times. But ever since I was around your age I didn't wait for luck to come to me. I made sure I made the most of my opportunities and most of the time I got off my arse and found them. Let me just say that I'm not perfect: I have failed and struggled in areas of my life – one being religion – but I thank God every day regardless and I have never stopped trying to be a positive example for under-privileged kids both black and white because I know how hard it is for you. So don't ever be afraid to ask for help. The teachers around you and the people you see here are addicted to helping Indigenous kids reach their dreams, but it can never start with them believing in you because what they have to offer won't mean a damn thing unless you believe in you and start making some of the hard decisions in life. You know, of all my friends and family that are in jail or have passed away, there's only one thing that separates me from them. Can anyone guess what it is? I will tell you now: it isn't the two inches of steel cage that surrounds them or the six feet of dirt that engulfs them. The only thing that separates me from them is choices and you can make a choice right here today about where you want your life to go – and let's not beat around the bush here, guys: it will be hard. It will be hard because you'll be going against the grain. I guarantee that even some of the people sitting right next to you will do everything in their power to keep you at their level. But if you make the tough choices and you push through the cracks you will become a rose that grew from concrete. I mention that image a lot; it's from a poem that has helped me stick to the hard road. It was written by Tupac Shakur (see introduction).

You know, I love Tupac. I love hip hop and I love sad, sad country music but that's where it stops for me. You see, there is nothing worse than becoming a second-hand version of someone else's culture. Especially when our culture is the oldest surviving culture in the world. Be proud to be Black Australians and don't try to be Black Americans. We have a rich history that is built squarely on one principle, our ability to adapt. You can go out to the centre of Australia, to the desert country, to some of the driest unliveable conditions on the planet and there's blackfellas living there because a long time ago they learned to turn their environment to their favour. Now you kids are coming from some pretty tough environments yourselves, so take some lessons. Push it, bend it, break it, mould it into an environment where you are king. Like I said, guys, it will be tough, but in all fairness I didn't come here to talk to the weak. I came here to talk to the strong. I didn't come here to find followers. Use my experience as a guide, but I am not here to find followers. No. I came here hoping to God to find leaders. I came here to find young Indigenous men and women that are willing to take the knocks and the bumps and still stay on their feet. Because if there is anything that our kids need to see, it's leaders. If you have little brothers and sisters, I can tell you now that what they need to see is that you are willing to forge a path for them to walk, that you are willing to light a candle in the dark. Make a choice to make a change and, who knows, hopefully one day most of you will be standing right where I am trying to convince a bunch of students to become everything that they should be.

Finally, don't ever think this is a one-way street. Let me finish by telling you what I said to a Former Origin Greats gathering of corporate heavies who invest time and effort in Aboriginal employment and training – real jobs for you fellas:

> I thank the FOGs for giving me this opportunity to speak tonight. I can honestly say this is a highlight of my life. I consider it a huge privilege to be able to rub shoulders with the likes of Big Geno [Gene Miles] and other Origin Greats and I consider it an even greater privilege to be able to bump heads with companies

and organisations like yours that are actively invested in recruiting and retaining Indigenous Australians. You know, looking around this room tonight and at the people here it kind of makes me feel like a small fish in a really big river but I grow confidence knowing that we are all swimming in the same direction – because just like you I am committed to igniting a revolution in the minds of our Indigenous youth. It's time for them to rise up and to start taking ownership of their lives and their talents and if there is one thing I would like you to know tonight, it's this. That you guys hold all the cards and you carry all the power to promote change and believe me when I say that your continued support is well and truly going a long way towards closing the gap. You know, I don't want to ruin the mood here tonight and I apologise if I'm weighing in a little heavy – but if you've had the chance to hear me speak to our Murri and Koori kids then you would know that there is a fire within me and it demands that I make the most of this opportunity.

# 21
# Our People Need Careers[1]

*Warren Mundine*

On Australia Day in 1972, four men took a regular beach umbrella and created the Tent Embassy. It is an image that has been embedded into the history of Australia.

When Michael Anderson, Billy Craigie, Bertie Williams, and Tony Coorey formed the Tent Embassy 40 years ago – they put themselves into the history books and became members of a long line of Aboriginal activists. At the time these activists were fighting for sovereignty, as a displaced nation of Aboriginal peoples.

I was 15 years old at the time, and the Tent Embassy symbolised the broader fight for equality for all Aboriginal people – to enable us to make free and informed choices about our lives, about the lives of our children, and for the generations of Aboriginal people to come after them.

We must pay tribute to what the Tent Embassy activists did for us. Their radicalism, and the activism of the people that joined them, brought Aboriginal Rights into the national spotlight. The radicalism of the Tent Embassy was necessary at the time and matched the size of the change that was needed in this country.

But in 2012, radicalism has now moved to the fringes of activism – and I think that is a positive step forward for all Australians. Earlier this year we saw the impact that radical activism had. On Australia Day this

---

[1] This chapter is an edited version of the Yarramundi Address delivered by Warren Mundine at the University of Western Sydney on 29 June 2012.

year we saw a small number of people hijack the Tent Embassy for their own agenda which resulted in ugly scenes in Canberra, including security guards whisking our Prime Minister away into a car, losing her shoe on the way.

These scenes were broadcast all over the country, and all around the world. When those scenes unfolded in Canberra the message of what these activists were calling for was lost in the chaos.

This only damaged the reputation of our country and these radical activists negatively portrayed all Aboriginal people, nationally and internationally.

When a small number of sovereignty activists called for people to take to the streets a very small number of people showed up. Like most other people, the majority of Aboriginal people were home with their families, preparing their kids for the coming school term, or getting ready for work the next day.

Forty years on, and what most people really want to see and want to be part of is a positive change that allows all Australians to play a role in education, employment, economic development, and ending the disparity between Indigenous and non-Indigenous Australians.

And in honouring the spirit of the Tent Embassy forty years later it is up to us, the whole of Australia, to take the opportunities that are now available because of the people who fought for us. We must take those opportunities with both hands, and make them our reality.

When I got the phone call from Andrew Forrest about becoming the CEO of GenerationOne – I knew it was the next logical thing for me to take on. I believe there is only one way to tackle welfare dependency in Indigenous communities and that's to give people the best alternative – a career.

GenerationOne is a national movement of people that believe that employment may not change everything but without it nothing will change. This isn't radical, but it works.

Employment is the single most important factor to economic development and we want Aboriginal people to be training and working in the roles that were seen to be untouchable for so long. As more and more of our young people graduate and become doctors, lawyers, teachers, and political leaders, our focus must remain on those who believe there is no opportunity for them in the modern economy. We must bust that myth, and shake the cycle of hopelessness by helping our people to believe in themselves, and the power they have to live the change they want to see. The change that the Tent Embassy activists and others like them, fought so hard to achieve.

For the first time in our nation's history employers from across Australia have come together through the Australian Employment Covenant to build a demand for an Indigenous workforce.

The 330 employers that have signed covenants are from a wide range of industries: government, hospitality, corporate, education, retail, and telecommunications and many more. From the boardrooms to the shopfronts employers have committed 62,600 jobs, 10,670 people have already taken up the opportunities, with a 70% retention rate to 6 months.

And governments are working towards ending the disparity with us.

The time for welfare reform is now. We need to campaign to help people take up employment and end the handouts that tie them to government – the belief that government will fix all their problems. By embracing the spirit of the Tent Embassy, employment and education become the drivers, with employers enabling people to move off welfare and into employment. Government is a critical partner, and through their policies, must act as an enabler, not an inhibitor. Welfare should not be a safety net, it should be a trampoline sending people back into employment and self-determination.

Warren Mundine didn't arrive here in a vacuum. I got here because my grandfather got a job as a rural worker. Not a pretty job. Not a high paying job. My grandfather got up in the morning, went to work, finished work in the afternoon, and went home. He gave his money to my grandmother who paid the bills, fed the kids, kept the house clean, and sent the kids to school.

My father grew up thinking that was normal. When he left school, he got a job as a plant operator. He got up in the morning, went to work, finished work in the afternoon, and went home. He married and when he got home he gave his money to my mother who paid the bills, fed the kids, kept the house clean, and sent the kids to school.

I grew up thinking that was normal. When I left school, I got a job as a factory worker and trained as a fitter and turner. I got up in the morning, went to work, finished work in the afternoon, and went home. I married and when I got home I gave some of my money to my wife who paid the bills, fed the kids, kept the house clean, and sent the kids to school.

My children grew up thinking that was normal. When they left school, half of them went to uni and half of them went into trades. Half of my children own their own business. They get up in the morning, go to work, finish work in the afternoon, and go home. In their world there is no concept of not working or not getting an education.

That is four generations of employment because my grandfather got a job.

After two years of consultation with Indigenous people, employers and governments in January this year GenerationOne launched the Skills and Training for a Career: Vocational Training and Employment Centres Policy. This policy calls for governments to stop pouring funding into employment programs that do not lead to jobs for Indigenous people.

The VTEC model advocates for employer-directed training; this means the process identifies an employer with a specific job, finds an Indigenous jobseeker, and then trains them to meet the needs of the role and start their career. This would be the reverse of the current process, which identifies the person, then the training, and then hopes there will be a job. As one employer told us, training for training's sake "is like jumping through hoops of hope".

The VTEC model has been used in Western Australia to ensure that Indigenous people who have been long-term unemployed can be supported into employment.

GenerationOne and the AEC have jointly called on the government to fund four Vocational Training and Employment Centres as a trial, with the hope of developing 25 VTEC sites around the country to ensure that the opportunity to engage in the country's economy is open to all people, that training leading to real jobs and opportunities is open to all our children.

If we take a step back and examine the big picture, the activism of our forefathers has contributed to the climate of change that we are currently living in. The education of our children is crucial and just as important as supporting their parents and families into employment.

Thirty-seven per cent of all Indigenous people in Australia are under the age of 15. We have a generation of people who are aspiring to be the next generation of professionals, politicians, tradespeople, and educators. Perhaps the more important role that each of those people will play is inspiring other young Indigenous people to take up the challenge of building a career, undertaking training, and changing the destructive stereotype that is often portrayed in the media.

One of the key roles of GenerationOne is to share success stories about employment, education, and training – showcasing people and organisations that have taken the opportunities and made the choice to move from welfare to work.

In December 2011 GenerationOne published *Case Studies of Success*. This document showcases six of the many employers who are working with the Australian Employment Covenant to end the disparity between Indigenous and non-Indigenous Australians. The pre-employment programs and supported mentoring that are taking place in businesses like Woolworths have seen over 350 people move through the pre-employment training and into positions.

These are the opportunities our people are seizing; these are the opportunities that our children are taking up; and our people will continue to be the change that we want to see – and in the spirit of the Tent Embassy, they too will take up the challenge facing their generation.

## 22

## Real Education, Real Jobs[1]

*Alison Anderson*

I see people, not categories, divisions, or races. I see people and the potential for us all to work together to bring clarity and progress into the world we share. Our task as politicians is to represent the whole community, and that I pledge to do. This is a moment of hope, a hinge in time. It is a long delayed day of promise for all Territorians and for all Australians. The nation is watching us today and it will be watching in the months to come as we chart the course ahead. We will bring resolve and advancement to the bush and knit the different worlds of our Territory more closely together. We are in this together. We are one Territory.

There is a weight on the shoulders of all of us. It is the weight of the failure of most of those who have sat in these seats before us. They failed to educate most of the Indigenous people of the Territory; failed to make them healthy or create jobs for them. It is a failure shared by both parties here and in Canberra, and shared by people outside of politics. It is a failure of Australia. I include in that all Indigenous people who have not taken up the opportunities which were offered to them. It will be hard for some of my friends, for members of my family, to hear that but it has to be said. There are few heroes in this story.

I mention these things not out of despair but to remind all of us there is no point in being in this place unless we have something new to contribute. Much of what has been done before has failed and it is our

---

[1] This chapter is based on speeches delivered by Alison Anderson, Minister for Indigenous Advancement, in Parliament in late October-early November 2012.

job, the one for which we were elected, to do things differently. The first step is to think differently. Behind most failed actions are failed ideas. Often starting life as noble ideas and becoming corrupted along the way. This is what happened in the way Australia treated Aboriginal people. In the 1960s and 1970s, there was a great moral awakening when white Australia realised what it had done to us and began to make amends.

That move to acknowledge our sufferings and our dispossession was a noble one. The laws to return land to us and encourage independent development were fine initiatives that grew out of the best intentions. Yet all this produced the twin corruptions of welfarism and the belief Aboriginal people ought to live forever in a cultural Stone Age. It did not happen quickly; those corruptions crept up on us over time and became entrenched. They have proved almost impossible to change. Now we have the sicknesses and abuse, the ganja and the crowded gaols, the empty schools and the suicides. How did all this happen? For the usual reason: because we continued to judge our ideas by their noble intentions instead of by their results. We did this for many years after those results proved the ideas had failed. They also became entrenched because government passed laws and set up agencies and funded them to create jobs. Those jobs were filled by people who built careers based on ideas that separate development was the way forward for Indigenous people. As the American writer Upton Sinclair wrote: "It is difficult to get someone to understand something when their salary depends on not understanding it." That is true everywhere and it is true in the Northern Territory. The idea that separate development was the answer provided hope for many and jobs for an increasingly powerful few. However, it has failed. I suggest the past 40 years of Aboriginal policy has been a sort of experiment, an experiment with human lives costing billions of dollars. Walk through Alice Springs after dark or visit Papunya and speak with my relatives: the people are sick in their bodies and in their souls. They are uneducated, orphaned, and widowed. They are in gaols and in cemeteries. It was a great experiment, perhaps even a necessary one, but it has failed.

Three per cent of Australians are Indigenous. In the Territory that rises to 30%. It does not just rise; it explodes and creates a whole new society, one this nation is still coming to terms with. We are different. What does it mean to be Indigenous here? Many things, of course, but some of the raw averages are interesting. It means we are young. For every non-Indigenous child in the Territory there are 4.5 non-Indigenous adults aged 20 to 59. To put that another way, over four adults to look after each child. However, for an Indigenous child there are only 1.5 Indigenous adults. In other words, there are far fewer adults to care for our children, to protect and inspire them, to feed, and look out for them. Where are the missing adults? There is no way to put this gently: they are dead. This is like the reverse of the old story of the Pied Piper: here it is the adults who have gone in places like Lajamanu, where 29% of people are younger than nine years old. Something has spirited away many of the parents, the uncles, and the aunties.

As I say, we are different. We are also remote. In all Australia 24% of Indigenous people live in remote or very remote areas. In the Territory that proportion is 81%. When I speak of remoteness, I mean not just remote from Darwin or Alice Springs, but remote from each other. In service delivery, remoteness makes everything harder – everything. Take transport, with road cuts during the Wet Season and prohibitively expensive public transport. A return trip from Katherine to Lajamanu costs $320 and runs just twice a week. Plus 527 homelands and outstations funded by my department – by definition even more remote. There will never be enough money to fund all this, not here or anywhere else in the world. That is something we ignore, but we ignore it at our peril. Again and again, I see programs that do not factor in the true cost of remoteness: the travel time needed to reach communities, and the cost of planes to access them during the Wet.

I can put a price on those costs. According to the Commonwealth Grants Commission's 2011 update, the cost of delivering welfare and housing services in the Northern Territory is 3.4 times higher than the national average. That is the price of remoteness. It is a price the government cannot afford to pay – not fully – which is why those services are usually deficient. That is one of the reasons for the problems we have in most communities: inadequate infrastructure and housing, poor health, and education. I point to these problems because there is no sense in denying them. There is no sense in denying our difference from the rest of Australia.

However, it is not all bad. There are problems with differences, but there are benefits too. Difference can become strength if it is treated with respect. This government respects the importance of cultural connections to land. We support the right of people to live on their country. One of the things this means is housing. At the moment, about 10,000 Indigenous people live in around 2,400 houses in homelands and outstations. Statistically, not overcrowded but, then, people are not statistics. The reality is very different.

There are two goals I will strive for: real education and real jobs. I am not the education minister and I am not the employment minister, I am the Minister for Indigenous Advancement. Those are the two areas, in particular, where I will be throwing my weight behind the efforts of my colleagues. Let me tell you why.

A major problem is education, starting with language. In 2008, 64% of Indigenous people in remote areas of the Northern Territory spoke an Aboriginal language as their main language at home. There is nothing wrong with that; it happens with many cultures around Australia. The problem is that many of those children failed to learn to speak and write English properly at school. That meant they could never get mainstream jobs. That meant they could never have access to opportunities for travel and living in other places, for getting better jobs in their places. It denied them choice, it meant they did not have the choices that most Australian young people have. Something else that shows what it means to be Indigenous in the Northern Territory: to be denied choice. It does not have to be that way, you can be different and still have choice and that means being different and strong, not different and weak.

This government intends to make our Indigenous children stronger, not by providing stronger crutches, more interpreters and welfare workers and police and jailers, but by making them more independent. The first step in independence is education and the first step in education is language. All Indigenous people will be taught English just like the children from all other cultures in Australia. This government is committed to making education normal for all children, no matter where they live. Real education for real jobs. There will be more boarding school places, more School of the Air, more experienced teachers everywhere. We are different to the rest of Australia in where we live, but we have to be identical in what we learn. That sort of difference builds strength not weakness. It creates choice not limitations.

We need to teach English so that the education a child receives here will be as good as in Sydney or Brisbane. I know the majority of kids in remote communities do not begin school with the same level of English as kids in our cities, and I know we need to work with the language that kids come into the classroom with to bring them up to speed in English as quickly as possible.

This is not controversial. This is common sense. This is about our kids having a proper grasp of English and receiving the same standard of education as any other kid in Australia. Real education and real jobs. This government is going to listen a lot and fix a lot. Even if we only made progress in the schools it would be something to be proud of. It would be much more than has been achieved in many decades.

One of the things we have to do to make schools normal is introduce normal curriculum just as they have in Melbourne, London, or New York. I am not suggesting we abandon our traditional culture or language, but teaching them should not be done in schools. It should be done after school and on weekends and during the holidays. That is when most of the other cultures in Australia teach their children traditional ways.

The job of the teachers in our schools will be to teach what is taught in normal schools around Australia. You can buy the curriculum off the shelf from any state you like. That is the only way our children will grow up to be able to compete for jobs and work alongside people educated in other places.

Another thing we have to do to make schools normal is to stop holding events that take kids away – no more sports events that go on for days. To say nothing of funerals for weeks. Some people say these events are traditional, but I have my doubts about that. Some have traditional roots, but they have grown because of the welfare world, because people have had so much empty time to fill. We need to educate parents to see that a new approach to education will involve some hard choices. No more excuses for children missing school. This is something government and local councils can help with. There should be no more support for any type of event that takes children away from home during school term.

Let us imagine we can improve education, we can make it real. That will take many years even if the changes I am describing come in. It will be many years before the first group of kids to receive a real education leave school. However, let us imagine that happens. Where will they go? I see them going for interviews for jobs now automatically filled by non-Indigenous people who often come to the Territory from other places. I see Indigenous people starting to fill those jobs because they are well educated and, sometimes, because of their local knowledge. They understand this place and its people better than the other applicants for the position. That happens in many places: locals have an advantage. It should happen here. I am talking about real jobs, not what we call 'blackfella ones'.

For example, my sister-in-law has been a teaching assistant for 25 years and, although she is a good worker, it is a dead end. She can never use that experience to move up or on. We need to phase out all the jobs we created for Aboriginal people: the teaching assistants and the special positions for Aboriginal police and healthcare workers, and all the rest.

They imply that Aboriginal people cannot do normal jobs. We need to replace them with real jobs that require real education, jobs that are not dead ends but that could lead on to other jobs, including jobs in other places if that is what some people want.

In that way, education can set us free. It can make us independent for the first time of all the non-Indigenous advisors who have tried to control our lives. At the moment we are being advised into the grave by people better educated than us. This needs to change. We need education to set us free – free of dependence, unemployment, welfare, and victimhood. Education has set billions of human beings free; it can do the same for us. Once we are independent we will have choices. Most 25-year-olds in Sydney can work anywhere in the world. They have the education and the work experience. I want our 25-year-olds to have the same choices.

Of course, many young people will want to stay in their communities, but even that requires education if they are to take advantage of the job opportunities that exist. There are opportunities, both existing ones and jobs we can create – to grow food, make bread, and fix cars. For people who can read and write and use computers to keep learning, there are plenty of job opportunities in the communities.

There are plenty of jobs in the Territory, in the communities and in government, in tourism and national parks, and mining. My dream is simple: to see Indigenous people filling more of those jobs in the future because of the quality of our education and because we make ourselves the best people for those jobs. Having a job is not mainly about money. It is about getting up in the morning and looking after yourself. It is about staying in the same place five days a week. It is about wanting your children to be educated so that they can get a job one day. It is about pride and respect – but we cannot put the cart before the horse. Many people who have been to Indigenous schools in the past generation are so poorly educated they have never had a real job. In employment terms, they are the lost generation. Our schools stole their futures from them. All we can do now is fix the problem for the next generation. It is a huge challenge but I believe we can do it.

It always surprises me how hard it is to get fresh food in remote places. There has to be a potential to change that. We have the land and the sun, and we have the example of the old mission market gardens where food was grown successfully across the Territory. I see hundreds of new jobs in that one area. Again, we will need help. Again, I suggest we ask other Australians to assist us. Not bureaucrats or soldiers, but gardeners, bakers, and mechanics to stay with us for six months and share their knowledge. However, that is a vision for the future. First we need to make our communities places outsiders would want to live in.

Jobs are there at this moment in the national parks. Anyone with dark skin has to have a head start going for a job in the tourism industry in the Northern Territory. Let us face it: the tourists have not come here to go to the opera or for shopping. They are here in large part because of Indigenous culture. And the landscape and art, animals and plants – that our people know intimately. Who better to share it with them than us? Some Indigenous people work in that industry already and there could be so many more.

And of course there is mining. Big companies are desperate for the opportunity to pay Indigenous people over a hundred thousand a year to work for them. Of course, we need education first if we are to go for those jobs but the jobs are there and that is a huge piece of good fortune. Australia is going through some economic good times. According to the Commonwealth government's new report on Asia, those good times are likely to continue. Indigenous people need to be part of that by improving basic education. This government is determined that many more Indigenous children will be able to get real jobs and take advantage of this prosperity and break the welfare cycle.

I admit that sometimes I despair at the reluctance of some Indigenous people to take the jobs that are already there. I look at the men of Yirrkala and ask why they will not drive the 20km to Nhulunbuy to earn excellent money in the mine and the processing plant there. These are the kinds of questions the rest of Australia has been asking for years as it tries to connect the dots. Tries to understand why a long-running mining boom can exist literally next door to a culture of entitlement and welfare dependency. As I travel around I will be asking questions – why so many Indigenous communities have become welfare traps where somewhere along the way from poverty to prosperity we took a side road and got stuck in a hell from where there seems to be no escape.

It is not good to live off welfare forever, just as it is not good to live off mining royalties if it means you do not work. This applies to people around the world, not just us. In the twenty-first century people need paid jobs, particularly men. It is not just about the money although the money is good. It is about status and respect, about responsibility and dignity. It is also about growing up and not being a child any more, about becoming an adult, so that children, real children, can depend on you. We need more of such adults in our Indigenous communities. When I am out bush I hope that this is one of the things that many people would want to talk about. How we can help people grow up. Sometimes in Indigenous matters we can despair because it can seem like we are always starting from scratch, never making any progress. But this government has policies that will work. The most important for me is fixing the schools to improve the quality of our teachers and their teaching.

There is another type of conversation where I grow impatient. I'm talking about this culture of complaint that hangs over so many Indigenous communities. We have to be wary of that, but we also have to be wary of many of the solutions that are offered – the frequent failures of the NGOs because they do not understand the communities where they work – the need for more culturally appropriate delivery of services by Indigenous people. Let me make one thing perfectly clear: that does not mean simply throwing dollars at communities and telling them to fix problems themselves. There has been some of that over the years and we know too often it does not work.

It seems to me that despite all that has been written about efforts to help Indigenous people, all the evaluations and the reports, we do not know very much about what works. Too often we read something that tells us a real project worked and should be introduced anywhere. But why did it work well in that one place? We are almost never told. There are too many anecdotes in public policy making for Indigenous people and not enough data. Some people have calculated that thousands of pages of evaluations, reports, and submissions are now written each week on Indigenous Australia. Never has so much been written for so little result.

The quantity is enormous, but the quality is poor. We have been let down by too many of our advisers, too many bureaucrats, and academics. I will always listen but I am getting sick of the poor quality research and poor quality evaluations. There is too much noise and not enough content. Here is an evaluation that will not need a doctoral thesis. People with jobs = 100% employed. People on welfare = 100% unemployed. We have all been avoiding the facts for too long now, avoiding the evidence, thinking it was not necessary because Indigenous people were different or because we were scared of what the facts might show. The time for that is over. I ask the NGOs and bureaucrats from those other places who come here to apply the same standard to us as they apply back home. When you write your reports and your evaluations, be as tough as you would be if you were evaluating progress in your own communities.

One of the reasons I spend so much time talking about education is the evidence is in on education. The facts are clear and we know what works. What works are teachers and schools, like those in Bunbury, Port Augusta, Bathurst, and Gladstone. The same approach to education works everywhere and it is time we tried it here in every school in the Territory.

I travel a great deal. I have visited so many remote communities and too often they are like nursing homes, full of illness, complaints, and death. Too often they are places where nothing gets done, no toilet is unblocked, no child taken to school unless someone from outside does it. I say they are like nursing homes; perhaps I should say nurseries – because everyone is a child, even the adults.

It is time to change that for the sake of our respect and our dignity. It is not as though the system we have works well. The non-Indigenous NGOs, or not-for-profits, are easy for government to deal with, especially the Commonwealth government which takes a long view all the way from Canberra. Often these NGOs are bright and shiny, run like clockwork, and fill in all the paperwork perfectly. They are good at lobbying and writing submissions. I do not mock that, however, they are not as good at providing services because they do not understand the communities they go into. Like so many non-Indigenous advisors over the years, so many experts are cursed by the combination of noble intentions and utter ignorance.

I suggest a greater role for Indigenous organisations. There is growing evidence community-based and controlled organisations can do better. We need to judge them by the same high standards we apply to non-Indigenous NGOs. However, when we do that we will find many of our own are up there with the best: local knowledge, there is nothing quite like it.

What is the way forward? I offer no magic solution, no silver bullets. My basic approach is real education for real jobs, and to keep travelling and doing what I can to make them reality, to keep visiting and keep listening to what people tell me. And keep in mind there is no reason Indigenous people cannot excel in schools and the workplace.

We are struggling with our history and, in some cases, with obstacles in our own hearts and minds. Much of what has happened to us is deeply unfair. Much we have witnessed and suffered has been terrible, but it is a struggle we must embark on and a struggle we can win.

I have been listening for a long time now to people in remote communities and I like to describe two types of conversations that are common, but dangerous. Common, even understandable, but dangerous.

The first is the conversation of endless complaint – where a person offers to do nothing for themself and demands everything be done for them. In the rest of Australia, people pick up the rubbish in their yards, they fix their own blocked toilets. When they turn on their TVs and see remote communities covered in litter and able-bodied men complaining about lack of maintenance on the houses they live in, they wonder why Indigenous people in these communities will not do things for themselves. Of course, in many places they do, but in many places they do not – in far too many. The rest of the world is looking and wondering why. It is wondering why so many Indigenous people have the sense of entitlement – the sense that everything will be done for them. I say to these people, to those in the communities and those watching, that everything will not be done by government, everything cannot be done. There are not the resources and everything should not be done by government because adults are not children. Adults are capable human beings who need to be strong so they can care for the real children – all those kids who should be safe and warm and in school.

Too much of the public discussion about Indigenous people has assumed, whatever the problem, government is the answer. It has been assumed that any problem can be solved with the right policies and the right amount of money. I would have no issue with that if it was correct but the history of the past 40 years, including the Intervention, shows it is wrong. I believe it failed because it came over time to treat Indigenous people as passive and, by treating us as passive, it helped make us passive. It also treated us as different and encouraged us to live in a parallel world that was supposed to be a dreaming but became a nightmare. The time has come to reject those beliefs and say that Indigenous people need to engage with other Australians. In particular, we need jobs and, for jobs, we need education. I mean real education and real jobs. Any policies that interfere with these two goals need to be thrown on the scrap heap.

Of course, we will need government to help achieve this but it needs to be help designed to liberate us, to make us independent human beings

– and this is possible. Governments can do bad things – we have seen enough of that in the Territory – but can also be a force for good. We Indigenous people need to be more like other Australians. I do not mean we should abandon our beliefs or our language but, like dozens of other cultures in Australia, we must learn to combine our own identities with participation in the broader society. That will not weaken us. It will make us stronger in who we are. To preserve the old ways, we must embrace the new ones.

I know there is much to be done; however, I believe the rest of Australia cares about what happens here and is just waiting for us to take the first step. Australia has more to offer us than a view of Indigenous people defined by their victimhood – more than welfarism or the Intervention. We need to convince it that the Territory is not a museum and is not a nightmare. Above all, we need to show our fellow Australians we want to be normal. We want the right to be just like them and keep our identity, but to live fully in the 21st century.

I have been describing a dream, but it is not a romantic dream. I hope it is not an impossible one. It is a dream based on looking at the past and being honest about what has gone wrong. It is a dream that does not aspire to the creation of some Utopia of a sort that has never been seen on the face of the earth before. My dream is we should get real and, for the first time since Europeans came to this land, Indigenous people should be thought of and treated just like everyone else. To someone in Melbourne, Shanghai, or New York, that might sound like a very modest dream, however, as all of us know, it is actually a big one to suggest that Indigenous people in the Northern Territory should live normal lives with real education and real jobs. That is the most radical dream of all.

I finish on a personal note about real children. Our Indigenous children have far fewer adults in their lives compared with other Australian children. We owe our children everything, and if we keep them at the centre of the picture we cannot go far wrong. Children need education and they need parents – dads as well as mums. Dads need jobs, not gaols, and for jobs they need education. That is why, in my mind, so much comes back to our schools. I believe if we get them right, much else will follow – not everything but a lot. That is my plan. It is a journey I intend taking over the next year as I visit as many of those 527 homelands and outstations as possible. I promise to do everything I can to make it a journey into a better future for all Indigenous people.

# 23
# Towards a Reconciled Australia[1]

*Mick Gooda*

My priorities as Aboriginal and Torres Strait Islander Social Justice Commissioner are underpinned by two unshakeable personal commitments: the first one is my commitment to addressing the disadvantages still faced by Aboriginal and Torres Strait Islander peoples today and the second is my commitment to doing all in my power to achieve a truly reconciled Australia. I am driven by the possibilities of change; the core of the change needed relates to people and their relationships. Any change rests with the capability of people to realise their potential and building this capability means building our human capital.

Many people are uncertain of what my role as Social Justice Commissioner entails. Briefly, I'm required to provide to the Australian Parliament a Social Justice Report and a report on Native Title. I'm also required to:

- review the impact of laws and policies with regard to Indigenous peoples;
- promote an Indigenous perspective on issues; and
- monitor the enjoyment and exercise of human rights of Indigenous Australians.

In a real sense, I'm handed these general directions and it's up to me to sort out my priorities in terms of how I do what the legislation requires of me. I quickly realised that I can't pick even one of the myriad

---

[1] This is an edited version of a speech that was delivered by Commissioner Gooda at the National Press Club, Canberra, on Wednesday, 3 November 2010.

challenges facing Aboriginal and Torres Strait Islander peoples – housing, health, education, etc – and expect to fix it by 2015 when my term expires. I believe that fixing these issues will require intergenerational commitment of the whole nation. But there is a way to reframe this approach: by shifting our focus to those issues that are foundational to an agenda of hope.

An agenda which, at its core, aims to unleash the potential of Indigenous Australians; that maximises the capabilities of each and every Indigenous Australian; that tackles the root causes of Indigenous health and social inequality. This requires a nation-building exercise. One which builds the healthy relationships necessary for this agenda of hope. So, at the centre of my priorities is the belief that we need to firstly develop stronger and deeper relationships between Aboriginal and Torres Strait Islander peoples and the rest of Australia.

Secondly, we need to develop stronger and deeper relationships between Aboriginal and Torres Strait Islander peoples and all levels of government. And, perhaps even more importantly, we need to develop stronger and deeper relationships between ourselves as Aboriginal and Torres Strait Islander peoples. Relationships are built on understanding, dialogue, tolerance, acceptance, respect, trust, and reciprocated affection. Relationships are destroyed by misunderstanding, intolerance, lack of acceptance, lack of dialogue, mistrust, and lack of respect.

So let's start with relationships between Aboriginal and Torres Strait Islander peoples and the rest of Australia. A non-Indigenous mate of mine hadn't ever had very much to do with Aboriginal or Torres Strait Islander people. In 2008 he found himself working for the Anangu board of an organisation based in Alice Springs for eight months. Both he and the Anangu approached eight or nine months of what was going to be a working relationship with open minds and open hearts but there was, understandably, some stand-offishness on both sides. The Anangu mob offered their traditionally soft handshakes with averted eyes. My mate offered his firm handshake, puzzled at the averted eyes. Gradually though, after some weeks of working together, learning a bit about each other's cultures and ways of going about things, eyes met, smiles crept onto faces, names were remembered, jokes were shared – tentatively at first – then they got more robust! Tucker was shared, families introduced, and invitations extended.

It's now almost three years since they worked together but the friendships remain. The Anangu mob would ring him when they came to Adelaide. Eyes light up when they meet – there's laughter and smiles and shared stories and tucker and beer. My mate travelled up to one of the remote communities to attend the funeral of one the board members' wives. He was invited to speak. He was welcomed into the mob in a way he could never have imagined. He reckons his time with the Anangu mob was one of the joys of his life and the friendships survive to this day. I read somewhere the following observation which has stayed with me for a lot longer than the name of the person who made it. It's this: Sometimes our closest friend is the one who has travelled the greatest distance to be our friend. So it was with my mate from Adelaide. So it will be with regard to the relationship between Aboriginal and Torres Strait Islanders and the rest of the Australian people.

When the National Apology was made in February 2008, I believed Australia was ready for a new, stronger, deeper relationship. On that day there was a palpable sense of us coming together as a nation for the first time. Indigenous and non-Indigenous Australians sat together, held each other and cried together. The nation took a great leap forward together – but somehow we lost momentum soon after. Despite much goodwill on both sides of the paddock, there are several tough issues we all have to confront as a nation if we are going to reset this relationship.

Recent surveys conducted among 12,000 people found that about 80% of Australians consider that racial prejudice is still a problem.[2] Three thousand respondents expressed some sort of prejudice themselves against Aboriginal and Torres Strait Islander peoples in particular.[3]

---

[2] University of Western Sydney. *Challenging Racism* (2009).
[3] Reconciliation Australia. *Australian Reconciliation Barometer* (2009).

Other national research reveals that about 20% of Aboriginal and Torres Strait Islander adults report regular experiences of racism.[4] Racism – hatred or intolerance of another race or races – results in much more than humiliation, embarrassment, and hurt feelings. Racism has serious health, social, and economic consequences for individuals, communities, and societies. It's been associated with depression, anxiety, high blood pressure, heart disease, smoking, alcohol and substance abuse, as well as poor employment and educational outcomes.[5] Racism has the potential to do plenty of damage regardless of who perpetrates it. So it's for these reasons, among others, that I've decided to focus on re-establishing trust and building positive relationships. We can't go about re-setting these relationships without a clear focus on the human rights of Aboriginal and Torres Strait Islander peoples in this country. Human rights are not just abstract concepts that exist in documents such as treaties, conventions, and declarations. And we are advised to remember this: human rights only become meaningful when they are able to be exercised.

Bishop Desmond Tutu once said: "I am not interested in picking up crumbs of compassion thrown from the table of someone who considers himself my master. I want the full menu of rights."[6] We have available to us in Australia one of the most important documents that sets out our human rights as Indigenous peoples – the United Nations Declaration on the Rights of Indigenous Peoples.[7] I will use the Declaration to guide my work. And I am committed to working with government to ensure that full implementation of both the spirit and intent of the Declaration is achieved in Australia. In my view, it should form the platform upon which a truly reconciled Australia is built.

---

[4] ABS. *National Aboriginal and Torres Strait Islander Health Survey Australia 2004-05* (no. 4715.0) (2006).

[5] Larson, A. *et al.* 'It's Enough to Make You Sick' (2007).

[6] Tutu. D. *If There Is Only One Message of Wisdom You Could Leave behind for Humanity What Would It Be?* (no date).

[7] United Nations. *United Nations Declaration on the Rights of Indigenous Peoples* (2008).

When it comes to human rights in Australia – and the denial of them which, as Professor Mick Dodson points out, is where the real harm is done – Aboriginal and Torres Strait Islander people are the most vulnerable group in this country. A few examples: Aboriginal and Torres Strait Islander people were not counted as citizens of Australia until 1967. We do not enjoy the same standards of education: in 2008, only 63% of Year 5 Indigenous students achieved the national minimum standard for reading compared with 93% of non-Indigenous students – a gap of 30%. As a result of the Northern Territory Intervention, the very instrument which is supposed to protect the most vulnerable in our society, the Racial Discrimination Act 1975 (Cth) was suspended in 73 communities. This is more than painfully ironic. In this country's history the Racial Discrimination Act has been compromised on only three occasions. Each time it has involved Aboriginal and Torres Strait Islander issues.

While it's easy to litanise the disadvantages, the injustices, the denial of rights, and the oppressions, we must not forget the progress. In 1967, 91.7% of Australians voted to count Aborigines and Torres Strait Islanders as Australians. It was a time when the goodwill and innate decency of the Australian people triumphed.

We've had a 20 year reconciliation process; the Royal Commission into Aboriginal Deaths in Custody; and the findings of Bringing them Home, just to name a few. In 1992, the High Court Mabo judgement finally put to rest the myth of 'terra nullius'. But I believe now is the time for that recognition to go further. I firmly believe the time is right, here and now, for the Australian people to formalise at least the recognition of the special and unique place of Aboriginal and Torres Strait Islander people in our nation, in our Constitution.

During the 2010 federal election campaign, Labor, the Coalition, and the Greens committed to a referendum to facilitate such recognition. The prospect of this referendum recognising Aboriginal and Torres Strait Islander people in the Australian Constitution provides us all with a great opportunity to reframe and reset our relationship as a nation. It's been said to me that a referendum to change the Constitution will suck up a lot of oxygen and resources, and perhaps even goodwill. These resources and goodwill could be put to be better use closing the gap between Indigenous and non-Indigenous Australia. Maybe that's true.

Certainly, we can't underestimate the immensity of such a challenge. Because of the double majority needed – an overall majority Yes vote, and a Yes vote from a majority of people in a majority of the states – only eight out of 44 referenda have been passed in Australia's history. We also know that bipartisan support at the political level will be absolutely essential and we know just how easy it is to get politicians to agree – especially if either side reckons there's a possible wedge in there somewhere.

But to those who doubt the importance of what amounts to a form of words, I say this. This process will give this generation of Australians the opportunity to say 'yes' – an opportunity to demonstrate goodwill and innate decency, just like over 90% of Australians did in 1967. In real terms this means we need between 12-13 million voters on our side. Yes, there will be debates, speeches, opinions in all the media, people prowling the parliamentary corridors, constitutional lawyers at 10 paces, yea- and nay-sayers, documentaries, panel discussions, arguments at dinner parties, barbecues and in front bars – all of these things. And it's precisely all of these things that will build awareness, focus minds and hearts, and help move us all forward as a nation.

By finally and formally settling and affirming the place of Aboriginal and Torres Strait Islander peoples in our nation, all of us grow in stature. During the next three years, I commit myself to working closely with our political leaders and, more importantly, the people of Australia to achieve a successful referendum. This will be a long hard journey. But it's the journey that will mark our maturity as a nation, not just the destination – important as it might be. This referendum about a change to our Constitution is not just about Aboriginal and Torres Strait

Islander peoples. It's not about looking back. It's about looking forward and moving forward as one, united nation. One mob under the Southern Cross.

I now turn my attention to the relationship between Aboriginal and Torres Strait Islander peoples and governments at all levels. I've travelled pretty widely. I've listened and I've learned. I know from my conversations with Aboriginal and Torres Strait Islander people around the country that there's hurt in our communities and relationships between Aboriginal and Torres Strait Islander people and governments are not good. There are lots of reasons for this. A lot stem from the treatment of Aboriginal people in those 73 communities that bear the brunt of the Northern Territory Emergency Response – the Intervention. There is always a sense of solidarity between Aboriginal and Torres Strait Islander peoples – and that sense of solidarity 'arcs up' when some of us are subjected to injustice and denied the rights that all other Australians enjoy.

The Intervention and the suspension of the Racial Discrimination Act affected us all deeply, regardless of where we actually live. It triggered in our collective memories all the past injustices that we experienced in our communities and in our families. Not for one minute will I argue that the situation in the Northern Territory didn't demand action. I'm on the record as saying action needed to be taken and the great majority of Aboriginal people I know agreed with me. However, that action should have been taken on a case by case basis. Painting everyone in a community with the same brush is neither helpful, nor fair – particularly to those many people doing the right thing. Each of the Intervention communities had big blue signs erected outside them which, amongst other things, loudly proclaimed restrictions on alcohol and pornography – as if everyone living behind those signs are alcoholic, perverts, and perpetrators!

I invite the residents of Yarralumla, Redhill, Woollahra, Mosman, and Toorak, to name just a few well-known, middle-class suburbs, to contemplate how they would feel with similar signs erected at the entrance to their communities. These signs continue to diminish the people living behind them and they diminish us as a nation. It gives me absolutely no pleasure to say that I fear relationships between governments and Aboriginal and Torres Strait Islander peoples have been badly damaged by the Intervention particularly. So let's not mince words here: it's going to take a lot of work to overcome the hurt and to fix the relationships that have broken down as a result.

Now that's been said, I happily acknowledge that the Australian Government has recently made significant commitments to addressing Aboriginal and Torres Strait Islander disadvantage – particularly through its Closing the Gap Agenda. In 2008, the Council of Australian Governments (COAG) – set specific and ambitious targets. I endorse these targets and now call for the development of a national plan to implement them. Nevertheless, these targets, however worthy, will not be achieved if we don't have a foundation of respectful and trusting relationships upon which to build. Trust enables governments and Indigenous Australians to work together to tackle the challenges of implementing change whether this be through new programs, tackling lifestyle changes needed for health, addressing poverty, or addressing problems within government systems.

If there's one thing I heard over and over in the early days in this job – and I continue to hear – it's that our relationship with all governments must improve. The *Little Children are Sacred* Report, the Report of the Review of the Northern Territory Emergency Response, the reports of the Special Rapporteur on Indigenous Issues, James Anaya, and the Coordinator General for Remote Indigenous Services, Brian Gleeson, all speak of the necessity to build relationships between governments and Aboriginal and Torres Strait Islander peoples which are based on trust and mutual respect. I draw your attention to part of the first recommendation of *Little Children are Sacred*: It is critical that both governments commit to genuine consultation with Aboriginal people in designing initiatives for Aboriginal communities.[8] Sadly, the people who used that Report to justify and design the Intervention must have overlooked this part of the Report.

Government agencies also need to have a good, hard look at themselves. These agencies must try to develop a sensible, co-operative, and culturally appropriate interface with communities. There is no place and no time for the sort of bureaucratic territorialism that, sadly, still marks much inter-departmental and community engagement. Governments have a responsibility to ensure that society's structures, laws, and processes facilitate a full and open engagement with Aboriginal and Torres Strait Islander citizens. Structures and processes that allow our people to be treated less equally than other Australians, consciously or unconsciously, are simply unacceptable.

I encourage you all to look at the work that has been done in the Fitzroy Valley. It's living proof that hard work and time can achieve effective community development. The Fitzroy Valley approach requires coordination, goodwill, and mutual respect at both community level and at all levels of government. And progress like this doesn't happen overnight. For the Fitzroy Valley, it's been a 10-year journey.

Our new national organisation, the National Congress of Australia's First Peoples, will also be a crucial part of building and strengthening relationships between governments and Aboriginal and Torres Strait Islander peoples. I look forward to working closely with it as it develops over the next few years.

I am advised that former Prime Minister Kevin Rudd was eager for every government agency with an Aboriginal and Torres Strait Islander responsibility, however slight, to develop an engagement strategy with the Congress. That sort of top-down commitment, from the very pinnacle of the administrative food-chain is a great start and one we should applaud. As Social Justice Commissioner, it will be my job to

---

[8] Wild, R. & Anderson, P. *Little Children are Sacred* (2007).

facilitate real communication between governments and Indigenous communities. And by this I don't mean glib exchanges in which each side says what it thinks the other side wants to hear.

Truth is a critical element in all good relationships. I'll work hard to build a framework for engagement that's predicated on truthful, respectful, exchanges where we, as Indigenous people, participate as equals. I'll also work with governments to develop legislation, policies, and practices that will improve rather than burden the lives of Aboriginal and Torres Strait Islander peoples. And through my Social Justice and Native Title Reports, I will monitor the effectiveness of these mechanisms frankly and fearlessly.

The third set of relationships on my priority list is the relationships we Aboriginal and Torres Strait Islander peoples have with each other: at the community, family, organisation, and individual level. Just as it is vital to prevent the harms caused us by the racism of others, it is also imperative that we create the enabling and nurturing relationships within our communities that are so pivotal to the agenda of hope that I wish to champion.

I've been pretty brutal about the dysfunctional relationships between Aboriginal and Torres Strait Islander people, governments and the rest of the Australian people. And I've been pretty upfront about where I think the faults lie. Well, it's now time for me to be brutal and upfront about the relationships between Aboriginal and Torres Strait Islander people. Sometimes these relationships are not good and unfortunately, at times, we can be our own worst enemies. I've been working in Indigenous affairs for nearly 30 years. I am not, nor should anyone else be, surprised when there are disagreements. They are a natural part of relationships. However, at times these disagreements can get very personal and very hurtful. And the hurt can end up affecting the whole community.

One of my non-Indigenous mates said me to that, with the best will in the world, working in Aboriginal and Torres Strait Islander Affairs can be very bruising. Some people will argue that they are so committed to fixing things that the conflicts that wound us are easily justified as 'collateral damage'. They'll say it's but a small price to pay for changing the status quo. Anyone who has anything to do with native title work in communities will relate to this. Anyone who has attended a contentious AGM of an Indigenous organisation will relate to this. Recent research conducted by the Office of the Registrar for Aboriginal Corporations found that internal disputes are the third most prevalent cause of Indigenous corporate failure.[9]

In 2006, I came across a concept the Canadian First Nation peoples call Lateral Violence. It's the name given to this bullying, harassing, and intimidating among ourselves. It's well attested around the world that oppressed people will eventually internalise their oppression and turn on each other. The notion of 'lateral violence' says that this behaviour is often the result of disadvantage, discrimination, and oppression and that it arises from working within a society that is not designed for our way of doing things. But whether that theory is sustainable or not, this is abuse and there's no excuse for it. We must have zero tolerance for any type of abuse.

Initially, I was concerned that a frank airing of this issue might well cause me some grief. I was prepared for being accused of airing our dirty laundry in public – this is just the way things are done in the Indigenous world and that I'm just making another rod for our backs with which non-Indigenous people can beat us up. However, I've been encouraged by the responses I have received when I have raised this issue with Aboriginal and Torres Strait Islander people. People recognise this is a real issue. And one we need to address.

In our communities there seems to be a considerable appetite to confront it and deal with it. I am immensely heartened by this. The work being done in places like Cairns and Yarrabah with the Family Well-being Empowerment Program – which is designed specifically to

---

[9] Office of the Registrar of Indigenous Corporations. *Analysing Key Characteristics in Indigenous Corporate Failure* (2010), 46.

overcome community conflict through building support within families and communities – shows us that, given the right opportunities, people are prepared to challenge and defeat these behaviours. Governments cannot and should not intervene to fix our internal relationships. Frankly, governments have more than enough of their own relationship problems to contend with. But governments can work with us and our communities as enablers and facilitators. They can also work to remove existing structural and systemic impediments to healthy relationships within our communities.

So ... to sum up. My priorities focus on strengthening relationships at three key levels. To reset these relationships, I will:

1. work with the Australian community to address racism in our country;
2. work towards a successful referendum that recognises the special place of Aboriginal and Torres Strait Islander peoples in our nation;
3. work to build proper and mutually respectful engagements between governments and Indigenous peoples; and
4. work towards a zero tolerance policy with regard to any type of abuse within our communities – bullying, harassment, intimidation, and violence.

Our agenda of hope can only be sustained when Aboriginal and Torres Strait Islander people are able to achieve our potential – able to realise our personal and collective capabilities. Striving to reach this vision through our work, our education, or our commitments to our families and communities. This work will be underpinned by a strong reliance on the values and standards derived from human rights frameworks, taking specific guidance from the Declaration on the Rights of Indigenous Peoples. These are my priorities. But what does this mean for us as a nation?

My friend Glenn Pearson from Perth, when asked what type of future he'd like to see for us, put it like this. It's a vision that I share and I want to share it with you:

> I want for me and my children – as I do for you and your children – to grow really, really old together – having led fantastic lives that have allowed us to make a lifetime contribution to the health and well-being of the broader community and our families.
>
> I want to know that when we were tested by life's challenges, we pulled together to face them as a people; that we drew upon the best of what we had, to find positive solutions to the things that have tested us along the way.
>
> I want to know that, purposively, we took on and changed those things that we felt do not reflect what we want in a fair, honest, respectful, and harmonious society.
>
> I want that we learn to hold and to celebrate Aboriginal and Torres Strait Islander culture and history as an essential part of the Australian story because we see ourselves as part of it – connected to it, proud of it, and centred by it.

I want a truly reconciled community: a truly reconciled Australia. And I want that we all want it.

# 24
# Together We Can't Lose: Seeding Success to Ensure Australia Flourishes

Rhonda Craven and Nigel Parbury

*Australia is far better than it once was for Aboriginal people but not as good as it might become.*[1]

This astute analysis by Australia's first published Aboriginal historian, James Wilson-Miller, remains enduringly poignant and apt. Despite well-meaning attempts by all governments and a plethora of non-Aboriginal and Aboriginal agencies, numerous national and international research studies have demonstrated that Aboriginal Australians remain the most disadvantaged Australians on all socio-economic indicators. There can be no more dramatic and salient indicator than the fact that Aboriginal people's life expectancy is not commensurate with that of non-Aboriginal Australians. Clearly, in our ever increasingly technological and complex world, halting the sheer wastage of Aboriginal talent and harnessing the full potential of our Aboriginal human and intellectual capital is vital for Australia. This makes sense in regard to: ensuring Australia flourishes as a nation; Australia's reputation as one of the most egalitarian and successful multicultural nations on Earth; our national ethos of a fair go for all; adding materially to Australia's socio-economic well-being; and forging a genuinely better future for all Australians based on mutual respect, understanding, and common goals. However, how to get agreement on viable and fresh ways forward remains problematic, such

---

[1] Personal communication with James Wilson-Miller (2013).

that Australia remains at the crossroads.

Fundamentally, Australia has been unable to reap the rewards of harnessing the full talents of her Aboriginal Australians largely due to a historical legacy and a continuing over-reliance on deficit thinking about Aboriginal Australians, with lower expectations widely entrenched in organisations and many Aboriginal and non-Aboriginal people's minds. Deficit thinking has enduringly bedevilled our shared history and still adversely impacts upon explicating and implementing potentially potent research-derived drivers of seeding success across the lifespan. So entrenched and pervasive are deficit thinking and lower expectations that their adverse impact is plainly visible from perspectives as diverse as: early childhood well-being (e.g., health provision, access to pre-school education); education; health; employment; government policy at all levels in Australia (local council, State, Commonwealth); and the psycho-social maladaptive dysfunction of many Aboriginal individuals and communities, with generation to generation welfare dependence such that people no longer see the way to independence and self-reliance. In this chapter, the thesis is that there are salient, research-derived, fresh ways forward that require a fundamentally different ethos and mindset to those of deficit models. Further, it is argued we need to direct Australia's resources and energies to ensuring Australia flourishes by explicating what seeds success, and we discuss some potentially potent strategies to make a real difference in furthering Australia's future.

## Together We Can't Lose

In the 1990s, when even a just republic seemed possible and reconciliation a moral certainty, a Council for Aboriginal Reconciliation (CAR) poster pictured athletes Cathy Freeman and Melinda Gainsford-Taylor wrapped in the Aboriginal and Australian flags. The message was clear: 'Together We Can't Lose'. In fact, the decade of reconciliation, to be in time for the 2001 Centenary of Federation, began with the surely possible and positive vision of creating "A united Australia that respects this land of ours, values the Aboriginal and Torres Strait Islander heritage, and provides justice and equity for all".[2] However, this vision did not eventuate. By the time of the *Corroboree 2000* ceremony at the Sydney Opera House, the nation's leaders had to put their ochred handprints on the vision statement on the wall - it was, quite simply, all that could be agreed. Who were to blame for the abject failure of reconciliation may never be agreed. However, clearly it is essential for Australians to work collaboratively, as together we can: realise all the potential of our commonwealth; achieve all our promise; and make Australia the country we always should have been.

As a nation it can be argued that we need to focus more on what unites us – what makes us all Australian – rather than insisting on difference. There also should be more attention to what Aboriginal people have in common – what makes them Aboriginal – for the simple reason that the more difference is highlighted, the more commonality – that is, Aboriginality – is sidelined, off the agenda. While ever Aboriginal and non-Aboriginal are seen as at opposite ends of the spectrum, "a united Australia"[3] will remain an aspiration. In fact, Aboriginal and non-Aboriginal people have much more in common than most people suppose. For example, Parbury suggests that many 'typical-Aussie' traits derive from both Aboriginal and European life.[4] For example: welcome-stranger friendliness; egalitarianism; Australian humour such as laughing at the absurd; vivid images in vernacular speech; make-do 'bush' improvisation; creativity; the sporting life; and having a good time. It is this commonality that should bind us all together as Australians and be the solid foundation on which to forge Australia to flourish as a common goal. Clearly, together we can't lose.

---

[2] Council for Aboriginal Reconciliation (CAR). *Walking Together* (1992).
[3] Ibid.
[4] Parbury, N. *History* (2005), 7, 8.

## Education is the Key

Recent research has found that Aboriginal Australians are one of the most disadvantaged Indigenous populations in the world.[5,6,7] The factors that underpin the current educational inequities between Aboriginal and non-Aboriginal Australian students are diverse.[8,9,10] These educational inequities are of grave concern, particularly given they are pervasive, extending across pre-school through high school.[11,12,13] For example, across three waves of the Programme for International Student Assessment (PISA) (2000, 2003, 2006) results, Australia as a whole was consistently ranked well above the Organisation for Economic Co-operation and Development (OECD) average, however Aboriginal students' results were consistently below the OECD average for: reading literacy, mathematics, and science.[14] Alarmingly, across the three timeframes there was no improvement in Aboriginal student performance. Given education predicates life's opportunities and well-being, this state of our nation is untenable and needs to be addressed to ensure Australia flourishes.

In 1819, Maria Lock, a daughter of the legendary Yarramundi placed at the Native Institution School, 'topped' the colony in the Anniversary Schools Examination. That surely should have proved once and for all

---

[5] Cooke, M. et al. 'Indigenous Well-being in Four Countries' (2007).
[6] Hill, K. et al. 'Excess Indigenous mortality' (2007).
[7] Ring, I. & Brown. N. 'Aboriginal and Torres Strait Islander Health-implementation, not more Policies' (2003).
[8] Craven, R. & Bodkin-Andrews, G. 'What research can tell us' (2011).
[9] Gray, J. & Partington, G. 'Attendance and non-attendance at School' (2012).
[10] Howard, D. 'Family, Friends and Teachers' (2012).
[11] De Bortoli, L., & Thomson, S. 'Contextual Factors that Influence the Achievement of Australia's Indigenous students' (2010).
[12] DEEWR. *National Report to Parliament on Indigenous Education Science and Training* (2006).
[13] Purdie, N., & Buckley, S. 'School Attendance and Retention of Indigenous Australian Students' (2010).
[14] De Bortoli, L., & Thomson, S. op. cit.

Aboriginal intellectual capacity and why a focus on what seeds success is critical. However, almost 200 years on we still lose potential every day largely thanks to deficit models and mindsets. For example, we still need to empower all of our teachers with the knowledge, skills, and attitudes to understand and teach all Australians about Aboriginal Australia which is fundamental for ensuring all Australians work together to seed success.[15, 16] Yet this could be readily addressed and we suspect it would be willingly addressed by stakeholders. Empirical studies have demonstrated that providing inservice professional development opportunities and mandatory Aboriginal Studies preservice courses are effective in seeding success and ensuring our teachers' talents are harnessed to ensure all Australian children flourish.[17] It would only take a mandated government policy to make this a reality.

It also needs to be well understood that the majority of parents of Aboriginal children share the same educational goals for their children as do the parents of non-Aboriginal children. In fact often Aboriginal students have both an Aboriginal and non-Aboriginal parent, as is the case of the children of the first author. There are still also far too many parents of both Aboriginal and non-Aboriginal children who are inadequate and dysfunctional to the point they cannot look after their own best interests, let alone those of their children. In an era that rightly in our view advocates the universal human rights of the child, and in the teeth of Australia's child protection laws, why such parents continue to have custody of children is unfathomable. It can only be supposed that deficit thinking and reduced expectations prevail – and the children suffer. Quite simply, the laws pertaining to child protection should be enacted to ensure that all Australian children are in environments conducive to flourishing in their educational pursuits. A more proactive approach could readily ensure that all Australian parents are able to

---

[15] Craven, R.G. 'Aboriginal Studies' (1999).
[16] Craven, R.G. 'Seeding Success' (2012).
[17] Craven, R.G. 'Shaping a Glad Tomorrow' (2003).

access positive parenting courses to empower them to be effective; and note that such courses do not need to be costly, particularly if they are online. Further, there are too many people involved in Aboriginal education, who advocate that Aboriginal students need massive and costly specialised institutional support to even survive in mainstream educational settings, let alone achieve! Such deficit thinking has resulted in a lack of focus and emphasis on educational excellence and therefore on what works. Compounding this is the fact that rarely are the voices of children and young Aboriginal adults sought, heard, and capitalised upon to explicate the drivers of success that can be emulated systemically to propel Australia to flourish. Even more salient, there are now many Aboriginal Australians, as well as other Indigenous people all over the world, who despite adversity have triumphed, competed, and succeeded in diverse mainstream settings – they have seen and lived the way to success and have flourished as a result thereof. As a nation we have much to learn and gain from empirically synthesising and analysing what these successful Aboriginal Australians, and other Indigenous people, identify as drivers of their success.

It could also be better appreciated and understood that what works to seed success for Aboriginal students is also highly likely to work for non-Aboriginal students and vice-versa. Australian educational researchers advancing the effective schools tradition have now established clearly that quality teaching is a prime factor in promoting improvements in student outcomes.[18,19,20] As such, examination of findings in the educational literature based on research with non-Aboriginal students, offers potentially powerful insights on seeing the way forward to seed success. For example, Hattie has synthesised over 800 meta-analyses, incorporating over 50,000 studies of the effects of various influences

---

[18] Hattie, J. 'Teachers Make a Difference' (2003).
[19] Hill, P. W., & Rowe, K.J. 'Modeling Student Progress in Studies of Educational effectiveness' (1998).
[20] Rowe, K. J. 'The Importance of Teacher Quality' (2003).

on student achievement.[21,22] Based on this rich research evidence, Hattie concluded that "It is what teachers know, do, and care about which is very powerful in this learning equation".[23] Similarly, Rowe (2003) in summing up the findings of next generation school effectiveness studies concluded "the quality of teaching and learning provision are by far the most salient influences on students' cognitive, affective, and behavioral outcomes of schooling – regardless of their gender or backgrounds".[24] Put simply, quality teachers make a real difference to students' lives and as such Australian teachers are ideally positioned to make one of the most powerful contributions to cultivating Australia's capability and generating well-being to result in Australia flourishing. Clearly both our most gifted and most disadvantaged Aboriginal and other Australian students need access to quality education and excellent teachers at all education levels from pre-school to university. However, currently our educational systems have not been enabled to successfully innovate to address this need. In this new technological era this is simply absurd as barriers preventing access to quality education and excellent teachers can be readily overcome in a cost-effective manner. For example, universities have been highly successful in utilising the advantages of the internet to deliver quality tertiary education to meet the needs of local, broader domestic, and international students. Hence it would be far from difficult to re-conceptualise the delivery of quality education by capitalising on our best teachers in a cost-effective manner by capitalising on the leaps and bounds of technological advances that have been delivered in Australia and internationally. As such, it would not be hard to deliver our very best quality educational practices and teachers to gifted Aboriginal and non-Aboriginal students via the internet. In fact, this could be more effective in respect to cost, as well as from an educational excellence perspective.

---

[21] Hattie, J. 'Teachers Make a Difference' (2003).
[22] Hattie, J. *Visible Learning* (2009).
[23] Hattie, J. 'Teachers Make a Difference' (2003), 2.
[24] Rowe, K.J. op. cit., 1

Overall, what drives success for Australia are our teachers and we have some of the best and most dedicated teachers in the world that we as a nation should be capitalising upon, respecting, and remunerating appropriately.

## Research Matters

Furthering Australia's future through creative thought about Aboriginal education is also plagued by a paucity of data-driven empirically-based research. This is evinced by Bin-Sallik et al. in their seminal review of Aboriginal Education research where they concluded that much of the literature they reviewed was descriptive;[25] in general "there is almost no empirical research";[26] there is "a noticeable absence in the current literature, of analysis of how 'to get things done'",[27] and few references to the schooling sector. A decade later, Mellor and Corrigan similarly lamented the lack of empirical research noting that: "There is not, in Australia, a research tradition of quantitative measurement in the Indigenous education literature. To ignore such measurement only continues to do injustice to the gravity of the problem".[28] They also emphasised that the research methodology employed in current research suffers from methodological flaws including: small case studies; focusing on a small subset of the population (e.g., communities with a high Aboriginal population); isolating Aboriginal education research from the broader discourses rather than embedding it in them; and asserting rather than demonstrating empirically the relation between cause and effect.[29] Clearly, there is a dearth of useful research being undertaken nationally in Aboriginal Education, yet:

---

[25] Bin-Sallik, M. et al. *Review and Analysis of Literature Relating to Aboriginal and Torres Strait Islander Education* (Vol 1, 1994a).

[26] Ibid., 7.

[27] Bin-Sallik, M. et al. *Review and Analysis of Literature Relating to Aboriginal and Torres Strait Islander Education* (Vol 2, 1994b), 19.

[28] Mellor, S. & Corrigan, M. *The Case for Change* (2004), 46, 47.

[29] Ibid., 46.

Scholarly research can make an important difference and identify much needed fresh insights on how to address critical educational issues of our time ... there is indeed a dire need to establish a concerted national programme of Indigenous Education research to develop a body of scholarly literature that can really put to the test presumed successful strategies, identify causal mechanisms that make a difference, and generate new solutions that are demonstrated by research to result in tangible outcomes.[30]

Clearly research matters and is direly needed to ensure that we develop our full capacity and enable Australia to flourish.

## Summary

The thesis in this chapter has been that as a nation we need a new intellectual mindset and new and dynamic focus upon ensuring Australia flourishes by explicating what seeds success. Fundamental to achieving this goal is putting a stop to the wastage of Aboriginal talent by explicating what seeds success to result in Australia flourishing. This chapter presented some examples of potentially potent innovative ways forward. Overall this chapter has emphasised that to ensure Australia flourishes and becomes as good as it can become, together we can't lose.

---

[30] Bin-Sallik, M. (2005).

# Bibliography

Aboriginal and Torres Strait Islander Education Action Plan (2010-2014). (2011). *Ministerial Council for Education, Early Childhood Development and Youth Affairs.* Carlton South, Victoria: Ministerial Council for Education, Early Childhood Development and Youth Affairs, and Education Services Australia.

Adermann, J., & Campbell, M. (2007). Big Worry: Implications of Anxiety in Indigenous Youth. *Australian Journal of Indigenous Education*, 36 Supplement, 74-80.

Altman, J. (1985). Gambling as a Mode of Redistributing and Accumulating Cash Among Aborigines: A Case Study from Arnhem Land. In G. Caldwell, B. Haig, M. Dickerson & L. Sylvan (Eds). *Gambling in Australia* (pp. 50-67). Sydney: Croon Helm.

Altman, J. (1987). *Hunter-gatherers Today: An Aboriginal Economy in North Australia.* Canberra: Australian Institute of Aboriginal Studies.

Altman, J. (2012). People on Country as Alternate Development. In J. Altman & S. Kerins (Eds.), *People on Country, Vital Landscapes, Indigenous Futures* (pp. 1-22). Sydney: Federation Press.

Altman, J., Biddle, N., & Hunter, B. (2008). *How Realistic are the Prospects for "Closing the Gaps" in Socioeconomic Outcomes for Indigenous Australians?* Centre for Aboriginal Economic Policy Research, Discussion Paper, no. 287. Canberra: ANU.

Altman, J., Buchanan, G., & Larsen, L. (2007). *The Environmental Significance of the Indigenous Estate: Natural Resource Management as Economic Development in Remote Australia.* Centre for Aboriginal Economic Policy Research, Discussion Paper, no. 286. Canberra: ANU.

Altman, J., & Fogarty, B. (2010). Indigenous Australians as 'No Gaps' Subjects: Education and Development in Remote Indigenous Australia. In I. Snyder & J. Nieuwenhuysen (Eds.), *Closing the Gap in Education: Improving Outcomes in Southern World Societies.* Melbourne: Monash University Publishing.

Altman, J., & Hinkson, M. (2010). *Culture Crisis: Anthropology and Politics in Aboriginal Australia.* Sydney: University of New South Wales Press.

Altman, J., & Hunter, B. (2003). Evaluating Indigenous Socioeconomic Outcomes in the Reconciliation Decade, 1991-2001. *Economic Papers*, 22(4), 1-15.

Altman J., & Kerins S. (Eds.). (2012). *People on Country, Vital Landscapes, Indigenous Futures*. Sydney: Federation Press.

Altman, J., & Martin, D. (Eds.). (1993). *Power, Culture, Economy, Indigenous Australians and Mining*, Canberra: CAEPR. Australian National University.

Amrein, A.L., & Berliner, D.C. (2002). High-Stakes Testing, Uncertainty, and Student Learning. *Education Policy Analysis Archives*, 10(18), 1-74.

Anthony, D. (2007). *The Horse, the Wheel and Language: How Bronze-Age Riders from the Eurasian Steppes Shaped the Modern World*. Princeton University Press.

Appiah, K.A. (2005). *The Ethics of Identity*. Princeton, NJ: Princeton University Press.

Ariely, D. (2009). *Predictably Irrational: The Hidden Forces That Shape Our Decisions*. London: Harper

Asmar, C., Page, S., & Radloff, A. (2011). Dispelling Myths: Indigenous Students' Engagement with University. *AUSSE Research Briefings*. Australian Council for Educational Research. Retrieved from www.acer.edu.au

Austin-Broos, D. (2006). "Working for" and "Working" Among Western Arrernte in Central Australia. *Oceania*, 76(1), 1–15.

Austin-Broos, D. (2009). *Arrernte Present, Arrernte Past: Invasion, Violence and Imagination in Indigenous Central Australia*. University of Chicago Press.

Australian Bureau of Statistics. (2001). *Measuring Wellbeing Frameworks for Australian Social Statistics* (no. 4160.0). Retrieved from http://www.abs.gov.au

Australian Bureau of Statistics. (2004). *National Aboriginal and Torres Strait Islander Social Survey, Northern Territory, 2002* (no. 4714.7.55.001). Retrieved from http://www.abs.gov.au

Australian Bureau of Statistics. (2006). *National Aboriginal and Torres Strait Islander Health Survey Australia 2004-05* (no. 4715.0). Retrieved from http://www.abs.gov.au

Australian Bureau of Statistics. (2010a). *National Aboriginal and Torres Strait Islander Social Survey: Users' Guide, 2008* (no. 4720.0). Retrieved from http://www.abs.gov.au

Australian Bureau of Statistics. (2010b). *Population Characteristics, Aboriginal and Torres Strait Islander Australians, Northern Territory, 2006* (no. 4713.7.55.001). Retrieved from http://www.abs.gov.au

Australian Bureau of Statistics. (2011). *Directory of Family and Domestic Violence*

*Statistics* (no. 4533.0). Retrieved from http://www.abs.gov.au

Australian Bureau of Statistics. (2012a). *Aboriginal and Torres Strait Islander Peoples (Indigenous) Profiles Datapack, First Release* (no. 2069.0.30.003). Retrieved from http://www.abs.gov.au

Australian Bureau of Statistics. (2012b). *Australian Demographic Statistics*, Mar 2012 (no. 3101.0). Retrieved from http://www.abs.gov.au

Australian Bureau of Statistics. (2012c). *Corrective Services Australia* (no. 4512.0). Retrieved from http://www.abs.gov.au

Australian Bureau of Statistics. (2012d). *Schools Australia 2011* (no. 4221.0). Retrieved from http://www.abs.gov.au

Australian Curriculum, Assessment and Reporting Authority (ACARA). (2012). *National Assessment Program: Literacy and Numeracy. Achievement in Reading, Persuasive Writing, Language Conventions and Numeracy. National Report for 2012.* Sydney: ACARA.

Australian Database of Indigenous Violence: www.indigenousviolence.org/dnn

Australian Government. (2012). *National Food Plan Green Paper.* Canberra: Department of Agriculture, Fisheries and Forestry.

Australian Institute of Health and Welfare. (2011). *Life Expectancy and Mortality of Aboriginal and Torres Strait Islander People.* Canberra: Australian Institute of Health and Welfare. Retrieved from http://www.aihw.gov.au

Australian Institute of Health and Welfare, and Australian Institute of Family Studies (no date). *Closing the Gap Clearinghouse.* Retrieved from http://www.aihw.gov.au/closingthegap

Australian National Council on Drugs. (2013). *An Economic Analysis for Aboriginal and Torres Strait Islander offenders: Prison vs Residential Treatment.* Canberra: Australian National Council on Drugs, National Indigenous Drug and Alcohol Committee.

Australian New Zealand Policing Advisory Agency's 2008 Report (2008). Melbourne: ANZPAA. Retrieved from www.anzpaa.org.au

Australian Senate. (2005). *Indigenous Education Funding: Final Report.* Canberra: Employment, Workplace Relations and Education References Committee.

Baarda, W. (1994). The Impact of the Bilingual Program at Yuendumu 1974 to 1993. In D. Hartman & J. Henderson (Eds.), *Aboriginal Languages in Education.* Alice Springs: Institute for Aboriginal Development Press.

Behrendt, L. (2012). *Review of Higher Education Access and Outcomes for Aboriginal and Torres Strait Islander People. Final Report.* Retrieved from http://www.innovation.gov.au/HigherEducation/IndigenousHigherEducation/ReviewOfIndigenousHigherEducation/FinalReport/index.html

Belanger, Y.D. (2006). Gambling with the Future: The Evolution of Aboriginal Gaming in Canada. Purich's Aboriginal Issues Series. Saskatoon, Canada: Purich Pub.

Belanger, Y.D., Williams, R.J., & Arthur, J.N. (2011). Casinos and Economic Well-being: Evaluating the Alberta First Nations' Experience. *Journal of Gambling Business and Economics,* 5(1), 23–46.

Bellavia, G.M., & Frone, M.R. (2005). Work-Family Conflict. In J. Barling, E.K. Kelloway & M.R. Frone (Eds), *Handbook of Work Stress* (pp. 113-147). Thousand Oaks, CA: Sage.

Beresford, Q., & Omaji, P. (1996). *Rites of Passage: Aboriginal Youth, Crime and Justice.* Fremantle, WA: Fremantle Arts Centre Press.

Biddle, N. (2012). Australian Census: Indigenous Australia Improves, but Closing the Gap is a Long Way off. *The Conversation.* Retrieved from http://theconversation.edu.au.

Bin-Sallik, M. (2005). Preface in Craven, R.G., Tucker, A., Munns, G., Hinkley, J., Marsh, H.W., & Simpson, K. *Indigenous Students'Aspirations: Dreams, Perceptions and Realities.* DEST. Canberra: Commonwealth of Australia.

Bin-Sallik, M., Blomeley, N., Flowers, R., & Hughes, P. (1994a Vol.1; 1994b Vol. 2). *Review and Analysis of Literature Relating to Aboriginal and Torres Strait Islander Education.* Part 1 Summary. Canberra: DEET.

Blagg, H. (2005). *A New Way of Doing Justice Business? Community Justice Mechanisms and Sustainable Governance in Western Australia (background paper no. 8).* Perth: Law Reform Commission of Western Australia.

Bloom, P. (2011). *How Pleasure Works: Why We Like What We Like.* London: Vintage.

Bohanna, I., & Clough, A.R. (2012). Cannabis Use in Cape York Indigenous Communities: High Prevalence, Mental Health Impacts and the Desire To Quit. *Drug and Alcohol Review,* 31(4), 580-584.

Bradley, D., Noonan, P., Nugent, H., & Scales, B. (2008). *Review of Australian Higher Education. Final Report.* Canberra: Commonwealth of Australia.

Brady, M. (1998). *The Grog Book: Strengthening Indigenous Community Action on Alcohol*. Canberra: Department of Health and Family Services.

Brady, M. (2004). *Regulating Social Problems: The Pokies, the Productivity Commission and an Aboriginal Community*. Centre for Aboriginal Economic Policy Research, Discussion Paper, no. 269. Canberra: ANU.

Breen, H. (2012). Risk and Protective Factors Associated with Gambling Products and Services: Indigenous Gamblers in North Queensland. *International Journal of Mental Health and Addiction*, 10(1), 24–38.

Brook, J., & Kohen, J.L. (1991). *The Parramatta Native Institution and the Black Town: A History*. Kensington, NSW: University of New South Wales Press.

Broome, R. (1983). *Aboriginal Australians: Black Response to White Dominance 1788–1980*. Sydney: Allen and Unwin.

Brough, M. (2010). *Our Generation* [Documentary]. S. Sabam & D. Curtis (Directors), D. Gondarra & J. McMullen (Co-Producers). www.ourgeneration.org.au

Burbank, V. (2006). From Bedtime to On Time: Why Many Aboriginal People Don't Especially Like Participating in Western Institutions. *Anthropological Forum: A Journal of Social Anthropology and Comparative Sociology*, 16(1), 3-20.

Calma, T. (2006a). *The Integration of Customary Law into the Australian Legal System*. Australian Human Rights Commission. Retrieved from http://humanrights.gov.au/

Calma, T. (2006b). *Social Justice and Native Title Report, 2006*. HREOC. Australian Government Press.

Cape York Institute for Policy and Leadership. (2005). *Freedom, Capabilities and the Cape York Reform Agenda*. Cairns: Cape York Institute for Policy and Leadership. Retrieved from http://www.cyi.org.au.

Carstairs, J.R., Myers, B., Shores E.A., & Fogarty, G. (2006). Influence of Language Background on Tests of Cognitive Abilities: Australian Data. *Australian Psychologist*, 41(1), 48-54.

Casey, D. (2007). *Report on the Review of the Department of Indigenous Affairs*. Perth, WA: Department of the Premier and Cabinet.

Catts, R., & Gelade, S. (2002). *Rhetorics and Realities: Equating the Delivery of Indigenous VET to the Demands of its Context: Commonalities from Two Research Projects*. Paper presented at the Australian Vocational Education and Training Research Association Conference, Melbourne.

Central Australian Aboriginal Congress Inc. (2008). *Aboriginal Male Health Summit 2008: Inteyerrkwe Statement*. Retrieved from www.caac.org.au/malehealthinfo.

Chikritzhs, T., Gray, D., Lyons, Z., & Saggers, S. (2007). *Restrictions on the Sale and Supply of Alcohol: Evidence and Outcomes*. Perth: National Drug Research Institute Curtin University of Technology.

Childe, V.G. (1958). *The Prehistory of European Society*. Harmondsworth: Penguin.

Chomsky, N. (2002). *Chomsky on Democracy and Education*. New York: Routledge.

Christie, M. (1993). Constructing a Galtha Curriculum. *Education Australia*, 22, 15-18.

Christie, M., Greatorex, J., Gurruwiwi, D., Djirrimbilpilwuy, F., Galathi, J., Gapany, D., Guyula, Y. et al. (2009). *Regulated Gambling and Problem Gambling Among Aborigines from Remote Northern Territory Communities: A Yolŋu Case Study* Workshop report. Darwin: School for Social and Policy Research, Charles Darwin University.

Christie, M., & Martin Y. (2011). The Public Problem of "Aboriginal Gambling": Winning the Struggle for an Urban Space. *Australian Journal of Social Issues*, 46(3), 253.

Chronology: The Bilingual Education Policy in the Northern Territory. (no date). *Four Corners* [Television show]. Australian Broadcasting Corporation.

COAG Reform Council. (2012). *Indigenous Reform 2010-2011: Comparing Performance Across Australia*. Sydney: COAG Reform Council.

Coleman, J.S., Hoffer, T., & Kilgore, S. (1982). *High School Achievement: Public, Catholic, and Private Schools Compared*. New York: Basic Books.

Collier, P., & Horowitz, D. (1997). Introduction. In P. Collier & D. Horowitz (Eds.), *The Race Card: White Guilt, Black Resentment, and the Assault on Truth and Justice*. USA: Prima.

Collingwood, R.G. (1962). *The Idea of History*. Oxford: Clarendon Press.

Commonwealth of Australia. (1997). *Bringing Them Home: National Inquiry into the Separation of Aboriginal and Torres Strait Islander Children from Their Families*. Canberra: The Human Rights and Equal Opportunity Commission.

Commonwealth of Australia. (2000). *Review of the Indigenous Education Direct Assistance (IEDA) Programme – October 2000*. Canberra: Department of Education, Science and Training.

Commonwealth of Australia. (2003). *Review of Indigenous Education Consultative*

*Bodies: Final Report.* Canberra: Department of Education, Science and Training.

Commonwealth of Australia. (2008). *Parent School Partnerships Initiative: Audit Report No.29 2007-08 Performance Audit.* Canberra: Australian National Audit Office.

Commonwealth of Australia. (2009). *Indigenous Education (Targeted Assistance) Act: Annual Report.* Canberra: Department of Education, Employment and Workplace Relations.

Commonwealth of Australia. (2012). *Our Land Our Languages: Inquiry into Language Learning in Indigenous Communities.* House of Representatives Standing Committee on Aboriginal and Torres Strait Islander Affairs. Canberra: Parliament of the Commonwealth of Australia.

Community Development and Justice Standing Committee. (2010). *Making Our Prisons Work: An Inquiry into the Efficiency and Effectiveness of Prisoner Education, Training and Employment Strategies: Report No. 6 in the 38th Parliament.* Perth, WA: Legislative Assembly, Parliament of Western Australia.

Connerly, W. (2000). *Creating Equal: My Flight against Race Preferences.* San Francisco: Encounter Books.

Cooke, M., Mitrou, F., Lawrence, D., Guimond, E., & Beavon, D. (2007). Indigenous Well-Being in Four Countries: An Application of the UNDP's Human Development Index to Indigenous Peoples in Australia, Canada, New Zealand, and the United States. *BMC International Health and Human Rights,* 7(9), 1-39.

Cooke, P. (2012). A Long Walk Home to the Warddewardde. In J. Altman & S. Kerins (Eds.), *People on Country, Vital Landscapes, Indigenous Futures* (pp.146-161). Sydney: Federation Press.

Coombs, H.C. (1994). *Aboriginal Autonomy: Issues and Strategies.* Cambridge University Press.

Coombs, H.C., Brandl, M.M., & Snowdon, W.E. (1983). *A Certain Heritage: Programs for and by Aboriginal Families in Australia.* Canberra: Centre for Resource and Environmental Studies, Australian National University.

Cordner, G.W. (1999). Elements of Community Policing. In L.K. Gaines & G. Cordner (Eds.), *Policing Perspectives: An Anthology* (pp. 137-149). Los Angeles, CA: Roxbury.

Cornell, S. (2008). The Political Economy of American Indian Gaming. *Annual Review of Law and Social Science,* 4(1), 63–82.

Cornell, S., & Kalt, J. (Eds). (1992). *What Can Tribes Do? Strategies and Institutions in American Indian Economic Development?* Los Angeles: American Indian Studies Center, UCL.

Cosby, B., & Poussaint, A.F. (2007). *Come on People.* Nasville: Thomas Nelson.

Council for Aboriginal Reconciliation (1992). *Walking Together, 1.* Canberra: AGPS

Craven, R.G. (1999). Aboriginal Studies: A National Priority. In R.G. Craven (Ed.), *Teaching Aboriginal Studies* (pp. 13–26). Sydney, NSW: Allen & Unwin.

Craven, R.G. (2003). Shaping a Glad Tomorrow: Mandatory Indigenous Studies Teacher Education Courses an International Educational Priority! In D.M. McInerney & S. Van Etten (Eds.), *Sociocultural Influences and Teacher Education Programs* (Vol. 3, pp. 165–197). Greenwich, CT: Information Age Publishing.

Craven, R.G. (2012). Seeding Success: Getting Started Teaching Aboriginal Studies Effectively. In Partington, G., Beresford, Q., & Gower G. (Eds.) *Reform and Resistance in Education: Fully Revised Edition.* Crawley, WA: UWA Publishing.

Craven, R. & Bodkin-Andrews, G. (2011). What Research Can Tell Us. In R. Craven (Eds.), *Teaching Aboriginal Studies: A Practical Resource for Primary and Secondary Teaching* (pp. 210-228). Australia: Allen & Unwin.

Cruickshank, J. (2008). 'To Exercise a Beneficial Influence over a Man': Marriage, Gender and the Native Institutions in Early Colonial Australia. In A. Barry, J. Cruickshank, A. Brown-May & P. Grimshaw (Eds.), *Evangelists of Empire? Missionaries in Colonial History.* Melbourne: Unniversity of Melbourne eScholarship Research Centre. Retrieved from http://www.msp.unimelb.edu.au/missions/index.php/missions

Cunneen, C. (2006). Racism, Discrimination and the Over-Representation of Indigenous People in the Criminal Justice System: Some Conceptual and Explanatory Issues. *Current Issues in Criminal Justice,* 17(3), 329-346.

Cunneen, C., & McDonald, D. (1997). *Keeping Aboriginal and Torres Strait Islander People out of Custody: An Evaluation of the Implementation of the Recommendations of the Royal Commission in [ie. into] Aboriginal Deaths in Custody.* Canberra: Office of Public Affairs, ATSIC.

Davidson, B.R. (1965). *The Northern Myth: A Study of the Physical and Economic Limits to Agricultural and Pastoral Development in Tropical Australia.* Melbourne University Press.

Davis, J. (1988). Slum Dwelling. In K. Gilbert (Ed.), *Inside Black Australia: An Anthology of Aboriginal Poetry* (p. 55). Ringwood, Victoria: Penguin Books.

Days, L. (2011). Family Violence and Homelessness in Aboriginal and Torres Strait Islander Communities. *Right Now: Human Rights in Australia*. Retrieved from http://rightnow.org.au

De Bortoli, L., & Thomson, S. (2010). Contextual Factors that Influence the Achievement of Australia's Indigenous Students: Results from PISA 2000-2006. *OECD Programme for International Student Assessment (PISA)*, 7.

De Plevitz, L. (2007). Testing the Social Justice Goals of Education: A Role for Anti-Discrimination Law. *Australian Journal of Indigenous Education*, 36 Supplement, 98-107.

Department of the Attorney General and Justice, Northern Territory. (2012). *Northern Territory Domestic Violence Act*, 1 July.

Department of Corrective Services WA. (2010). *Annual Report: 2009-2010*. Retrieved from http://www.correctiveservices.wa.gov.au

Department of Corrective Services WA. (2012). *Weekly Offender Statistics, 16th August 2012*. Retrieved from http://www.correctiveservices.wa.gov.au

Department of Education, Employment, and Workplace Relations (2008). *National Report to Parliament on Indigenous Education Science and Training, 2006*. Canberra: Commonwealth of Australia.

Department of Families, Housing, Community Services and Indigenous Affairs (DFHCSIA). (2011). *Annual Report, 2010-2011*. Canberra: Australian Government.

Devansesen, D., & Briscoe, J. (1980). The Health Worker Training Program in Central Australia, *Lambie Dew Oration*. The Sydney University Medical Society.

Devlin, B. (2009). Bilingual Education in the Northern Territory and the Continuing Debate over its Effectiveness and Value. Paper presented to the AIATSIS Research Symposium *Bilingual Education in the Northern Territory: Principles, Policy and Practice*. Canberra.

Dillon, A. (2010). Self-esteem (Liking Ourselves). *Aboriginal and Islander Health Worker Journal*, 34(3), 23-24.

Dillon, S. (2007). Maybe We Can Find Some Common Ground: Indigenous Perspectives, a Music Teacher's Story. *Australian Journal of Indigenous Education*, 36 Supplement, 59-65.

Dineen, T. (2001). *Manufacturing Victims: What the Psychology Industry is Doing to People*. Montreal: Robert Davies.

Discrimination Commissioner. (1995). *Alcohol Report: Racial Discrimination Act 1975 Race Discrimination, Human Rights and the Distribution of Alcohol.* Canberra: Australian Government Publishing Service.

Dulfer, N. (2012, November 26). Testing the Test: NAPLAN Makes for Stressed Kids and a Narrow Curriculum. *The Conversation.* Retrieved from http://theconversation.edu.au.

Edgell, S. (2006). *The Sociology of Work: Continuity and Change in Paid and Unpaid Work.* London: SAGE.

Edwards, B., Gray, M., Baxter, J., & Hunter, B.H. (2009). *The Tyranny of Distance? Carers in Regional and Remote Areas of Australia.* Melbourne: Australian Institute of Family Studies.

Ehrlich P.R., & Ehrlich, A.H. (1981). *Extinction, the Causes and Consequences of the Disappearance of Species.* New York: Random House.

Elder, L. (2009). *What's Race Got to do With It?* New York: St Martin's Griffin.

Evans, W.N., & Topoleski, J.H. (2002). *The Social and Economic Impact of Native American Casinos.* Working Paper. National Bureau of Economic Research, September 2002. Retrieved from http://www.nber.org/papers/w9198.

Family Responsibilities Commission. (2012). *Annual Report: 2011-12.* Cairns: Family Responsibilities Commission.

Faragher, E.B., Cass, M., & Cooper, C.L. (2005). The Relationship between Job Satisfaction and Health: A Meta-analysis. *Occupational and Environmental Medicine,* 62(2), 105–112.

Federal Court of Australia's Indigenous Dispute Resolution & Conflict Management Case Study Project. (2009). *Solid Work You Mob Are Doing.* Retrieved from http://www.nadrac.gov.au

Ferguson, J. (2002). Global Disconnect: Abjection and the Aftermath of Modernism. In J.X. Inda & R. Rosaldo, (Eds.), *The Anthropology of Globalization* (pp. 136-153). Malden, MA: Blackwell.

Findlay, M., Odgers, S., & Yeo, S. (1994). *Australian Criminal Justice.* Melbourne: Oxford University Press.

Fitzpatrick, J.P., Elliott, E.J., Latimer, J. Carter, M., Oscar, J., Ferreira, M., & Hand, M. (2012). The Liliwan Project: Study Protocol for A Population-based Active Case Ascertainment Study of the Prevalence of Fetal Alcohol Spectrum Disorders (FASD) in Remote Australian Aboriginal Communities. *BMJ Open,* 2(3).

Fleming, J., & O'Reilly, J. (2008). In Search of Progress: Community Policing in Australia. In Williamson, T. (Ed.), *The Handbook of Knowledge Based Policing: Current Conception and Future Directions* (pp.139-156). Sussex: Wiley.

Fletcher, J. (1989). *Clean, Clad and Courteous: A History of Aboriginal Education in New South Wales*. Sydney: J Fletcher Desktop Publisher.

Flinders, M. (1814). *A Voyage to Terra Australis Undertaken for the Purpose of Completing the Discovery of that Vast Country and Prosecuted in the Years 1801, 1802 and 1803 in His Majesty's Ship the Investigator and Subsequently in the Armed Vessel Porpoise*. Pall Mall, London: G and W Nicol.

Flinders Institute for Housing, Urban and Regional Research (FIHURR). (2008). *Women, Homelessness and Domestic Violence: A Synthesis Report*.

Fogarty, B. (2012). Country as Classroom. In J. Altman & S. Kerins (Eds.), *People on Country: Vital Landscapes, Indigenous Futures*. Sydney: Federation Press.

Fogarty, B., & Schwab, J. (2012). *Indigenous Education: Experiential Learning and Learning through Country*. Centre for Aboriginal Economic Policy Research, Working Paper, no. 80. 1-24. Canberra: ANU.

Foote, R.J. (1996). *Aboriginal Gambling: A Pilot Study of Casino Attendance and the Introduction of Poker Machines into Community Venues in the Northern Territory*. Darwin: Centre for Social Research, Northern Territory University.

Ford, C., (2012). Great Expectations: A Bold Social Experiment on Cape York is in its Fifth Year. *The Monthly*, November, 22-33.

Fordham, A., Fogarty, B., Corey, B., & Fordham, D. (2010). *Knowledge Foundations for the Development of Sustainable Wildlife Enterprises in Remote Indigenous Communities of Australia*. Centre for Aboriginal Economic Policy Research, Working Paper, no. 62. 1-59. Canberra: ANU.

Franklin, J. (2012). The Missionary with 150 Wives. *Quadrant*, 56(7-8), 31-32.

Freiberg, A. (2001). Problem-Orientated Courts. *Journal of Judicial Administration*. 11, 8-27.

Gasper, D. (2004). *Human Well-being: Concepts and Conceptualizations*. WIDER Discussion Papers, No. 2004/06. United Nations University World Institute for Development Economics, Helsinki.

Gelade, S., & Stehlik, T. (2004). *Exploring Locality: The Impact of Context on Indigenous Vocational Education and Training Aspirations and Outcomes*. Adelaide: National Centre for Vocational Education Research.

Gibson, L. (2010). Making a Life: Getting Ahead, and a Living in Aboriginal New South Wales. *Oceania*, 80(2), 143-160.

Goldsmith, A.H., Sedo, S., Darity W. Jr., & Hamilton, D. (2004). The Labor Supply Consequences of Perceptions of Employer Discrimination during Search and On-the-job: Integrating Neoclassical Theory and Cognitive Dissonance. *Journal of Economic Psychology*, 25(1), 15-39.

Gooda, M. (2011). *Social Justice Report 2011*. Canberra: Australian Human Rights Commission, 58.

Goodale, J.C. (1987). Gambling Is Hard Work: Card Playing in Tiwi Society. *Oceania*, 58(1), 6–21.

Gore, A. (2007). *The Assault on Reason*. London: Bloomsbury.

Goulding, D. (2007a). *Recapturing Freedom: Issues Relating to the Release of Long-term Prisoners into the Community*. Sydney: Hawkins Press.

Goulding, D. (2007b). Violence & Brutality in Prisons: A West Australian Context. *Current Issues in Criminal Justice*, 18(3), 399-414.

Goulding, D., Hall, G., & Steels, B. (2008). Restorative Prisons: Toward Radical Prison Reform. *Current Issues in Criminal Justice*, 20(2), 231-242.

Government of New South Wales. (1814). *Establishment of the Native Institution 1814 – Government and General Order*. Retrieved from http://ww.records.nsw.gov.au.

Grant, E. (1998). *My Land, My Tracks*. Innisfail: Innisfail and District Education Centre.

Grant, E. (2005). *Holistic Planning and Teaching Framework* [videodisc]. Clifton Beach, Qld.: Critical Mass Media.

Gray, J. & Partington, G. (2012). Attendance and Non-Attendance at School. In Q. Beresford, G. Partington, & G. Gower, (Eds.) *Reform and Resistance in Aboriginal Education* (pp. 261-303).WA: UWA Publishing.

Green, J., & Morrison, J., facilitated by Kerins, S. (2012). 'No More Yardin' Us Up Like Cattle', In J. Altman & S. Kerins (Eds.), *People on Country, Vital Landscapes, Indigenous Futures* (pp.190-201). Sydney: Federation Press.

Greenhaus, J.H., Allen, T.D., & Spector, P.E. (2006). Health Consequences of Work-family Conflict: The Dark Side of the Work-family Interface. *Research in Occupational Stress and Well Being*, 5, 61–98.

Greenhaus, J.H., & Beutell, N.J. (1985). Sources of Conflict between Work and Family Roles. *Academy of Management Review*, 10(1), 76-88.

Greening, T. (2000). Pedagogically Sound Responses to Economic Rationalism. *ACM SIGCSE Bulletin*, 32(1). 149-156.

Gregory, S. (2007). *The Devil behind the Mirror: Globalization and Politics in the Dominican Republic*. Berkley, CA: University of California Press.

Grieves, V. (2009). *Aboriginal Spirituality: Aboriginal Philosophy, the Basis of Aboriginal Social and Emotional Wellbeing*. Discussion Paper No. 9. Darwin: Cooperative Research Centre for Aboriginal Health.

Groome, H., & Hamilton, A. (1995). *Meeting the Educational Needs of Aboriginal Adolescents*. Commissioned Report (Australia: National Board of Employment, Education and Training) no. 35, Canberra: Australian Government Publishing Service.

Gruenewald, D.A. (2008). Place-Based Education: Grounding Culturally Responsive Teaching in Geographical Diversity. In D.A. Gruenewald & G. A. Smith (Eds.), *Place-Based Education in the Global Age: Local diversity*. New York: Lawrence Erlbaum Associates.

Gruenewald, D.A. (2006, April). *Why Place Matters: The Everyday Context Everywhere of Experience, Culture and Education*. Paper presented at the Annual Conference of the Association of Educational Research in America, San Francisco.

Gsell, F.X. (1956). *"The Bishop with 150 Wives": Fifty Years as a Missionary*. Sydney: Angus and Robertson.

*Hales v Jamilmira* [2003] NTCA 9.

Halliday, M.A.K. (1995, December). *Language and the Reshaping of Human Experience*. Paper presented at the Fourth International Symposium on Critical Discourse Analysis, Athens.

Hambleton, R., & Rodgers, J.H. (1995). Item Bias Review. *Practical Assessment, Research & Evaluation*, 4(6). Retrieved from http://pareonline.net/getvn.asp?v=4&n=6

Harris, S. (1980). *Culture and Learning: Tradition and Education in Northeast Arnhem Land*. Darwin: Northern Territory Department of Education.

Harris, S. (1990). *Two-way Aboriginal Schooling: Education and Cultural Survival*. Canberra: Aboriginal Studies Press, eBooks.com Retrieved from http://www.ebooks.com/287022/two-way-aboriginal-schooling/harris-stephen/

Harris, E., & Morrow, M. (2001). Unemployment is a Health Hazard: The Health Costs of Unemployment. *The Economic and Labour Relations Review*, 12(1), 18-31.

Harvey, D. (2005). *A Brief History of Neoliberalism*. Oxford University Press.

Hasluck, P. (1988). *Shades of Darkness: Aboriginal Affairs 1923-1965*. Melbourne University Press.

Hasluck, P. (1994). *Mucking About: An Autobiography*. University of Western Australia Press.

Hattie, J. (2003). *Teachers Make a Difference. What is the Research Evidence?* Paper presented at the Joint New Zealand Association for Research in Education and Australian Association for Research in Education conference, Auckland, December.

Hattie, J. (2009). Visible Learning: A Synthesis of over 800-Metal-Analyses relating to Achievement. London: Routledge.

Heath, S.B. (2010). Family Literacy or Community Learning? Some Critical Questions on Perspective. In K. Dunsmore & D. Fisher (Eds.), *Newark International Reading Association*, DE, 2010. Retrieved from http://www.shirleybriceheath.net/pdfs/SBH_bringingLiteracyHome.pdf

Herbert, B. (2012). Spate of Suicides Grips Aboriginal Community. *ABC News*, 6 September.

Hill, K., Barker, B., & Vos, T. (2007). Excess Indigenous Mortality: Are Indigenous Australians more Severely Disadvantaged than other Indigenous Populations? *International Journal of Epidemiology*, *36*, 580-589.

Hill, P.W., & Rowe, K.J. (1998). Modeling Student Progress in Studies of Educational effectiveness. *School Effectiveness and School Improvement*, *9* (3), 310-333.

Hitchens, C. (2001). *Letters to a Young Contrarian (Art of Mentoring)*. New York: Basic Books.

Holderhead, S. (2012, May). Protest against NAPLAN Tests by Academics. *News.com.au* Retrieved from http://www.news.com.au

Holmes, J. (2010). The Multifunctional Transition in Australia's Tropical Savannas: The Emergence of Consumption, Protection and Indigenous Values. *Geographical Research*, August, 48(3), 265-280.

Homelessness Australia. (No date). *Homelessness and Indigenous Australians*. http://www.homelessnessaustralia.org.au

Hope, A.N. (2008). *Record of Investigation into 22 Deaths in the Kimberly*, Coronial Inquiry. Perth: WA Department of Health.

House of Representatives Standing Committee on Aboriginal and Torres Strait Islander Affairs. (2011). *Doing Time – Time for Doing: Indigenous Youth in the Criminal Justice System*. Canberra: Parliament of the Commonwealth of Australia.

Houston, J. (2007). Indigenous Autoethnography: Formulating Our Knowledge, Our Way. *Australian Journal of Indigenous Education*, 36 Supplement, 45-50.

Howard, D. (2002). Family, Friends and Teachers: Why Indigenous Students Stay at or Leave School. *The Australian Journal of Indigenous Education, 30*(2), 8-12.

Hudson, S. (2008). *CDEP: Help or Hindrance? The Community Development Employment Program and its Impact on Indigenous Australians.* CIS Policy Monograph 86. Sydney: The Centre for Independent Studies.

Hudson, S. (2009). *From Rhetoric to Reality: Can 99-Year Leases Lead to Homeownership for Indigenous Communities?* CIS Policy Monograph 92. Sydney: The Centre for Independent Studies.

Hudson, S. (2011). Straddling Black-Fella and White-Fella Laws. *Ideas@TheCentre.* Newsletter. Sydney: The Centre for Independent Studies, 25 March.

Hughes, H. (2007). *Lands of Shame: Aboriginal and Torres Strait Islander 'Homelands' in Transition.* Sydney: Centre for Independent Studies.

Hughes, H. (2008). Who are Indigenous Australians? *Quadrant*, 52(11), 26-32.

Hughes, H., & Hughes, M. (2012a). The Denial of Private Property Rights to Aborigines. *Quadrant*, 56(5), 25-29.

Hughes, H., & Hughes, M. (2012b). *Indigenous Education 2012*, CIS Policy Monograph. Sydney: Centre for Independent Studies.

Hughes, H., & Warin, J. (2005). *A New Deal for Aborigines and Torres Strait Islanders in Remote Communities.* Issue Analysis 54, Sydney: The Centre for Independent Studies.

Hughes, P. (1988). *Report of the Aboriginal Education Policy Task Force.* Canberra: Department of Employment, Education and Training, Australian Government Printing Service.

Hunt, J. (2012). North to South. In J. Altman & S. Kerins (Eds.), *People on Country, Vital Landscapes, Indigenous Futures* (pp. 94-114). Sydney: Federation Press.

Hunter, B.H., & Schwab, J. (2003). *Practical Reconciliation and Recent Trends in Indigenous Education.* Centre for Aboriginal Economic Policy Research, Discussion Paper, no. 249. 1-35. Canberra: ANU.

Hunter, E. (1993). *Aboriginal Health and History: Power and Prejudice in Remote Australia.* Melbourne: Cambridge University Press.

Hunter, E. (2006). *Back to Redfern: Autonomy and the 'Middle E' in Relation to*

*Aboriginal Health. Discussion Paper Number 18.* Canberra: Australian Institute of Aboriginal and Torres Strait Islander Studies.

Hunter, E., Brady, M., & Hall, W. (1998). *Services Relating to Alcohol in Indigenous Communities.* Canberra: Office of Aboriginal and Torres Strait Islander Health Services.

Hunter, E., Gynther, B., Anderson, C., Onnis, L.-a., Groves, A., & Nelson, J. (2011). Psychosis and its Correlates in A Remote Indigenous Population. *Australasian Psychiatry,* 19(5), 434-438.

Hunter, E., Gynther, B.D., Anderson, C.J., Onnis, L.L., Nelson, J.R., Hall, W., Baune, B.T., & Groves, A.R. (2012). Psychosis in Indigenous Populations of Cape York and the Torres Strait. *Medical Journal of Australia,* 196(2), 133-135.

Hunter, E., Hall, W., & Spargo, R. (1991). The Distribution and Correlates of Alcohol Consumption in A Remote Aboriginal Population. Monograph No 12. Sydney: National Drug and Alcohol Research Centre.

Hunter, E., Onnis, L.-a., & Pritchard, J. (in press). Gardens of Discontent: Health and Horticulture in Remote Aboriginal Australia. Canberra: Australian Institute of Aboriginal and Torres Strait Islander Studies.

Independent Media Centre, Australia. (2011). *Town Camp Leader Outraged by Bess Price Claims on ABC Television's Q and A,* media release.

Indigenous Economic Development Strategy 2011–2018. (2011). Canberra: Australian Government. Retrieved from http://www.fahcsia.gov.au

Izzard, J. (2010). The Trial of Andrew Bolt: I – Designer Ethnicity [Electronic version]. *Quadrant Online,* 54(12), 15-19. Retrieved from www.quadrant.org.au

Jahoda, M. (1982). *Employment and Unemployment: A Social-psychological Analysis.* Cambridge University Press.

Jajirdi Consultatnts. (2009). *Should Customary Law Be Recognized by the Courts.* Retrieved from http://jajirdi.com.au

Jarrett, S. (2013). *Liberating Aboriginal People from Violence.* Ballan, Victoria: Connor Court.

Johns, G. (2011). *Aboriginal Self-Determination: The White Man's Dream.* Ballan, Victoria: Connor Court.

Jones, D.J. (1988). *A Source of Inspiration and Delight: The buildings of the State Library of New South Wales Since 1826.* Sydney: Library Council of NSW.

Jordan, K., Bulloch, H., & Buchanan, G. (2010). Statistical Equality and Cultural Difference in Indigenous Wellbeing Frameworks: A New Expression of an Enduring Debate. *Australian Journal of Social Issues,* 45(3), 333-362.

Kahneman, D. (2011). *Thinking Fast And Slow*. London: Allen Lane.

Kahneman, D., & Krueger, A.B. (2006). Developments in the Measurement of Subjective Well-being. *Journal of Economic Perspectives*, 20(1), 3–24.

Kays, M., & Romaszko, J. (1995). *Away Yesterday and Today: Back Tomorrow: A One-week Snapshot of Attendance Patterns in Tasmanian schools*. Tasmania: Education Planning Branch, Department of Education and the Arts.

Keeley, L.H. (1996). *War before Civilization: The Myth of the Peaceful Savage*. New York: Oxford University Press.

Kerins, S. (2012). Caring for Country to Working on Country. In J. Altman & S. Kerins (Eds.), *People on Country, Vital Landscapes, Indigenous Futures* (pp. 26-44). Sydney: Federation Press.

Kimm, J. (2004). *A Fatal Conjunction: Two Laws Two Cultures*. Sydney: Federation Press.

Kinnane, S. (2003). *Shadow Lines*. Fremantle, WA: Fremantle Arts Centre Press.

Klein, N. (2008). *The Shock Doctrine: The Rise of Disaster Capitalism*. London: Penguin Books.

Kral, I. (2007). *Writing Words – Right Way! Literacy and Social Practice in the Ngaanyatjarra World* (Unpublished Doctoral Thesis). Canberra: The Australian National University.

Kral, I. (2010). *Generational Change, Learning and Remote Australian Indigenous Youth*. Centre for Aboriginal Economic Policy Research. Working Paper, no. 68. Canberra: ANU.

Kutay, C. (2007). Knowledge Management as Enterprise. *Australian Journal of Indigenous Education*, 36 Supplement, 137-144.

Lahn, J. (in press). Aboriginal Urban Professionals and 'Middle Classness'. In D. Howard-Wagner, D. Habibis & T. Petray (Eds.), *Theorising Indigenous Sociology: Developing Australian and International Approaches*. University of Sydney.

Lamb, D., & Young, M. (2011). 'Pushing Buttons': An Evaluation of the Effect of Aboriginal Income Management on Commercial Gambling Expenditure. *Australian Journal of Social Issues*, 46(2), 119–140.

Lane, J. (2009). *Indigenous Participation in University Education*, Issue Analysis. Sydney: Centre for Independent Studies.

Lane, J., & Lane, M. (2008). *Hard Grind – The Making of an Urban Indigenous Population*. Melbourne: Bennelong Society Conference.

Lang, S. (2009). Learning a Second Language is Good Childhood Mind Medicine,

Studies Find. *Chronicle Online*, May. Retrieved from http://www.news.cornell.edu/stories/may09/bilingual.kids.sl.html

Langton, M. (2008). Trapped in the Aboriginal Reality Show [Electronic version]. *Griffith Review*, 19.

Langton, M. (2010). The Resource Curse [Electronic version] *Griffith Review*, 28.

Langton, M. (2012a). Counting Our Victories: The End of Garvey-ism and the Soft Bigotry of Low Expectation. *The Boyer Lectures*, Australian Broadcasting Corporation.

Langton, M. (2012b). *Indigenous Exceptionalism and the Constitutional 'Race Power'*. Melbourne Writers Festival, 26 August.

Larson, A., Gilles, M., Howard, P.J., & Coffin, J. (2007). It's Enough to Make You Sick: The Impact of Racism on the Health of Aboriginal Australians. *Australian and New Zealand Journal of Public Health*, 31(4), 322-329.

Lasorsa, T. (2011). Bilingual Programs with Special Reference to the Northern Territory. *Aboriginal Child at School*, 18(4), 10-18.

Law Reform Commission of Western Australia. (2004). *Aboriginal Customary Laws: Project No 94*. Perth, WA: Law Reform Commission of Western Australia.

Lawrence, R. (2005). Governing Warlpiri Subjects: Indigenous Employment and Training Programs in the Central Australian Mining Industry. *Geographical Research*, 43(1), 40–48.

Lawton, J.H. (1994). What Do Species Do in Ecosystems? *Oikos*, 71, 367-374. Copenhagen.

Lea, T. (2008). *Bureaucrats and Bleeding Hearts: Indigenous Health in Northern Australia*. Sydney: UNSW Press.

Lea, T. (2012). When Looking for Anarchy, Look to the State: Fantasies of Regulation in Forcing Disorder Within the Australian Indigenous Estate. *Critique of Anthropology*, 32(2), 109–124.

Lea, T., Young, M., Markham, F., Holmes, C., & Doran, B. (2012). Being Moved (On): The Biopolitics of Walking in Australia's Frontier Towns. *Radical History Review*, 114, 139–163.

Lee, L., & Thompson, A. (2007). Working Productively with Indigenous Communities, *Australian Journal of Indigenous Education*, 3, 32-38.

Levinson, D. (1989). *Family Violence in Cross-Cultural Perspective* (Vol 1). Newbury Park, CA: Sage.

Liu, C., & Spector, P.E. (2005). International Issues. In J. Barling, E.K., Kelloway, & M. R. Frone (Eds.). *Handbook of Work Stress* (pp. 487-515). Thousand Oaks, CA: Sage.

Lowe, J.B., Woodward, A., & Daly, J. (2012). The Plain Facts about Tobacco's Future. *Australian and New Zealand Journal of Public Health*, 36(5), 403.

Macoun, A. (2012). Aboriginality and the Northern Territory Intervention. *Australian Journal of Political Science*, 46(3), 519-534.

MacWilliam, H. (2001). *Aboriginal Over-representation Project*. Paper presented at Best Practice Interventions in Corrections conference, Australian Institute of Criminology, Sydney.

Maddock, K. (1988). Myth, History and a Sense of Oneself. In J.R. Beckett (Ed.), *Past and Present: The Construction of Aboriginality*. Canberra: Aboriginal Studies Press.

Makuwira, J. (2007). The Politics of Community Capacity Building: Contestations, Tensions and Ambivalences in the Discourse in Indigenous Communities in Australia. *Australian Journal of Indigenous Education*, 36 Supplement, 129-136.

Manne, R.A. (2007). Pearson's Gamble, Stanner's Dream: The Past and the Future of Remote Australia. *The Monthly*, August, 30-40.

Manne, R.A. (2011). Bad News: Murdoch's Australian and the Shaping of the Nation. *Quarterly Essay*, 43, 1-119.

Manne, R.A. (2012). Dark Victory: How Vested Interests Defeated Climate Science. *The Monthly*, August, 22-36.

Marchetti, E., & Daly, K. (2004). *Indigenous Courts and Justice Practices in Australia*. Canberra: Australian Institute of Criminology.

Marika, B., Munyarryun, B., Munyarryun, B., Marawili, N., & Marika, W., facilitated by Kerins, S. (2012). Ranger Djäma? Manymak!, In J. Altman & S. Kerins (Eds.), *People on Country, Vital Landscapes, Indigenous Futures* (pp.132-145). Sydney: Federation Press.

Marika, M., & Roeger, S. (2012). Dhimurru Wind Bringing Change, In J. Altman & S. Kerins (Eds.), *People on Country, Vital Landscapes, Indigenous Futures* (pp.119-131). Sydney: Federation Press.

Markham, F., Doran, B., & Young, Y. (in press). Estimating the Spatial Extent of Casino Catchments in Australia Using a Trade-area Model. *Growth and Change*.

Martin, D. (1993). *Autonomy and Relatedness: An Ethnography of Wik People of Aurukun, Western Cape York Peninsula* (Unpublished Doctoral Thesis). Australian National University, Canberra.

Martin, D. (2011). *Is Welfare Dependency 'Welfare Poison'? An Assessment of Noel Pearson's Proposals for Aboriginal Welfare Reform.* Centre for Aboriginal Economic Policy Research, Discussion Paper, no. 213. Canberra: ANU.

Marx, K. (1993 [1857]). *The Grundrisse.* London: Penguin Books.

Maynard, J. (2007). Circles in the Sand: An Indigenous Framework of Historical Practice. *Australian Journal of Indigenous Education*, 36 Supplement, 117-120.

McCallum, K. (2011). Journalism and Indigenous Health Policy. *Australian Aboriginal Studies*, 2, 21-31.

McClelland, A. (1993). Long-term Unemployment: Costs and Responses. *Australian Economic Review*, 26(2), 26-30.

McElrea, F. (1999). Taking Responsibility in Being Accountable. In J. Consedine, & H. Bowen, (Eds.), *Restorative Justice: Contemporary Themes and Practice.* Lyttleton, New Zealand: Ploughshare.

McGregor, R. (1993). Protest and Progress: Aboriginal Activism in the 1930s. *Australian Historical Studies*, 25(101), 555-568.

McKnight, D. (2002). *From Hunting to Drinking: The Devastating Effects of Alcohol on an Australian Aboriginal Community.* London: Routledge.

McMullen, J. (2001). *A Life of Extremes: Journeys and Encounters*, Sydney: HarperCollins.

McMullen, J. (2011a). Correspondence on the Intervention. *Arena Magazine*, 111, April/May, 31-35.

McMullen, J. (2011b). The Promised Land. *Tracker*, October, 23.

McMullen, J. (2012a). The New Land Grab. *Tracker*, March, 19. http://tracker.org.au/2012/03/the-way-ahead-the-new-land-grab/

McMullen, J. (2012b). Protector Macklin's Intervention. *Arena Magazine*, 117, April/May, 21-25.

McMullen, J. (2012c). The Search for Common Ground. *Journal of Indigenous Policy*, Issue 13, University of Technology Sydney, 35.

McRae, D., Ainsworth, G., Cumming, J., Hughes, P., Mackay, T., Price, K., Rowland, M., Warhurst, J., Woods, D., & Zbar, V. (2000). *What Works? Explorations in Improving Outcomes for Indigenous Students.* Canberra: Australian

Curriculum Studies Association and National Curriculum Services.

McRae-Williams, E., & Gerritsen, R. (2010). Mutual Incomprehension: The Cross Cultural Domain of Work in a Remote Australian Aboriginal Community. *The International Indigenous Policy Journal*, 1(2), Retrieved from: http://ir.lib.uwo.ca/iipj/vol1/iss2/2.

McWhorter, J. (2001). *Losing the Race.* New York: Free Press.

Mead, L. (2012). Welfare Reform and the Family: Lessons from America, In P. Saunders (Ed.), *Reforming the Australian Welfare State*, (pp. 44-61). Melbourne: Australian Institute of Family Studies.

Mellor, S. & Corrigan, M. (2004). *The Case for Change: A Review of Contemporary Research on Indigenous Education Outcomes.* Melbourne: ACER.

Meyers, N. (2000). *Global Security*, In H. Newbold (Ed.), *Life Stories: World-Renowned Scientists Reflect on Their Lives and the Future of Life on Earth* (pp. 169-182). Berkley, Los Angeles: University of California Press.

Millennium Ecosystem Assessment. (2005). *Ecosystems and Human Well-being: Biodiversity Synthesis.* Washington, DC: World Resources Institute.

Miller, C. (2005). *Aspects of Training that Meet Indigenous Australians' Aspirations: A Systemic Review of Research.* Adelaide: National Centre for Vocational Education Research.

Ministerial Council for Education, Early Childhood Development and Youth Affairs. (2011). *Aboriginal and Torres Strait Islander Education Action Plan 2010 – 2014.* Melbourne: Department of Education, Employment and Workplace Relations. Retrieved from http://deewr.gov.au

Morphy, F. (2007). Uncontained Subjects: 'Population' and 'Household' in Remote Aboriginal Australia. *Journal of Population Research*, 24(2), 163-184.

Mullighan, Hon. E.P. QC. (2008). *Children on Anangu Pitjantjatjara Yankunytjatjara (APY) Lands: Commission of Inquiry: A Report into Sexual Abuse* (Mullighan Inquiry), presented to the South Australian Parliament, April 2008.

Mununggurr, Y. (2010). Our Generation [Documentary]. S. Sabam & D. Curtis (Directors), D. Gondarra & J. McMullen (Co-Producers). www.ourgeneration.org.au

Myers, F. (1986). *Pintupi Country, Pintupi Self: Sentiment, Place and Politics Among Western Desert Aborigines.* Washington, DC: Smithsonian Institution Press.

Naeem, S. (1998). Species Redundancy and Ecosystem Reliability. *Conservation Biology*, 12(1), 39-45.

Nagel, T., Hinton, R., Thompson, V., & Spencer, N. (2011). Yarning About Gambling in Indigenous Communities: An Aboriginal and Islander Mental Health Initiative. *Australian Journal of Social Issues*, 46(4), 371.

National Centre for Vocational Education Research. (2010). *Australian Vocational Education and Training, Indigenous Students*. Retrieved from www.ncver.edu.au

National Curriculum Services. (2012). *What Works. The Work Program. Improving Outcomes for Indigenous Students. Success in Remote Schools: A Research Study of Eleven Improving Remote Schools*. Abbotsford: National Curriculum Services.

National Health Strategy Working Party. (March, 1996). Reprint. *A National Aboriginal Health Strategy*.

National Indian Gaming Commission. (2012). *NIGC Tribal Gaming Revenues*. Washington DC: NIGC Tribal Gaming Revenues.

Nazemi, S. (2009). Sir Robert Peel's Nine Principles of Policing. *Los Angeles Community Policing*. Retrieved from http://lacp.org/2009-Articles-Main/062609-Peels9Principals-SandyNazemi.htm

Nicoll, F. (2009). On Talking about Indigenous Gambling and Economic Development in Australia, the US and Canada: Rights, Whiteness and Sovereignties. *International Journal of Critical Indigenous Studies*, 2(1), 49–61.

Northern Territory Department of Education and Training. (2012). *Enrolment and Attendance Statistics*. Retrieved from http://www.det.nt.gov.au.

Northern Territory Second Reading Speeches, Sentencing Amendment Bill 2003. Retrieved from http://www.austlii.edu.au/au/legis/nt/bill_srs/sab2003211/srs.html

Nowra, L. (2007). *Bad Dreaming: Aboriginal Men's Violence Against Women and Children*. Melbourne: Pluto Press.

Nugent, M. (2009). *Captain Cook Was Here*. Melbourne: Cambridge University Press.

Office of the Registrar of Indigenous Corporations. (2010). *Analysing Key Characteristics in Indigenous Corporate Failure:* Research Paper (2010), p 46. Retrieved from http://www.oric.gov.au/

Osborne, B. (2003). Preparing Preservice Teachers' Minds, Hearts and Actions for Teaching in Remote Indigenous Contexts. *Australian Journal of Indigenous Education*, 31, 17-24.

Parbury, N. (2005). *Survival: A History of Aboriginal Life in New South Wales*. Sydney: David Ell.

Parbury, N. (2005). *Survival: A History of Aboriginal Life in New South Wales.* (2nd Edition). NSW: Allen & Unwin.

Parish, D.F.G. (1990). *Minj Kabirridi: School Non-Attendance in Two Traditionally Oriented Aboriginal Communities in the Northern Territory.* Armidale: University of New England.

Partington, G. (2000). Non-Indigenous Australians and Indigenous Autonomy. *Australian Journal of Indigenous Education,* 28(2), 15-19.

Partington, G. (2001). Current Orthodoxy in Aboriginal Education. *National Observer,* 50, 20-28.

Pascoe, E.A., & Richman, L.S. (2009). Perceived Discrimination and Health. *Psychological Bulletin,* 135(4), 531-554.

Pearson, N. (2000a). *Our Right to Take Responsibility.* Cairns: Noel Pearson and Associates.

Pearson, N. (2000b). Passive Welfare and the Destruction of Indigenous Society in Australia. In P. Saunders (Ed.), *Reforming the Australian Welfare State* (pp. 136-155). Melbourne: Australian Institute of Family Studies.

Pearson, N. (2001). Outline of a Grog and Drugs (And Therefore Violence) Strategy. *Cape York Partnerships.* Retrieved from http://www.cyp.org.au/useful-links/noel-pearson-papers

Pearson, N. (2006). Layered Identities and Peace, Earth Dialogue Brisbane Festival. *Cape York Partnerships.* Retrieved from http://www.cyp.org.au/useful-links/noel-pearson-papers

Pearson, N. (2009a). Radical Hope: Education and Equality in Australia. *Quarterly Essay,* 35.

Pearson, N. (2009b). *Up From the Mission: Selected Writings.* Collingwood, Victoria: Black Inc.

Pearson, N. (2011). *Radical Hope: Education & Equality in Australia.* Collingwood, Victoria: Black Inc.

Pearson, N., Denigan, B., & Götesson, J. (2009). *The Most Important Reform: Position Paper.* Cairns: Cape York Partnerships.

Perry, S. (2005). *Man up! Nobody is Coming to Save Us.* Middletown: CT: Renegade Books.

Pholi, K. (2012a). Silencing Dissent inside the Aboriginal Industry. *Quadrant,* 56(12), December, 6-15.

Pholi, K. (2012b). Why I Burned My 'Proof of Aboriginality'. *ABC The Drum*, 27 September. Retrieved from http://www.abc.net.au/unleashed/4281772.html

Pholi, K. (2013). The Final Insult. *The Spectator Australia*. Retrieved from http://www.spectator.co.uk/australia/australia-features/8810021/the-final-insult/

Pinker, S. (2002). *The Blank Slate: The Modern Denial of Human Nature*. London: Penguin Books.

Playford, P. (1964). Report on Native Title Welfare Expedition to the Gibson and Great Sandy Desert. *Records of the Geological Survey of Western Australia*.

Pollack, D. (2001). *Indigenous Land in Australia: A Quantitative Assessment of Indigenous Landholdings in 2000*. Centre for Aboriginal Economic Policy Research, Discussion Paper, no. 221. Canberra: ANU.

Pollard, D. (1988). *Give & Take: The Losing Partnership in Aboriginal Poverty*. Sydney: Hale & Iremonger.

Porter, R. (1994). *Paul Hasluck: A Political Biography*. University of Australia Press.

Prause, J., & Dooley, D. (1997). Effect of Underemployment on School-Leavers' Self-Esteem. *Journal of Adolescence*, 20(3), 243-260.

Procopius. (2007). *The Secret History* (P. Sarris, Trans.). London: Penguin Classics.

Productivity Commission. (2007). *Overcoming Indigenous Disadvantage: Headline Indicators*. Canberra. Retrieved from www.pc.gov.au/gsp

Purdie, N., & Buckley, S. (2010). *School Attendance and Retention of Indigenous Australian Students*. Closing the Gap Clearinghouse Issues Paper, no. 1, 1-25.

Ramsay, A.W. (1969). *Sir Robert Peel: Makers of the Nineteenth Century*. University of California: Constable and Co.

Ranzijn, R., McConnochie, K., & Nolan, W. (2009). *Psychology and Indigenous Australians: Foundations of Cultural Competence*. Melbourne: Palgrave MacMillan.

Read, P. (2006). Shelley's mistake: The Parramatta Native Institution and the Stolen Generations. In M. Crotty (Ed.), *The Great Mistakes of Australian History*. Kensington, New South Wales: University of New South Wales Press.

Reconciliation Australia. (2009). *Australian Reconciliation Barometer: Comparing the Attitudes of Indigenous People and Australians Overall*. Retrieved from http://www.reconciliation.org.au

Rephann, T.J., Dalton, M., Stair, A., & Isserman, A. (1997). Casino Gambling as An Economic Development Strategy. *Tourism Economics*, 3(2), 161–183.

Reynolds, R.J. (2009). "Clean, Clad and Courteous" Revisited: A Review History of 200 Years of Aboriginal Education in New South Wales. *The Journal of Negro Education*, 78(1), 83-94.

Ring, I., & Brown, N. (2003). Aboriginal and Torres Strait Islander Health-implementation, not more Policies. *Journal of Australian Indigenous Issues*, 6(3), 3–12.

Roberts, T. (2005). *Frontier Justice, A History of the Gulf Country to 1900*. Brisbane: Queensland University Press.

Roberts, T. (2009). *Black-White Relations in the Gulf Country to 1950*: Blackheath History Forum, Saturday 29 August 2009. Retrieved from http://www.abc.net.au

Robinson, M., & Yu, P. (1975). A Note on Kuns: An Aboriginal Card Game from the North-west of Western Australia. *Department of Aboriginal Affairs Western Australia Newsletter*, 11(3), 41–49.

Rose, D.B. (2000). *Dingo Makes us Human: Life and Death in an Australian Aboriginal Culture*. Oakleigh, Victoria: Cambridge University Press.

Rose, N. (1996). *Inventing Our Selves: Psychology, Power, and Personhood*. New York: Cambridge University Press.

Rostron, V., Campion, W., & Namarnyilk, I., facilitated by Fogarty, B. (2012). Countrymen Standing Together, In J. Altman & S. Kerins (Eds.), *People on Country, Vital Landscapes, Indigenous Futures* (pp.162-173). Sydney: Federation Press.

Rowe, K.J. (2003). The Importance of Teacher Quality as a Key Determinant of Students' Experiences and Outcomes of Schooling. Paper presented at the Australian Council for Research in Education conference, Melbourne, 19-21 October, 2003.

Rowse, T. (1996). *Traditions for Health: Studies in Aboriginal Reconstruction*. Darwin: NARU.

Rowse, T. (2002). *Indigenous Futures: Choice and Development for Aboriginal and Islander Australia*, Sydney: UNSW Press.

Royal Commission into Aboriginal Deaths in Custody (1991). National report volume 1. Canberra: Australian Government Publishing Service

Royal, T.A.C. (2009). 'Māori—Urbanisation and Renaissance' *Te Ara—the Encyclopaedia of New Zealand*. Retrieved from http://www.teara.govt.nz/en/maori/page-5.

Russell-Smith, J., Whitehead, P., & Cooke, P. (Eds.). (2009). *Culture, Ecology, and Economy of Fire Management in North Australian Savannas: Rekindling the Wurrk Tradition.* Melbourne: CSIRO Publishing.

Sachs, W. (1992). Introduction. in W. Sachs (Ed.). *The Development Dictionary: A Guide to Knowledge as Power* (pp. 6-25). London: Zed. Books.

Sackville, R. (Justice) (2002). *Traditional Knowledge, Intellectual Property and Indigenous Culture.* Conference Paper, Benjamin N Cardozo School of Law Yeshiva University, New York.

Sammut, J. (2011). Custody for Indigenous Kids More than Black and White. *ABC The Drum*, 1 June. http://www.abc.net.au/unleashed/2740350.html

Sammut, J. (2012). Is Preventing 'Another Stolen Generation' Racist? *Ideas@TheCentre*. Newsletter. Sydney: The Centre for Independent Studies, 6 July.

Sanders, W. (1996). Local Governments and Indigenous Australians: Developments and Dilemmas in Contrasting Circumstances. *Australian Journal of Political Science*, 31(2), 153-174.

Sanders, W. (2002). *Towards An Indigenous Order of Australian Government: Rethinking Self-Determination as Indigenous Affairs Policy.* Centre for Aboriginal Economic Policy Research Discussion Paper, no. 230. 1-32. Canberra: ANU.

Sanders, W., & Morphy, F. (Eds.). (2001). *The Indigenous Welfare Economy and the CDEP Scheme.* Centre for Aboriginal Economic Policy, Research Monograph No. 20. Canberra: ANU.

Sansom, B. (1980). *The Camp at Wallaby Cross: Aboriginal Fringe Dwellers in Darwin.* Canberra: Australian Institute of Aboriginal Studies.

Sarra, C. (2009). *Challenging the Tide of Low Expectations in Indigenous Education: NAPLAN Data,* 2009. Retrieved from http://chrissarra.wordpress.com/2009/09/11/2009-naplan-data/

Sarra, C. (2010). 'Beyond the Victim', *National Indigenous Times* (Issue 214, Vol 9), 17.

Schama, S. (2000). *A History of Britain, Part 8, the Two Winstons*, BBC Television Series. London: BBC.

Schools Council, National Board of Employment, Education and Training. (1992). *Aboriginal and Torres Strait Islander Education in the Early Years. Compulsory Years of Schooling Project, no. 4.* Canberra: Australian Government Publishing Service.

Schwab, R.G. (2001). 'That School Gotta Recognise Our Policy!' The Appropriation of Educational Policy in An Australian Aboriginal

Community. In M. Sutton and B. Levinson (Eds.), *Policy as Practice: Toward A Comparative Sociocultural Analysis of Educational Policy*. Westport, CT: Ablex Publishing Corporation.

Schwab, R.G. (2006). *Kids, Skidoos and Caribou: The Junior Canadian Ranger Program as a Model for Re-Engaging Indigenous Australian Youth in Remote Areas*. Centre for Aboriginal Economic Policy Research Discussion Paper, no. 281. 1-34. Canberra: ANU.

Schwab, R.G. (2012). Indigenous Early School Leavers: Failure, Risk and High-Stakes Testing. *Australian Aboriginal Studies*, 1, 3-18.

Schwab, R.G., & Sutherland, D. (2003). Indigenous Learning Communities: A Vehicle for Community Empowerment and Capacity Development. *Learning Communities: International Journal of Learning in Social Contexts*, 1, 53-71.

Scrymgour, M. (2008). *Education Restructure Includes Greater Emphasis on English*. Northern Territory Government Media Release.

Shakur, T. (1999). *The Rose that Grew From Concrete*. New York: MTV Books/Pocket Books.

Shaw, W. (2012). Indigenous 'Solutions' Just Disempower Us Further. *ABC The Drum*, 6 June. http://www.abc.net.au/unleashed/

Shergold, P. (2009, July 11). Devolve Power to the People. *Weekend Australian*.

Shergold, P. (2012). Welfare to Work: The Indigenous Challenge. In J. Healey (Ed.), *Welfare Reform Debate*. Thirroul, NSW: Spinney Press

Simpson, J., Caffery, J., & McConvell. P. (2009). *Gaps in Australia's Indigenous Language Policy: Dismantling Bilingual Education in the Northern Territory*. Australian Institute of Aboriginal and Torres Strait Islander Studies Discussion Paper, no. 24, 1-48.

Smallwood, G. (2011). *Human Rights and First Australians' Well-being* (Doctoral Thesis). James Cook University.

Smallwood, G. (2012). Sovereign Union – First Nations Interim National Unity Government [audio file]. *Townsville Professor Blasts Australia over Land Rights and Intervention at International Conference*.

Sowell, T. (2004). *Affirmative Action around the World: An Empirical Study*. New Haven: Yale University Press.

Sparks, K., Cooper, C., Fried, Y., & Shirom, A. (1997). The Effects of Hours of Work on Health: A Meta-Analytic Review. *Journal of Occupational and Organizational Psychology*, 70(4), 391-408.

Spezzano, C. (2001). *If It Hurts, It Isn't Love*. London: Hodder and Stoughton.

State of the Environment Committee. (2011). *Australia: State of the Environment 2011*, Independent Report to the Australian Government Minister for Sustainability, Environment, Water, Population and Communities. Canberra: Department of Sustainability, Environment, Water, Population and Communities.

Steele, S. (2006). *White Guilt: How Blacks and Whites Together Destroyed the Promise of the Civil Rights Era*. New York: Harper Perennial.

Steels, B. (2009a). *Declared Guilty: A Never Ending Story*. Germany: VDM Verlag.

Steels, B. (2009b). Imprisonment of the Many: Capacity Building or Community Demolition? In *Ngoonjook: A Journal of Australian Indigenous Issues*, no. 32.

Stevens, M., & Young, M. (2009). Betting on the Evidence: Reported Gambling Problems Among the Indigenous Population of the Northern Territory. *Australian and New Zealand Journal of Public Health*, 33(6), 556–565.

Stevens, M., & Young, M. (2010). Independent Correlates of Reported Gambling Problems amongst Indigenous Australians. *Social Indicators Research*, 98(1), 147–166.

Stewart, J. (2007). Grounded Theory and Focus Groups: Reconciling Methodologies in Indigenous Australian Research. *Australian Journal of Indigenous Education*, 36, Supplement, 32-37.

Summary of Australian Indigenous Health. (2012). *Health Infonet*. Retrieved from http://www.healthinfonet.ecu.edu.au

Sutton, P. (2011). *The Politics of Suffering: Indigenous Australia and the End of Liberal Consensus* (2nd ed.). Melbourne University Publishing.

Sydney Gazette. (31 December 1814). First Aboriginal Day at Parramatta 28 December 1814. Lachlan and Elizabeth Macquarie Archive. Retrieved from http://www.lib.mq.edu.au/digital/lema/1814/sydgaz31dec1814.html

Sykes, C.J. (1992). *A Nation of Victims: The Decay of the American Character*. New York: St. Martin's Press.

Taylor, J. (2001). Postcolonial Transformation of the Australian Indigenous Population. *Geographical Research*, 49(3), 286–300.

Taylor, J. (2010). *Demography as Destiny: Schooling, Work and Aboriginal Population Change at Wadeye*. Centre for Aboriginal Economic Policy Research Working Paper, no. 64. 1-64. Canberra: ANU.

Taylor J., & Biddle, N. (2008). *Locations of Indigenous Population Change: What Can*

*We Say?* Centre for Aboriginal Economic Policy Research Working Paper, no. 43. Canberra: ANU.

Tebtebba Foundation. (2008). *Indicators Relevant for Indigenous Peoples: A Resource Book*. Baguio City, Philippines: Tebtebba Foundation.

Thaler, R.H., & Sunstein, C.R. (2009). *Nudge: Improving Decisions about Health, Wealth And Happiness*. London: Penguin.

*The Queen v GJ* [2005] NTCCA.

Thomson, G. (2006, September 12). Former Social Club Set for Bush Camp. *Centralian Advocate*. Alice Springs. 4.

Trigger, D. (1982). *Nicholson River (Waanyi/Garawa) Land Claim* (unpublished). Northern Land Council, Darwin.

Trimble, C., Sommer, B., & Quinlan M. (2008). *The American Indian Oral History Manual: Making Many Voices Heard*, California: Left Coast Press.

Trudgeon, R. (2000). *Why Warriors Lie Down and Die*. Darwin: Aboriginal Resources and Development Services Inc.

Turner, P., & Watson, N. (2007). The Trojan Horse. In J. Altman & M. Hinkson (Eds.), *Coercive Reconciliation: Stabilise, Normalise, Exit Aboriginal Australia* (pp. 205-212). Melbourne: Arena.

Tuttle, L. (1987). *Encyclopedia of Feminism*. London: Arrow Books.

Tutu. D. (no date). *If There Is Only One Message of Wisdom You Could Leave behind for Humanity What Would It Be?* Retrieved from http://www.tutufoundationusa.org/

Tyler, T. (2006). Restorative Justice and Procedural Justice: Dealing with Rule Breaking. *Journal of Social Issues*, 62(2), 307-326.

United Nations. (2008). *United Nations Declaration on the Rights of Indigenous Peoples*. Retrieved from http://www.un.org

University of Western Sydney. (2009). *Challenging Racism: The Anti-racism Research Project*. Retrieved from www.uws.edu.au

Victorian Health. (2012). *Mental Health Impacts of Racial Discrimination in Victorian Aboriginal Communities, Experiences of Racism Survey*: A summary. VicHealth.

Vygotsky, L.S. (1978). *Mind in Society: The Development of Higher Psychological Processes*. Cambridge, MA: Harvard University Press.

Wade, N. (2006). *Before the Dawn, Recovering the Lost History of Our Ancestors*. London: Penguin Books.

Walker, J., & McDonald, D. (1995). *The Over-representation of Indigenous People in Custody in Australia: Trends & Issues in Crime and Criminal Justice no. 47.* Canberra: Australian Institute of Criminology.

Warner, W.L. (1958) (Revised edition. First edition in 1937). *A Black Civilization: A Social Study of an Australian Tribe.* New York and London: Harper and Brothers.

Warr, P. (1987). *Work, Unemployment and Mental Health.* Oxford: Clarendon Press.

Watts, B.H., & Gallacher, J.D. (1969). *Report on an Investigation into the Curriculum and Teaching Methods used in Aboriginal Schools in the Northern Territory: To the Honourable C. E. Barnes, Minister of State for Territories.* Darwin.

Wax, A. (2009). *Race, Wrongs, and Remedies: Group Justice in the 21st Century.* Lanham, MD: Rowman & Littlefield.

Weatherburn, D., Fitzgerald, J., & Hua, J. (2003). Reducing Aboriginal Over-Representation in Prison. *Australian Journal of Public Administration,* 62(3), 65-73.

Wenz, M. (2008). Matching Estimation, Casino Gambling and the Quality of Life. *The Annals of Regional Science,* 42(1), 235–249.

Wild, R., & Anderson, P. (2007). *Little Children are Sacred: Report of the Northern Territory Board of Inquiry into the Protection of Aboriginal Children from Sexual Abuse.* Darwin: Northern Territory Government.

Willis, E. (1984). Has the Primary Health Worker Program Been Successfully Exported to the Northern Territory? *Aboriginal Health Project Information Bulletin,* 6 August, 13-18.

Wilson, E. O. (2012). *The Social Conquest of Earth.* NY: Liveright.

Windschuttle, K. (2009). *The Fabrication of Australian History, Vol. Three: The Stolen Generations 1881-2008.* Sydney: Macleay Press.

Winick, B. (2003). A Therapeutic Jurisprudence Model for Civil Commitment. In K. Diesfeld & I. Freckelton, (Eds.), *Involuntary Detention and Therapeutic Jurisprudence.* New York: Ashgate Publishing.

Winkelmann, L., & Winkelmann, R. (1998). Why are the Unemployed so Unhappy? Evidence from Panel Data. *Economica,* 65(257), 1-15.

Woinarski, J., & Dawson, F. (2001). Limitless Land and Limited Knowledge: Coping with Uncertainty and Ignorance in Northern Australia. In J. W. Handmer, T. W. Norton, & S. R. Dovers (Eds.), *Ecology, Uncertainty and Policy – Managing Ecosystems for Sustainability* (pp. 83-155). Harlow, England: Prentice Hall.

Woinarski, J., Mackey, B., Nix, H., & Traill, B. (2007). *The Nature of Northern Australia. Its Natural Values, Ecological Processes and Future Prospects*. Canberra: ANU E Press. Retrieved from http://epress.anu.edu.au/nature_na_citation.html.

Wooden, M., Warren, D., & Drago, R. (2009). Working Time Mismatch and Subjective Well-being. *British Journal of Industrial Relations*, 47(1), 147–179.

Wright, W.E. (2002). The Effects of high Stakes Testing in an Inner-City Elementary School: The Curriculum, the Teachers, and the English Language Learners. *Current Issues in Education*, 5(5). Retrieved from http://cie.asu.edu/volume5/number5/index.html

Yilli Rreung Regional Council. (2001). *Annual Report, 2000-2001*. Darwin, N.T.

Young, M., Doran, B., & Markham, F. (in press). Gambling Spaces and the Racial Dialectics of Social Inclusion: A Case Study of a Remote Australian Casino. *Geographical Research*. Advance online publication. doi: 10.1111/j.1745-5871.2012.00787.x

Young, M., Lamb, D., & Doran, B. (2011). Gambling, Resource Distribution, and Racial Economy: An Examination of Poker Machine Expenditure in Three Remote Australian Towns. *Geographical Research*, 49(1), 59–71.

Young, E., Ross, H., Johnson, J., & Kesteven, J. (1991). *Caring for Country: Aborigines and Land Management*. Canberra: Australian National Parks and Wildlife Service.

Yunupingu, M. (1995). National Review of Education for Aboriginal and Torres Strait Islander Peoples: Final Report. Canberra: Australian Government Publishing Service.

Zubrick, S.R., Silburn, S.R., De Maio, J.A., Shepherd, C., Griffin, J.A., Dalby, R.B., Cox, A. (2006). *The Western Australian Aboriginal Child Health Survey: Improving the Educational Experiences of Aboriginal Children and Young People* (Vol 3). Perth: Curtin University of Technology and Telethon Institute for Child Health Research.

Zur, O. (2005). The Psychology of Victimhood. In R.H. Wright & N.A. Cummings (Eds.), *Destructive Trends in Mental Health: The Well-intentioned Path to Harm* (pp. 45-64). New York: Routledge.

# Contributors

**Alison Anderson**

The Hon. Alison Anderson MLA is currently Minister for Regional Development, Indigenous Advancement and Women's Policy in the Northern Territory. She has spent her life trying to improve the conditions of Aboriginal people living in Central Australia.

**Nicholas Biddle**

Nicholas is a Fellow at the Australian National University's Centre for Aboriginal Economic Policy Research. He also has a PhD in Public Policy from the ANU where he wrote his thesis on the benefits of and participation in education of Indigenous Australians.

**Paddy Cavanagh**

Paddy was a member of the original NSW Aboriginal Education Unit that developed Australia's first Aboriginal Education Policy in 1982. Since then he has been there done that in a lifetime spent in promoting Aboriginal education and a better understanding of the shared history of Aboriginal and non-Aboriginal Australians.

**Rhonda Craven**

See editors' biographies.

**Anthony Dillon**

See editors' biographies.

**Bruce Doran**

Bruce is a researcher at the Centre for Aboriginal Economic and Policy Research at the Australian National University. He is currently chief investigator on an Australian Research Council Linkages Grant examining the impacts of gambling in remote Australia.

## Thomas Draper

Born on a mission in Moree, north-west New South Wales, Thomas learned a strong work ethic from his father, won boxing titles and played professional Rugby League in England. His drive to succeed made him a construction supervisor with Arrow Energy. He gives back by talking up life messages for school and corporate audiences.

## William Fogarty

Bill has a 15-year history as an educator and researcher working in remote communities in Northern Australia. His research focuses on the nexus between Indigenous and Western knowledge in education and remote development. He is currently a Research Associate at the National Centre for Indigenous Studies (ANU).

## Mick Gooda

Mick is the Aboriginal and Torres Strait Islander Social Justice Commissioner. He is also currently a Board Member of the Centre for Rural and Remote Mental Health Queensland, and the Australian representative on the International Indigenous Council which focuses on healing and addictions.

## Dot Goulding

Dot is a Senior Research Fellow at Curtin University and a co-director of the Asia Pacific Forum for Restorative Justice and Coordinator of the Institute for Restorative Justice & Penal Reform, Australia. Her research has been mainly in the area of imprisonment, restorative justice and domestic violence.

## Sara Hudson

Sara was a researcher with the Centre for Independent Studies. Since 2008 she has published widely on a range of Aboriginal issues focusing on employment, welfare, housing, 99-year leases and home ownership, and the lack of accountability in Aboriginal health.

## Helen Hughes and Mark Hughes

Helen is Emeritus Professor, Economics, Australian National University. She is a senior fellow at the Centre for Independent Studies, for which both she and her son Mark have researched and written extensively on Indigenous issues.

## Ernest Hunter

A medical graduate in Australia, and trained in adult, child and cross-cultural psychiatry and public health in the US, Ernest has worked for two decades in remote Aboriginal Australia. He is Regional Psychiatrist with Queensland Health, and Adjunct Professor with the University of Queensland, based in Cairns.

## Stephanie Jarrett

Stephanie is the author of *Liberating Aboriginal People from Violence*. This book critically assesses the policy and judicial responses to the problem of Aboriginal domestic violence, particularly within the limits of community self-determination precepts.

## Kirrily Jordan

Kirrily is a Research Fellow at the Australian National University's Centre for Aboriginal Economic Policy Research. Her work focuses on Indigenous employment and its relationship to wellbeing, as well as analysis of 'what works' in Indigenous employment programs and policy.

## Seán Kerins

Seán is a Research Fellow at Centre for Aboriginal Economic Policy Research at the Australian National University. He has worked with Indigenous peoples and local communities for the last 20 years on cultural and natural resource management issues. Previously he managed the Northern Land Council's Caring for Country Unit in Darwin.

### Francis Markham

Francis is a research associate at the Menzies School of Health Research and a PhD candidate at the Australian National University. His PhD research concerns the political geography of service delivery in regional and remote Australia.

### Jeff McMullen AM

Jeff is a highly respected Australian journalist, author, and film maker who works with Aboriginal communities as honorary chief executive of Ian Thorpe's Fountain for Youth and is a director of the Australian Indigenous Mentoring Experience. He campaigns tirelessly for the rights of Aboriginal people.

### Warren Mundine

Warren is a former national president of the ALP, and the former CEO for GenerationOne. His life and career have been shaped by personal commitment to community, both Indigenous and non-Indigenous, and he has more than 26 years' experience working in the public, private, and community sectors.

### Nigel Parbury

See editors' biographies.

### Geoffrey Partington

Geoffrey was a teacher, headmaster, education officer and adviser, and teacher educator in England. He has carried out commissioned research into teacher education and social studies teaching in the UK, New Zealand, Australia, and Canada.

### Kerryn Pholi

Kerryn is a former Aboriginal public servant and social worker, currently based in Canberra. She worked for various government agencies on data collection and reporting on Aboriginal health and wellbeing. Her articles on identity politics and freedom of speech have appeared in *Quadrant*, *Spectator Australia* and *The Drum*.

## Dave and Bess Price

Dave is Anglo-Celtic. Bess is Warlpiri, born and raised at Yuendumu, now MLA for Stuart. As well as her first languages, Warlpiri and English, she speaks four other Aboriginal languages. Dave and Bess have worked extensively in education, public administration, community development, social and educational research, cross-cultural awareness training, and translation and interpreting.

## Brian Roberts OA

Brian has been teaching and researching in tertiary education since 1956, specialising in land management. His long experience with African Homelands and his role in the Cape York Peninsula Land Use Study led to a 20 year study of Aboriginal policy. He is currently Adjunct Professor at James Cook University, Cairns.

## Jonny Samengo

A former advertising executive, Jonny was inspired to volunteer for the Indigenous Program at Scots College, Sydney, where his son was enrolled. Since 2010, he has been Director of the program. In this time the program has expanded to have 18 Aboriginal boys on scholarships at Scots, from around Australia, La Perouse to Arnhem Land.

## R.G. (Jerry) Schwab

Jerry is a Fellow at the Centre for Aboriginal Economic Policy Research at the Australian National University and carries out research on Indigenous education, literacy, and youth policy. He has been involved with educational research and development in Australia and overseas since the mid-1980s.

## Patricia Shadforth

Patricia is the white-Australian matriarchal head of a large Indigenous family. She has spent the last 42 years living with Aboriginal people of all descriptions in the Top End, including remote traditional tribal people, whilst continuing her work as a paediatric nurse.

**Brian Steels**

Brian is a researcher at Curtin University and co-director of the Asia Pacific Forum for Restorative Justice. His work for penal reform as a Critical Criminologist as well as an activist sets him apart from many of his peers; he sits among the world's foremost convict criminologists.

**Martin Young**

Martin is a Senior Lecturer in the Centre for Gambling Education and Research, Southern Cross University. His research agenda centres on a critical approach to gambling as a form of contemporary capitalist development, particularly in regional and remote contexts.

# Editors' Biographies

**Professor Rhonda Craven** is Director, Centre for Positive Psychology and Education, University of Western Sydney, which is ranked seventh in the world and first in Australia for Educational Psychology. She is the editor of the best selling text *Teaching Aboriginal Studies* (1999, 2011), the National Project Co-ordinator of the highly successful Teaching the Teachers Indigenous Australian Studies Project of National Significance, and has served as an invited expert for the National Experts Closing the Gap Forum for the Menzies Foundation.

**Dr Anthony Dillon** is a Postdoctoral Fellow at the Centre for Positive Psychology and Education, University of Western Sydney. He has worked as a data analyst, analysing Aboriginal health datasets for ten years, and currently lectures on psychology, and Aboriginal health and well-being at the University of Western Sydney. He is often asked by various media for his views on Aboriginal affairs and has contributed to *The Australian* and the ABC's *The Drum*.

**Nigel Parbury** is author of the acclaimed *Survival: A History of Aboriginal Life in New South Wales* (1986, 2005). He has worked in Aboriginal education for 25 years, for NSW AECG (Aboriginal Education Consultative Group) 1990-99, 2005-10, and been involved in: the schools reconciliation rock musical *1788: The Great South Land* and, with Rhonda Craven, *Teaching the Teachers: Indigenous Australian Studies* Project of National Significance and the best-selling text *Teaching Aboriginal Studies* (1999, 2011). He is now with the Centre for Positive Psychology and Education, University of Western Sydney, passionate about Aboriginal talents, dreaming what Australia can be.

www.ingramcontent.com/pod-product-compliance
Lightning Source LLC
Chambersburg PA
CBHW032014230426
43671CB00005B/77